SO-AFN-032

Professional Practices

in association management

The Essential Resource for Effective Management of Nonprofit Organizations

Executive Editor and Contributing Author

John B. Cox, CAE

Written by leading industry experts

★asae
association management press

WASHINGTON, DC

The authors have worked diligently to ensure that all information in this book is accurate as of the time of publication and consistent with standards of good practice in the general management community. As research and practice advance, however, standards may change. For this reason it is recommended that readers evaluate the applicability of any recommendations in light of particular situations and changing standards.

ASAE: The Center for Association Leadership
Association Management Press
1575 I Street, NW
Washington, DC 20005-1103
Phone: (202) 626-2723; (888) 950-2723 outside the metropolitan Washington, DC area
Fax: (202) 408-9633
E-mail: books@asaecenter.org
We connect great ideas and great people to inspire leadership and achievement in the association community.

John H. Graham IV, CAE, President and CEO, ASAE
Susan Sarfati, CAE, President and CEO, The Center for Association Leadership and Executive
  Vice President, ASAE
Susan Robertson, Senior Vice President, ASAE: The Center for Association Leadership
Keith C. Skillman, CAE, Vice President of Publications and Editorial Director,
  ASAE: The Center for Association Leadership
Baron Williams, CAE, Director of Book Publishing,
  ASAE: The Center for Association Leadership

Cover design by Beth Lower
Interior design by Troy Scott Parker, cimarrondesign.com

This book is available at a special discount when ordered in bulk quantities. For information, contact the ASAE Member Service Center at (202) 371-0940.

A complete catalog of titles is available on the ASAE website at www.asaecenter.org.

ISBN-13: 978-0-88034-363-3
ISBN-10: 0-88034-363-X

Printed in the United States of America.
10 9 8 7 6 5 4 3 2 1

Contents

Preface to the Second Edition vii

1 Association Governance and Structure 1
   Wayne E. Leroy, CAE

2 Developing Policies and Procedures 13
   Jone R. Sienkiewicz, CMP, CAE

3 Defining the Future 21
   Bruce Butterfield, CAE, APR

4 Sustainability: Associations as Agents of Change in the
   Collaborative Economy 31
   Richard C. O'Sullivan

5 Strategy Management 47
   James Dalton

6 Legal Issues 57
   Jefferson C. Glassie, J.D.

7 Building Strong Component Relations 67
   Adrienne Antink, CAE

8 Subsidiary Corporations 73
   William T. Robinson, CAE

9 Leadership 79
   Carla Balakgie, CAE

10 Negotiating More Effectively 95
    Jack W. Kaine

11 Ethical Practices for Associations and the Professionals
    They Serve 105
    Scott R. Sturzl

12 High-Yield Tactical Planning **117**
   Crisis Management **128**
   John B. Cox, CAE

13 Budget and Finance **131**
   Kathie Berry, CAE

14 Human Resource Management **143**
   Michael R. Losey, SPHR, CAE

15 Fundraising **191**
   James P. Gelatt

16 Supplier Relations **201**
   Stacey Riska

17 Research and Statistics **209**
   Michael Sherman, CAE

18 Managing Information Technology **225**
   Maynard H. Benjamin, CAE

19 Knowledge Management **235**
   Richard V. Lawson

20 Facilities Management **243**
   Wayne E. Leroy, CAE

21 Government Relations **249**
   Janis L. Tabor, CAE

22 Public Relations **263**
   Barbara Hyde, CAE

23 Diversity **275**
   Velma R. Hart, CAE

24 Coalition Building **287**
   John J. Mahlmann

25 Community Service **297**
   Randolph R. Schools, CAE

26 Education Programs **303**
   Ralph J. Nappi, CAE & Deborah B. Vieder

27 Publishing Professional Magazines, Books, and Other Media . . . **313**
   Debra J. Stratton

28 Science, Technical, and Medical Publications **333**
   Don Hemenway

29 Association Marketing. **349**
   Alan R. Shark, D.P.A., CAE

30 Membership Recruitment and Retention **363**
   Mark Levin, CAE, CSP

31 Going International. **375**
   Carolyn A. Lugbill, CAE, MAM

32 Meeting Planning and Management **391**
   Dawn M. Mancuso, MAM, CAE

33 Legal Issues in Association Standard Setting, Certification and
   Accreditation Programs, and Codes of Ethics **419**
   Jeffrey S. Tenenbaum & Beth A. Caseman

34 Certification and Accreditation Programs. **433**
   Michael S. Hamm, CMC

35 Affinity Programs. **445**
   Matthew J. Rowan

CAE Content Outline **455**

Index **467**

Organizational Units

Nearly two thirds of associations (62 percent) grant their members direct voting privileges. Submitting every decision to the entire membership, however, would soon prove unwieldy. Instead, associations establish a structure of organizational units to make the decisions that lead to the implementation of their missions and goals.

Those organizational units may include the following:

Board of Directors

Board sizes vary, with the median being 16 voting members according to the latest *Policies and Procedures in Association Management* survey. In addition, more than half of associations (58 percent) have *ex-officio* board members who do not vote; those people tend to be the chief executive officer (CEO) or the chief elected officer who just completed his or her term.

A variety of methods are used to select board members, ranging from direct election by the membership, to selection by various constituency groups within the association (such as regions, chapters, or special interest groups), to selection by a nominating committee. The most common length of board tenure, preferred by nearly half of associations (49 percent), is three years or longer; two-year terms would be the next most common length of time for board members to serve.

To ensure stability and continuity, while at the same time injecting new ways of thinking into a board, most associations use a rotation method for selecting board members. A three-year cycle, for instance, allows for one out of three board members to be new each year, while two-thirds remain experienced board members. Still, a majority of associations (81 percent) allow a board member to succeed himself or herself for an additional term or two.

Officers

Leading the board work are officers, whose duties are typically specified in the association bylaws. The number of board officers usually ranges between four and seven, including these positions:

- *President/Chair(man) of the Board.* This is the chief elected or appointed volunteer position which, in nearly two thirds of associations (63 percent), has a one-year term. (To avoid confusion, associations often assign the title of chairman to the chief elected officer if the chief executive officer carries the title of president).

- *First Vice President/Vice Chair(man)/Chair(man)-Elect.* This person is next in succession for becoming the chief volunteer officer.

- *Secretary/Treasurer.* This officer is responsible for maintaining the fiscal and official written records of the association. Instead of combining this office, some organizations treat it as two separate positions. Others designate the chief executive officer as the secretary, thus removing that position from elective office.

- *Vice Presidents/Directors.* These positions are usually designated by program or service functions (for example, Director of Education or Membership Vice President) or by geographic designation (for example, Vice President of Professional Development or Eastern Regional Director).

Executive Committee

This smaller governing body, which averages seven members, has the authority to act on behalf of the entire board of directors. It may comprise the board officers, or it may include other members of the board in the interest of achieving balance and harmony. For instance, members of the executive committee might include the chief executive officer, the incoming chief elected officer, and the immediate past elected officer. Most associations use executive committee meetings as an interim decision-making measure between meetings of the full board of directors.

House (or Assembly) of Delegates

Some associations, usually individual membership organizations, mirror the legislative branch of the United States government by having a delegate representational system that may be based on geography, special interest area, or other appropriate criteria. For instance, a national association of attorneys might have a delegate from each affiliated state association, as well as delegates who represent the interests of a particular region or type of legal practice. Because of the larger size of this organizational unit, it may convene only once or twice a year.

Standing Committees

The majority of associations have 5 to 10 standing committees—ongoing groups that continue from one year to the next. Usually described in the bylaws, these committees focus on the long-term needs of the association as identified in the mission statement or strategic plan. Some common standing committees, in addition to the Executive Committee described above, are: budget or finance, nominating, membership, government affairs, and education.

A committee's composition should reflect the association's membership. If committee membership isn't representative of the general membership, either the committee or the members at large might feel disenfranchised from the association. This balance is especially important for the nominating committee, which is charged with identifying future leaders who reflect the organizations constituencies.

As on the board of directors, terms of service may last three years, with about one-third of the committee turning over each year. Some associations make annual appointments, with the provision that effective and productive committee members can be re-appointed for multiple years. To emphasize the committee's importance and accountability to the board of directors, many associations appoint a board member to chair each standing committee.

Ad hoc Groups/Task forces

To keep pace with today's rapidly changing environment, many associations have increased their use of ad hoc groups, such as task forces or teams. They are often appointed by the chief elected officer, with input from the executive committee or board of directors.

These groups are self-limiting in both time and scope; they focus on short-term, specific needs—such as generating a solution to an organizational problem or the association's response to an emerging issue—and then disband when their work is complete. In fact, those characteristics make it somewhat easier to recruit volunteers who may be unable to make a greater commitment to the organization.

Because most ad hoc groups are formed for special purposes or functions, they require detailed objectives and desired outcomes. Electronic communications such as e-mail and conference calls can enable ad hoc groups to accomplish their short-term tasks without time-consuming, face-to-face meetings. This conserves the association's financial resources while involving more of the membership.

Special Interest Groups

These groups represent a specialized or focused area of the industry or profession represented by the association. Special interest groups are usually transitional: They relate to a newly identified need or perhaps to an area where membership or interest is declining. By serving as an incubator, the association provides the support, resources, and volunteers that the group needs to identify and fulfill its mission. Once that mission has been achieved, the special interest group and its leaders are often absorbed into other organizational structures of the association. But if the association hasn't supported the group, such as by assisting with meetings and providing a staff liaison, the group may break away and form a separate organization or form an alliance with a competing association.

Membership Sections

A special interest group may evolve into a permanent membership section that represents a geographic or functional area—for instance, a U.S.-based trade association may maintain an international section for its members who do business abroad. In some associations, sections operate much like an "association within an association" with their own elected leaders, budgets, and designated staff. Volunteer leaders may represent the sections interest within the associations overall governing body.

Strengthening the Volunteer Leader Relationship

Associations depend upon volunteers to provide leadership within their organizational structures as well as to assist with events and programs, such as contributing articles to the association's publication, giving a presentation at its annual conference, or helping raise funds for its educational foundation. Activities related to attracting—and keeping—those valuable volunteers must be incorporated not only into the strategic plan but also into the culture of the association.

Those activities include:

Recruitment

Getting involved in the association by attending or helping with events can get someone noticed, but it may take some effort to encourage that person to assume a leadership role. Current leaders—especially those who serve on the nominating committee—should always be on the lookout for knowledgeable, talented, and enthusiastic people who could eventually take over the responsibilities of top-ranking volunteers. By meeting and talking with members, both staff and current leaders will get some idea of their leadership potential and availability.

Volunteer Orientation

Once potential leaders have agreed to become part of the governance structure, the association must acquaint them with their new roles and responsibilities. The board of directors, for instance, may have the responsibility of approving the association's financial and investment statements; an introduction to how those documents are organized and what they communicate would enable new board members to make well-informed decisions.

Three types of documents prove useful for providing volunteers with an understanding of the association's structure and operations:

1. *Legal,* including articles of incorporation and bylaws.
2. *Management,* such as association policies and procedures, financial reports, minutes of past meetings, and job descriptions for both volunteers and staff.
3. *Internal,* such as the association's code of ethics, organizational chart, and strategic plan.

Although many associations rely on staff and current leaders to conduct orientation and training, some are increasingly turning to outside consultants who have a working knowledge of governance structures and systems. In fact, a number of association chief executive officers trade the function of training one another's volunteer leaders. Whether the trainer comes from another association or a consulting firm, the rationale is that someone from the "outside" can deliver appropriate messages with a greater degree of objectivity.

Also gaining in popularity is mentoring—pairing an experienced board member with a newly elected one to answer questions, provide information, and simply serve as a friendly face in a possible sea of strangers.

While training is more task-oriented, orientation provides an overview of the association and identifies how and where the new leader fits into the picture. Orientation—whether handled by one person or by a team of experienced leaders and staff—should provide new leaders with guidance on the specific task their committee, task force, or other organizational unit is to accomplish during their tenure.

What It Takes

Although by no means a complete list of leadership attributes and characteristics, the following list serves as a starting point for selecting volunteers to lead the association:

- **Proven performance.** Leadership requires knowledge, talent, skill, vitality, and the ability to make a difference. In the association environment, that translates into a solid track record of contributing to the success of programs, events, or projects.

- **Commitment.** Serving as an association leader is an honor and a reward—but it requires a demonstrated commitment to the organization and its mission and goals.

- **Time to serve.** Participating fully in association activities requires extra time to prepare for, travel to, and attend meetings.

- **Good health.** The often hectic and strenuous pace of volunteer leadership requires a good mental and physical condition.

- **Understanding of team work.** Many people contribute their efforts toward the realization of an association's goals and objectives—no one does it alone. Well-developed interpersonal and communication skills are essential to effective team work.

- **Sound judgment and integrity.** In many instances, popularity brings potential leaders into the limelight of the association. But popularity must be tempered with good judgment and integrity: Decisions may need to be made that are not popular among the members.

- **Ability to think strategically.** This is for the good of the whole organization and not particularly for a constituency they may represent. Volunteer leaders must be able to leave personal agendas and politics at the door in order to work on behalf of the organization.

- **Communication and "teaching" skills.** By virtue of their position, current leaders serve as mentors and teachers to future leaders. Enthusiasm and a passion for the mission and goals of the association are visible characteristics that people can emulate.

- **Organizational experience.** People who have served on other nonprofit boards and developed skills on committees, working with budgets, raising funds, and promoting the image of the organization are good candidates for leadership roles.

- **Ability to subordinate special interests.** Leaders often emerge because of their special expertise or effective representation of a specific membership constituency. Leadership, however, may require subordinating those special interests for the greater good of the entire association.

- **Exemplary personal conduct.** Leaders' behavior and attitudes can greatly influence others in the association. As a result, it's vital for them to have and exhibit a sensitivity to race, ethnic, gender, age, and other human differences and good listening skills.

- **Support systems.** The extra efforts required of volunteer leaders involve a substantial time commitment. Not only does this need to be understood by the person's employer but also by his or her family and friends.

- **Visionary leaders must see past daily operations to focus on the larger needs.** This provides momentum to move the organization's mission and goals forward with effective governance.

The final consideration relates to the end of a volunteer's leadership tenure: the ability to bow out gracefully. Nothing can be more fractious to an association than a leader who continues to lead after his or her term has concluded.

Recognition

For the many hours association volunteers spend away from their families, friends, and jobs—not to mention the weekends in airplanes or hotel rooms—they deserve recognition. Of course, volunteers gain recognition among their peers and even the public by contributing to association publications, giving presentations at conferences, and serving as a spokesperson for the association. Still, all leaders should be formally recognized for their service and contributions when their volunteer commitment ends.

The award need not be elaborate or expensive but should be appropriate and presented with sincerity. Recognition may be as simple as providing a special ribbon for all volunteer leaders to wear at the convention. Or, it might entail arranging upgraded accommodations or special in-room amenities for those who travel to association meetings. One association might provide volunteers with desk items (mugs, letter openers, and so forth) carrying its logo, while another might host a thank-you reception and give engraved plaques to volunteers.

Because many volunteers serve in order to make a contribution to their fellow members, recognition of their efforts should take place in the presence of their peers—the associations members.

Support

As *Policies and Procedures in Association Management* points out, more than half of associations don't reimburse committee members for the travel, food, and lodging expenses incurred to attend board meetings (the majority, however, do reimburse those expenses for the chief elected officer). Yet associations that aren't in the position to reimburse expenses can still demonstrate support of their volunteers.

For instance, volunteers accept the risk of personal liability when they accept a position as an officer or director. Although successful legal action against association officers and directors is rare, the potential consequences of an action initiated in today's litigious society might warrant the purchase of professional liability insurance. A com-

---

Worth Watching

Several trends that may affect organizational structure and volunteer involvement emerged in the 2006 survey titled *Policies and Procedures in Association Management*. They include the following:

- Online voting increased significantly with 29 percent of organizations reporting this as an accepted method in 2005, up from seven percent in 2001.

- More than one out of two associations (52 percent) reported having an audit committee, 24 percent of those organizations creating the committee after Sarbanes Oxley was enacted.

- Nearly a quarter of respondents (22 percent) reported having a whistleblower policy with 74 percent adopting a policy after Sarbanes Oxley.

---

prehensive director and officer's insurance plan can shield volunteers from being held personally liable for actions taken on behalf of the association.

The most visible means of volunteer support, however, is staff assistance. In addition to serving as the liaison to the chief executive officer, staff can lighten a volunteer leader's load by preparing meeting materials; handling logistics for meetings; drafting and distributing minutes; and providing information on association policies, procedures, and programs.

The Staff-Volunteer Relationship

A balance between volunteer and staff involvement is needed for the overall mission and goals of the association to be achieved. Volunteers have "real world" experience and expertise because they operate in—and are therefore sensitive to—the environment that influences members' needs. Staff has the experience and expertise needed to administer and operate the association so it can meet those needs.

To put it simply:

- The role of volunteers is to ensure that the association serves the needs of its members, by establishing direction and policies for programs, products, and services. They focus on longer term, strategic issues.

- The role of staff is to keep the association moving ahead in the direction and according to the policies established by volunteers, by implementing procedures that deliver the programs, products, and services to the members. They focus on shorter term, operational issues.

In some associations, achieving an appropriate balance between the volunteer and staff roles and responsibilities is fraught with anxiety and causes much consternation and frustration to both volunteers and staff. As noted above, a delineation that clarifies the value and appropriate role of each party can help avoid or alleviate such situations.

Role clarification, for instance, should emphasize that committees, task forces, sections, special interest groups, and the chief executive officer are accountable to the board of directors.

Committee and board members should be expected to sign a commitment form, conflict of interest statement, and understand the goals of the committee. In turn, the board answers to the membership for how the association is governed and managed.

Open and frequent communication—through newsletters, periodicals, annual meetings, chapter or section gatherings, and so forth—provides accountability back to the membership. E-mail is used by almost all associations, as well as reliance on Web sites to disseminate information and provide 24/7 resources. In addition, many associations issue annual or quarterly reports, long used by business and industry, to communicate their financial and strategic decisions to their stakeholders—their members.

Partners in Leadership

Achieving open communication depends greatly on appointing a liaison between the board of directors and the various organizational units. The chief executive officer typically assumes this role of liaison along with his or her other responsibilities to ensure that the board receives timely and accurate information regarding the activities of the various organizational units.

The chief executive officer may channel much of that information through the chief elected officer, which is why the two people should function as a true team for the association to remain on a positive and forward course. If, for example, one withholds information from the other, or if the two have widely differing opinions about the association's strategic direction, confusion may result among the volunteers as well as the staff.

Working as a team entails learning about one another's strengths, weaknesses, hopes, and aspirations. That may be accomplished by attending seminars aimed at building partnerships between the chief elected and executive officers or by observing one another in action. For instance, some associations have a tradition of inviting the newly elected officer to their offices to meet staff and observe how board policies are carried out at the operational level. Likewise, other organizations routinely send the chief executive officer to visit the chief elected officer in his or her work environment.

On an ongoing basis, many chief elected and chief executive officers spend several hours on the phone every week or two—or trade frequent e-mail messages—to coordinate their schedules, discuss upcoming activities and emerging concerns, and brainstorm solutions to problems that may have arisen. By becoming familiar with the other's personality, working style, and decision-making preferences—and by remaining in frequent contact—the two parties can build a partnership that avoids power struggles and advances the work of the association.

References and Suggested Reading

ASAE & The Center for Association Leadership, *Policies and Procedures in Association Management,* Washington, D.C., 2006.

Able, Edward H., Jr., *Future Perspectives,* Foundation of the American Society of Association Executives, Washington, D.C., 1985.

Conners, Tracy D., *The Nonprofit Organization Handbook,* McGraw-Hill Board Co., New York, 1980.

Drucker, Peter R, *Management,* Harper & Row, New York, 1973.

Dunlop, James J., *Leading the Association: Striking the Right Balance Between Staff and Volunteers,* Foundation of the American Society of Association Executives, Washington, D.C., 1989.

Eadie, Douglas C., *Boards That Work: A Practical Guide to Building Effective Association Boards,* American Society of Association Executives, Washington, D.C., 1995.

Foundation of the American Society of Association Executives, *Critical Competencies of Association Executives,* Washington, D.C., 1979.

Greif, Joseph, *Managing Membership Societies,* Foundation of the American Society of Association Executives, Washington, D.C., 1979.

Imming, Bernard J., *Fundamentals of Association Management: The Volunteer,* American Society of Association Executives, Washington, D.C., 1982.

——, *Getting Involved: The Challenge of Committee Participation,* American Society of Association Executives, Washington, D.C., 1980.

——, *A Special Responsibility,* Foundation of the American Society of Association Executives, Washington, D.C., 1984.

Jacobs, Jerald A., *Association Law Handbook,* American Society of Association Executives, Washington, B.C., 1996.

Levitt, Theodore, *The Third Sector: New Tactics for a Responsive Society,* AMACOM, New York, 1973.

Schlegel, John F., *Enhancing Committee Effectiveness,* American Society of Association Executives, Washington, D.C., 1994.

Snyder, David Pearce, and Gregg Edwards, *Future Forces,* Foundation of the American Society of Association Executives, Washington, D.C., 1984.

Webster, George D., *The Law of Associations,* Mathew Bender Company, New York, 1982.

About the Author

Wayne E. Leroy, CAE, is president and CEO of W&N, LLC, a consulting company for non-profit associations and organizations. Prior to that, he was executive vice president of the Association of Higher Education Facilities Officers.

Beth Brooks, CAE, president of the Texas Society of Association Executives, reviewed this chapter and, with the author's permission, updated information as appropriate.

Review Questions

1. While bylaws may vary in length and complexity, there are several components in all bylaws. What are five of the most common issues noted in bylaws?

2. Why would an association consider being incorporated?

3. Name four leadership characteristics.

4. What are four common ways that associations communicate with members?

2

Developing Policies and Procedures

Jone R. Sienkiewicz, CMP, CAE

A SSOCIATIONS WITHOUT POLICIES AND procedures are like ships without rudders. They may experience smooth sailing on calm days, but the minute a storm begins brewing, they risk losing their way in troubled waters. Policies and procedures keep an association on course by giving members and staff the guidelines for making consistent and logical decisions as critical issues arise.

Understanding the difference between the two is essential to ensuring an association's success:

- Policies, which spell out standards of conduct and decision making, articulate the strategy and philosophy of an organization's governing body, be it a board of directors, executive council, or assembly of delegates. Developed and adopted by volunteer leaders, policies provide the framework upon which the association builds its procedures. Do not forget with the revisions of Sarbanes-Oxley that it is prudent to include not only what should be done but also what are prohibited activities. This is especially true of associations and societies that use government grants and contracts.

- Procedures delineate how to administer the policy; in other words they spell out the steps needed to turn a particular concept into reality. Both volunteers and staff can develop procedures, although staff implements them as part of the association's operations. In order for this to be done efficiently, the staff and board must define the core competencies of the organization to assure the operations and activities are correctly defined for maximum impact. Staff, committees, and the board must plan to ensure that quality-control measures are in place in each of the written procedures.

For example, an association's board of directors may propose and adopt a policy stating that the annual convention will take place every year on the third weekend in May. The corresponding procedures, which provide staff with a plan of action to follow, might dictate that the meeting occurs in a particular set of days or hours, and with a particular schedule (general sessions, educational seminars, recreational activities, and so forth).

Involving officers, board members, committee leaders, and staff in the development and review process helps shape usable, enforceable policies. To provide consistency as staff and volunteer leadership changes—and to lessen the possibility of misinterpretation—written procedures should accompany each policy. Although they can be elaborate, written procedures don't have to be complicated to get the job done.

Once supporting procedures have been drafted and approved—by either the governing body or, more likely, by the chief executive officer—legal counsel should review the total package to ensure that the policies and applicable procedures comply with all applicable federal and state laws.

In general, association policies and procedures address three areas: governance, operations and management, and public image and public policy.

Governance

Policies in this area relate to how the governing body governs both itself and the association. They include the following:

Membership and organizational structure. Such policies define the categories of membership (regular, associate, affiliate, and so forth) and corresponding dues structures, as well as such things as whether the association is incorporated, its nonprofit tax code, and whether legal counsel is hired, retained, or used as needed.

Because the Internal Revenue Service (IRS) has begun to question whether associate members are truly members—as opposed to vendors buying access to a specialized market or services—more associations are refining their membership policies to spell out what roles associate members may fill within the governance structure. The more involved associate members are in leadership roles, the less likely the IRS seems to take their membership dues.

Volunteer leadership. Associations use these policies to spell out terms of office, explain the selection or election process (including guidelines for campaigning or the role of the nominating committee in preparing a slate of candidates), and describe any reimbursements available to volunteers for board or committee service.

Related entities. Many associations establish for-profit subsidiaries for generating non-dues revenue or set up nonprofit foundations for advancing the industry or profession through research and educational activities. In either case, the parent association should develop separate policies and procedures for governing and operating the spin-off organization, such as the size and composition of its governing body. Keeping records—and possibly personnel—exclusive to the subsidiary or foundation will facilitate compliance with tax code regulations and minimize confusion in day-to-day operations.

In addition, the parent association should establish a set of policies that explain the relationship between it and the subsidiary or foundation. Especially helpful are policies that outline the management fee, if any, paid to the parent organization; the percentage of shared overhead; the amount of dividends or royalties to be paid and to whom; and reporting responsibilities.

Association management. The chief executive officer is accountable to the association's governing body; it, in turn, reviews his or her performance and determines the appropriate compensation and benefits. To ensure consistency in the review process as volunteer leaders change, governance policies often outline the volunteer positions that participate in the process—for example, the chief elected officer and his or her successor may conduct the review each year on behalf of the entire board.

Although not often discussed, a succession policy helps protect the association in the event of the death or abrupt termination of the chief executive officer. The chief executive officer should work with the board to develop the staff leadership succession plan. The plan would cover areas such as which staff person, department vice president, or director would be in charge on an interim basis; what salary or benefit payments would be paid to the estate of the departed executive; and what procedure would be followed to seek the services of another executive. (Note: a succession policy must be consistent with the terms of any employment contract that exists between the association and chief executive officer, primarily in the area of severance or death benefits.)

It's helpful to have policies in place to guide the work of a search committee, even though the committee is ad hoc in nature. The policy may, for example, designate the incoming elected chairman or president as the head of the group charged with finding and evaluating the next chief staff executive. The accompanying procedures should spell out the time frame for the search, how the candidates will be presented to the board, and any reimbursement of volunteer expenses associated with the search.

Finance. At the governance level, policies generally address the association's fiscal year, the amount of money targeted for or maintained in reserves, what types of investments are to be considered, and who has the authority to invest the funds.

Operations and Management

These policies, which deal with day-to-day operations of the association, include the following:

Credentialing. Many associations offer a credentialing program—accreditation, certification, licensure, or standardization—as a means of ensuring professional competence in the field they represent or to establish standards. Policies must spell out eligibility requirements (such as the minimum number of years working in the industry or profession or passing an exam), as well as any criteria for renewal of the credential (such as attending a specific number of continuing education seminars within a certain number of years). Legal counsel should review the policies with an eye toward antitrust concerns and the potential for legal or tax liability.

Finances. Sound financial policies can reduce costs by putting effective accounting practices in place. Topics addressed are the method of accounting used (cash, accrual, or a combination of the two), the number of signatures needed on checks (and who can sign them), the content of and schedule for financial reports presented to the governing body, and the method of reporting annually to the general membership. In addition, the establishment of an independent audit committee that oversees the audit function (selection of the audit firm, scope of the audit/review, timing, internal controls, reports, and process for resolving any discrepancies) is essential. This committee should include those with the knowledge and experience to effectively serve.

Government affairs. These policies encompass such issues as who serves as the lead lobbyist for the association, at what levels the association monitors legislation or regulatory actions, and whether the association operates a political action committee (PAC). In the latter case, procedures might cover how the PAC is administered, at what level PAC contributions could be made, and how contributions are acknowledged.

Meetings/Conventions. Policy issues include the number and type of meetings to be held, whether an exhibition or trade show will take place in conjunction with one or more meetings, the geographic pattern of site selection, and who has the authority to select the site. Other issues of concern might be the design and content of the educational program, related activities (golf tournaments, family programs, and so forth), and who has the authority to enter into contracts on behalf of the association.

Policies for international meetings or world congresses must take into consideration the secretariat of those events. For instance, the host organization's meeting

---

Under Review

After policies have been developed and put into place, it's important to ensure they continue to serve the association's ever-changing needs. Some guidelines to consider are:

1. Set an annual date to review all existing policies and procedures—and stick to it. An obvious time might be during the annual review of the bylaws. In most cases, if bylaws changes are needed or recommended, policies and procedures will be affected and may need to be modified or even abolished.

2. Involve staff in reviewing the association's policies and procedures. The people who must enforce, carry out, and be responsible for and to the policies are the ones who can most efficiently and effectively see the needed changes. The end result is not only better policies and procedures but also a staff "buy-in" to facilitate adherence to them.

3. Consider using past presidents to review policies and procedures that affect external entities, such as members, the general public, and the industry or profession.

4. Set aside a short period of time to try out the new policies and procedures before finalizing them. It is easier to change something that is temporary than to revise something the board has approved and made a permanent part of the association's structure.

policies may not coincide with those of the co-sponsoring association. The production of a world congress can be time-consuming and nerve-racking. Imagine planning an annual meeting in three, four, or five different countries for people of such diversity that the most innocent of remarks, slights, or omissions can ruin the event. Policies established for these events must transcend those of any single organization within the secretariat. To achieve a balance that provides the most advantageous position for all groups involved, tact and diplomacy are essential.

The host organization might naturally assume a leadership role in not only contracting with vendors but also in setting the policies and procedures for administration of the congress itself. A trap to avoid is assuming that the policies and procedures in place for the host organization's annual event(s) are acceptable to the co-hosts.

For example, the host organization may have a policy that allows exhibitors to set up their booths on Saturday and Sunday for a Monday opening. One of the co-hosts may not allow such practices on the basis of religious beliefs. In order to have the exhibits set up and ready for Monday, a compromise may have to be reached that, while the activity will be allowed, it will not be posted or publicly announced. In other words, those who need to know will know, and those who may be offended and need not know would not be included in the information loop. Another example might be the use of first names or nicknames on badges. Some cultures welcome this informality as a way of "breaking the ice." Other cultures consider it an insult to call people by their first names before becoming well acquainted.

In addition to discussing cultural likes and dislikes, it might be appropriate to simply designate which group's policies take precedence in instances where cultural considerations are not part of the equation.

Membership and dues. While governance policies outline who members are, operational policies outline how those individuals or companies are treated. For instance, an association may have a policy of answering a member's question within 24 hours or communicating with all members at least once a month.

Associations with chapters require policies for serving and communicating with them. Items for consideration include the costs of services provided by the national to each chapter, which level has the responsibility for invoicing or rebating membership dues, and how chapters are represented at national meetings.

Some associations stipulate that their members pay dues based on a calendar year; others tie dues payments to their fiscal year or to the member's anniversary date. The amount of dues can be flat, sliding, or a percentage of some tangible number related to the industry (such as sales volume, number of employees, and so forth).

Whatever dues criteria are established, supporting procedures should outline how the association handles late-paying or non-renewing members. For example, procedures might address when and how many times dues will be billed, how to accommodate members who wish to stretch dues payments over several months or quarters of the year, and when non-paying members will be removed from the active membership list.

Office administration. Issues range from the hours of operation to the use of computer equipment by staff, from the way the phone is answered to which employees are covered by liability insurance. A strong document-retention policy and a backup of data policy are needed to maintain the historical perspective of the organization.

Personnel. These policies set the tone of the workplace: If they're strict and unyielding, they may alienate employees. On the other hand, liberal policies can weaken the position of management and jeopardize professionalism. Personnel policies usually cover sick and annual leave (how it's accrued, the number of paid holidays, and so forth); employee dispute resolution and insurance benefits; reimbursement of staff travel expense; and grounds for termination, leaves of absence, outplacement services, and severance pay.

Because this area is heavily regulated, it's best to consult with both a human resources professional and an attorney to ensure policies comply with both federal and state laws.

Publishing. The vast majority of associations publish at least one periodical. Whether it's a one-page, one-color newsletter or a slick, four-color magazine or journal, the print vehicle requires policies such as whether advertising is accepted and from whom, how sales representatives are compensated, how—and whether—members review materials before they are printed, and the requirements for submitting material for publication.

Services. Policies in this area might spell out who can have access to the association's information services, library, fax-on demand service, referral program, Web site, or group insurance plan. Antitrust concerns dictate that associations consult with legal counsel when drafting policies that relate to pricing structures and participation in group-purchasing plans.

If the association maintains relationships with suppliers through affinity programs, this area would also include guidelines for selecting the suppliers, promoting or marketing the product or service, and determining royalties.

Public Image and Public Policy

Every association serves or comes into contact with a number of publics, ranging from its elected leaders to its general membership, from the narrow niche of the specialized trade press to the general public. With that in mind, policies typically cover the following:

Media relations. The designation of an official spokesperson for the association is, unfortunately, often omitted from the policy manual. Many associations limit the role of spokesperson to the CEO or the chief elected officer—either exclusively or in tandem. For instance, a trade association might designate the CEO to speak on issues affecting the industry, while the top elected leader addresses association-related issues. Another policy might identify exceptions, such as when other staff members or volunteers take on the role of association spokesperson while testifying before a regulatory or legislative body.

Guidelines for Development

Having a list of questions to answer will help define policy concerns and set the stage for drafting the supporting procedures. Additionally, developing a format for a written policy manual will provide consistency throughout the association.

Here is a simple, six-step methodology for setting policies and procedures; the smallest organization can use it to develop and maintain guidelines, or a larger organization with more complicated needs can expand upon it. To illustrate the process, consider the example of the Anything For A Buck Association (AFABA):

1. **Define the question or problem requiring a policy statement.** AFABA wants to form a foundation to award college scholarships to the children of members.

2. **Analyze the alternative solutions.** Questions might include: Should students be entering freshmen in college or can they be at any level? Is the scholarship based solely on academics, or does community service play a role? What is the timetable for receiving and reviewing applications? How many scholarships should be given? In what amount? Will the money be paid directly to the college or to the student?

3. **Select the most reasonable alternative.** After analyzing the alternatives and choosing the answers that best suit the association's needs, drafting the policy and related procedures is easy.

4. **Develop the policy that speaks to the accepted alternative.** For instance, AFABA's policy statement might read: The AFABA Scholarship will be awarded to entering college freshmen. The children of all members will be eligible for this award. The scholarship will be awarded in May. Deadline for receipt of applications will be the last Friday in March.

5. **Develop procedures that will implement the policy.** In this example, the procedures might read as follows:

   - AFABA staff will design an announcement and application that incorporate the criteria for the scholarship.

   - The draft application and announcement will be sent to the AFABA Scholarship Committee for review and comment.

   - Upon approval from the committee, AFABA staff will proceed with production of the application and announcement.

   - Scholarship announcements and applications will be sent to all members with the January issue of the AFABA Journal and again in a stand-alone mailing in February.

   - Scholarship applications received in the AFABA office will be date-stamped on the cover and held for forwarding to the Scholarship Committee for its April meeting.

   - Completed applications will be sent to the committee for review not later than two weeks before its meeting.

6. **Evaluate the results to identify the need for change.** AFABA might build this step into its procedures as follows.

   - AFABA staff and the Scholarship Committee will review the policy and administrative procedures for this scholarship annually.

   - Changes in this policy require the approval of the AFABA Board of Directors.

   - Changes in administration require the approval of the Scholarship Committee.

Media relations policies may also spell out what media receive which type of news. For instance, some association news releases may be appropriate for distribution to the trade press exclusively, while other news with more effect on the general public would warrant releases to the national media.

Crisis management. Most associations, at one time or another, face a negative situation within their industry or profession—or perhaps within the organization itself. Having a crisis management policy, coupled with a set of procedures that define what to do in specific circumstances, not only helps maintain the association's image but also assists staff in fulfilling their roles. Policies need to designate a spokesperson, describe who will serve on the task force that sets the ground rules for a response, and list who must be contacted immediately and in what order.

Supporting procedures should outline which board and staff positions do what and, more important, which ones should do nothing at all.

In conclusion, it is important to establish and utilize a strong peer review network to maintain knowledge of current association practices. While most organizations rely on internal staff to serve this function, it can be helpful to have a focus group of staff and members to serve as this review team. This inclusive approach will assure that the practices work well with member expectations.

About the Author

Jone R. Sienkiewicz, CMP, CAE, serves as executive director of the Real Estate Educators Association and the American Association for Paralegal Education. She is also director of the exhibits/marketing division at Talley Management Group, Inc., an association management company in Mt. Royal, New Jersey.

Review Questions

1. What areas in your association have policies but no procedures?

2. How can you update your policies or procedures to bring them up-to-date with your internal/external practices?

3. How long has it been since you reviewed your crisis management policies and procedures? What new areas should be addressed?

4. How many of your new initiatives have not yet been incorporated into your policies and procedures manual? How long will it take you to incorporate them?

5. What practices are you using that should be made into formal procedures?

6. Who in your office is responsible for setting procedures? How does the information needed to update, change, or incorporate new procedures get transmitted to them?

Defining the Future

Bruce Butterfield, CAE, APR

I T IS NO NEWS that the world of associations is on the cusp of fundamental change. The unanswered question is what to do about it. This change is being driven by globalization; the creation of modular relationships that supersede industry and professional boundaries; the technology of connection that permits wide and instantaneous sharing of information and knowledge; and the entrance of the Millennial generation, the most collaborative generation in human history, into the workforce.

Today's association leaders can very much empathize with Christopher Columbus' chandler. He had no idea where they were going, how long it would take, or what they would need when they got there. But he had to supply the ships nonetheless. We, like him, need to imagine what new opportunities and challenges will arise in a new world, about which we know only that it will bear little resemblance to the old one.

Getting a Grip on the Future

When asked how he made such accurate predictions, the late management guru Peter Drucker said, "I don't forecast. I look out the window and identify what's visible but not yet seen." This is the purpose of an ongoing futures analysis process: to identify what is visible but not yet seen in order to avoid being blindsided. For example, in the mid 1990s, a large U.S. association built a multimillion-dollar proprietary portal that was quickly overshadowed by the Web and abandoned. Had it identified the Web, which its president called "the lion on the other side of the hill," and assessed its implications, the association might have seen that the open architecture of the Internet would supplant proprietary systems and avoided its huge loss.

To prepare for the future and implement any positioning strategy, associations must understand how their members' needs will change, not in the murky and distant future, but in the years that lie immediately ahead. Member needs assessments and customer satisfaction surveys, however, only show how well you performed in the past. They are notoriously poor in advising how you should perform in the future. Associations must concern themselves with the emerging member needs being created by external forces and what changes their organizations need to implement to help their members respond to them.

In order to determine what is driving the future, associations must examine not just their customers, but also their customers' customers. The very best one can expect from a study of one's own customers is to react to changes sooner. However, by studying its customers' customers, an organization can anticipate emerging needs of its immediate customers or members. Schematically, the process can be described as follows:

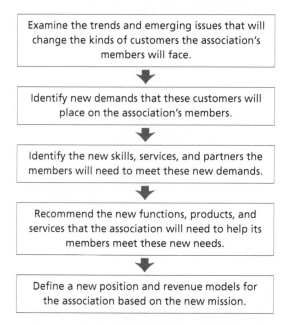

The result of this approach is a proactive, market-driven solution that responds to the long-term needs of the members' market rather than solely the short-term concerns facing today's members. There is more information on this methodology in the chapter that follows by Rick O'Sullivan.

Associations have always been information gatherers and producers. But there are many other sources of information today, so associations no longer have a franchise. Now they need to be intelligence digesters, abstracters, and analysts. This has high value because their members often are too busy to do this for themselves. The new cry for help is, "Just tell me what's in my in-box that I should pay attention to and what it means!" This requires futures analysis. Note the use of the word "futures," not "future" analysis. There is no one future to be divined from the vantage point of today. To attempt to do so leads to forecasts and predictions, which are usually incorrect. The future does not project from today in a straight line. It spins out in overlapping tiers.

Components of Futures Analysis

There are five primary activities involved in futures analysis:

- Identifying and monitoring change;
- Considering and critiquing the impacts of change;
- Imagining conceivable alternative futures;
- Envisioning preferred futures; and
- Planning and implementing desired change.

The means of accomplishing these activities are environmental scanning, identification of change drivers, scenario planning, and strategic planning.

Any futures analysis system should have four extremely important objectives: (1) Issue and trend identification and analysis are ongoing; (2) Implications are determined, (3) Implications lead to actions, and (4) The scanning process yields salable products. Here is an example of a futures analysis process used by a healthcare association:

Consider and Critique the Impacts of Change
The Futures Analysis Cycle

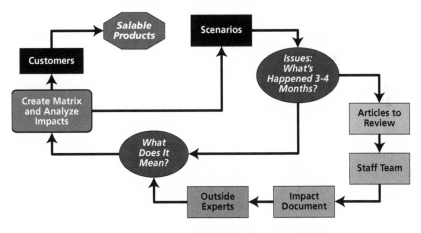

In this model, staff and selected volunteers analyze quarterly what has happened with major issues confronting the industry. Staff members are assigned publications, Web sites, blogs, and other resources to review pertaining to the forces having an impact on the major issues. A senior staff team headed by a full-time director reviews the submissions and determines which are pertinent to be abstracted for a quarterly impact document that is provided to a group of 30 to 40 outside experts from diverse disciplines inside and outside of the healthcare field that meets semiannually. The incentive for their participation is early access to intelligence and the opportunity to interact with people they might not otherwise meet in a free-ranging dialogue.

These experts offer options about additions and subtractions from the impact document, determine priorities of issues, and discuss their meaning to the industry and the association. The senior staff team creates a matrix that lists the issues and whether they have a positive, negative, or neutral impact on the industry. The development of this matrix leads to the creation of new products and services that help members address the issues and scenarios that play out the issues to a point in time, usually fives years out. The scenarios then suggest strategies and impacts that lead back into the issues analysis process. It becomes a virtuous circle.

Environmental Scanning

There are three primary concerns in constructing an effective environmental scanning process:

1. Scanning is a labor-intensive process that is difficult for hard-worked staff and part-time volunteers to perform well.

2. The effectiveness of the scan is a function of *what* is being scanned and *for what purpose*. The more outlets, the richer the scan will be and the greater the likelihood of correctly identifying emerging issues and trends.

3. However, scanning volumes of information is a daunting task. There are several types of change (see "Types of Change"), with two—emerging issues and trends—being the most crucial to identify in a scanning process, as these are the change areas most effectively leveraged.

Futurists are most interested in emerging issues because they are the seeds of trends, the changes that will initiate a trend over time. Identification of an emerging issue leads to potential for real leverage in how that issue eventually affects an organization. The goal is to effectively focus your association's environmental scan.

Types of Change

- **Cycles**—changes that occur over an observable time period and are rather predictable (i.e. seasons, ice ages, El Niño)

- **Wildcard events**—sudden, discontinuous change (i.e. the fall of the Berlin Wall, the September 11 tragedies, the threat of a worldwide pandemic)

- **Trends**—changes that move in a direction over time. Trends are not new; there is much data and information about them and they have been observed for a period of time (i.e. global warming, population changes)

- **Emerging issues**—the type of change that, ideally, a futures analysis process will uncover and focus on (i.e. the effect of religious fundamentalism on energy supplies, time-shifting, and place shifting of information)

Futurists often scan STEEP categories (sociodemographics, technology, economics, environment, and politics). Rich scans produce volumes of "hits" that must be analyzed and assessed for implications. How do you focus on what is important? Use panels of experts in each field to vet scanning "hits," and advise you on their relative impact and immediacy. These vetted "hits" can be displayed on a scanning gauge (shown in the figure below). "Hits" with high impact and immediacy are recommended for action by the association or its constituents and intensely tracked. High impact and low immediacy and low impact and high immediacy "hits" are simply tracked. Low impact and low immediacy "hits" would no longer be tracked, but would be on a watch list and periodically revisited to see if they have changed intensity and because some may be weak signals that will develop into significant trends.

Scanning gauges can be assembled into a dashboard of business fields that allows a quick overview of each scan and enables discussions of commonalities and tie-ins. In other words, this is where the dots get connected. Business fields could be the STEEP categories described above or more sector-specific fields. For example, ASAE & The Center's business fields might include what is happening in the worlds of convening, communication, education, organization, and structure or customership. The display of information can be facilitated by dashboard software programs, and there are many on the market.

Due to the changing and continuous nature of tracking, the association can offer online subscriptions for accessing the scanning results. Since this is intelligence and highly valuable in helping members head off threats and take advantage of emerging opportunities, subscriptions can generate significant income streams, perhaps in the high six figures or more depending on the association's membership.

The Scanning Gauge
Copyright © 2006 The Forbes Group

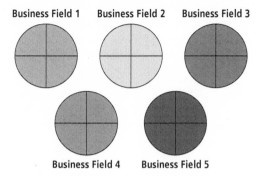

The Scanning Dashboard
Copyright © 2006 The Forbes Group

Business Field 1   Business Field 2   Business Field 3

Business Field 4   Business Field 5

Identifying Change Drivers

Through the environmental scanning process, decision-makers can identify emerging forces able to reshape or overwhelm existing institutions and, consequently, promote different behaviors that may not appear rational within today's structure. The output of environmental scanning can be a daunting array of these change drivers. It is important to narrow the number of change drivers because they will be used to define alternative future scenarios.

The paradigm for explaining individual and organizational behavior is: Structure → Conduct → Performance. Organizational structures create the rigidities that guide conduct and make market performance predictable. When determining change drivers, test them against the Structure → Conduct → Performance model and look for those that are structural.

A healthcare organization wanted to create some alternative future scenarios. Their environmental scan revealed two extremely significant structural change drivers—the type of healthcare that would be delivered in the future and the means of that delivery. Each of these drivers had polar opposite outcomes. The type of healthcare delivered in the future could focus on wellness or disease treatment. The means of delivery in the future could be institutional delivery of care (hospitals, clinics, physicians' offices) or community delivery of care (senior centers, schools, malls).

In another example, when Y2K threatened, predictions ranged from no effect to total disaster. Some futurists built scenarios based on two change drivers—the response of technology (isolated failures vs. widespread failures) and the response of society (social coherence vs. social breakdown).

In the association world, there are two powerful structural change drivers that are increasingly being discussed by association leaders. They are technological change and demographic shifts. The spectacular deployment, unplugging and portability of the Internet and the convergence of communications delivery technologies (from PC to laptop to PDA to cell phone to IPod® to TIVO® [TV time shifting] to Slingbox® [TV place shifting]) challenges associations, which are not known as early adopters. Couple this with the arrival in the workforce and association membership of the huge Millennial Generation (born since 1982 and who have never not used instant messages, text messaging, blogs, vlogs, and wikis) and you have the ingredients of dramatic change.

Scenario Planning

When change drivers have been identified, they can be used to create potential future worlds where planners can work at minimum risk. This methodology was initially developed by The Rand Corporation and refined by Royal Dutch Shell. It has been successfully used worldwide by companies, governments, and associations.

It is human nature to restrict our thinking to the known and the comfortable. However, history has demonstrated time and again that profound change comes in surges and jerks instead of sustained moderate trends. Rather than committing to the rules of conduct dictated by a single structure, scenarios create alternative structures that allow decision-makers to play out alternative futures. Scenarios are not stories about the way things are but alternatives about what they could be.

The Value of Scenarios

Scenario stories are told from a particular point in time and look back to the present. Scenario planners work with them by adding their thinking about how the stories might evolve and then creating strategies that will advance desirable futures and prevent undesirable ones. While the real future will emerge from all of the scenarios and more, scenario planning helps leaders to move past barriers and, as the earlier Drucker quote says, identify what is visible but not yet seen.

Scenario planning is an approach to strategy development and decision-making that acknowledges, then structures, the inherent uncertainty in the societal, public policy, and business environment and aims at achieving maximum feasible resilience in strategy. It is predicated on the fact that in an uncertain environment, single-point forecasts, which most leaders tend to rely on, are inherently inaccurate and strategies based on them will almost certainly be misdirected.

Scenarios are not predictions: They are carefully structured descriptions of alternative possible futures. They are not just variations around a base case: They are significantly, often structurally, different views of the future. And they are not generalized views of feared or desired futures: They are specific decision-focused views of the future. The benefits of scenario planning, properly conceived and executed, are that the scenarios provide

- a more thorough understanding of the dynamics of change
- better consideration of the full range of opportunities and threats
- reduced vulnerability to surprises

- more resilient, flexible strategy
- better assessment of risks

Scenarios closely examine what forecasts take for granted, the structural drivers that determine trends in the first place. The scenario process examines how changes in the underlying structure can play out into radically different behaviors.

Scenario Principles

There are two principles required for scenario planning to work:

- Planners must agree that the scenario stories are only plausible, not probable.
- They must be willing to suspend disbelief when confronted by stories that challenge their current thinking.

The word "never" should not be used when developing and working with scenarios. For example, people once thought that the Cold War would *never* end, that the Soviet Union would *never* collapse, that the United States would *never* be attacked, and that the Internet would *never* be anything but a fad.

Creating Scenarios

Because there are unlimited possible combinations of the effects of fact, issues, and trends, scenarios usually are limited to a manageable number—two to four, with four being ideal for richness and nuance. Two scenarios lead to a best case/worst case, either/or type of approach, which is limiting. Three scenarios lead to a best case/worst case/most likely approach that encourages planners to take the easy and familiar, most likely path. More than four scenarios are unmanageable and often lack sufficient contrast to be useful.

Scenarios can project far out into the future, fifteen years or more. Long-term projections are essential for longer-term investments such as factory locations, drug development, hospital construction, and road building. However, scenario building takes practice, and long future projections can be difficult. Longer-term scenarios risk playing guessing games and injecting *wildcards,* the unexpected events that disrupt the scenarios.

Scenarios also are three dimensional. Like the Rubik's Cube puzzle with its movable facets that was popular years ago, scenarios can be changed by changing assumptions, drivers, or the facts and trends chosen to describe them. In fact, scenarios are not static. Once developed, they need to be constantly refreshed as new facts and trends emerge, and the strategies that grow from them should be reviewed for continuing relevance and updated.

Scenario development begins with selection of two powerful and intersecting change drivers identified in the environmental scan. Each change driver becomes an axis that defines a four-pronged matrix of alternative future worlds. Each axis has opposite poles that have an equal chance of occurring. Using the association sector drivers of adoption of technological change and response to demographic shifts, we can create a matrix like this:

Fast
Technology Adoption

New Generation Needs
Embraced

New Generation Needs
Resisted

Slow
Technology Adoption

The quadrants of the matrix create future worlds. Each one contains a story. In the upper left quadrant, associations quickly respond to new technologies for interaction and give new generations a place at the table in policy making and product-service design. In the upper right quadrant, associations quickly respond to new technologies for interaction but resist the demands of younger members for participation in leadership and policy development. In the lower left quadrant, associations recognize and meet the participation needs of younger members but are slow to acquire the new tools of connection because of budget constraints or difficulty in persuading older members to relinquish reliance on older means of interaction. In the lower right quadrant, associations are hidebound and fail to respond either to changing means of connecting or the needs and demands of their young, technology savvy members.

In creating scenario stories for each of these alternative future worlds, a five-year timeline makes sense. Within that period, there will be flashpoints of technology advancement the equal of the Internet, and the Millennial Generation will be flooding the job market. Scenario stories should be short—no more than two or three pages—compelling, and bold. It is difficult to write scenario stories in planning sessions. It is better to create the stories offline and vet them in a facilitated session. At that session, planners should identify strategies that might work in several scenarios. Such strategies enable the association to quickly respond as the real future evolves because the scenarios have been thought through in advance.

Working with Scenarios

Since scenarios identify strategies, they feed naturally into the association's strategic planning process. Scenarios expose gaps in the association's policies, value equation, and organizational structure that should be addressed in the strategic plan. Take, for example, the lower right quadrant of the association matrix. One could argue that it describes a bleak potential future filled with dissatisfaction and, perhaps, dissolution. Viewed through a different lens, it can be a harbinger for change. A task force of traditional and newer member cohorts could look at ways to address apparently colliding desires. Here is a place for younger members to mentor older ones about the value of new technologies for interaction and older members to mentor younger members about how to approach policy setting. Conversely, the upper left quadrant of the matrix appears to be Nirvana. But is it? If associations in this world jump on new technologies, are they being thoughtful and prudent in use of resources? Are new generations' needs being addressed at the expense of older ones'? The same task force addressing the bleak scenario can address the Nirvana scenario. It is good to have people work in conflicting scenarios to challenge their conventional wisdom and encourage them to think differently.

In addition, alternative future scenarios are the means for determining a preferred future for an organization. Too often, associations indulge in the creation of meaningless vision statements, such as "…be the premier association for (fill in the blanks)." Such so-called visions offer no direction to staff and leaders about how to proceed. On the other hand, preferred futures are a series of ends that create a timeline of milestones to achieve by a certain date. Here's an example from a professional association:

By 2009, the Association

- has defined the discipline as a specialty
- is a catalyst for improving procedural outcomes and patient safety
- has a global reach
- is sought by policy makers in making decisions about products, procedures, and reimbursement
- defines evidence-based best practices

Preferred futures describe what the association is and does at a defined future point in time. The milestones of a preferred future are goals and objectives along the road to a desired end. Each one can be made living with implementation strategies that are specific, achievable, and timely.

American baseball legend and cracker-barrel philosopher Yogi Berra once advised, "When you get to the fork in the road, take it." The futures analysis process does just that. It enables associations to explore pathways to the future risk free. It creates valuable intelligence that is salable and exciting for participants. Moreover, it puts you in charge of defining your future rather than being defined by it.

About the Author

Bruce Butterfield, CAE, APR is president of The Forbes Group, Fairfax, Virginia.

Review Questions

1. How would you change your association's environmental scanning system to give your leadership better decision-making intelligence?

2. What are the most significant drivers of change in your association's industry or profession that grow from the Structure → Conduct → Performance model?

3. How is your association responding to those change drivers and is that response effective?

4. How is your association involving the next generation of potential members and leaders in setting your future course?

4

Sustainability

Associations as Agents of Change in the Collaborative Economy

Richard C. O'Sullivan

Associations designed along traditional linear supply-chain relationships will not survive in the 21st century. Thanks to Just-in-Time (JIT), Quick Response (QR), e-commerce, and a host of other business practice innovations since the 1980s, the supply chain is dead. And changing the wording to "value chain" does not resurrect it. "LEGO-relationships" in which businesses couple and uncouple partnerships with each deal, which take advantage of the electronic communications technologies but are not dependent on them, have turned commercial security on its head. Associations simply cannot expect to protect members' commercial or professional interests by defending narrowly defined immediate business relationships.

The more fluid markets of the 21st Century demand that association leaders shift their thinking away from the linear *supply chain* or *value chain* relationships that have dominated association planning and operations for decades. Now associations need to think in terms of *demand networks* in which their **members' customers,** not the members themselves, command the focus of association business planning. The association's members' needs are better understood as one of several providers to the end-customer and not in isolation. Today's association leaders must reach beyond just members to directly engage a diverse range of stakeholders whose vested interests align with the association's goals and members' success in the marketplace. The cast of characters that now command association executives' attention include not only their members' customers, other suppliers and regulators of the members' customers' markets, but also key players in other businesses and professions that govern other activities that serve the final consumer of the markets in which the members participate. By working through more holistic nonlinear relationships, associations are able to more readily identify emerging competitors, partners, and allies in their members' markets and to expand their sources of revenue, and thereby assuring both the associations' and their members' success.

This approach requires a far more entrepreneurial management style through which the association identifies and exploits the value its success brings to the *entire* marketplace. While entrepreneurship has always been important to effective association leadership, this approach, which I call *Customers' Customer Analysis*, helps associations to identify how their activities bring value to businesses and institutions, including other associations, who never directly consume the associations' services. Called "capturing positive externalities" in economics, this practice identifies the means for third parties who profit from these activities to pay for the benefits received.

On the upside, greater entrepreneurship reduces the association's dependence on dues without reaching into its members' pockets through additional fees as well as engages a broad range of stakeholders and allies in meeting the association's advocacy goals. On the downside, *Customers' Customer Analysis* creates financial conflicts of interest between the association and its core members by increasing the association's financial dependence on these alternative stakeholders whose interests may sometimes be at odds with those of the membership base. As *social* entrepreneurs, association executives must constantly balance the financial stability of their organizations for which they have stewardship responsibility and the commercial/social success of their members. This *double bottom line*, which distinguishes social entrepreneurs from their commercial peers, creates one of the unique dimensions of association management, unknown in the traditional commercial world. The balance of this chapter discusses these ideas in greater depth.

Drivers of Association Market Change That Make Demand-Networks Necessary

Three revolutionary trends emerged at the end of the 20th century that have changed how, why, and with whom people and businesses want to associate:

- The development of Just-in-Time business relationships
- The "professionalization" of the American workforce
- Globalization

Their impacts on association management, financing, and marketing have been equally revolutionary. Understanding these trends is crucial to developing successful association business models that tap the power of demand networks.

1. The Development of Just-in-Time Relationships: Associations in the Post-information Economy

The Information Revolution of the 1990s began a decade earlier with association-led standardization initiatives in Just-in-Time (JIT) supply-chain management and Quick Response (QR) business relationships. Associations, collaborating across industry supply chains, developed and promoted the Electronic Data Interchange (EDI) data sharing practices and cross-firm decision-making that laid the foundation for Electronic Commerce and defined the dizzying economic transformation of the 1990s. Practitioners, however, soon discovered that these innovations did not merely streamline business transactions; they fundamentally altered business relationships. Former Federal Reserve Chairman Alan Greenspan observed that the greatest changes brought by the technological advances of the last 20 years have been the ways in which "their implementation has fundamentally altered economic relationships and business practices that, in turn, have blurred the boundaries" of economic activity.[1]

An example of this blurring is contract manufacturing, which has uncoupled product design from productive capacity and helped firms to greatly accelerate product innovations, reduce design-to-market cycles, and reduce the risk of intellectual piracy. Applying Just-in-Time (JIT) and Quick Response data sharing practices with contracting to independent manufacturing operations around the world and focusing on the high added value of the design, apparel manufacturers slashed the design-to-delivery cycle by nearly half a year resulting in lower prices for the customer and reduced market risk to themselves. Technology Forecasters (TFI) estimates that in the first decade of the 21st century, contract manufacturing in the electronics industry has grown by more than 20 percent a year, more than twice as quickly as the electronics industry as a whole.[2]

The result of two decades of strategic outsourcing across numerous industries has been the emergence of what Timothy Sturgeon of MIT's Industry Performance Center calls "co-evolutionary shared networks," in which inter-firm collaboration has led to analysts thinking of competencies at *the industry level* instead of *within individual firms*.[3] Helping to design and manage these networks is both the greatest opportunity and challenge to association executives. Rather than thinking vertically, with each firm managing productive, marketing, administrative, and logistical capacities, businesses now think horizontally and focus on delivering these functional capacities *across multiple firms*. Sturgeon labeled this phenomenon "vertical disintegration."

Ironically, associations, through which businesses created these practices, have been slow to identify how the shift in business relationships from smoke-stacked industry organizations to cross-sector coalitions has fundamentally redefined the demand for association services.

---

[1] Remarks of Alan Greenspan to 21st Century Workforce Conference, June 20, 2001, www.frb.gov.

[2] Five Year Forecast—Electronics Manufacturing, 2005 annual study, Technology Forecasters, Inc., Alameda, CA, www.technologyforecasters.com.

[3] Sturgeon, Timothy J., Industry Co-Evolution and the Rise of a Shared Supply-base for Electronics Manufacturing, Cambridge, MA, Massachusetts Institute of Technology, Industrial Performance Center, May 2001.

Emergence of Cross-sectoral Coalition Networks

One of the most remarkable outcomes of the "collaborative economy" has been the downsizing of American business. In 1965, one in four Americans worked for a Fortune 500. By 2005, that figure had fallen to one in fourteen.[4] By 2002, businesses with fewer than 100 employees accounted for half of all jobs in the U.S. (for the first time in 100 years) and an even greater share of Gross Domestic Product (GDP). MIT's Sturgeon argues that contrary to conventional wisdom, the drive to outsourcing is not merely to cut labor costs. "The ultimate goal of inter-firm collaboration is to maximize *the overall value,* not merely limit the costs, of inter-firm linkages ... [that] can only be realized through the dynamic process of interaction among economic actors."[5] Having outsourced all but "competitive competencies," the smaller more flexible businesses that emerged in the 1990s and 2000s need to develop collaborative relationships with other complementary suppliers to their markets to assure the competitiveness of their products and services.

Richard Langlois of the University of Connecticut, examining the needs of downsized firms, concluded that outsourcing caused a "loose coupling" of essential support services needed to create products and bring them to market. Langlois argues that organizations, having "sacrificed control of key resources in exchange for speed and efficiency, need outside help to recruit and manage such resources."[6] Therefore, the greatest value that associations can offer its members in a world of "vertical disintegration" is **to manage those key resource relationships**.

To mirror those new relationships in their own structures and services, associations need to place greater emphasis on *partner* rather than *peer* relationships and focus more on cross-sector coalitions and networks and less on traditional industry-specific links that defined most associations through the 20th century. **The key to effective association leadership in the future is to focus on developing those network relationships around the members' key customers rather than solely promoting current members' market positions.**

Managing Process No Longer Internal to Members' Organizations

For many industry associations, the transition from large, vertically integrated member firms to small, flat specialized firms was seminal. Their traditional role of protecting their members' market advantage was incompatible with the emerging need for cooperation in "shared network environments."

Associations had to quickly shift their priority setting systems to accommodate a broad and diverse group of younger and leaner businesses whose needs are quite different from a small group of older, larger members that dominated many associations in

---

[4] The Small Business Economy, SBA Report to the President, 2006, Small Business Administration, Washington, DC, September 2006.

[5] Ibid.

[6] Langlois, Richard, *The Vanishing Hand: The Changing Dynamics of Industrial Capitalism,* 2003, University of Connecticut, Center for Institutions, Organizations, and Markets.

the past. For many associations, small firms went from being the hangers-on relegated to occasional specialized interest groups to the growth engines of the industries that the associations represent. Small firms' competitive interests depend on coordinating business relationships with a whole range of *indirect* suppliers, partners, and intermediaries such as technology developers, financial services providers, transportation infrastructure, and marketing services as well as with traditional *direct* supply chain providers of raw materials and intermediate products.

The dramatic transformation of the National Business Forms Association (NBFA) is an excellent example of how JIT and EDI fundamentally changed an association. With a membership comprised of business form wholesalers and distributors, NBFA was extremely vulnerable to both JIT and e-Commerce. The need for paper business forms first began to decline as more transactions were conducted over proprietary EDI value-added networks (VANs). The market erosion of paper forms accelerated with the emergence of the open-ended architecture of the Internet. Additionally, thanks to Just-in-Time delivery capabilities and the introduction of high-speed digital printing, forms manufacturers began to directly manage forms inventories for their largest clients.

NBFA's members realized that they were never really in the business of managing the office paper inventories but rather in the business of providing the tools to help businesses manage administrative and financial processes. To survive, business forms distributors needed to first reinvent themselves as problem solvers instead of product providers and then realign themselves with other businesses with similar objectives. For its part NBFA, renamed the Document Management Industries Association (DMIA), opened membership up to accountants, lawyers, bankers, payroll processing firms, and other businesses engaged in managing what could be called "nonproductive" (as in not directly related to the production of a product or service) business activities. Having shifted from a vertical to a horizontal organization, DMIA flourished.

2. The "Professionalization" of the American Workforce

Professional societies were not immune to structural changes driven by outsourcing and electronic commerce. The 1990s witnessed an explosion in new occupations and professions the likes of which has not been seen since the second Industrial Revolution in the late 1800's. According to the U.S. Bureau of Labor Statistics' Occupational Projections Office, one in three jobs created in the decade ending in 2014 will be in occupations that did not exist prior to 1990. Some labor experts have projected that workers entering the workforce today will change *careers*—not *jobs*—four times before they retire.[7] In stark contrast to past generations that identified with the industries or firms that employed them, by the 1990s, worker loyalty to career gained priority as workers identified more with their *professions* or *occupations* and focused on "portable skills" that transferred from one employer to another.

---

[7] 2002 Economic Census of the United States, Washington, DC, U.S. Bureau of the Census.

This shift in worker priorities led to a pronounced change in the composition of the association sector. The growth of professional societies far outstripped the growth rate of business associations, dramatically altering the balance between the two. According to the U.S. Census Bureau, between 1997 and 2002, revenues at professional societies grew at twice the rate as those of business associations while employment in professional organizations increased more than three times as fast. Professional societies also became larger with employment per organization increasing 14 percent in the same five-year period, compared to just under 3 percent for business associations. Revenues per association jumped 31 percent for professional societies, compared to 13 percent for business associations (before discounting for inflation).[8]

The introduction of new technologies and new business practices that drove these changes in professional markets does not simply change *how* one does something. It fundamentally changed *what* is done and for whom. To remain relevant in this environment, professional societies must help their members constantly reinvent themselves, expand members' skills, and enhance their value to clients by linking with complementary service providers rather than increase members' revenue by limiting entry and exit through rigid rules.

Interventional radiologists (IRs) faced growing competition from cardiologists and vascular surgeons who also mastered the catheter, IRs' primary tool. By focusing, not on competing suppliers, but on the patient, The Society for Interventional Radiology (SIR) learned that their non-invasive technique, which reduced the physical shock to the patient, allowed for earlier hospital releases that created new shocks for the patient and his primary care providers at home. Rather than take the traditional approach of pushing for turf-protection legislation, SIR partnered with GPs and home nurses to solve the new challenges created by "interventional medicine," a term SIR coined, in order to secure its members' position as the providers of choice by referring physicians.[9]

3. What Globalization Really Means for Associations

Finally, the redefining of corporate functions that fueled the drive to outsourcing has, in turn, led to a globalized view of product and service sourcing. Crucial competitive functions are now performed closer to the time for delivery. Coordination and communication take place around the globe and—in the case of intellectual property development—around the clock as globalized teams pass design work from time zone to time zone, earning the description "sunrise production scheduling."

To do so, however, industry associations changed emphasis to *harmonizing* standards internationally rather than *differentiating* local ones. Where businesses once encouraged associations to pursue local regulations to create non-tariff barriers (NTBs)

---

[8] Hecker, Daniel, "Occupational employment projections to 2012", Monthly Labor Review, pp. 80-105, Washington, DC, U.S. Bureau of Labor Statistics.

[9] The Forbes Group, *In a New Vein: Finding a New Role for Interventional Medicine*, April 2001, www.forbesgroup.com.

to foreign competitors, they now see such strategies as compromising their effectiveness as a competitive participant in increasingly globalized shared networks.

The "Viagra™ Lesson"

The counter-productive impact of differentiated local standards was most keenly experienced in what Europeans now call the "Viagra Lesson." European and Japanese pharmaceutical manufacturers encouraged national regulators to withhold licensing Viagra in order to buy time for local manufacturers to create competing products. The World Trade Organization (WTO), however, allows for "parallel" imports of an unlicensed product as long as the patient has a valid prescription from a doctor in a country where the drug is legally prescribed. The purpose of this regulation was to allow international travelers to access prescribed medications from anywhere on the planet regardless of local restrictions.

Neither the WTO nor the European or Japanese authorities anticipated local patients, eager to obtain Viagra, capitalizing on this loophole by electronically finding an American doctor who could examine lab tests remotely thanks to recent advances in telepathology and provide both an accurate diagnosis and a valid prescription. The traditional NTBs against Viagra proved impotent. Healthcare regulators were forced to reverse their decision so local physicians could learn how to properly dispense the product.

The lesson to associations should be clear. In today's globalized world, using local regulations as artificial market barriers not only fails to protect the product being regulated, it also tears at the "shared networks" the local market needs. Rather than differentiating standards, harmonizing licensing requirements across national borders is now needed to assure both the safety of the consumer and the economic viability of local services (such as diagnosing and prescribing, in this case) that can otherwise be obtained electronically.

It's the Information—Not the Technology

In a globalized environment, information is shared not only across organizations but also across legal systems. Participants need to be assured that proprietary information remains protected regardless of where it goes. India and not China has emerged as the software capital of the developing world because rampant software pirating in China has made it too risky a place to create intellectual capital.

Global associations must manage the flow of information and knowledge across the entire demand-network that supports their members' products. Karen Katen, president of Pfizer Pharmaceutical Group, Pfizer's global pharmaceutical operation, notes, "At a fundamental level what pharmaceutical firms do is transfer scientific knowledge to physicians, and increasingly to patients, their families and their communities." In order to assure the safe use of their products, firms such as Pfizer must also participate in local medical training. Through its Learning and Development Center, Pfizer now offers on-site and distance learning, satellite transmission, and videoconferencing to medical and healthcare staff in markets around the world. But this solution is too overwhelming for most businesses with smaller profit margins. Associations must take the lead in the next stage of globalization and focus on developing the demand networks that influence the competitiveness of their members' products rather than advocacy to assure product-friendly support infrastructures and the safety of the customer across borders.

The *Customers' Customer* AND Demand Network Building

Having demonstrated that the success of associations' members depends on the health of the environment for their members' customers, we now examine how to best identify a demand-driven network. In the world of "blurred borders," most changes, challenges, and opportunities defining market sectors usually come from outside existing market boundaries. By examining only the healthcare industry in the early 1990s, we would not have seen the emergence of assisted living facilities, birthed by the hospitality industry.[10]

To assure members' success, associations need to look beyond their immediate customers and markets and study the new kinds of environments that are emerging and the new customers they create. By focusing on the end-users of the markets in which their members participate, association executives can *anticipate* rather than *react* to change.

Building customer-centric demand networks through *Customers' Customer Analysis* consists of four stages:

- Broaden the definition of whom you serve
- Redefine your members based on the new definition
- Re-examine and identify your partners and competitors
- Re-engineer the association business model

First, the association must examine the trends influencing their members' market with a cold, analytical eye. The founder of The Forbes Group, Paul Forbes, once observed, "The reason most strategic planning fails is that people are reluctant to discuss their own death." Most organizations are interested in examining change only to the point where it finds opportunities for continuing current activities. This "solution in search of a problem" approach unfortunately is applicable to many associations and their volunteer leadership. Never forget that those who have risen to the top of their professions or industries and populate associations boards usually have the most to lose from profound change!

---

[10] O'Sullivan, Richard, "Customer's Customer Analysis and Demand Driven Association Strategies," *Journal of Association Leadership*, ASAE & The Center for Association Leadership, Washington, DC Winter 2004.

Customers' Customer Analysis intentionally seeks out those trends that could change the needs of the customers who currently use your members' products or services as currently designed, offered, or supported in the marketplace. Following the traditional Structure-Conduct-Performance paradigm, association leaders begin by asking:

- How could changing market structures, regulations, technologies, or social priorities change our members' customers' needs?
- How will these needs be met?
- Can the association's members meet those needs?
- What capabilities will the member need in order to do so?

Graphically these steps can be presented as follows:

> Identify economic, political, technological, and social trends that are shaping the markets into which your members sell

> Determine how these trends could change what your members' customers will demand

> Assess your members' capacities to meet these new customer needs

> Identify key supplier and allied industries needed to competitively serve the end-user market both now and in the future

> Identify support industries, business service providers (e.g. consulting, training, technology specialists), and other private-sector firms that need to be developed or enhanced to make the targeted cluster competitive

> Determine the infrastructure requirements and public policies that need to support members in delivering the new products and/or services

For example, the case of Interventional Radiology above demonstrated that the solution for SIR was in better understanding the patients' needs—not the hospitals'.

Selection of Channels of Distribution

At this point the association has identified the products and services that members need to succeed with these new customers. Now it must decide if it should:

1. Meet those needs directly
2. Encourage public policy or government services
3. Leave it to the marketplace

Associations need to think of the three sectors of the economy, the public, private, and nonprofit as different channels of distribution to meet members' needs. Associations should not try to meet all their members' needs, only those for which it has an unassailable competitive advantage. Associations tend to limit management of their members' market environment to only those functions that they can directly control or finance. Thus, if a newly identified member need is outside its scope or ability, the leadership tends to abdicate responsibility for its development.

If Not You, Then Who?

If the association is not able to address the newly identified needs directly then it should determine who will and then encourage others to take up the task. Therein it will find its next member, ally, or competitor. Those services that the association does choose to undertake directly become the new member products and services. Those identified as "public goods" by government organizations become the new advocacy objectives. Those better left to the competitive market become new opportunities for commercial partnerships.

To be sure, fee-for-service income is not new to the nonprofit sector in general nor to associations in particular. Associations have long depended on fee-for-service income by differentiating between dues-supported product and service bundles and those sold individually to members and the public. Yet, this is much more than outsourcing association services to a third party. Very often, other firms in the marketplace that are better positioned to meet new member and members' customers' needs more efficiently will pay the association for its assistance in opening up new markets.

Caution—The Privatization of Government Services

The role of the government in managing the business environment has been seriously challenged since the late 1970s. Contrary to the accelerating pace of change elsewhere in the economy and society, "governments, built in the industrial model with their sluggish centralized bureaucracies, preoccupation with rules, and their hierarchical chains of command" were unresponsive to change.[11] A popular solution to "reinvent" government embraced by both Republican and Democratic administration was to contract government service development and delivery to civil society organizations, such as associations.

While associations see some obvious benefits to accepting the role of social or public service provider, particularly in increased non-dues revenue and greater control through self-regulation, this is also fraught with dangers. In many cases, the "oppor-

---

[11] Osborne, David and Ted Gaebler, 1992, *Reinventing Government: How the Entrepreneurial Spirit is Transforming the Public Sector,* Reading MA, Addison-Wesley Publishing Co., p. 12.

tunity" of contractual relationships with government agencies has changed association management strategies, practices, priorities, and skill sets—not always for the better.

Greater direct regulatory responsibility for industry or professional standards has brought four fundamental changes to an association:

- First it has dramatically changed the sources of revenue from donation and dues to fee-for-service activities. In the association world, the total budget drawn from dues has fallen from over 60 percent in the 1980s to 35 percent today.[12] Many association leaders now believe that even that figure is too high and have set a 20 percent cap for dues as the new benchmark.

- Secondly, this shift has profoundly altered associations' advocacy roles. The very organizations that pushed hardest for government activism were selected to take on the role of delivery provider. In extreme cases, associations who chose this path found their relationships with government agencies transformed from adversarial to financially dependent. (A discussion on using *portfolio planning* to mitigate this risk follows.)

- Thirdly, the association may find itself in an adversarial relationship with noncompliant members and must be prepared to face the potential financial and political consequences of disciplining even the most powerful members.

- Finally, it has greatly expanded both the number and types of recipients of services well beyond core constituency. In the case of an association, engaging as a supplier of public goods, such as testing labs, research, and standards development, the associations' influence expanded beyond those who voluntarily support the organization by compromising the exclusivity of the relationship with dues-paying members.

The Risks of a Customers' Customer Strategy

While creating new, nondues revenue from outside the membership base represents the most enticing aspect of *Customers' Customer Analysis*, it could potentially be the most perilous. Generating income outside the association membership is extremely attractive. It generates profits that can then be used to subsidize member activities. That does not mean that the association gets a free lunch.

The Double Bottom Line

It may seem obvious that an association *should* charge commissions or royalties to third-party suppliers in exchange for their help in creating products or services that the third-party firm then sells to the association's members or members' customers. However, if these services move the market toward a path advantageous to the industry or profession represented, the association may choose to forgo profits on the service

---

[12] Operating Ratio Report, 12th edition, vol 1, 2003, American Society of Association Executives, Washington, DC. p. 2.

to assure their widest possible adoption. This is especially true if the organization or consumer, whose decisions you are trying to shape, either cannot afford or is reluctant to purchase the new service.

For example, in the 1980s, the American Fiber Manufacturers Association, The American Textile Manufacturers Institute, and the American Apparel Manufacturers Association collectively spent considerable sums to create electronic data interchange (EDI) standards to help make its members more competitive in the face of foreign competition. While software producers would have willingly paid substantially for the use of these standards, the three organizations chose to put them in the public domain, essentially giving away three years' work. Why? They realized that to sell the product would have limited their distribution to a handful of software houses that could then restrict their distribution and use. To be sure that software would be developed not only for large firms but also for small ones that would now be crucial participants in the "value network," the members were best served by allowing specialty software firms to have free access to the standards. In this way, the associations had to place their members' commercial interests before their own financial interests.

Adverse Selection Problem

In offering fee-for-service products, associations also face the dilemma of adverse selection bias. An association may discover that those members or customers who will most benefit from the change are least able to pay. By protecting its own commercial interests and withholding services, the association risks acting as a barrier to market growth and innovation instead of a promoter, which is not only contrary to associations' purpose but also possibly risks anti-trust action if withholding the service proves a barrier to market entry or exit.

When creating new products and services, the association needs to identify all of the beneficiaries and then assess to what degree the financial stability of the association must be balanced against the commercial success of its members.

Therefore, the final steps are:

> Define a strategic direction based on the newly identified purpose and new relationships with government and market sectors

> Determine how the new association products and services will be financed, taking into account which should be dues supported and which should be fee-for-service

> Develop a strategic plan and business model that determines how, when, and by whom these new services will be delivered

Its Not About ALL of Your Members, Just the Survivors

"But that's not what our members do!" is one of the most common observations made by those who will restrict themselves to their current member base. As noted earlier, one needs to encourage members to respond to new customers, not to try to get new customers to accept what members offer. This criticism most often comes from the association's board members themselves. Association executives need to consider that the current board is populated by those who have been most successful in meeting the challenges and needs of today's customers—not necessarily tomorrow's. In fact, those whose capacities are best suited for current market conditions may be the ones most threatened by a change in those conditions. Association executives must remind themselves that they serve the membership, not the board. In the end, they must concern themselves with those members who will survive change and be able to distinguish between honest and reasonable skepticism of market prognostications and an unwillingness to face potential threat.

Addressing Conflicts of Interest: Portfolio Analysis in a Nonprofit Context

The Adverse Selection problem mentioned earlier is only one example of potential conflicts of interest that emerge when an association shifts its primary focus from its members to its members' customers. Once the association develops business relationships with other suppliers or stakeholders in its members' markets, it develops financial interests and possible financial dependence on their success. The association needs to carefully balance these interests to be sure that it does not sacrifice its members' success for its own.

In the for-profit world, this balance is easily achieved through portfolio analysis; however, for associations, this is much more difficult. In fact, several organizations, most notably Bridgespan, a provider of consulting services to the nonprofit sector, have tried to develop portfolio analysis criteria appropriate to nonprofits. Experts agree that, like an investment portfolio, associations need to distribute earnings across sufficient revenue sources as to not be dependent on any one for the organization's survival. Yet, to date, there is no real agreement on how to quantifiably measure the balance of the organization's financial goals and social benefits. Bridgespan, itself incubated as a 501c(3) firm by Bain & Company, has undertaken the most innovative work in this field but has yet to create a systematic nonprofit portfolio model.

The best advice is to observe the organization's behavior. Association executives need to carefully assess if, when, and where conflicts could arise and create structural barriers to preemptively prevent unacceptable behavior. The American Society for Interior Design (ASID), for example, created standards for interior design service quality. Because the society charges certified members a higher dues payment than that for non-certified members, ASID faced an implicit conflict of interest. Clearly, ASID would benefit from having as many certified members as possible while its members would benefit from having a more restrictive certification process. To resolve the conflict ASID created a completely separate organization, the National Council for Interior Design Quality (NCIDQ) to develop standards and administer the certification exam. Because NCIDQ has no vested interest in a high or low passing rate, it insulated ASID from charges (or the temptation) of watering down the standards to increase dues income.

Conclusion

The JIT/QR globalized environment of the 21st Century, in which the boundaries between industry sectors, markets, and even public and private sectors have blurred, has fundamentally changed the forces to which associations must respond. These changes were developed to reduce barriers to innovation and to accelerate the pace of change. Unless associations base their financial survival on fostering change, they risk compromising the future of the members and undermining their own survival. By employing *Customers' Customer Analysis*, designed to identify emerging needs of members' customers and easing members' adoption of the products and services needed to accommodate change, association executives will assure the most success for their members and for themselves.

To do so, however, they need to develop sources of revenue closer to the members' markets and create fluid partnerships that will allow for rapid adoption of new ideas and products, carefully balancing these new sources to minimize potential conflicts with their members.

This demands that associations engage in developing demand-driven networks that focus on promoting greater efficiency *across* enterprises. This is a far different challenge than in the traditional focus on enhancing the competitive capacities *within* their members. While in the end associations need to engage a broader range of economic stakeholders both for their own financial survival and for their members' ultimate benefit, association executives must be prepared to cope with the inherent conflicts of interests. The role of associations in the years ahead will be to foster cross-sector collaborative relationships that help their members harness the forces of change rather than protect them from it.

About the Author

Richard C. O'Sullivan is an economist and business environment analyst with 30 years experience in the public, private, and civil society sectors in the U.S., European, and Asian markets. He created the *Customers' Customer Analysis* approach to association strategic planning and program development discussed in this chapter. From 2004-2006, Mr. O'Sullivan introduced new self-sustaining association development models in Southeastern Europe. From 2002-2004, he served as assistant director of Johns Hopkins University's Center for Civil Society Studies and before that as chief economist and senior vice president of The Forbes Group beginning in 1994.

Review Questions

Rather than review questions for this chapter, do your own *Customer Analysis*.

Putting Customers' Customer into Practice

Ready to begin? *Customers' Customer Analysis* starts by answering the following questions:

- Who are the major customers of your members' products or services?
- What are the current technological, economic, regulatory, and social forces that can change
  - Who those customers are
  - What they will demand
- What new capacities (skills, partners, products, etc.) will future members need in order to stay competitive with these new customers?
- Looking at each capacity, which ones are best provided by
  - The association?
  - Government agencies?
  - Private sector firms?
- What is the association's role in managing each?

Strategy Management

James Dalton

T HE NOTION THAT STRATEGIC planning isn't what it used to be is now widely accepted. Unfortunately, there's much less agreement on what it has become. A symposium held at MIT's Sloan School of Management looked back at strategic planning's 40-year evolution from a cutting-edge concept in the early 1960s through its calcification into a fixed template that inadequately addressed the need for flexibility in rapidly changing environments. In the leading MBA programs the subject has evolved to a point where the term "strategic planning" rarely appears in either the titles of the courses or the textbooks students use.

The association executive's awareness of this changing perspective on planning was documented in a series of focus groups done as a part of an ASAE Foundation research project that led to the publication of *From Scan to Plan: Managing Change in Associations* (2004). When asked to describe their thoughts on the subject, focus group participants made the following observations:

- There was a point in the not-too-distant past when everyone used a similar approach to planning, but there is no longer any uniform understanding of how it should work or whether it is even worth it.

- The making of strategy, by whatever name or process, must be far more inclusive than before, yet faster and more flexible.

- Some means of anticipating the future and building consensus on what should be done about it was essential.

These three observations pretty well summarize the current challenge. There is no longer any single template for all, but every association must engage a broader spectrum of participants in a dialogue on how the environment is changing and how the association and its profession or industry should adapt—preferably before the consequence of environmental change has affected everyone else. And in this adaptive framework one point is clear: Having a strategy is more important than having a document called "The Plan". The concept of strategy and the process of strategy making are front and center.

Good Strategy Evolves Gradually

The need to reconsider our understanding of strategy making under rapidly changing conditions is captured by James Brian Quinn, a management guru from Dartmouth's Tuck School of Business, in what he calls logical incrementalism. Quinn's thesis is that the development of strategy in successful organizations is not at all like the rational-analytical systems portrayed in the management literature. He thinks it is fragmented, evolutionary, and intuitive. Good strategy evolves over time in a stream of activities that include conversations, planning, serendipity, failed initiatives, persistence, more conversation, and, yes, technique.

This last element may seem to be at odds with the mix that preceded it. If technique is understood to be a systematic procedure by which a complex task is accomplished, isn't it a bit like that rational-analytical system that Quinn and others seem to reject? Yes and no. In the traditional approach to strategic planning, a large batch of information is poured into a rational-analytical model, and a plan is produced. In this alternative, which might be thought of as strategy management, a rational-analytical technique is applied to information flow that percolates through a wide variety of events and yields strategies.

Strategy Involves Ongoing Programs, Not Just New Ones

Two models illustrate how this might work in an association context. The first provides an overall framework that distinguishes strategic initiatives from established programs. The second puts the concept of strategy into a consistent format that captures its dynamism and makes it easily manageable.

The following diagram illustrates the framework used to distinguish strategic initiatives from ongoing programs. This is important because too often that which is said to be strategic includes an assortment of things such as new initiatives, established activities thought to be critically important, programs that need strengthening, and even some very tactical to-dos. This inconsistency is made worse by what is missing. Most of the ongoing programs that deliver value to the customer are not accounted for or are referred to dismissively as being a part of ongoing operations. Even if there is an operating plan that makes them explicit, rarely is there a systematic connection between established programs and strategic initiatives.

In this framework there are two dimensions, vertical and horizontal. The vertical dimension represents the stable portion of an association. In it, the mission and goals give purpose and direction to the programs that deliver value to customers in the

current budget year. These programs have what might be thought of as rolling momentum, cyclical activities that generate value year after year.

Although the content delivered by programs such as the annual meeting or the monthly magazine changes with each edition, their function and purpose are consistent through time. The managers of these programs will adjust them on a regular basis in what is thought of as continuous improvement, but the basic value proposition is stable. Even programs with high variability, like government relations, are fairly stable in terms of their purpose, execution, and resource requirements. As a rule of thumb, 80 to 90 percent of an organization's resources go into these activities.

The horizontal dimension portrays a dynamic that is the opposite of stability. In it we identify the strategic issues that drive the need for change as well as the initiatives that are launched to address them. The improvements that program managers make in the vertical dimension deal with the effectiveness of the programs. The strategic initiatives in the horizontal dimension change the fundamental nature of the value that the association delivers. To adapt in this significant a manner is to surrender stability and enter into uncertainty. New programs may be created, established ones may morph into something else, and in some cases these adaptations may alter the mission and goals of the organization.

Management and leadership in this framework are opposite but complementary functions. We manage to accomplish specific objectives on time and on budget. We lead when we help people see the need for change, arrive at a common vision, and deal with uncertainty as we explore the best way of achieving it. These efforts account for the other 10 to 20 percent of the organization's resources.

Peter Drucker came to believe that organizations should have two budgets. An operating budget allocates resources to established programs over a set period. A strategic budget allocates resources for adaptations that address the future viability of the organization and play out over an unpredictable period. This is not a contingency fund for things that may or may not come up. It is for strategic initiatives that must come up.

The horizontal dimension symbolizes the crosscurrents of change and lays out a spectrum of events that move from initial efforts to see the forces of change to an understanding of them and then to priority setting that leads to action. Environmental

scanning is used to identify these change agents. The ways of conducting a scan include formal future studies, market research, brainstorming sessions with leaders, "town hall" conversations with rank-and-file members, and focus groups with member suppliers and clients or customers.

The challenge in managing these activities lies in the highly varied types of information that they consider. Studies produce recommendations. Some methods of analysis produce lists. Market trends render data. Conversations generate observations. All of this information needs to flow across the horizontal dimension in a sorting and refining process that clarifies, compares, and selects. In the end, a few highly refined issues will compete for limited strategy making resources.

From Information Overload, Strategic Issues Emerge

Critical to this process is the concept of a strategic issue, the interaction of two variables that are affecting each other in ways that demand your attention. A strategic issue is expressed in a single-sentence statement that is carefully crafted to highlight tension between the variables. The strategy will be designed to convert this tension into an opportunity. One example of a statement that has these attributes comes from the association that accredits engineering programs:

The growing demand for accreditation of engineering degree programs delivered entirely by distance learning…

brings into question the site-specific requirements of the laboratory experience.

In this display, the two variables are separated to highlight the distinction. Some people confuse an issue with a topic, which has only one variable. They assume that the topic must be hot enough for everyone to understand why it must be addressed. This is a dangerous assumption that leads to misunderstandings. It is important to note that a strategic issue provides no hint of what should be done. That comes with the strategy. The issue itself provides a clear declaration of motivation for taking actions.

There are more strategic issues in the association's environment than any leader can deal with collectively, so the sorting out process comes in the form of a radar screen.

It imposes an arbitrary limitation on the number of issues that will be considered at any point in time. That limit is, simply, the number of issues that fit on a single piece of paper, which amounts to about 15 or 20.

The broadest spectrum of members possible should be involved in the identification of issues that will compete for a position on the radar screen. This process can include focus groups, cafe conversations, town hall meetings, surveys, committee input, and more. In the end, the issues that qualify for the radar screen will do so based on two criteria. Strategic issues are those that (1) will have the greatest impact on the association's membership and (2) are within the association's ability to act upon effectively.

Issues Can Be Classified by Clarity and Importance

The issues that do make it onto the radar screen fall into several categories based on their clarity and importance. Typically this involves three groups. Some of the issues will require additional research to understand them more clearly or resolve disagreements on their importance. These issues are referred to the appropriate committee or task force for research.

In the second category are those issues that are clear enough but not urgent or high enough on the importance ranking to justify action at the current time. They are, however, on the radar screen because they warrant monitoring for possible action in the future. As a matter of course, program managers may be asked if and how they may be addressing some aspect of these issues. The collective response will probably not amount to a succinct strategy, but the association staff is very likely addressing elements of the issue, which should be encouraged and tracked.

The third group includes those issues that are ready for prime time. These top-priority issues are candidates for strategy making. Everyone is invited to participate in the discussions that identify issues and consider their relative importance, but ultimately the board owns the tool and sets the priorities. This is an extension of the board's fiduciary responsibility because the strategies they drive typically require a significant investment and are apt to alter the association's fundamental value propositions.

Strategy Has Four Elements

From Scan to Plan: Integrating Trends Into the Strategy-Making Process (ASAE Foundation, 2003) considers several definitions of strategy from the management literature and develops one based on the demands placed on the association by virtue of the need to orchestrate the efforts of staff, elected officers, and volunteer committee members. Strategy is defined as a series of causes and effects aimed at a desired outcome. A model can help with the initial development of the strategy and the monitoring of its progress over time.

The model treats strategy as a single initiative with four interacting elements that account for the strategy's intelligence:

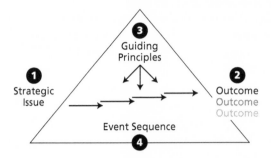

1. Issue. In constructing a strategy, you start with the strategic issue or motive to act. Strategic issues may have reams of analysis behind them, but the succinct, single-sentence structure provides a clear focal point of agreement on the force that is driving the strategy.

This focus is important because two things happen as the strategy proceeds. The strategy manager's understanding of the issue may sharpen as a result of what is learned along the way, and the dynamics associated with the issue itself change because issues are not stationary. The adage in baseball comes to mind: Keep your eye on the ball. In this case, the issue is the ball, and the three remaining elements constitute your swing.

2. Outcome. The second element determines the endgame or desired outcomes. These can be expressed in two or three short, crisp statements that provide clear images of what will be accomplished if the strategy is successful. Well-crafted outcome statements are measurable and give the strategy its performance metrics. In the illustration, the outcomes are shown in shades of gray to make the point that these too may shift as a result of what is learned as the strategy advances.

3. Principles. The third element sets boundaries on the strategy manager's prerogatives and introduces a critical relationship between those who approve the strategy and those who manage it. Boards approve strategies and turn the management of them over to the staff, a committee, or a task force created exclusively for that purpose. For the strategy to be intelligent, that is, to learn as it goes, managers must be free to make adjustments in real time. Nevertheless, the board has ultimate responsibility for changes of this magnitude. The guiding principles make cautionary statements on pitfalls that should be avoided or policies that should be respected. They should not be prescriptive to a point where they dictate how the outcomes will be achieved.

4. Event Sequence. The fourth element is the action plan that defines the tasks necessary to achieve the outcome in a manner that respects the principles. Quinn refers to the action plan as an event sequence to make the point that successful strategy rarely goes according to plan. Strategies may have a fixed set of actions when they deploy, but part of being intelligent is recovering from missteps and finding ways around blind alleys. In the end a strategy will have exhibited a distinct set of causes and effects that moved it from the issue to the outcomes, but it probably won't look like the initial action plan. The term event sequence is intended to convey the point that it's not about the plan so much as it is about getting there.

The other distinction between an action plan and an event sequence has to do with the difference between management and leadership. Leaders communicate in a manner that can simplify the complex. While the manager needs to deal with the details, this model provides a strategy sketch that simplifies what may at the detail level be a complicated endeavor. It does so because it is designed to serve the needs of the leaders who approve strategy. They need to maintain the big view. Quinn believes that most complex strategies can be captured in four to seven major thrusts. The purpose is to show the strategy's viability and give some scope of the resource requirements. It's a sketch.

For example, one association had a desired outcome that would diversify the membership by including a new demographic group of technicians that were emerging as a result of a new technology that was affecting their industry. The outcome statement called for a specific number of new members from this group by a certain point in the future. The event sequence or causes and effects that would make this happen were summarized as follows:

- Develop a database of a thousand prospects.
- Send complimentary copies of the magazine to them for three months prior to the annual meeting and include feature stories on the issues they care about.
- Schedule several annual meeting sessions that address these issues and highlight them in the magazine issues they receive before the meeting.
- Send customized marketing appeals to persuade them to attend the meeting.
- Initiate a membership marketing campaign once the complimentary subscription and annual meeting tactics play out.
- Assess the effectiveness of the effort and propose phase-two initiatives and more research on their particular needs.

Those who manage this strategy will require much more detail to make these steps happen. But from the perspective of those who approve the strategy, it gives enough of a sketch for them to see the viability and understand the magnitude of the cost.

One of the primary points behind this model is that the four elements—issue, outcome, principles, and event sequence—can be analyzed separately or as a unified force. The model places these elements in a model that is linear in the construction phase, but becomes iterative once the strategy deploys.

Looking at them separately makes it easier to deconstruct the strategy when it goes awry. Each element carries its own opportunity to misinform the others and that will be the culprit that needs fixing. The strategy may fail because the issue driving it was not understood accurately or because the desired outcome was unrealistic, the guiding principles were too restrictive, or the event sequence was unrealistic or under-funded.

The need for dialogue between the board that launched the strategy and the managers responsible for its execution is structured around the interactive nature of these

Managing a Radar Screen

Leaders can limit the number of objects on their radar screens—that is, limit the number of issues that vie for their attention—as they reason their way to agreement on the forces that warrant strategic investments. The American Society of Civil Engineers (ASCE), Reston, Virginia, is developing a radar screen that, in its work-in-progress state, provides a view of this ongoing process.

In the first round of ASCE's process, information on potential issues flowed from regional meetings, committee recommendations, research initiatives, staff input, and other sources to a planning committee that then refined the issue statements. When the ongoing process is up and running, the board will annually review similar input, discuss the issues, make possible edits, and agree on a set of issues that will be addressed in the course of the year. During the year, board members plan to engage the membership in conversations designed to edit ASCE's collective understanding of these issues and identify new issues for possible inclusion in the next iteration.

Boards are considering ways to reach beyond the membership, and even beyond conventional thinking, to gather insights that members don't have. They might invite critics of the profession—and every profession has them—to offer their thoughts. Once a year, the board members will take a snapshot of this moving picture to inform the strategy-making process that is attached to the annual budget cycle. This fixed connection point is critical to the stability of the organization, but it is not the only time an issue can advance to the strategy-making stage. The board could consider having a strategic fund that allows the freedom to launch a strategy at any point in the year if it is urgent and clearly understood.

In ASCE's process, still very much under development at press time, issues typically fall into three categories: priority, monitor, and research. Priority issues are important to the association's constituents and within the organization's ability to address. Issues in the second category are not as urgent, so they are acknowledged and monitored. At some point they could graduate to priority status or fall off the radar screen to make room for other issues that win this competition for attention.

The third and final category includes issues that require more research. Information theory lays out a spectrum of clarity that ranges from equivocal to unequivocal. Equivocal information contains uncertainty or noise. They typically generate consternation when we are struggling to phrase them accurately or include them at all on the radar screen.

The following three issues are being considered by ASCE for inclusion in what will be the organization's first radar screen. Because the following three issues represent only a preliminary

Continued on next page

four elements. The strategy section of *From Scan to Plan* provides guidelines on the roles and responsibilities of the board and the strategy managers with respect to the elements. This is something that will vary according to the cultural norms of the association. As a rule of thumb, the board has the final say on the characterization of an issue that frames the strategy, but all were welcome in the process that identified it and placed it on the radar screen. The outcome statements must be approved by the board, but they should ask the managers to draft them as a part of their initial work in creating the sketch. This will drive a dialogue that will make sure both parties understand each other and agree on where the strategy is bound. The principles are the

draft, these examples reflect only a possible disposition. Whether they will appear in ASCE's radar screen, in what form, is still to be decided.

Priority Issue

Years of deferred infrastructure investment and maintenance place public safety at risk and hinder the nation's economic growth and competitiveness.

ASCE has pursued infrastructure as a priority issue for some time, so the new radar screen is simply recognizing a force that is responsible for a significant expansion in the society's government relations program in recent years.

Monitor

Engineering services are increasingly seen as a commodity due to
- *The perceived influence of certain technologies on design services;*
- *The outsourcing of engineering services to offshore providers; and*
- *The hourly basis of pricing that fails to reflect the value delivered.*

ASCE members express serious concern about this issue, but it is not yet clear if the association is in a position to do something about it. Member expectation may demand an acknowledgment and that alone may drive this issue into the monitoring category. If the board concludes that ASCE cannot act on it effectively, they will develop a communication plan to convey this to those members who feel strongly about it.

Research

The career commitment and work ethic of engineering's current leaders may not be in sync with a younger generation whose members may
- *Have different quality-of-life expectations;*
- *Seek more immediate gratification from the tasks they are given;*
- *Place more emphasis on the social significance of the profession's work; and*
- *Be more willing to make abrupt career changes if they see other opportunities that meet their expectations.*

The mere length of this issue in its early stage of development provides the first indication that it may be carrying some noise, meaning not all of the information is accurate or warrants strategic attention. It is highly conjectural and based on opinions that may not have won widespread support. Nevertheless, if strategy is about the long-term viability of a constituency, this has the earmarks of something that may pass the tests for priority status. A board may refer an issue like this to a committee and direct them to conduct research.

exclusive domain of the board because they place boundaries on the managers. The event sequence should be the exclusive domain of the managers, but it must pass the tests for viability and affordability.

In the life of the strategy, this sketch, which easily fits on a single piece of paper, is used to keep the board informed. If the managers think that the issue or the outcomes need editing, they would seek approval for this from the board. Board approval would also be required if the event sequence was altered in a way that requires more resources than were allocated. Otherwise the sketch is a simple means of keeping the board informed. For example, the strategy managers might provide the board with a progress report that says the first three of the seven sequence events are now complete, but there are a few issues regarding progress on the fourth. It isn't something that requires board approval, but the managers want a conversation with the board simply to keep them in the loop. The strategy sketch helps to organize this kind of dialogue.

As strategic planning sheds its rigid, elaborate, and somewhat imperial procedures and becomes a fast-moving way of maintaining conversations on the future and launching initiatives to sustain the organization, a simpler set of tools is needed to capture the action. The framework to distinguish established programs from adaptation pursuits and the strategy model are intended to serve this purpose. Regardless of what we wind up calling it, associations must maintain stability, evolve, and document these opposite but complementary requirements.

About the Author

James Dalton is president of Strategic Counsel, Derwood, Maryland.

This chapter was excerpted and adapted from an article the author wrote for the Fall 2006 issue of the *Journal of Association Leadership*.

Review Questions

1. Describe the four elements of strategy.
2. What is the appropriate dialogue between the board, staff, and members during strategy making?
3. How can associations involve different stakeholders in strategy making?

Legal Issues

Jefferson C. Glassie, J.D.

I N THIS LITIGIOUS SOCIETY, chief executive officers and all staff must remain on alert to protect their associations from risks of liability. Lawsuits and government enforcement actions can be devastating—financially and organizationally— particularly if the association doesn't have proper legal risk-protection measures in place. In light of the Sarbanes-Oxley inspired obligations of responsibility, transparency, and accountability, careful attention to legal issues is crucial. Sarbanes-Oxley is legislation adopted by Congress that applies to publicly traded companies and imposes strict financial accountability requirements; the law is generally not applicable to nonprofit organizations, but its principles of accountability and responsibility have affected views of appropriate nonprofit governance.

Legal Audits

In a perfect world, every association would commission a formal and comprehensive legal audit to review all aspects of its programs and activities to determine whether significant legal exposure existed. Then, in that perfect world, the association would undertake a routine "legal check-up" every year or so to review ongoing and developing legal issues and problems.

Like a financial audit, a legal audit can help protect an association against unexpected liability. In addition, a legal audit can point out trouble spots that deserve board or staff attention and may even trigger the development and implementation of key association policies that will help minimize potential liability (for instance, an antitrust compliance policy).

Undertaking a legal audit of association activity also demonstrates the board's or CEO's good faith and due diligence in taking reasonable steps to identify and avoid potential liability. Even a less formal but thorough legal review of specific high-profile areas, such as certification programs, can highlight some of the more problematic risks and generate recommendations for minimizing those risks.

Of course, it is often not possible to have outside counsel conduct a full legal audit. Both seasoned veterans and those new to association management can use the following summary to review legal considerations important to most associations. (Note that this is not an exhaustive review and cannot replace legal advice, counsel, or a formal legal audit; it may, however, help avoid some of the legal potholes associations may encounter.)

Corporate Status

The association's corporate status offers a good starting point for a legal review. An incorporated association has Articles of Incorporation on file with the state or jurisdiction (such as the District of Columbia) in which incorporation occurred. Periodically, association staff or the relevant volunteer committee should review the Articles of Incorporation to ensure that they remain consistent with current activities. For instance, changes made in the bylaws or other structural aspects of the association—such as the number of directors and officers, membership criteria, and voting requirements—may make Articles of Incorporation out of date.

In addition, the legal status of the association in its state of incorporation must be up to date—otherwise known as keeping the corporation in "good standing." Most states require the filing of annual or other periodic reports in order for associations to obtain the limited liability protection available through the corporate form.

An association incorporated in one state but with offices in another state usually needs to file reports in the other state, too. Failure to file the annual reports can result in revocation of corporate status or authority, with subsequent liability exposure to the individual officers, directors, and staff members of the association. Therefore, all annual corporate filings in any jurisdictions where the association is incorporated or has offices should be made routinely and on time.

The bylaws—the general governing document that applies primarily to day-to-day association activities—should be consistent with state law and the Articles of Incorporation. The bylaws usually cover such organizational aspects as membership, meetings, voting, officers, directors, and committees. Provisions authorizing the existence of chapters also may be included.

Many associations have specific committees charged with ensuring that the bylaws are up to date and consistent with the association's current practices and procedures. In turn, it's important for associations to follow their bylaws. For example, membership voting and proper notice of meetings should be accomplished in accordance with the bylaws. Otherwise, failure to follow the policies and procedures of the association as outlined in the bylaws and other governing documents can result in challenges by members. Legal counsel can review preparation of notices for meetings, voting materials, and agendas to ensure compliance with legal requirements.

It is also important to address governance and board issues and ensure that meetings follow applicable law. Sarbanes-Oxley inspired principles argue for adopting conflict of interest and whistle-blower policies. Board and committee education and orientation sessions are also advisable.

Finances

Practically speaking, strong and healthy finances greatly influence the success of an association. Legally speaking, strong policies that protect against improper financial activities are essential as well. Legal liability can arise if association finances are mishandled, whether through incompetence, inadvertence, or deliberate fraud or embezzlement.

The board of directors generally has the responsibility for overseeing the development of budgets and for reviewing the finances. In fact, directors owe certain fiduciary duties to the organization to manage its affairs in good faith and in its best interests. The board, however, must remain apprised of important financial developments and receive periodic financial reports. Otherwise, the CEO or staff could possibly be accused of misleading the board, and liability could be imposed on individual staff members.

Accountants can help develop procedures and policies to prevent against embezzlement or other misuse or misappropriation of association funds (for instance, employees who handle funds should be bonded). Other useful policies relate to the investment of operating and surplus funds and the routine handling of deposits and writing of checks.

The preparation of audited financial reports also is recommended for associations. These reports give the board, members, and the general public confidence that the association's finances have been carefully and professionally prepared and audited. If the cost of hiring an outside professional (specifically, a certified public accountant) seems cost-prohibitive, the association should have an independent third party review its accounting and financial policies and procedures to ensure that appropriate protections are in place. Again, Sarbanes-Oxley principles suggest that associations should have an audit committee—or an executive or finance committee—that specifically reviews and monitors the audit and interacts independently with auditors.

Tax

Carefully, correctly, and accurately compiled financial information must form the basis for annual reports to the Internal Revenue Service (IRS). Tax-exempt associations with annual revenues that exceed $25,000 per year must file an annual information report with the IRS on Form 990.

The majority of trade associations and professional societies are exempt from federal income tax under Section 501(c)(6) or 501(c)(3) of the Internal Revenue Code. Section 501(c)(6) covers membership organizations with professional industry interests, such as business leagues, boards of trade, and other organizations that exist to promote a specific profession or line of commerce. Section 501(c)(3) organizations have primary purposes that are charitable, educational, or scientific; because donations to such organizations are tax-deductible to the donors, additional legal requirements apply.

The determination letter from the IRS granting (c)(3), (c)(6), or other 501(c) tax status should remain part of the association's permanent records. In the absence of a determination letter, the association should immediately seek legal counsel to ensure that it fulfills appropriate filing and reporting requirements. In addition, most states require tax-exempt organizations to file annual reports, and some (such as California and the District of Columbia) even require that an association submit a formal application to obtain such an exemption.

If tax-exempt organizations fail to conduct their activities in accordance with the tax-exempt purposes described under the Internal Revenue Code, they may face the imposition of taxes, penalties, or even revocation of their tax-exempt status. In addition, if an association's nonexempt activities—such as marketing particular services for members or selling non-related products—become substantial, they may jeopardize the organization's tax exemption. More commonly, activities that are unrelated to the association's purpose or mission, are "regularly carried on," and constitute a "trade or business" under IRS definitions will result in unrelated business income subject to tax (UBIT).

If unrelated revenues subject to UBIT rise to within 30 or 40 percent of the association's annual budget, the IRS may question its tax-exempt status. Associations in that situation often spin off some of their activities into a for-profit subsidiary (see Chapter 8).

One way to avoid UBIT is to structure activities in such a manner that they will not be subjected to tax. For example, many association affinity programs can be appropriately characterized in legal agreements as generating "royalty" income for associations: Passive revenues, such as dividends, interest, and royalties, are exempt from UBIT provided certain rules are observed. In addition, sponsorships of activities can generate tax-free revenues if the association recognizes and acknowledges the sponsor in accordance with IRS guidance.

Insurance

Associations can take many steps to reduce potential liability. Yet, in the current legal environment, there is no way to prevent an aggrieved member or other person from suing the association to seek compensation or relief from allegedly harmful behavior. Therefore, associations must have adequate insurance coverage to protect against liability arising from a wide variety of legal claims. Given the sophisticated insurance policies on the market, associations do well to turn to a knowledgeable insurance agent or broker with experience in the association field for help in obtaining adequate and appropriate coverage.

Commercial general liability (CGL) insurance protects against basic theft, "slip and fall," or other activities that can occur in the association's office environment. Of perhaps greater value in protecting against liability that may arise from association programs is association professional liability insurance (APLI), often referred to as directors and officers (D&O) insurance. (The two policies are different, however; the traditional form of D&O isn't sufficient in today's environment.) APLI policies protect against negligence and other allegedly wrongful acts of the association, which provisions of CGL policies don't cover.

It's important to adequately disclose all association activities to the insurance company when obtaining insurance and to carefully review any endorsements or exclusions in the policy. For example, the policy may exclude damages or losses from antitrust, certification or standardization programs, or even employment practices. It often is worth paying additional amounts to ensure the coverage for the association is broad and without significant loopholes; the extra protection can pay off if a lawsuit is filed.

Litigation

Given the potentially high cost and time-intensity of litigation, ignoring any claims made against the association can prove foolhardy. Legal counsel must be involved in the analysis and handling of any claims that might lead to litigation. The CEO or other appropriate staff person should carefully monitor, with legal counsel, any litigation in process against the association. He or she can then ensure that all aspects of the litigation are handled carefully and in a timely manner, not only to avoid potentially serious damages but also to manage legal costs.

When litigation is either expected or in progress, it's important to have policies and procedures that preserve the association's confidences and "attorney/client privilege." Association boards of directors also should be kept informed of the status of any significant claims or litigation, but board members must be clearly warned against inadvertent disclosures that may harm the association's case.

Although insurance policies tailored to association activities should cover the costs of litigation, the insurer will require proper and timely notice of any claim to obtain coverage.

Contracts

A written contract or agreement should memorialize any important legal obligation owed by, or to, an association. This is important not simply from the legal perspective, but also to confirm that the parties entering into arrangements for the sale or purchase of goods or services know exactly what is required of each. Most associations have policies stating that legal counsel must review and approve all contracts, which can be signed only by authorized officers.

All contracts are subject to negotiation. In other words, an association doesn't have to accept the exact contracts submitted by hotels, vendors, or others. In fact, it's helpful for associations to develop standard-form contracts to use with hotels, vendors, affinity program sponsors, and other vendors. A standard form makes it easier to always include contractual provisions that protect the association.

Important provisions include the following: warranties or specifications with respect to the goods or services to be provided, licenses for any use of intangible property (such as trademarks or copyrights), payment terms, indemnification or limited liability provisions, and termination or cancellation clauses. An "out" clause always is advisable because a vendor relationship—no matter how good it appears at the start—can turn sour. It's better to think about contract termination before the contract is signed than have to fend off claims of loss or damage if a contract is terminated inappropriately without adequate terms.

Personnel

Personnel- or employment-related claims often present a difficult area for associations because personal relationships may become bitter when employees depart on the association's terms rather than on their own. Allegations of discrimination based on age, sex, or race are commonplace, whether in fact any discrimination occurred.

A well-written, clear, and legally sufficient employee manual offers the best protection against difficult disputes with employees. Courts look to a manual as the basis for the terms and conditions of the relationship between employer and employee. As such, it should govern all aspects of employment, including termination, and be kept up to date to reflect the current practices of the association. The association should also conduct objective and consistent personnel evaluations and maintain them in appropriate files.

Employment-related claims may arise in a number of areas other than discrimination. For example, some associations have been subject to legal liability for failing to pay proper overtime for nonexempt employees, instead substituting compensatory time. Vacation policies also are important; in most circumstances, unused vacation time must be paid upon termination.

A well-written employee manual, followed closely, can minimize the potential for long, expensive, and divisive suits based on employment practices. At least one association employee should be specially trained in employment matters, including proper methods of hiring and firing, as well as employee benefits. Legal advice should be sought in advance of any proposals to terminate employees.

Intellectual Property

What is the most important property held by an association? Perhaps an office building—but many lease space. And most associations are not likely to own cars, boats, or extensive art collections. Therefore, "intellectual property" often represents an association's most valuable property.

Also referred to as "intangible property," intellectual property consists of patents, trademarks, service marks, trade names, certification marks, copyrights, and mailing lists (which can be considered trade secrets). From a legal standpoint, the association should take all reasonable steps to protect its intangible property, such as filing registrations with appropriate state and government authorities. Registrations can enhance the value of intangible property and provide important procedural protections in the event of any litigation.

In addition to ensuring that they use proper copyright or trademark notices, file registration applications, and properly attribute sources in association publications, staff must also make sure that the association has all rights to use anyone else's copyrighted materials that it includes in its publications or other materials. For instance, articles submitted by independent authors or speeches made at association meetings and published in conference proceedings have to be handled in a manner that grants the association adequate rights to use the material as it wishes.

For copyrighted publications, the general recommendation is to obtain full copyright assignments so that the association *owns* the rights to the materials. Otherwise, it is sufficient for the holder of the copyrighted work (usually the author) to grant a release or license that is broad enough to cover any potential uses by the association. It's preferable that all who write for association publications or make presentations at association meetings submit standard-form copyright assignments or releases. Also, any agreements with independent contractors should include provisions assigning copyright to the association.

Intellectual property rights command increased attention as associations move further into the world of cyberspace by creating Web sites, home pages, bulletin boards, listservers, and e-mail systems. Special legal issues apply to Internet activities, particularly in connection with intangible property rights, so associations should consult legal counsel before embarking on such activities.

Association Programs

The wide range of association activities and programs, different for each profession and industry, makes a full legal review of such programs impossible here. However, several themes run through the general collection of association programs and activities:

- **Antitrust.** The Sherman Act and other federal and state antitrust laws prohibit anticompetitive acts in restraint of trade. Among these are several commonly recognized illegal activities, such as price fixing, allocation of markets, and boycotting of competitors. But any activities considered unreasonably exclusionary or anticompetitive may give rise to problems. For instance; antitrust issues can crop up with respect to membership eligibility criteria, certification programs, availability of products and services to nonmembers, standard settings, promulgation of codes of conduct, statistical programs, and credit-reporting activities.

To avoid potential problems, associations need strong antitrust compliance policies that they routinely announce to members, particularly at association meetings. It's always advisable for legal counsel to attend meetings where sensitive topics are on the agenda and to remain apprised of any activities that potentially come within the jurisdiction of antitrust laws.

- **Due Process.** Association actions that are inherently exclusionary or may adversely affect members and others must be taken in accordance with basic due-process principles. In other words, association programs must be substantively and procedurally fair and reasonable.

  Furthermore, professional or product certification programs, standards setting, and other self-regulation programs should be developed in a fair and reasonable manner. They must not unfairly exclude those who should be entitled to participate or to receive credentials or other recognition from the association.

- **Membership.** Membership eligibility decisions and any disciplinary actions, particularly expulsion, must be undertaken in accordance with relevant due-process principles. It is recommended that members have the opportunity to appeal decisions to a neutral appeal panel.

- **Political and Lobbying Activities.** Special rules apply in this area. For instance, organizations that are exempt under Section 501(c)(3) of the Internal Revenue Code are absolutely prohibited from any political activities, such as supporting or opposing a particular candidate during an election campaign. Section 501(c)(3) also limits the amount of lobbying that organizations can conduct; lobbying cannot exceed an "insubstantial amount" or the specific limits established under Section 501(h) of the Internal Revenue Code.

Although Section 501(c)(6) organizations have more freedom to lobby, they're subject to new lobbying dues nondeductibility laws, whereby the portion of member dues allocated to fund lobbying activities are nondeductible. Alternatively, the association can pay a "proxy" tax on such lobbying expenditures.

In addition, Congress in 1996 enacted a Lobbying Disclosure Act that requires registration of those lobbying the federal or executive branches of the United States government. The definitions of lobbying found in both the legislation and the Internal Revenue Code are broad and complex. To ensure compliance, associations may wish to seek the assistance of legal counsel.

Finally, under the Federal Election Campaign Act, it is illegal for corporations to participate in federal elections, except through political action committees (PACs). The rules for participation in federal elections and solicitations for PAC contributions are complex, and some states have laws with similar restrictions. Any associations engaging in political activity should consult legal counsel—except Section 501(c)(3) organizations for which such activities are not permitted.

Appropriate Protection

Association executives face numerous legal issues and obstacles in the daily course of their activities. That's why it's important for CEOs and staff to ensure that appropriate policies and procedures are in place to protect the association against potential liability. In situations where numerous, complicated, and often-times convoluted rules and regulations apply, however, CEOs may wish to seek legal counsel for assistance in devising appropriate steps or responses. In some cases, responding in the wrong manner may be worse than doing nothing.

Like it or not, one of the hats an association executive must wear says "Legal" on it, and he or she needs an adequate knowledge of legal issues to handle the job professionally and competently.

References and Suggested Reading

CCH Exempt Organizations Reporter.

CH Federal Election Campaign Financing Guide.

Glassie, Jefferson C., *International Legal Issues for Nonprofit Organizations*, American Society of Association Executives, Washington, D.C., 1999.

Hopkins, B., *The Law of Tax-Exempt Organizations, 8th ed.*, John Wiley & Sons, 1992.

Jacobs, Jerald, *Association Law Handbook, 4th ed.*, American Society of Association Executives, Washington, D.C., 2007.

Jacobs, Jerald and Glassie, Jefferson, *Certification and Accreditation Law Handbook*, 2nd ed. American Society of Association Executives, Washington, D.C., 1992.

Jacobs, Jerald, *Federal Lobbying Law Handbook, 2nd ed.*, American Society of Association Executives, Washington, D.C., 1993.

Jacobs, Jerald, and D. Ogden, *Legal Risk Management for Associations*, American Psychological Association, Washington, D.C., 1995.

Oleck, H., and M. Stewart, *Nonprofit Corporations, Organizations & Associations*, 6th ed., Prentice-Hall, Inc., Englewood Cliffs, NJ., 1994.

About the Author

Jefferson C. Glassie, J.D., is a partner in Pillsbury Winthrop Shaw Pittman's nonprofit organizations group and represents associations and nonprofit organizations on a wide range of legal matters, including antitrust, tax, certification, accreditation, contracts, employment, merger, intellectual property, and corporate issues. He has significant experience in international legal issues and is the author of *International Legal Issues for Nonprofit Organizations,* published by the American Society for Association Executives. He is also co-author with Jerry Jacobs of *Certification and Accreditation Law Handbook, 2nd edition.* He is the former chair of the ASAE & The Center's Legal Section Council and a former member of the ASAE & The

Center's International Section Council. He also serves as an instructor for the ASAE & The Center's online electronic course on legal issues for associations and as faculty for the ASAE & The Center Virtual Law School.

Review Questions

1. What have you learned from this chapter that you can implement in your association to minimize legal risks?

2. If you don't have policies that follow from Sarbanes-Oxley principles in your association, such as whistle-blower and conflicts of interest policies, what can you do to encourage the board of directors to adopt them?

3. Do you think it's important for your association to conduct a legal audit?

4. What type of legal review and compliance program do you have in your association to avoid legal problems?

CHAPTER

7

Building Strong Component Relations

Adrienne Antink, CAE

VERY ASSOCIATION HAS SUBSETS—THEY may be chapters, special interest groups, sections, committees, task forces, work groups, advisory panels, affiliates, allied societies, regions, virtual forums, e-mail lists, and a plethora of others. These are all components. Typically components are geographically based, but functionally based components are also common. They may be separate legal entities or part of a federation or integrated into the corporate structure of the lead association. Whatever their form or structure, the relationship between the lead association and its components must be mutually beneficial if it is truly to be a positive partnership.

Understanding the Importance of Components

Associations dedicate significant resources—money, volunteer effort, and staff time—to creating and maintaining positive component relations. Why do they do this? What do they see as the return on investment? For members, components provide continuing education and networking opportunities at the state, local and/or global level. In addition they often actively influence legislative and regulatory issues. For the lead association, a strong volunteer base guarantees the future success of an association. It is through the components that the lead association builds the leadership pool that allows continual fresh blood to course through the organization, which ensures that new ideas and fresh perspectives are infusing the association so it is poised for the future.

Components also keep the organization in touch with the grassroots of the membership. It is from the trenches that new trends, emerging concerns, changing member needs, and innovative ideas bubble up. This gives the organization the future intelligence it needs to advance the association's profession and mission. In addition, components provide the lead association additional marketing channels for products and services. Extending the lead association's brand to the components increases awareness and strengthens the organization's identity at the state, local, and global levels.

In turn components benefit from affiliation by piggybacking on the lead association's reputation and brand name. Also, component officers look to the lead association for new arenas in which to serve in leadership positions after completing service at a state or local level. Most lead associations provide leadership training that would not usually be available at the component level. In addition, many components receive administrative support services from the lead association.

Working Effectively with Components

There are eight key steps to working effectively with components:

1. **Clearly define the roles and responsibilities of the lead association and the component.** Who does what? What can each expect of the other? The objective is to eliminate duplication. Articulating what each level is responsible for allows the lead association and components to be more effective and facilitates working as a coordinated team to carry out their shared mission. Although defining roles and responsibilities is typically driven by the lead association, ideally components are engaged at appropriate points in the process. It should be more of a friendly negotiation than an arbitrary direction from the lead association.

2. **Codify these roles and responsibilities in an affiliation agreement.** This document may also be called a charter. In addition to delineating responsibilities, there are important legal requirements that will also need to be addressed in an affiliation agreement, such as the use of the association's logo, liability and incorporation requirements, etc.

3. **Spell out in the affiliation agreement any reporting requirements that the components will be expected to complete on a scheduled basis.** This could be reports on membership numbers, financial performance, notifications of new officers, or samples of the component's use of the association logo. Many associations also set performance expectations. For example, a component may have to offer a specific number of education activities each year. State the consequences for non-compliance for all requirements described in the affiliation agreement.

4. **Specify the criteria to be used in recognizing a new component and the process for dissolving a component.** Like any organizational unit, components have a life-cycle that begins with the identification of an emerging need and the creation of the component followed by a spurt of rapid growth which transitions into a period of stability. When the environment changes and the original need is no longer present, the component may be retired. The component's lifecycle may be of short duration

or it may operate effectively for an indefinite period. It is more likely that special interest groups will have a shorter life span than geographically based components.

Often associations are reluctant to sunset a component, thinking it will be seen as a failure on the part of either the volunteer leadership or staff. However, in reality it is important to recognize that components do not necessarily need to live forever. By retiring components when they have completed their work and bringing new ones on line, an association shows its nimbleness in responding quickly to member needs and to a changing environment.

5. **Provide an orientation for new component leaders to clarify roles and responsibilities.** The orientation is usually conducted by the lead association and may be held at the headquarters of the lead organization, or staff may travel to the component. Be sure component leaders know who has been assigned as their liaison at the lead association and what support they can expect. Components often have their own professional staff. Defining roles between the staff of the lead association and the component staff is also important.

6. **Clarify expectations for working together.** Orientation is also a good opportunity to clarify expectations. Most association leaders have had previous volunteer experience in their communities or in other professional societies before reaching their current positions with the association. Each organization will have a different leadership culture with different performance standards, approaches for rewarding and recognizing volunteers, and ways of working with staff.

7. **Identify staff to manage the lead association's relationship with its components.** A key competency of component relations professionals is managing multiple relationships. Component relations professionals are ombudsmen, advocating simultaneously for both the lead association and the component at multiple intersections. This includes interaction with other staff at the lead association, board members and other volunteer leaders at the lead association, and component leaders, staff, and members. Truly, component relations professionals are the face of the association as they work with all of these important stakeholders.

8. **Identify which services the lead association will offer its components.** All associations have to address what services they will offer their components based on organizational culture, member needs, resources, and the maturity of the component. To quote the conventional wisdom of component relations professionals, "If you've seen one component relations strategy, you have seen one component relations strategy." They're all different—and for a good reason. They must be flexible and take into account the uniqueness of the association's components and the needs of their members and leaders.

Every association supports its components differently. There is no one preferred set of services. One association may provide extensive association management support services—database, Web page, and publications support—while another association may choose to focus its resources on more global support like leadership training and mentoring or insurance purchasing programs. There is no right or wrong approach. It all comes back to the association articulating the role components play in achieving the organization's goals—and the resources available.

Communicating with Components

The secret to successful component relations is simple, but like so many simple things, it's not that easy to carry out. Continual, effective, and sensitive communication is the foundation of strong component relationships. The communication vehicles used and how messages are crafted—to include the words and tone—must be appropriate to the member and staff culture of the particular association. The mechanics of communicating are not hard. The trick is in composing the message and delivering it. The bottom line is to engage in consistent, honest, and ongoing communication within the context of the association's organizational dynamic.

Typical outreach to components includes one-on-one conversations by phone and e-mail, leadership conferences, and field visits. At any one time, a combination of these methods will be in play. There is no one-size-fits-all in deciding what kinds of communication work best for an association and its components. The use of leadership conferences and field visits depends on the association's budget and staff resources. If an association has limited funding for these activities, regularly scheduled conference calls and frequent e-mail dialogue are always available. Continually communicate with component leaders with multiple touches—phone calls, e-mail messages, face-to-face meetings—whatever the association can afford and works well for staff and volunteers.

Consistency, honesty, and most of all, doing what you say you will do, builds trust. At the end of the day, it is trust that defines the component's perception of the lead association. The trust factor is the gauge of the relationship. Without trust there is no partnership, regardless of whatever paper requirements and written documentation may be in place. The lead association may think it has the big stick, but in reality it is simply a twig if there is no trust.

Building trust is more than the amount of communication. It is about dependable follow-up. It is being sincere in seeking feedback and actually using it. If you get input that cannot be acted on for whatever reason, acknowledge that the message was heard and that the lead association understands the component's position, even if it doesn't agree with it. Volunteer leaders do not want to waste their time talking to the lead association if they are only going to pay lip service to the thoughts the components took the time to express. Components are important stakeholders in your association's future. Distinguish between asking for input and seeking a decision. Openly acknowledge the value of components and what they are accomplishing.

Contact component leaders on a regular basis to share information, ask for input, and brainstorm ideas as well as to request assistance. It is easy for lead association staff to get a reputation of only calling the component when they want something. Conduct in-house training for all association staff on how to work with volunteer leaders. This should include organizationally articulated expectations of how staff will communicate with member volunteers, including response times, messaging, and tone.

There are many times when it is necessary to deliver a message components do not want to hear. Bad news is better received if the lead association is candid and explains why it is taking a particular plan of action. This is not a time for vagueness and innuendo. If component leaders feel they have been treated fairly and honestly in the past, they will continue to respect the association through any difficult discussions.

All associations have different structures for their components, provide different services, and have different member and staff cultures, but all will be successful if there is ongoing transparent communication delivered with genuine respect and political sensitivity.

Recommended Reading

Component Relations Handbook: Tools and Tips for the Component Relations Professional (ASAE & The Center, 2005)

"Bright Lights and Vibrant Components" by Peggy Hoffman, *Association Management*, February 2004

"Components as Colleagues" by Adrienne Bien, CAE and Cynthia D'Amour, *Association Management*, May 2005

About the Author

Adrienne Antink, CAE, is vice president for learning and networking for the Medical Group Management Association, Englewood, Colorado.

Review Questions

1. What are the key steps an association must take to work effectively with its components?

2. What kinds of information should be included in an affiliation agreement?

3. How does the lead association build trust with its components?

8

Subsidiary Corporations

William T. Robinson, CAE

W HEN ASSOCIATIONS WISH TO expand their scope of activities—by offering group-purchasing arrangements, insurance programs, investment services, books and journals, or travel services to name just a few possibilities—they often establish a subsidiary or an affiliate organization. The difference is mainly one of ownership: Subsidiaries are owned, while affiliates are independent corporations.

In either case, the association's legal counsel must be involved in establishing the corporation because of the many federal, state, and possibly foreign laws and regulations that may pertain. For instance, a general business corporation in Delaware is substantially different from one in California or from a captive insurance company in Vermont.

Generally speaking, associations form subsidiary corporations for five reasons. They are to:

1. **Allow the association to engage in activities not permitted by its purpose, charter, or bylaws.** The Internal Revenue Service (IRS) does not exempt from taxes non-related business income of trade associations and individual membership societies that fall under Section 501(c)(6) of the Internal Revenue Code. Nor can these organizations receive tax-deductible contributions from donors. One solution is to form an affiliate and qualify it as a 501(c)(3) organization, which can receive gifts or grants that are tax-deductible to the donor.

   Similarly, state and federal regulatory agencies have long maintained authority over certain businesses and would prevent an association from engaging in those businesses directly. One example is insurance underwriting—the association itself could not be an actual insurance company, but it can form a separate corporation to act as one.

2. **Enable the association to offer services to niche markets.** A specific set of members may express a desire for something that other members aren't interested in, such as a geographic-based facility or service. Rather than use all members' dues to fund something that not all would benefit from, an association could establish a subsidiary to meet those specific needs. Only those using the service would pay for it, and the association would charge related staff time to the subsidiary's budget, not its own.

3. **Provide additional revenue sources.** Some members might argue that association dues are similar to a tax, and there's a limit to how much they're willing to be taxed. Rather than increase membership dues, associations can generate revenues through profit-seeking, tax-paying enterprises. (Because these association-related enterprises usually compete with tax-paying businesses, they are also subject to taxes, according to the IRS.)

4. **Increase the association's capacities and scope.** An association that can provide a wide range of additional services makes itself more valuable to members. Although additional staff are often needed to manage and operate an association's various business enterprises, they bring an expertise that can be of great value in other areas.

5. **Protect the association from the consequences of an activity's financial failure.** Any activity has a risk associated with it. Financial risks, in particular, increase with an activity's size and complexity. This is especially true when significant capital expenditures are required, along with expert (and expensive) personnel. But if an association carries on its high-risk activities through a separate corporation, the bankruptcy of one won't necessarily damage the financial viability of other activities or of the association itself.

Patterns of Governance

Generally speaking, an association can choose from four patterns of control or governance. Each has its pluses and minuses, as explained below:

1. **After forming the new company, the association turns it over to the participating members.** The association may maintain a presence by having its chief executive officer (CEO) or an elected leader sit on the subsidiary board.

    Advantages: The association will have performed a service for its members by establishing the company. Turning the new organization over to participants enables the association to avoid further operational responsibility and to remain focused on its principal mission.

    Disadvantages: The association will eventually lose identification with the enterprise, along with its ability to use the company for new purposes. Additionally, the association loses a potential source of additional revenue and staff expertise.

2. **The association board serves as the board of the subsidiary.** The two boards may be identical, or the subsidiary's board may have a few of the same officers and directors.

Advantages: All the necessary business of the subsidiaries can be conducted at regular meetings of the association's board. In this way, board members become familiar with the activities of the subsidiaries, and the association avoids the additional costs of separate board meetings for the subsidiary.

Disadvantages: As the subsidiary grows in size, the number of issues requiring attention by the governing board increases. These can reach the point where time is not available to accommodate the agendas of both the association and its subsidiaries. More important, the experience required to serve on an association board is not necessarily the same as that required to serve on the board of a complex subsidiary, such as an insurance company.

Lastly, by design, association governing boards have a regular turnover in membership. The same rate of turnover, however, is not necessarily good for subsidiary boards, where stability and accumulated experience are valuable from a business perspective.

3. **The association appoints the board of the subsidiary.** Usually selected are people with experience in the subsidiary's activities—perhaps some from the participating members—plus a representative of the association's governing board or executive committee and the CEO. This pattern is frequently used when an association has more than one subsidiary or when its subsidiary has a high level of activity.

Advantages: The subsidiary company is free to take on a life of its own, often independent of the association. The potentially heavy hand of over-governance by the association's board is avoided.

Disadvantages: The association incurs additional expenses to hold separate board meetings. Also, taking on "a life of its own" can so distance a subsidiary from its parent association that control issues emerge; subsidiary real estate operations or insurance companies, for instance, can have financial statements that dwarf the association's other resources.

4. **The association creates a holding company to oversee the subsidiaries' work.** The governing board of the holding company may be drawn from the association's executive committee or from the boards of the subsidiaries. Or, it might include senior staff officers of the association and the CEOs of the subsidiaries.

Advantages: When subsidiaries have become numerous, a holding company can summarize all activities in one report to the association's board. This permits the board to devote its time and attention to the normal association business.

Disadvantages: Subsidiary activities can become increasingly remote from the functions of the association, as perceived by its governing board.

For any of these structures, the parent organization can exert additional control by appointing its CEO, chief financial officer, or general counsel to serve in the same capacity for the subsidiary.

Management and Staffing

If a subsidiary engages in a minor activity, the association may assign managerial responsibility to a current staff member on an "additional duties" basis. If the subsidiary operates within a complex or fast-changing field, however, an expert in that area is required. He or she will eventually come to understand the parent association and associations in general, while providing valuable expertise.

One large professional association tried to sidestep the need for such expertise by appointing its executive committee as the board of the subsidiary company and its public relations director as the subsidiary company's manager. The public relations director's duties included liaison with the parent association's local societies, which were the intended beneficiaries of the subsidiary. The company manager did not report to the subsidiary company's board but to executives within the association.

While the company manager was learning about the subsidiary's business, the new company missed major opportunities for service and growth. A few years later, the manager retired and was succeeded by an executive experienced in the subsidiary's field. At this point, the subsidiary's business markets collapsed due to external forces. The association's subsidiary was financially unprepared for this, and the new executive requested large infusions of capital.

The executive committee of the association, however, in its role as the subsidiary's governing board, had turned over several times and had gradually lost interest in the affairs of the company. No one on the board recalled the crisis that had resulted in the subsidiary's formation. As a result the board did not provide additional capital. The company failed.

This example illustrates the necessity of employing trained personnel for each major subsidiary activity, as well as the importance of continuity among members of the subsidiary's governing board. Additional considerations for staffing subsidiaries include the following:

- **Experts should receive compensation based on the industry from which they have been recruited.** Compensation of association staff tends to reflect the patterns within the industry or profession represented, with modifications based on the association's locale, size, and scope. The same is true of compensation within the industry of the subsidiary.

  Often the two systems clash, causing difficulties for the association's CEO. For example, incentives for attracting new business, prizes, bonuses for achievement of management objectives, and stock options are common in industry but seldom found in associations. Yet the association may need to offer these to subsidiary employees to aid in their recruitment and retention.

- **Experts need to continue associating with colleagues and events in their industry.** A subsidiary's specialized employees maintain their expertise by associating with their colleagues. The related expenses may exceed those for employees of the association, especially where extensive or international travel is involved. This situation may create jealousy, or perhaps a sense of unequal treatment, on the part of association employees. The association CEO should be prepared to address any morale problem that may arise.

- **"Outside" experts may find the association world confusing or less interesting than their own fields.** Associations are usually deliberative and feature committee-based decision making, which people from some industries may find unfamiliar. Generally speaking, associations are also risk averse. These differences can be a source of difficulty, especially in the early stages of a new enterprise.

Are subsidiaries worth the effort and the risk? The answer lies not in a simple yes or no but on individual circumstances. Timing, opportunity, finances, association leadership—even ambition—all play a role in the decision-making process.

Potential Perils

These three perils may affect associations that operate subsidiaries:

1. **Failure of the enterprise.** In establishing a new activity, it is often difficult to find members who are willing to take the risks associated with it—especially in areas where growth is essential to success.

   In other words, it's easy to find the people willing to go second but difficult to find those willing to go first. If growth is essential to the subsidiary's financial viability but doesn't occur, it's wiser to discontinue the effort and accept the early loss to avoid a constant drain on the association's resources.

   Association subsidiaries can also fail for lack of sufficient start-up capital or overly optimistic assumptions of early success.

2. **Failure to recognize the enterprise's obsolescence.** Members will seek the best price of a product or service. Even loyalty to the association eventually takes a back seat to better prices. When an outside agency can perform the services of an association subsidiary better or cheaper—usually because of the economies of greater volume or more sophisticated systems—it's wiser to discontinue the effort. Sometimes the association can sell its subsidiary to its more successful competitor.

3. **Turnover on the governing board or the arrival of "second guessers."** New members of the association's governing board bring different experiences from those in leadership positions when the subsidiary was established. In addition, the subsidiary may have solved a problem that existed years earlier but is no longer evident to new board members.

   To avoid the surprise of opposition surfacing at a meeting, the orientation of new board members should devote sufficient time to reviewing the nature, purpose, and activities of each subsidiary. Any antipathy on the part of a new board member can be identified early on and accommodated with additional information.

On balance, subsidiaries can increase the value of an association to its members, expand the capacities and scope of the association, build up the association's revenue and wealth, and position the association to accommodate unforeseen challenges and opportunities.

About the Author

William T. Robinson, CAE, is a retired senior vice president of the American Hospital Association.

Review Questions

1. What are the reasons that associations typically form subsidiary corporations?

2. Discuss the four patterns of governance that an association may choose for its subsidiaries.

3. What areas should be taken into consideration when staffing subsidiaries?

CHAPTER

9

Leadership

Carla Balakgie, CAE

"The quality of leadership, more than any other single factor, determines the success or failure of an organization."

– Fred Fiedler & Martin Chemers, *Improving Leadership Effectiveness*

The Leadership Chimera

"The quality of leadership, more than any other single factor, determines the success or failure of an organization," wrote Fred Fiedler and Martin Chemers in their 1976 publication titled *Improving Leadership Effectiveness*. As myriad books, articles and scholarly journals have attested in the intervening years, this statement is just as true today as it was 30 years ago. So why then, after decades of hypothesis, study, application, reinvention, and reapplication of leadership practices, are businesses and their leaders still grappling with how to get it right? In all probability the elusive answer lies in the fact that leadership is both a quantitative and qualitative equation; a social and an occupational discipline; a human and a business process; and an apt metaphor for the cliché "both an art and a science" that requires intellectual and emotional competency from individuals to direct the systems involved. This chapter explores the common and the unique leadership requirements for association leaders as stewards of the nonprofit business sector.

The Attributes of Leadership

Part of the challenge in solving the leadership enigma involves distinguishing the relationship between leaders and the organizational leadership systems in which they operate. Until the realization is made that the two components are synergistic and symbiotic, executives will continue to struggle in their pursuit of leader and leadership effectiveness. Let's first explore the structural requirements of successful leadership.

Association executives, like any business professional, must understand and effectively coalesce a number of complex organizational processes, which include:

- Establishing and engendering support for a strategic view of the future of where the enterprise wants to be;

- Designing the organization, which consists of the architecture, processes, and resources to support achievement of the desired end state as well as the efficacy and continuity of its operation;

- Creating effective business policies and processes to implement the related required actions; and

- Cultivating a corporate environment conducive to success.

Added to this substantive list are practices like leading and managing change, data-driven decision making, risk analysis and risk taking, ethical business behavior, negotiation, facilitation, consensus building, and nurturing a culture that is guided by and responsive to stakeholder needs. This is a sizeable charge for any leader, the accomplishment of which is enabled by yet another collection of skills in the personal realm.

So what are the individual requirements of leadership? In the third edition of *The Leadership Challenge,* James Kouzes and Barry Posner reveal a critical truth about

Five Practices and Ten Commandments of Leadership

1. **Practice:** Model the way.
   a. *Commandment:* Find your voice by clarifying your personal values.
   b. *Commandment:* Set the example by aligning actions with shared values.

2. **Practice:** Inspire a shared vision.
   a. *Commandment:* Envision the future by imagining exciting and ennobling possibilities.
   b. *Commandment:* Enlist others in a common vision by appealing to shared aspirations.

3. **Practice:** Challenge the process.
   a. *Commandment:* Search for opportunities by seeking innovative ways to change, grow and improve.
   b. *Commandment:* Experiment and take risks by constantly generating small wins and learning from mistakes.

4. **Practice:** Enable others to act.
   a. *Commandment:* Foster collaboration by promoting cooperative goals and building trust.
   b. *Commandment:* Strengthen others by sharing power and discretion.

5. **Practice:** Encourage the heart.
   a. *Commandment:* Recognize contributions by showing appreciation for individual excellence.
   b. *Commandment:* Celebrate the values and victories by creating a spirit of community.

The Leadership Challenge, Jossey-Bass 2003. Reprinted with permission.

leadership: Leadership is a relationship—a relationship between those who aspire to lead and those who choose to follow. To navigate the complexity of interaction between individuals and groups, today's leader must demonstrate mastery of numerous personal competencies: communication, authenticity, integrity, self-awareness and the awareness of their impact on others, compassion, listening, persuasion, confidence, humility, the willingness to take risks, be wrong and to fail—sometimes publicly—courage, decisiveness, vision, and the fortitude to "walk the talk" by modeling expected behaviors. Kouzes and Posner sum up these competencies in their hierarchy of the "Five Practices and Ten Commandments of Leadership."

Whether by living desired behaviors, instigating possibility thinking about the future, or acting as change champion, sculling coach, or chief morale officer, leaders bear the onus for the efficacy of their organizations. Successful leadership is a rich stew whose recipe includes individual acumen, interpersonal and group relationship management, and orchestration of various human and business processes. In correct measure, all of these ingredients support advancement of the enterprise of which leaders are endowed.

Making Right Decisions and Making Decisions Right

A unique element of the nonprofit management rubric is the concept of shared leadership among the chief staff officer, the governing board, volunteer structures, and at times, even members who consider themselves as owners of the organization. Often the most prized abilities of executives in the for-profit sector do not translate to the nonprofit arena where there is complex governance and diffuse power structures. In his monograph *Good to Great and the Social Sectors*, Jim Collins hypothesizes that there are two types of leadership styles—executive and legislative. He explains that in executive leadership, the individual has enough concentrated power to simply make the right decisions. In legislative leadership, no individual (not even the chief executive) has enough structural power to make the most important decisions by themselves. Legislative leadership relies more upon persuasion, political currency, and shared interests to create the conditions for the right decisions to be made. This has clear applicability to the means by which association executives achieve buy-in and agreement from their boards and stakeholders on key organizational decisions.

According to Collin's leadership hierarchy, Level 5 (great leaders) differ from Level 4 (good leaders) in that they are ambitious first and foremost for the benefit of the organization, cause, or mission and not for themselves. In addition, they possess the will to do whatever it takes to make good on that ambition. Said simply, they make sure that the *right* decisions happen—no matter how difficult or painful—for the long-term greatness of the institution and the achievement of its mission, independent of consensus or popularity. This principle is at the core of how accomplished association professionals must conduct themselves and those they lead in terms of decision making for membership associations.

While still a work in progress, the theory of executive and legislative leadership is expected to yield a management approach that blends both styles in ratios in accordance with the business environment to which it is applied. For either the for-profit or nonprofit sectors, it means knowing when to exercise the executive prerogative in decision making, and for association leaders, it means understanding in relation to the importance of the battle for the good of the association's mission. Many may contend that this is a competency that successful nonprofit executives have already mastered. Regardless, this concept has powerful applications for the shared governance—or legislative leadership—model of associations.

Sound decision making isn't exclusively about an ideal approach or environmental conditions, however. It also requires the discipline to gather and use data, through both formal and informal processes. This might be as structured as market research conducted through surveys, polls, and interviews or as unofficial as calling a few colleagues or members to explore ideas. Risk analysis, assessing the benefits and costs—both tangible and intangible—is also a critical component of data-driven decision making. These elements are what might be referred to as the science side of the process. Yet the art factor is also critical to reaching well-informed decisions.

The art of data-driven decision making is in knowing how to put the information into context and blend it with experience, intuition, common sense, and cultural considerations to reach well-rounded conclusions and to avoid falling into analysis paralysis. Everything cannot be quantified, and a good leader knows that decision making involves a certain level of ambiguity and the need to make decisions based on imperfect information. How then to mitigate the risks? Judgment, reason, experience, and trusting one's gut are integral to the process. Leaders must draw on these intuitive competencies and use them in combination with the data to formulate conclusions.

Checklist for Effective Decision Making

Have you:
- Demonstrated a clear link to the root issue?
- Canvassed and weighed the value of a wide range of alternatives?
- Considered possible consequences of each alternative, both positive and negative?
- Made a clear link to the full range of goals and the value added implicated by the choice?
- Searched for new information relevant to the decision?
- Challenged outworn decisions?
- Assimilated new, relevant information even if it did not support the course of action you initially preferred?
- Involved input about and from those affected?
- Been aware of the decision-making process and shared it with others if the decision is collective?
- Included a plan for adoption and contingency plans?

From *The Prepared Mind of a Leader—Eight Skills Leaders Use to Innovate, Make Decisions, and Solve Problems*, Bill Welter and Jean Egmon, ©2006

As the nursery rhyme chants, "the cheese stands alone." So the practice of testing one's thinking and theories with trusted allies or those integral to the process is essential to making things go more smoothly. Because decision making can be an evolutionary process, input from a reasonable number of key stakeholders along the way facilitates buy-in and eliminates barriers. Moreover, running the trap line with those who have a vested interest in order to check for unknown snags, ensure optimal positioning, and gather new perspectives can prevent missteps and mistakes for the process leader.

And finally, leaders must project confidence in their decisions and be ready, willing, and able to sell them to other stakeholders. Not everyone will agree with the conclusion, but if they were afforded opportunity for input and perceive the leader's confidence in the ultimate decision, the chances for success are significantly enhanced.

It Takes a Village

Association leaders are the epicenter for the synthesis of a unique set of resources, processes, and cultural norms required to run their equally distinctive businesses. They are leaders of communities—of practice, professions, and industries—and of myriad individuals with differing relationships to the association enterprise. As volunteer leaders cycle through their roles and time-bounded tenures, staff make inevitable career migrations, and members enter and leave the association sphere, the chief executive officer remains as the standard bearer for the organization's vision, mission, and goals as well as the guardian of its traditions. Success in this capacity requires some fundamental features.

In the *7 Measures of Success—What Remarkable Associations Do that Others Don't*, a study published by ASAE & The Center for Association Leadership with the direction of leadership expert Jim Collins, accomplished leaders are described as the "great go between." This moniker reflects the CEO's role as a broker of ideas for their organizations—among staff, the board, volunteers, and members. It goes on to explain that remarkable associations flourish under the guidance of remarkable leaders who are visionary in their own right but that also understand the greater importance of the stakeholders' vision for the future of the organization. This type of leader possesses the ability to listen and respond to other's ideas—setting aside or modifying their own as needed—and to stimulate energy and engagement among these individuals in coalescing a view of what is possible and then enabling it to happen. This is in opposition to the more autocratic practice of decreeing a course of action based on their individual vision and dictating the outcome. Put simply, great leaders inspire, instigate, and contribute to the realization of an association's vision by bringing together the best strategies from among the members of its community and engaging them in the actions to realize it.

In carrying out the service mission of their associations, leaders must ensure existence of an organizational ethos that is demonstrably aligned with and responsive to the needs, values, and interests of its constituents. As described under the attributes of legislative leadership, this requires that chief staff executives promote the greater good of the association in all of their individual actions and deeds and that they also establish a set of cultural values that require the same from staff and volunteers. Thankfully there are some simple yet powerful ways to accomplish these objectives.

First, a well-defined process for strategic planning should exist that allows for the inputs of the board, other volunteers, and the membership at large. Whether achieved through stakeholders' direct participation in the planning process or through surveying and feedback mechanisms, this influx of environmental data will make certain the alignment of organizational priorities with constituent interests and will mitigate the well-intended but sometimes arbitrary impacts of transient volunteer leadership. Institution of an ancillary process that links strategic and operational planning is also vital in making sure that the actions undertaken by the association—albeit by staff and/or volunteers—directly benefit its members.

Development of standards that reflect the expected behaviors and requirements of volunteers, staff, and members are also effective tools. For example, adoption of a code of conduct for the board of directors and committees clarifies the roles, responsibilities, and expectations of these vital resources in carrying out the work of the association. Establishment and promulgation of a member code of ethics sets forth the standards for the conduct of members in their profession and in their relationship with the association. A conflict of interest and fiduciary responsibility policy makes clear the moral and legal responsibilities of the board. Written job descriptions for officers, board, and board and standing committees are additional mechanisms for reinforcing the stewardship responsibilities of volunteers (e.g., setting strategic direction, ensuring adequate resources, duty of care, etc.), helping them to be successful in their work, and avoiding the challenges created when there is ambiguity about their roles and responsibilities in relation to staff. Left to interpretation, this void always will be filled but not necessarily in ways conducive to the enterprise. Other strategies include having well-defined processes for attracting, training, and directing volunteer efforts and for measuring the success of their performance against organizational goals.

Finally, the chief executive must actively attend to the ongoing refinement of the explicit and implicit policies, procedures, and traditions within their associations (e.g., bylaws, nominating procedures, planning processes, and "the way things are done"). Developing shared values, norms, and desired behaviors of staff and volunteers is an effective technique for attracting and retaining human resources that will support the preferred culture of the association. This may include things like service-level orientation, guidelines for interaction and conflict resolution, or even attitudinal archetypes. Associations, like any business, are organic entities that regularly change and evolve; this requires that the leader be aware and intentional about what will best serve the needs of the organization—and its constituents—on an ongoing basis.

Modeling the Way

In their book *Heart, Soul and Spirit: Bold Strategies for Transforming Your Organization*, authors Dr. Bill Maynard and Tom Champoux contend that good leaders lead by example, influence, and collaboration; poor ones lead by intimidation or at best by default. To say then that leaders must model the behaviors they expect of others may not be the obvious overstatement it appears.

Foremost is the requirement that association professionals maintain the highest degree of personal integrity and professional ethics. Whether in exercising discretion and confidentiality with information, ensuring transparency for association business and financial matters, negotiating agreements in good faith and the best interests of the association, or even the smallest gesture such as not employing corporate shipping services for personal use, leaders must hold themselves to impeccable standards of conduct. How else could they fulfill their other key obligation of identifying and resolving the ethical dilemmas involving others and/or that affect the association? As

Components of Culture Management

Define: For the leader, the process should begin by documenting core values and the related actions (behaviors) that support them. No one can meet unknown expectations so explicitness is critical. This may include work style matters such as whether outcome/productivity is more important than the means or number of hours worked; clarity on the organization's tolerance and value for change; expectations for the service of customers such as striving to make every interaction a one-stop event; or expected conduct for engaging volunteers and fellow staff through well-designed meeting agendas, preparedness, and honoring every participant's viewpoint.

Adapt: Almost any endeavor is enriched by the benefit of alternate views. Leaders should strive to be receptive to feedback and possible adaptation of institutional values and norms based on input from their partners—albeit in the staff, volunteer, or member environs. This accomplishes not only the first benefit of infusing the culture with diverse ideas but also creates a level of engagement in those who feel they've had a hand in creating the values and rules by which they must abide.

Assess: Measuring how well reality aligns with aspirations is a third and essential component in culture management. For example, staff performance evaluations should include assessment of how well their behaviors support the agreed upon corporate values and norms. The group leader is certainly not exempt from this process and in fact should be the most prominent in demonstrating openness to feedback on their conduct and success in sustaining these fundamental elements. Using tools such as a 360-degree performance evaluation is an effective way for executives to obtain candid input from subordinates, board members, and other volunteers and members on what they're doing well and areas of needed improvement. In addition, willingly undergoing this type of assessment demonstrates a keen level of authenticity and humanness by the leader and the ability to "walk the [values] talk." This in return will empower or require commensurate behavior in others.

– C.B.

individuals, association leaders should abide by the American Society of Association Executives Standards of Conduct in all aspects of their professional activities. As mentioned earlier, development of organizational standards for member, volunteer, and staff conduct are also effective tools for promoting good ethics institution-wide. Finally, remaining perpetually attuned to how one's actions are or might be perceived is a solid litmus test for how well a leader is living up to the expectations they have established for themselves and for others.

But beyond ethics, what else does modeling the way entail? In the *Leadership Challenge*, Kouzes and Posner expound that to effectively demonstrate what they want from others, leaders must first be clear about their guiding principles by letting people know what they really think and believe, clearly and distinctively giving voice to their values, and then leading from what they believe. In other words, values rhetoric is insufficient; a leader's talk and actions must match. One of the most potent ways leaders can fashion the desired outcome is by clearly articulating and nurturing a corporate culture that supports these specific values and one in which both they and their staffs can thrive. After all, according to Maynard and Champoux, the leader is the single most significant factor in determining the climate of the organization, and the climate directly impacts the level of performance and success of the people within an organization. So the association leader must attend to this tall but attainable order.

Lastly, how can culture affect the ultimate business and financial efficacy of associations? In their memorable study of corporate America, *Corporate Culture and Performance* (1992), Kotter and Heskitt assessed 200 firms from more than 22 separate

A Tale of Two Cultures

Successful Corporate Culture	Traditional Corporate Culture
Risk-taking and experimentation encouraged.	Maintenance of status quo and tradition honored practices.
Inquiry, trouble shooting, and feedback welcomed from/for all areas.	Control of information important; feedback channels limited/non-existent.
Employee development high priority institution-wide.	Development of individuals optional and discretionary by unit.
Individual contributions to development of core values and change supported.	Sustenance of status quo..."how things are done" the focus.
Change and adaptation to changing needs a way of life.	Change a threat and generally avoided.
Focus on member customer needs as reason.	Reluctance to change for any motivator for change.

Adapted from *Intentional Design and the Process of Change*, Patrick Sanaghan and Rod Napier; © 2002, National Association of College and University Business Officers

industries during an 11-year period. They sought the answer to the following question: "How does the culture of an organization influence its success according to certain measures (e.g. increasing revenues, an expanding work force, growth in stock value and net profitability)?" The findings have relevance for the leader of any organization seeking to be more responsive and competitive in a business climate that is increasingly bottom-line driven and associations are no exception to this paradigm. The most successful companies in the Kotter and Heskitt study had well-defined cultures where values like risk taking are encouraged and supported along with support for innovation and change. Most importantly, the leaders of these organizations focused heavily on meeting the needs of their external stakeholders as well as those of their staff and other human resources.

A Word about Diversity

As discussed above, fostering an environment where varying ideas, views, and contributions are valued is integral to a healthy and productive organizational culture. The association leader also must give particular attention to the principles of diversity in all aspects of the association's work, promoting a climate of inclusiveness that reflects understanding and respect for the differences among members of its community. This includes ensuring that all association services—communications, programs, and products—demonstrate sensitivity to race, ethnicity, gender, religion, age, sexual orientation, nationality, disability, appearance, geographic location, and professional level. Attention to diversity can take the form of an explicit policy statement articulating the association's commitment to all forms of diversity in every aspect of its work. Some organizations establish committees to oversee diversity efforts in volunteer and member activities such as the board nominations process, mentoring and scholarship initiatives, and association event planning (e.g. speaker selection, presentation guidelines, accommodation of dietary and religious requirements, etc.). Also important are the individual actions of members within the association community in honoring the espoused principles. Staff, volunteers, and members should be made aware of these expectations through orientation and training programs and held accountable for supporting adherence. However executed, association leaders must actively promote diversity through their personal actions and throughout all facets of the enterprises they lead.

The Relationships of Association Leadership

"In organizations, real power and energy is generated through relationships. The patterns of relationships and the capacities to form them are more important than tasks, functions, roles, and positions."
– Margaret Wheatly, *Leadership and the New Science*

According to Kouzes and Posner, success in leadership....business...and life...has been, is now, and will continue to be a function of how well people work and play together. Accomplished association leaders understand the intricacies of the interpersonal and group relationships they must manage and are masters of the methods for maximizing the potential from each. The following section outlines critical competencies for the association leader's interaction with key stakeholders such as the board and staff. It's important to note that the concepts detailed under each of the specific relationship categories that follow can be extrapolated and applied to the other categories. In other words, the effective management of interpersonal relationships and group facilitation is founded on a universal set of core principles. As you read the scenarios outlined below, challenge yourself to think how the doctrines might apply to other individuals or groups with whom association leaders must interact.

The Board

One of the most critical relationships for an association executive is the one he or she has with the board of directors. The efficacy of the governing body is integral to determining the success of the entire organization, and the CEO plays the primary role in effecting that outcome. According to author Doug Eadie in his book *High Impact Governing in a Nutshell—17 Questions that Board Members and CEOs Frequently Ask*, this is a high-stakes matter that deserves considerable time and attention from both parties. He cites the contributing factors to this equation as 1) members of this elite leadership team tend to be strong personalities with substantial egos and a propensity toward type-A behavior that can naturally cause a measurable level of friction and 2) the issues with which they must grapple are often complex and critical thereby creating a pressure-cooker environment that can stress and strain the CEO/board relationship. So what should association leaders do to nurture the most positive and productive relationship possible with the board? Said simply, help them be successful. Everyone wants to succeed and being the catalyst and enabler of that reality is a critical requirement of the association leader.

As discussed earlier, the first component is to ensure the existence of procedures for attracting and retaining the highest quality individuals to serve in the board role— those who can measurably further the strategic objectives of the organization. Also worth repeating is the importance to this equation of orientation, training, and achieving clarity on the roles and responsibilities between staff and volunteers. To quote a *Good to Great* axiom of leadership guru Jim Collins, these steps will "get the right people on the bus" and will help them to best organize resources in "figuring out the path to greatness."

There are several techniques for the ongoing development of the board/staff leader relationship. Foremost, the chief staff officer must establish his/herself as a partner and valued resource to the board for determining the items of strategic and operational importance on which it should spend its time and in helping the governing body be successful in its role as steward of the association. He/she must provide informed consultation to the board—impartially championing the best interests of the association by bringing to bear useful concepts, information, policies, and business strategies that will both protect and propel the association forward. Occasionally this can be an untenable role, especially when the CEO must take a position that is in part or in whole opposition to that of the board but in the best interests of the enterprise. While sometimes necessary, these moments are generally infrequent and navigable if the staff leader has successfully built the necessary trust and credibility by using the relationship management strategies discussed throughout this text.

In the process realm, the leader's purposeful design of meeting agendas is an essential strategy—albeit for planning retreats, regular board meetings, or conference calls— to guarantee fruitful discussion and decision making on appropriate matters. This includes selecting appropriate items for inclusion on the agenda, articulating intended outcomes, designing exercises or group process to yield desired inputs/outputs and providing appropriate background and information as required for decision making or discussion. Creating ground rules for behavior, group interaction, and decision making is also a useful tactic for optimizing outcomes and managing group dynamics (e.g., respect other's ideas/opinions, no question is stupid, refer tangential items to a parking lot for follow-up). It can also minimize the sometimes derailing attitudes that group members will adopt such as dominating, controlling, or seeking personal gain and recognition. Engaging participants in an evaluation of their work and interaction is another key process. This opens the door to needed improvements, gets buy-in for the required change, and provides the association leader with the opportunity to coach and mentor board members on best practices in governance and association management.

Personally, association leaders need to model sound individual and group facilitation skills. Demonstrating the willingness to listen, be influenced by other opinions, and to concede positions or decisions to the greater good are all examples. Fostering a sense of mutual dependence and camaraderie among the participants, each of whom believes he or she needs the others to succeed, is another method. Not surprisingly, using judgment and discretion and knowing when to exercise the facilitator's executive prerogative with regard to sustaining productivity are also on the competency list. Collectively these tactics enable contributions and viewpoints to be heard from all participants and help achieve agreement and/or mitigate deconstructive conflict. Effective group leadership also involves the ability to comprehend, interpret, and translate concepts that have emerged from the group and to reframe them to achieve clarity, shared understanding, consensus, or movement of the discussion to the next level. Heeding one's inner voice or tapping the power of intuition is another implicit but important facilitation aptitude. This involves monitoring the unconscious and often unspoken dynamics that transpire in a group setting and directing the process based on what is happening in the moment. Examples of this might be sensing when it is time for greater or lesser debate, taking a total timeout, or pursuing a change of direction that might lead to breakthrough thinking and new heights of group functionality.

"Before you are a leader, success is all about growing yourself. When you become a leader, success is all about growing others."
– Jack Welch

The Staff

Goethe said "treat people as if they were what they ought to be, and you will help them to become what they are capable of being." This is an apt edict for association leaders with regard to their role in developing the potential of their organization's human resources—albeit staff, volunteers, or members. Of particular importance is the cultivation of staff competency in carrying out the work of the association. As noted earlier, staff often provide the most consistent level of leadership to a nonprofit organization due to the transitory nature of volunteer and member roles. Therefore, maximizing the potential of employees of any kind— full-time, part-time, or contract— is essential and encompasses supporting both their professional and personal development through mentoring, career counseling and advancement, and leadership growth.

The importance of leaders in articulating and modeling desired behavior was detailed earlier in this text as was the need for them to create a corporate culture conducive to the achievement of organizational objectives and aligned with the organization's core values. Equally as important is the existence of an environment where staff can operate effectively and achieve personal and professional fulfillment. Attributes of such an atmosphere include a sense of achievement among employees, recognition for their contributions, the nature of the work itself, possessing responsibility and authority, and opportunities for advancement and growth. Leaders should spend time actively mentoring and coaching staff, rewarding and remediating their skills based on their unique competencies and areas of needed improvement.

Addressing individual and group needs for professional development is also important. This might involve supporting membership, volunteer activities, and/or participation in learning opportunities sponsored by association management or other specialty associations germane to their field of work (e.g., meeting management, information technology, human resource administration). Training designed to address the specific needs of the enterprise team should also be provided. This might be team building work to improve group cohesion, immersion education on the profession or industry the association serves, or general training on areas like effective meeting design and facilitation techniques. In short, staff must be equipped with the tools to help them be successful in their current roles and to expand their abilities and contributions in preparation for future roles. This provides the opportunity for them to grow as individuals, thereby delivering additional value to the association. Another aspect of staff development is providing professional advancement opportunities. Leaders should be vigilant in their attentions to the ever changing needs of the organization, the required resources to meet those needs, and the structures and resources that will accomplish these requirements. In this vein, aligning staff development opportunities with organizational needs and growth is a win-win proposition for everyone.

CEO Confidential
Increasing Your Chances of Being Remarkable

The following list describes practices that distinguish remarkable associations, and accordingly their leaders, from their counterparts.

- **Keep your eyes and your mind open.** Products and services should emanate from two sources—your mission and members' documented needs.

- **Develop and foster a strong customer service culture.** Keeping members front and center is everyone's job.

- **Keep your balance.** Remain firm about the *what*—your mission—and flexible about the *how*—your products and services.

- **Clean your plate.** As you add new programs and services, eliminate those that no longer serve a need. Have only one sacred cow—your mission.

- **Seek to influence, not control.** The CEO's job is to facilitate visionary thinking and be a broker of ideas, not to force others to adopt his or her vision.

- **Remain humble.** You don't know it all. The best source of what members need is the members themselves. Seek out their views often and in a variety of ways.

- **Be a good neighbor.** Seek out and foster relationships with organizations that may not share your overall mission but do share your desire to accomplish certain goals. Don't make friends for the sake of appearances or profits—do it for the sake of your mission.

Excerpted from *7 Measures of Success: What Successful Associations Do That Others Don't,*
ASAE & The Center, 2006

The staff's work environment is significant in determining their productivity and personal and professional achievement. Beyond training, coaching, and development are cultural elements such as work/life balance and taking time to celebrate and reward accomplishments. Certainly there are systems and processes that support these outcomes such as incentive-based compensation (i.e., commissions or bonuses), flextime, and telecommuting policies. The leader's contribution goes beyond these components to include modeling the behaviors and values that reinforce a healthy work setting. He/she fosters an atmosphere where excellence, innovation, and calculated risk-taking are valued and rewarded, thereby inspiring others to their personal best. They demonstrate support for a balance between the needs of the organization and the needs of the individuals therein and assure that in the end equation, both benefit equitably. Humility, giving credit to others and awareness of their personal strengths and weaknesses, and the courage to surround themselves with others of equal and complementary talent are the traits of accomplished leaders, and most likely accomplished organizations.

To Be or To Be Created

So what of the millennia-old debate about whether leaders are born or made? Perhaps in the final analysis, it is a distinction without a difference. Even if an individual is imbued—seemingly from birth—with exceptional leadership instincts and skills, those competencies can still be enhanced, expanded, and perfected. For those less propitiously preordained but of whom leadership is their decided lot, the attributes, successful methodologies, and characteristics of great leaders can be learned and adopted as their own. So, whether inherent or learned, good leadership—like good taste—can be continuously improved.

References and Recommended Reading

7 Measures of Success—What Remarkable Associations Do that Others Don't, ASAE & The Center for Association Leadership, Washington, D.C., 2006.

Champoux, Tom and Maynard, Bill, *Heart, Soul and Spirit: Bold Strategies for Transforming Your Organization*, The Effectiveness Institute, Redmond, Washington, 1996.

Collins, Jim, *Good to Great: Why Some Companies Make the Leap... and Others Don't*, HarperBusiness, New York, 2001.

Good to Great and the Social Sectors: A Monograph to Accompany Good to Great, HarperCollins, New York, 2005.

De Pree, Max, *Leading Without Power: Finding Hope In Serving Community*, Jossey-Bass, New York, 1997.

Dym, Barry Michael and Hutson, Harry, *Leadership in Nonprofit Organizations: Lessons From the Third Sector*, Sage Publications, Inc., Thousand Oaks, California, 2005.

Eadie, Douglas, *The Extraordinary CEO*, American Society of Association Executives, Washington, D.C., 1999.

High Impact Governing in a Nutshell—17 Questions that Board Members and CEOs Frequently Ask, American Society of Association Executives, Washington, D.C., 2004.

Goleman, Daniel, *Emotional Intelligence: 10th Anniversary Edition—Why It Can Matter More Than IQ*, Bantam, New York, 2006.

Hesselbein, Frances, *Hesselbein on Leadership*, Jossey-Bass, New York, 2002.

Hrebiniak, Lawrence G., *Making Strategy Work: Leading Effective Execution and Change*, Pearson Education, Inc., Upper Saddle River, New Jersey, 2005.

Marquardt, Michael J., *Leading with Questions: How Leaders Find the Right Solutions By Knowing What To Ask*, John Wiley & Sons, New York, 2005.

Napier, Rod and Sanaghan, Patrick, *Intentional Design and the Process of Change*, National Association of College and University Business Officers, Washington, D.C., 2002.

Posner, Barry and Kouzes, James, *The Leadership Challenge*, 3d ed., John Wiley & Sons, Inc., New York, 2002.

Roberto, Michael A., *Why Great Leaders Don't Take Yes for an Answer: Managing for Conflict and Consensus*, Pearson Education, Inc., Upper Saddle River, New Jersey, 2005.

Welter, Bill and Egmon, Jean, *The Prepared Mind of a Leader—Eight Skills Leaders Use to Innovate, Make Decisions, and Solve Problems*, Jossey-Bass, New York, 2006.

Wheatley, Margaret J., *Leadership and the New Science: Discovering Order in a Chaotic World*, 2nd edition, Berrett-Koehler Publishers, San Francisco, 1999.

About the Author

Carla Balakgie, CAE, is executive director of the Electronic Transactions Association, Washington, D.C., a position she has held since 2003. Prior to assuming leadership of ETA, she served as senior vice president and COO of the National Association of College and University Business Officers, where she also held numerous management and executive roles during the course of fifteen years. Carla began her career in association management in the publishing division of the American Society of Association Executives. Her 23 years in the association management profession have included numerous volunteer leadership positions. Most recently, she was selected to serve on the ASAE Board. She is also a current member of the Journal for Association Leadership Editorial Board. In 2000, Carla was named as an ASAE Fellow.

Review Questions

1. Of all the concepts discussed in this chapter, what do you consider to be the most important aspect of leadership? Why?

2. Regarding the born-or-made debate on leadership: What attributes lend themselves to the "born" side of the equation and which to the "made?"

3. Can all aspects of leadership be learned? Why or why not?

4. What are the personal responsibilities of the leader in facilitating the concepts outlined in this chapter? How do traits such as self-awareness, self-actualization, and behavior factor into the equation?

5. How should leaders cultivate other leaders, and how can you apply these practices in your association?

Negotiating More Effectively

Jack W. Kaine

NY TIME TWO OR more people are exchanging information with the intent of changing the relationship, they are negotiating. Some people are natural negotiators; those who aren't can still master the skill of negotiating. It begins with an understanding of the three requirements of a successful negotiation:

1. **The terms can be varied.** If the terms are all-or-nothing, take-it-or-leave-it, then it is not negotiating. It is selling. And any association chief executive officer (CEO) who is perceived as trying to sell the board on anything is headed for trouble.

2. **It centers on a scarce resource**—or what is perceived as scarce, such as money, time, talent, or information. In the association environment, where there never seems to be enough money, budgets and salaries must be negotiated. Too, because time always is in short supply, the CEO constantly negotiates priorities.

3. **Each party must have something to gain.** People often think of negotiation as a competition. When they feel as if they are competing with one another, people do not share any information—or if they do, the information is intended to mislead the other party. Another common problem is that some negotiators take too narrow a view of the negotiations: People see the negotiation as something that is done to simply reach agreement on an issue.

Negotiating is actually a process of getting and keeping agreements. A successful negotiation produces not just an agreement but one that will work for all parties. Getting an agreement is the easy part—keeping it is harder. An agreement that works only for one side ultimately works for neither side. If one side perceives itself as the loser, that person or group has no desire to keep the agreement and the negotiation fails. It then becomes the source of further conflict and negotiation.

A successful negotiation is win-win, which should never be confused with "equal win." The term win-win means mutual gain; very seldom can each party win equally. Following a principled approach to negotiations, however, ensures that all parties come out of the negotiation ahead.

Five Traits of Effective Negotiators

These are the five traits necessary to negotiate successfully:

- **Be a good planner.** Good negotiators do their homework, preparing a wide-ranging list of alternatives. The more alternatives that are available, the better the chance of finding a position that all parties find favorable. Preparation also builds confidence, which is an important element for establishing power in negotiations. In the association environment, the strategic planning process offers an excellent example of good planning—and of negotiation.

- **Have high expectations.** Executives, who expect more, get more. Entering a negotiation with high goals and a positive attitude greatly influences the final result. Negative attitudes and grudges can be easily revealed during the negotiation process, so it's important to set a positive tone from the start.

- **Have a high energy level.** It takes a great deal of energy and concentration to negotiate effectively. The tension involved in reaching a position can quickly drain one's levels of energy and alertness. As a result, always enter a negotiation rested and, conversely, never commit to a course of action when fatigued.

- **Be a good listener.** Negotiation involves the exchange of information to change a relationship. Information is power, and the most important way to gain information is to listen. Negotiators who listen to the other side's desires have a better understanding of what it will take to make a deal; they understand what will satisfy the other party's needs.

- **Be persistent.** Persistence—the ability to retain resilience after rejections and setbacks—is to negotiating as carbon is to steel: It's essential to building a solid agreement. Executives who are not satisfied with an impasse and continue to negotiate are able to move the discussion toward a positive outcome for everyone.

11 Golden Rules

These rules apply to every negotiation:

Rule 1: Begin from a position of trust. When people are angry or do not trust one another, they communicate poorly and don't share their information. Or, if information is shared, it will be designed to deceive or mislead the other party.

Principles of Negotiation

- **The person who speaks first sets the tone for the negotiation.** Don't worry about getting in the last word; work hard to get in the first word, and make it positive. The opening remarks represent the one part of a negotiation that must be scripted and rehearsed to the point of seeming spontaneous. Why? As Will Rogers, the American humorist, said, "You never get a second chance to make a first impression."

- **The person who asks the most questions determines the content and direction of the negotiation.** Questions provide information as well as a safeguard: It's impossible to say something wrong when listening. If you ask a question, however, you must listen to the answer. And note that there's a difference between questioning and interrogating; the former helps you understand the other party's real interest, while the latter makes the other party defensive and suspicious.

- **People do things for their reasons, not yours.** Most people prepare for the negotiation from their point of view. However, all good negotiators must be able to state the other party's case—and answer it as well. Leverage is important, and it cannot be gained without viewing the negotiation from all points of view.

It is a lot easier to get a negotiation off on a positive note than to overcome a bad start.

Rule 2: Avoid escalating a conflict. Conflict is inevitable. It can be positive, negative, or irrelevant; what makes the difference is how the conflict is handled. Like steam, conflict can be used to generate energy or cause an explosion.

Negotiations often become heated when the parties have a desire to win at any cost. This common mistake is fueled by biased perceptions and judgments, as well as egos, pride, and emotion. But when people get angry or do not trust one another, negotiations become stalled.

Many people view negotiations as a competitive endeavor where one party wins and the other party loses. As soon as a negotiation becomes competitive, the negotiator should stop it and reframe the discussion in a positive light. This can be done, for example, by saying, "How do you feel about this discussion we're having right now?" If the other party is being honest, he or she will probably reply, "I'm very uncomfortable." This opens the door to an agreement, if the first party acknowledges, "I am very uncomfortable as well."

In this way, agreement can grow out of argument. This situation would also give you an opportunity to take the lead in the negotiation by then saying, "I would like to suggest that we refocus our thinking on all the areas we agree on, and then let's build from there to see if we both cannot get more of what we need."

If repeated attempts to reframe the negotiation do not work, a cooling-off period in the form of a break may be necessary. A good rule of thumb is to break off negotiations for at least 12 hours; after that amount of time, it will be much easier to focus on the facts and not on the emotions. The cooling-off period, however, should not exceed 48 hours; conflict does not age gracefully.

Rule 3: Know when to walk away. Some people start a negotiation by seeing how far they can push the other party. If these bullies get away with their behavior, they will continue it. In other words, difficult people may never change because they have been rewarded for being difficult. They may have to change, however, if you resist the pressure to make a bad deal—generally by walking away.

To be able to do this, you must assess—*before* the negotiation begins—what you will do if you don't reach agreement. This is known as your walk-away position. Any agreement that is of higher value than your walk-away position is better than an impasse.

You also must be able to assess what the other party will do if an agreement is not reached. The party with the best walk-away position has a decided advantage in the negotiation.

Rule 4: Be a careful communicator. Expert negotiators are clear, concise communicators. One technique they use is "labeling" their communications.

Labeling signals a change of direction, much like using turn signals when driving a car. This makes it easier for the other party to follow and understand the conversation.

For example, before making a point, the expert negotiator says, "I would like to make a point." He or she also says, "May I ask a question?"—and then asks the question. Likewise, if the person has a concern, he or she will preface it by saying, "I have a concern." This technique not only clarifies the discussion but also creates receptivity. If you say, "may I ask a question?" the other person sounds rude if he or she says no. By asking for permission, you create a more receptive environment.

Good negotiators, however, do not label their disagreements. They do not say, "I disagree with you because...." When stated in that form, the disagreement comes first

---

Saving Face

One night, the CEO of a large trade association received a telephone call from a member who said, "Now before you say no, let me tell you about a great idea I have for a television commercial that the association should produce." He went on to describe a scene that was guaranteed to generate lots of awareness for the association—all bad, from the CEO's perspective.

Rather than argue with the member by telling him how wrong the idea was, the CEO asked questions: How long would it take to build a set for shooting the commercial? Where would it be built? How much would it cost? After some discussion, the real problem surfaced: The member had gotten tired of the association's commercials. The CEO proposed some research to determine whether the commercials were effective in gaining more business for the association's members. The results showed they were, so the commercials continued to be televised.

This is but one example of the "4-F" approach that you can employ when you disagree with someone yet don't want them to dislike you for it. The four Fs represent Feel, Felt, Found, and Facts. After listening to the other person's comments, you might say, "I can appreciate why you would feel that way. I felt that way myself, until I found out the following...." At this point, share the facts that prompted you to change your mind. In essence, you're saying, "I felt just like you until I learned the real facts. When I got them I changed my mind, and you will want to change yours as well." The 4-F method of disagreeing allows someone to change their mind without losing face.

and the reasons for it second. What is being said is, "Here I come. Get ready to disagree with me in return." The other person then starts listening for points to argue about. Instead, ask questions about the points of disagreement. These questions will weaken the other person's position by pinpointing flaws. Then you can make your proposal.

Another effective way to handle disagreement is to say, "I have this point I would like to discuss with you. It is..., and as a result, I disagree." In this case, reason comes first, then disagreement.

Rule 5: Lead by questioning. The way to control a negotiation, board meeting, or conversation is not by talking but by questioning: The person who asks the most questions controls the content and direction of the discussion. Questioning also produces information and gives you time to think—while depriving the other person of thinking time.

At times you may be called upon to negotiate without adequate preparation time. One technique that will gain you some time is to ask questions you already know the answers to. This also enables you to assess the honesty of the person answering: Proceed cautiously if the answers are not correct. In addition, asking questions may make it appear as if you are not well-informed—and people may tell you a lot if they believe they know more than you do.

In preparation for a negotiation, list all the questions that could be asked. Decide who will answer each question on the list, as well as the unanticipated questions that arise during the negotiation. This responsibility may fall to the CEO or chief elected officer, depending on who directs the negotiating team.

Next, develop an answer for each question. That helps control your response; the more you talk during a negotiation, the more likely you are to overexplain and thus weaken your position. Developing answers is best done as a group and with a tape recorder. The person to whom the question has been assigned answers it on the tape, which is then played back so the group can critique the response. The question is repeated and the group again critiques the revised response. This process continues until everyone is satisfied with the answer.

In this way, the person who is responsible for that question has a tape-recorded version of the perfected answer. He or she can review the answer repeatedly in preparation for the negotiation.

Rule 6: Avoid making counterproposals. Most negotiators put their proposals on the table too soon, in opposition to the other party's proposal. For example, an association may start with a low salary figure and the CEO with a high one.

When the other negotiator has advanced a proposal or taken an opposite position, he or she is in the least receptive frame of mind to hear your proposal. Rather than offer a counterproposal, ask questions about what was presented: How would this work? What does this mean? What would happen if...? After clearly identifying the proposal's shortcomings, make suggestions to resolve the problems that have become evident. Advance proposals not in opposition to the other side's proposal but as solutions to problems identified in the discussion.

This technique helps establish an atmosphere of trust and cooperation. Good negotiators do not think of themselves as negotiators but rather as problem solvers.

Rule 7: Focus on your strongest positions. Most people are taught that the more reasons they can find to support a position, the stronger it becomes. When most people negotiate, however, they advance too many reasons: Every argument put forth that isn't as persuasive as the strongest argument simply weakens their position.

Develop as many reasons as possible to support your position. However, use only the strongest ones during the negotiation. Here's the typical scenario: After the other party in a negotiation offers a reason to support his or her position, ask, somewhat skeptically, "Is that your only reason?" The other party then will offer half a dozen more supporting reasons. As soon as you hear one reason that sounds weak, say, "Now, just a minute, let's examine the last thing you said." At this point, the power in the negotiation switches, all because of the weak point that was advanced.

Rule 8: Settle on an agreement that is workable. An agreement that will not stand up to close examination will not last. Instead, it will become the source of further conflict and negotiation.

To ensure an agreement is workable, frequently summarize the negotiations proceedings to make sure all the parties involved understand it. Otherwise, the parties may both think they have an agreement, only to find out that their understanding of what had been agreed to was different. Testing understanding and summarizing can help avoid problems in the future.

In addition, skilled negotiators know it is not in their best interests to slip anything past the other party. In fact, if you believe that the other party has agreed to something not in its best interest, mention it. This not only helps build trust but also puts the obligation on the other party to make a concession in return to move the negotiation forward.

For instance, after the board or staff has agreed to something, ask, "Now if we are going to have a problem with this agreement, what do you think it will be?" At the moment of agreement, the trust level will be high because all parties want the agreement to work. It is at this point that people will bring out their hidden agendas. When a concern surfaces, agree that the point is valid and ask what other concerns the person may have. Also express any concerns you may have and then pose this question: "If this does occur (taking the concerns one at a time) how will we handle it?"

What makes this rule so powerful is that any solution worked out before a problem occurs will be fairer to the parties concerned. "Pre-negotiating" solutions allows you to be hard on problems yet soft on people.

Rule 9: Develop a power position. Power is a function of having options and being willing to take risks. Options give you the ability to make choices; risk is variously described as mental toughness, backbone, or fortitude.

In general, negotiators do not realize their full power when they:

- Focus on their limitations. What you think about in a negotiation is what you realize.
- Feel powerless. Power is very illusive: If you think you are powerful, you are.
- Are unwilling to take a risk. The party willing to take the greatest informed risk in a negotiation always has a decided advantage.
- Are intimidated by the power of the other party. To generate power, you must understand the limits of the other negotiator's power.

It's best to prepare for a negotiation as a group, because groups tend to take greater and more informed risks than individuals. In addition, a group can generate and anticipate more options and alternatives. The Japanese have an expression that's good to keep in mind for negotiations: "None of us is as smart as all of us."

Rule 10: Time is power. Every negotiation has a deadline that is either stated or implied. Deadlines pressure people to make decisions; without deadlines, very little movement would occur in a negotiation.

Although important, time is one of the least understood elements in a negotiation. The party with the longest deadline in a negotiation always has a decided advantage because time buys more options.

Before a negotiation begins, ask yourself these three time-related questions:

- What self-imposed or association deadlines am I under that will make it hard for me to negotiate?
- Are these deadlines real, or can I negotiate an extension with my own team? Most of the pressure a negotiator feels is generated internally.
- What deadlines make it difficult for the other party to negotiate? You cannot generate leverage in a negotiation until you can look at it from the other party's point of view.

Rule 11: Create a positive climate. Climate can best be described as what you do that makes people want to negotiate with you. It includes where you meet, when you meet, how you dress, who you bring, and any number of other factors. Good negotiators create a positive climate that is conducive to information exchange.

Where you meet depends on where you are in the negotiation. During the information collection stage, it is better to meet at the other party's place of business and to take as many people as possible with you. Members of the group should attempt to meet independently with the other party—people will share information when given a chance, especially if their boss is not present. If you're in the final stage of a negotiation, however, meet in your office. This gives you control: The door can be shut, the phones turned off, refreshments brought in at your request, and the room set up to your liking.

Power is an important element in negotiation, and it starts with dress. It is better to be overdressed than underdressed; you can take off a coat and tie, but it is hard to put one on at the last minute. A good rule is to dress like the other party, but marginally better.

Never negotiate without an agenda, which is the guiding force behind the information exchange. It keeps you organized and the negotiation on track. It does not have to be a formalized agenda—a checklist works fine—nor does it have to be shared with the other party.

If a formalized agenda is used, ask the other party to provide a list of the items they would like to discuss. At the same time, make your own list, then draft the agenda in the order you wish to maintain control. What appears on the agenda is as important as what isn't on it. Remember that one way to make issues nonnegotiable is to never allow them to reach the agenda.

Common Mistakes

Several pitfalls can doom negotiations and result in an undesirable agreement. The most common mistakes are:

1. **Believing that one person wins and the other loses.** This is called distributive negotiation and typically involves a single issue or a "fixed pie." Yet it's a misconception that only one party can win at the expense or loss of another. Very seldom is negotiating a zero-sum game.

   Rather than divide the "pie," focus on enlarging it. There always are things that you can do for the other party that will have a high value to them and a low cost to you. Likewise, the other party can do things that will cost them very little but mean a lot to you.

2. **Ego.** More negotiations are destroyed by ego than any other single factor. Ego comes into play when one of the parties starts acting emotionally—angry, hurt, insecure, or frightened—and not rationally. If you feel that either you or the other party has allowed emotions to take control of the negotiation, call for a break or cooling-off period.

3. **Being inflexible.** The negotiator who holds to an initial position or belief and fails to adjust as the negotiation proceeds doesn't achieve the best agreement. This type of negotiation often results in an all-or-nothing settlement where neither party is satisfied.

   The secret of a good negotiator is flexibility. There always is a better deal for all parties involved in a negotiation than is apparent at first.

4. **A negative approach.** The way a negotiation is framed can affect each party's willingness to reach an agreement. Presenting negotiations in a favorable light for the other party will build trust and understanding and help to achieve a sound agreement.

5. **Dissecting information.** Know the amount and the reliability of the information that is available. Learning to distinguish information that is relevant will improve the quality and success of the negotiation.

6. **Having a narrow point of view.** Negotiators who take the other party's perspective into account are more likely to reach a successful agreement.

7. **Making assumptions.** You must make assumptions to negotiate. Those assumptions, however, do not always hold up to reality. In preparing for a negotiation, list all your assumptions, as well as those you believe the other party will make. Test these assumptions for validity, and change any that don't ring true.

8. **Overconfidence.** Many biases can combine to inflate a negotiator's confidence and judgment. Assumptions, prejudices, and egos can impede the process. Minimize overconfidence by effective information gathering and never taking anything for granted. Most people believe they have more control over the outcomes of negotiation than they really do.

9. **Negotiating with yourself.** Most negotiators are harder on themselves than on the party across the table. If, in preparation for a negotiation, you write down your starting position but think, "They'll never buy that," you'll probably lower your position. That's negotiating with yourself.

   When you do this, you give away your "bottom line." The other side always will ask for concessions, some of which will have no value to you. When you give concessions before the other side asks for them, you deprive yourself of room to negotiate. An impasse often occurs as a result.

10. **Poor concession making.** Good negotiators know how to make concessions. Too quick a concession is viewed as a sign of weakness by a competitive win-lose negotiator. In addition, it will not bring you closer to agreement but will elevate the competitive negotiator's goals.

    Never give a concession the minute you realize that you can give it. When you do concede a point, always explain what new information led you to change your position. The stock and trade of a good negotiator is credibility, which will diminish quickly if you make concessions without explaining why.

Practice Makes Perfect

Sound negotiation skills can be learned and refined, most often through everyday business conduct. Practice these fundamentals to become a better negotiator and a more effective representative of your association:

- **Use direct, clear communications.** Good negotiators are easy to follow and are clear in their discussions.

- **Ask a lot of questions.** Use questions to gain information, establish the credibility of the other party, reframe an issue, and gain thinking time at the expense of the other party.

- **Test and summarize understanding.** All sides in a negotiation must understand what has been agreed to and be satisfied with the agreement. A successful agreement will stand the test of time.

• **Anticipate and plan how to handle problems before they arise.** Thinking ahead and addressing potential situations early during the negotiations creates a more solid agreement.

Redefining the Issue

It's often possible to remove an issue from a negotiation by asking a good question. For example, one association called a consultant when it became clear that board members were divided over whether to relocate the organization's headquarters. Upon hearing the consultant's fee, however, the association's executive director expressed concern about the cost.

In response, the consultant asked, "What will happen to you and your association if you do nothing?" The CEO responded, "We'd lose the entire West Coast membership. They are talking about starting another association if we do not make a move." The consultant replied that he couldn't leave the executive director and the association in a worse position than that. The consultant made price a nonissue by asking a question—and the association hired him.

By getting people to confront their most dreaded fear, you may convince them to accept a change you want. In 1988, for instance, Jim Baker was negotiating the formalities for the presidential television debates on behalf of George Bush. The staff of Michael Dukakis wanted their candidate to stand on a box behind the podium so he'd appear taller and more presidential. Baker simply asked if they planned to take a box along for Dukakis to stand on when he negotiated with Gorbachev. His question made the box a nonissue and quickly took it off the agenda for the debate.

About the Author

Jack W. Kaine is a consultant who specializes in teaching negotiating skills to the leaders of associations and corporations worldwide. Prior to forming his consulting firm, he was vice president and principal human relations consultant for Lawrence-Letter and Company, a management and association consulting firm.

Review Questions

1. What are the requirements of a successful negotiation?

2. When negotiating, is it preferable to have the first word or the last word? Why?

3. How should you handle a situation when emotions have taken control of the negotiations?

Ethical Practices for Associations and the Professionals They Serve

Scott R. Sturzl

AN IMPORTANT DEFINING CHARACTERISTIC of any profession is its set of ethical standards. Professional associations are in a key position to influence ethical behavior by establishing such standards whether they are called codes of ethics, conduct, professionalism, professional responsibility, standards of conduct, or by some other name.

A day rarely goes by without some significant report in the media exposing a lapse in ethical behavior. Perhaps more importantly, the media sometimes mentions worthy and positive ethical behavior. Recently several Coca-Cola employees attempted to sell a secret formula for a new product to Pepsi. Pepsi immediately contacted Coca-Cola and the Federal Bureau of Investigation to ensure a quick resolution of this matter rather than gaining unfair advantage over its archrival. In an example of cooperation, it was reported that major United States and European defense contractors will jointly develop the first set of voluntary ethical standards to apply to contracts on both sides of the Atlantic.

We're reminded in *Codes of Professional Responsibility* (Gorlin, 1999) that all ethical events affect people; daily interactions and decisions together determine the ethical impact on society as a whole. Ethics builds from person to group or team, to department, division, or organization. The common denominator always begins at the level of personal behavior and decision-making.

What is common in the relationship between doctor and patient, student and teacher, buyer and supplier, sales associate and customer, association executive and board member, government employee and citizen? Each, in turn, involves a relationship built on trust, honesty, and integrity. It is likely the professional or trade associations supporting such relationships and roles have developed and published ethical standards.

Often ethical standards become the foundation of a code for constituents and impact the environment in which professionals work. Professionals subscribe to the code, which guides both individual and group decisions and actions. A code can reach across professions, geography, organizations, and culture, and may even reach across country boundaries.

The Reach of a Code

Webster's New Collegiate Dictionary describes "ethic" as "a theory or system of moral values, the principles of conduct governing an individual or group." The scope of a code may be broad or narrow. Some codes are written for a subset of a profession (e.g., a medical subspecialty) while others have broad application across a profession (e.g., accounting). Geographically, a code may cover a small jurisdiction, a county or a state; yet others will be national or multinational.

The association community is in the position to positively influence the development, implementation, communication, and practice of a code of conduct for its constituents and the profession within which they work. In a number of cases, the association also elects to build required mechanisms to act as a code enforcer.

A Code's Integration with the Association's Mission and Objectives

Individual professionals and the organizations for which they work often look to the association community for guidance and leadership. An association can be a proactive and important influencer of ethical practices. However, such a commitment by an association must be squarely embedded in its mission and objectives and have the support of senior management and its board of directors. The following list and question set are designed to help an association considering the development a set of ethical standards ensure that its mission is being served. Associations that already have a published code can use the material for review purposes.

Possible goals for the development, publication, and ongoing support of an association's code might include the desire to:

- Lead the profession;
- Raise the profile of the profession;
- Add value for individual or organizational members;
- Become the recognized central repository of information, references, and best practice on the topic of ethics for the profession;
- Take a stance on matters important to the profession;
- Influence society;
- Support research on ethical practices;
- Shape and guide the behavior of professionals; and
- Provide a foundation of ethical practice from which employers can develop a unique code for their employees and those with whom they do business.

Social Responsibility

All professionals today deal with an environment that is complex and demanding. The concept of social responsibility is an example of how the world is changing and becoming more complex. While there is debate about the areas that fall under the umbrella of social responsibility, the Institute for Supply Management's program covers seven areas, one of which is the subject of ethics.

Commitment to socially responsible behavior is good business—in both the public and private sectors. Often payback can be quantified in financial terms. Socially responsible behavior may even ensure that an enterprise will avoid difficult or embarrassing scrutiny. However, soft payback in dignity, success, self-worth, and honor provides the real foundation and rationale for socially responsible behavior.

Social responsibility is defined as "a framework of measurable corporate policies and procedures and resulting behavior designed to benefit the workplace and, by extension, the individual, the organization and the community." For the Institute for Supply Management™, social responsibility covers seven specific areas.

I. Community
1. Provide support and add value to your communities and those of your supply chain.
2. Encourage members of your supply chain to add value in their communities.

II. Diversity
1. Proactively promote purchasing from, and the development of, socially diverse suppliers.
2. Encourage diversity within your own organization.
3. Proactively promote diverse employment practices throughout the supply chain.

III. Environment
1. Encourage your own organization and others to be proactive in examining opportunities to be environmentally responsible within their supply chains either "upstream" or "downstream."
2. Encourage the environmental responsibility of your suppliers.
3. Encourage the development and diffusion of environmentally friendly practices and products throughout your organization.

IV. Ethics
1. Be aware of *ISM's Principles and Standards of Ethical Supply Management Conduct.*
2. Abide by your organization's code of conduct.

V. Financial Responsibility
1. Become knowledgeable of, and follow, applicable financial standards and requirements.
2. Apply sound financial practices and ensure transparency in financial dealings.
3. Actively promote and practice responsible financial behavior throughout the supply chain.

VI. Human Rights
1. Treat people with dignity and respect.
2. Support and respect the protection of international human rights within the organization's sphere of influence.
3. Encourage your organization and its supply chains to avoid complicity in human or employment rights abuses.

VII. Safety
1. Promote a safe environment for each employee in your organization and supply chain. (Each organization is responsible for defining "safe" within its organization.)
2. Support the continuous development and diffusion of safety practices throughout your organization and the supply chain.

Source: Institute for Supply Management™ Web site (www.ism.ws/sr/Principles.cfm)

Several questions will help guide the association in developing a code:

1. What is the charter or mission of the association?
2. Has the mission or charter shifted over time? If so, how?
3. What guidance can the board of directors provide about the role of the association in setting ethical standards?
4. Will the concept of social responsibility be addressed at the same time as the ethical standards or later? (See sidebar "Social Responsibility.")
5. What are/were the goals and objectives for initially establishing a set of ethical standards? Are the goals and objectives still current for today's environment and today's professional?
6. What role will the standards have in the association's business? To what degree will the board of directors need to be involved?
7. What resources will be required for the development and ongoing support of a code?
8. Will the association take a stance on matters of ethics? If so, how will it be communicated to members? To professionals in the field? To the public at large?
9. What are the possible consequences and impact of establishing a set of standards? Of taking a stance on a particular topic or issue?
10. Will the code be treated as a model only? Will it be voluntary? Will it be mandatory?
11. Will the code be enforced? If so, how?
12. How might a code be benchmarked with others?
13. How will the association obtain input from its members and learn what members want or need?
14. Will members be required to agree to "live by the code" as a condition of membership? As a condition to hold a license or certification?
15. Should a committee be established to oversee the issue of ethics?

Management and "Ownership" of the Code

Management and ownership of the code plays an important part in how well the code is maintained, how credible it will be, and the degree to which the code is embedded in content throughout the profession's training as well as its licensure or certification programs.

1. Who will be responsible to ensure the code is included in course content, conferences, and leadership programs?
2. Where does the code belong in licensure or certification programs?
3. Who will have the authority for development and upkeep of the code?
4. How will access to the code be made available?

Frequently the association will appoint a committee to manage responsibilities from code development through code enforcement, if any. (See sidebar "Ingredients of a Code of Ethics.") Typically the committee will also be responsible for updating the code on a prearranged schedule (e.g., every three years).

Ingredients of a Code of Ethics

As the association works to establish a set of ethical standards, it will be necessary to determine the ingredients or standards to be covered in the code. Each column in the following chart lists categories at a high-level for five different associations and professions. A quick review and comparison shows some commonality of standards.

Association (1)	Marketing (2)	Supply Management (3)	Journalism (4)	Mental Health (5)
Personal Conduct	Honesty and Clarity of Offer	Perceived Impropriety	Seek the Truth and Report It	Provide Competent Service
Promote Ethics	Marketing to Children	Responsibilities to Employer	Minimize Harm	Deal Honestly with Patients and Colleagues
Maintain Loyalty	Special Offer and Claims	Conflict of Interest	Act Independently: - Avoid conflicts of interest - Disclose conflicts - Deny favored treatment	Respect the Law
Uphold Laws	Sweepstakes	Issues of Influence	Be Accountable	Respect the Rights of Patients, Colleagues, and Other Health Professionals
Strive for Excellence	Fulfillment	Confidential and Proprietary Information		Continue to Study, Apply, and Advance Scientific Knowledge
Use Only Legal and Ethical Means	Collection, Use, and Maintenance of Marketing Data	Supplier Relationships		Be Free to Choose Whom to Service
Serve All Members	Telephone Marketing	Reciprocity		
Maintain Confidentiality	Fund Raising	Applicable Laws		
Refuse Personal Gain	Laws, Codes, and Regulations	Socially Diverse Practices		
Do Not Discriminate		National and International Conduct		
Communicate Truthfully		Professional Conduct		
Cooperate to Advance the Profession		Responsibilities to the Profession		
Improve Public Understanding of Associations				

(1) ASAE & The Center
(2) Direct Marketing Association
(3) Institute for Supply Management™

(4) Society of Professional Journalists
(5) American Psychiatric Association

The Committee and Its Responsibilities

Practicing professionals add value to the committee by ensuring code relevance. Consequently, volunteers are often asked to serve on a committee and are appointed through the association's volunteer process. Professionals also have an in-depth knowledge of the field and bring weight to any published standards or code. Association staff have a role to play by supporting volunteers, ensuring the committee has the ear of senior management and the board, and providing the resources and tools to communicate its decisions and code to those inside and outside the profession.

When forming a committee to focus on standards or a code, an association's management should consider:

1. Who best represents the professional community?
2. What will be the committee's degree of authority, responsibility, and autonomy?
3. How will the committee conduct its business, document its work, and share outcomes with its constituents?
4. To whom will the committee report?
5. What role will association staff play?
6. How will the committee be funded?
7. What will be the length of members' terms?
8. How/should the association board be represented on the committee?
9. What other matters or issues will need to be addressed and resolved?

Code Enforcement

Deciding the issue of code enforcement within the association can be difficult. Enforcement has considerable implications, both practical and legal. The association will need to reach agreement on whether a formal enforcement process will be put in place.

If enforcement is to be an integral part of a program, some questions that need to be answered include:

1. Where will responsibility lie for code enforcement?
2. What resources will be required to manage enforcement?
3. What are the potential legal consequences associated with enforcement?
4. What are the potential legal consequences associated with non-enforcement?
5. How will enforcement be defined?
6. What will the consequences be for unethical behavior?
7. Are the standards clear and unambiguous?
8. When will legal advice be needed?
9. How will the association track ethical behavior of its members? Its profession?
10. What will the due-process procedure look like? Who will be responsible for its application including any required investigations?

11. What process will be in place for reporting, discovering, and investigating alleged unethical practices?
12. How might whistle blowing laws or other laws fit into enforcement?

These questions raised here will be helpful to associations and other organizations that need to address the issue of enforcement. Also, it is common for organizations to establish a helpline, appoint an ethics officer, and require employees to attend initial and annual training as well as sign an annual ethics pledge.

Two Key Concepts

There are two overarching concepts to be understood and addressed when developing a code and communicating the importance of individual behavior. The first key concept is called conflict of interest. The concept consists of the idea that an individual may not use his or her position in such a way as to cause another person to provide some type of benefit either for themselves or others. Professionals should avoid personal and business decisions and actions that create conflict between their personal interests and the interests of their employers.

It is common in ethical practice to require people to notify their employers (and in some cases others) about potential conflicts of interest and seek guidance on how to proceed. Such transparency will help ensure protection of the professional should there be a need to review actions and decisions at a later point, especially if documentation of the issue has been maintained.

The second key concept of ethical practice cautions against even the *appearance* of unethical behavior or decision. Professionals should be aware of this concept and take whatever actions are necessary to protect their integrity and ensure that the interests of their employers prevail. Unfortunately, the appearance of an ethical lapse or violation can be as damaging as an actual lapse or violation.

Research

Associations have the responsibility to determine when and how research should be accomplished in support of its ethical principles and standards. Research can be used to determine if the existing standards are up-to-date and applicable or if they need to be modified and updated in some way. Ongoing research is also an excellent way to watch for positive and negative trends and determine what can or must be done in support of ethical behavior and practices. Some questions for the association include:

1. Does the association conduct research in the area of ethics?
2. Who is assigned the responsibility for research activities?
3. How are research tools and methodologies determined and developed?
4. How are results published?
5. Where will the resources come from?

6. How can research further the mission and goals of the association? Of the profession?

Barriers and Drivers in Ethical Practice

A recent study uncovered a number of specific barriers and drivers to ethical practice (ISM, 2006). An association's or, an organization's management, can use this information to perform an audit (See sidebar "Ethics and Social Responsibility Program Audits.") with the goal to enhance the likelihood of ethical behavior by ensuring that barriers are removed and drivers are in place and supported.

Key barriers to ethical practice include:

- Lack of leadership;
- Ineffective training;
- Ineffective communications;
- Differing standards across functions/departments;
- Lack of internal consequences for unethical behavior;
- Misalignment of business priorities;
- Regulatory complexity;
- Pressure from peers, management, and suppliers; and
- Pressure to perform ("to meet the numbers").

Key drivers supporting ethical practice include:

- Clearly written and communicated policies and procedures;
- Top management support;
- Government regulations;
- Individual employee values; and
- Organizational culture (supporting organizational citizenship and longer-term orientation).

The understanding of barriers and drivers can be used by an organization to enhance the likelihood of solid ethical performance by its employees.

Auditing a Code

Associations should step back periodically and perform an audit of their codes. The audit should identify where content is current and where it needs to be modified, deleted, or added. For example, have there been laws or regulation changes that need to be included in the code? Has the profession changed in some significant way that impacts what should be included in the code? Perhaps a shift in what is acceptable has occurred and needs to be captured in the code.

The challenge will be to develop a plan of action and find the necessary resources to review and improve the code, thereby ensuring ongoing commitment to ethical behavior through the publication of an updated code of ethics.

Ethics and Social Responsibility Program Audits

Associations developing and communicating a code of ethics or a set of social responsibility standards can help their constituents on an ongoing basis by encouraging a periodic audit. The following partial set of questions is designed to help facilitate an audit within the association.

1. Is the association aware of standards and trends within its industry?
2. Does the association comply with applicable laws and regulations covering ethical practices in the profession?
3. Does the association have written policies in place that cover standards?
4. Are goals in place for each standard? What are they? How are improvements and changes incorporated?
5. How does the association disperse and communicate information on its ethical policies internally and to others as appropriate for adoption, understanding, and compliance?
6. Is training provided? What is the frequency and to whom is training provided?
7. Are standards and practices incorporated into contractual documents with those with whom the association does business?
8. Does the association measure its performance against standards and report results? Are auditable processes in place?
9. Are managers and appropriate employees measured on meeting goals? What are the rewards for outstanding performance and consequences for not meeting goals?
10. Are responsibilities for ethics assigned to specific individuals or groups of individuals? What is the level of accountability for making something happen within the association? Are those accountable made known within the association?
11. Is there a champion or process owner accountable for these standards?
12. What is the highest level of oversight or accountability within the association?
13. Are financial and human resources committed?
14. Is annual tracking in place? Does the association communicate accomplishments within the association, with stakeholders, and with the community?
15. Are internal and/or external recognition programs in place?
16. Are core values specific to the association, industry, or business incorporated into human resources policies, employee manuals, and job descriptions?

Laws, Regulations, and Executive Orders Affect Ethical Behavior

Frequently, ethical behavior is intertwined with laws, regulations, and executive orders, and it is common to find references to legal content in ethical codes. It is the responsibility of the practicing professional to become knowledgeable about such matters affecting practice and follow both the intent and letter of laws, regulations, and executive orders.

Some general categories that may impact ethical practice include:

- Antitrust laws;
- Trade regulations;
- Industry-specific laws and regulations;
- Patent, copyright, trade secret, and trademark laws;
- Employment laws and regulations;

- Financial laws and regulations; and
- Environmental laws.

One of the more complex and difficult aspects of ethical practice can arise when associations and practitioners need to address and reconcile customs, laws, regulations, and executive orders across international borders.

International Considerations: Part of the Ethical Puzzle

Culture, laws, and customs can complicate the development, practice, and enforcement of ethical standards. Some steps that can be taken to manage this issue include:

1. Reviewing ethical standards written by a sister association in another country.
2. Reviewing the ethical standards of multinational companies.
3. Involving and retaining international members on the ethical standards committee.
4. Subscribing to an international newsletter or magazine covering the subject of ethics.
5. Acknowledging that it is not always possible to reconcile each point and developing suggestions or recommendations on how to proceed.
6. Becoming clear about behavior(s), actions, and decisions that are clearly illegal in the country where the professional works or does business.

Associations and professionals are responsible for gaining an understanding of inherent conflicts and working to minimize them.

Conclusion

Matters of ethical codes and conduct are often complex and include a strong emotional component. While ethical behavior may be influenced by the environment in which the professional finds himself or herself, ethical behavior is first and always about personal behavior and decisions. Each association is in a position to play a pivotal role in helping its constituents understand what ethical practice is required within the profession it represents. Each association also has the responsibility to work with its members to ensure that a solid and workable set of principles and standards is developed and communicated.

References

Gorlin, Rene A., *Codes of Professional Responsibility, Ethical Standards in Business, Health, and Law*, Fourth Edition, 1999.

Principles and Standards of Ethical Supply Management Conduct with Accompanying Guidelines, Institute for Supply Management™ brochure, January 2005.

ISM Principles of Social Responsibility with Accompanying Supply Management Audit for Social Responsibility Principles, Institute for Supply Management™ brochure, 2004.

International Business Ethics Institute, *International Business Ethics Review*, Volume 7, Issue 2.

Social Responsibility and the Supply Management Profession: A Study of Barriers and Drivers to Ethical Practices, Institute for Supply Management™, May 2006.

About the Author

Scott R. Sturzl, vice president, Institute for Supply Management, has twenty years of experience in association management. He has international certification experience and currently leads the development and delivery of content for ISM's premier conferences, public seminars, and other product lines. He is responsible for international sales of ISM products and services for companies' internal programs. Sturzl obtained his lifetime Certified Purchasing Manager certification in 1997 and his master's in adult education in 1993.

Review Questions

1. What similarities do you think might exist across a spectrum of ethical codes of different industries or professions? What might account for the similarities?

2. What are your thoughts about enforcement of a code? Can you think of any risks involved in having an enforcement process that could result in some type of punitive action against an individual for unethical behavior?

3. What are your thoughts about the concept that an appearance of unethical behavior can be as damaging as actual unethical behavior?

4. Where would you go to find information on laws or regulations that might become a part of the material covered in your association's code of conduct?

5. What do you think about the complexity that may arise when writing or enforcing a set of standards that will be international in scope?

High-Yield
Tactical Planning

John B. Cox, CAE

S TRATEGIC PLANNING MUST BE a wonderful thing. All associations seem to do it. But if strategic plans are so good, why don't they consistently yield the stellar results their creators intend?

The answer is obvious and simple: The associations creating these plans did not take them to the next step, neglecting to design the tactical planning required to achieve the goals and objectives identified in the strategic planning process.

Time and again the author has either evaluated or consulted associations that have developed glittering, sometimes brilliant strategic plans. These plans contain admirable goals, attainable objectives, and remarkable vision. Each association had the goal to be the number-one representative of the widget industry or profession, with the objectives of presenting a loud and unified voice to elected representatives, capturing additional dues revenue, and—ultimately—providing still more benefits, programs, products, and services to members. And in each case, a carefully crafted vision statement said this will happen by 2010, 2020, or some future, undefined date.

When asked for the steps, methods, actions, and activities—in short, the tactics—that will accomplish these enviable goals, objectives, and visions, association staff and volunteers most often respond with a blank stare. Like retirement planning for too many people, it was almost quite enough just to have the idea. The details would some-how, sometime, take care of themselves. It doesn't have to be this way.

By taking the next logical steps after achieving vision, establishing goals, and defining objectives—by developing the tactical machinery to drive the dream—every association can realize its full potential and attain the promise established in its strategic planning.

There are as many different approaches to tactical planning as there are associations. As long as they lead to the same result, they are all worth the effort. The following model is proffered because in use after use, it has yielded the absolutely highest return on the investment of association time and human and financial resources. It is what the sciences call radially adaptive (i.e., highly malleable); it can be freely employed for almost any application an association needs, with or without a strategic plan backing it up. It can be used for a single purpose or program, or expanded to encompass an entire association wish list of goals and objectives. It is in the latter regard, however, that the tactical plan is most valuable. In its creation, obvious synergies between various operational functions, programs, and activities will surface, and it is in recognizing and cross-fertilizing these opportunities that the highest yields will occur. Stated simply, no association activity occurs in a vacuum. When various operations such as continuing education, annual meetings, publications, political activities, and press and communications programs are linked together in a tactical plan, a multiplier effect kicks in and the return on investment is far greater than on any activity undertaken alone.

Keep that multiplier effect in mind as you read the planning steps below. You will rapidly see that periodic and non-periodic publications are as integral to member recruitment and retention as are continuing education and conventions. They redouble when combined with political or representational activities and compound with public and media relations. Once you begin to think tactically, you'll realize that you can expand every beneficial program to serve four or six masters, and these expansions will interlock and cross-fertilize to produce even greater activity and return.

A thought or two before examining the linear steps in tactical planning.

More than one thoughtful association professional has noted that the problem with this whole enterprise is that most people don't plan to plan. That is, they simply don't set aside the time or the ideation that thoughtful, involved, productive planning demands. Don't make that mistake. Tactical planning requires a serious commitment and continuity; it is not an occasional thing. The yield will so far exceed the effort expended that any time allocated for it will be more than well spent. It will, quite literally, transform the association.

There are no bad ideas. Time and again, the author has heard one or another idea shot down during planning sessions as too risky, tried before, not right for the association's members, too advanced, too retro, too something. Nonsense! These same ideas, in the proper context, went on to become the engines that drove or accelerated successful tactical plans. You are about to read several references to "blue-sky" thinking. Heed them. Most often, it is the blue-sky idea—the thought from left field—that allows you to break out of the box.

"If you don't know where you're going, it doesn't matter which road you take."

Perhaps the White Rabbit didn't say it exactly that way to Alice during her travels. But he would have if he had been describing tactical planning. Besides, it's a nice segue to our first step. Because, if you don't know what you want or where you want to go, why do tactical planning at all? So...

I. Setting Goals and Objectives

This step will already be accomplished in the aforementioned (and much abused) strategic planning exercise that many associations engage in. But if not, the reader needs to understand that it is the prerequisite to tactical planning. Quite simply, it must answer questions such as, what does the association want to accomplish? Why? What strategies will take it there?

Stand by for blue-sky reference number one. If you haven't already defined your goal and objectives, do so. Now. Even if you have, revisit them. Ignore the obvious. Kick your way out of the box. In other words, avoid the predictable, easy-to-attain goals. Maybe it's time to think of a global presence. Of starting a for-profit subsidiary. Of opening that branch office in Tierra del Fuego.

In any case, in step one you define what you want to attain, your goal(s) in planning. Then you define why you think you want to achieve them, and what your objectives are for goal attainment. Finally, you think of the gross strategies to get you there. For example:

- The World Wide Widgets Association (WWWA) establishes a goal to have the greatest possible number of members, to represent the entire industry.

- Its objectives are to generate a lot of additional revenue to increase its political clout, to become the real voice of the industry, and to provide more programs, services, benefits, and activities to its constituents.

- WWWA's strategy will be to design and implement a major, ongoing member recruitment and retention program.

Now, that was easy, wasn't it?

In a couple of steps or so, we'll look at how tactics are required to drive strategies. But first this important announcement: Please plan to plan. Setting goals and objectives is best done in an atmosphere devoted to the enterprise. A retreat is usually the best venue and vehicle. Wherever and whenever, allow thinking to roam free. That's when breakthroughs occur.

II. Situation Analysis/Problem Definition

Remember those initial references to tactical planning as being linear and sequential? Here is where it begins to become obvious.

WWWA now has a goal, objective, and even a strategy. Before it can set about attaining its goal, it needs to carefully analyze its current status, its market position, the impediments to goal and objectives attainment, its strengths, and, most important, its weaknesses. Does it have the resources to proceed? If not, can it acquire them? What will be required to succeed, to realize its potential?

As, and after, it has analyzed and defined its current status, WWWA needs to define its problem areas—those impediments to achieving its goals. This is actually a two-part exercise:

Internal Problems

What elements will preclude realizing its goals? It is absolutely imperative to be brutally honest in this exercise. Anything less will doom the enterprise. In a nutshell, if there are roadblocks, identify them.

Typical references here include insufficient staff, insufficient financial resources, lack of the electronic resources that would make coordination of a member campaign possible, lack of real time to devote to the effort, and so on. If you don't candidly identify the barriers here, don't proceed with planning. The effort won't be successful.

External Problems

Surprisingly, these are less problematic than internal problems, but they must be recognized and overcome nonetheless. In marketing, it can be thought of as identifying and measuring the competition. Suppose there is a larger, stronger, longer-established association that predominates in member share, or there is a lack of recognition in the marketplace. Perhaps the association didn't prevail in an important political battle. Possibly, potential and former members consider its dues too high. Whatever the problems are, they must be identified, confronted, and, if possible, overcome to clear the way for any success with stated goals.

Something important will have transpired at this point. An association engaged in tactical planning and following the just-described steps will have established goals and knows why it wants to achieve them. It knows the strategies it will take to get there and has analyzed its current status including what is going right and where there are challenges. And, it has identified the problems, internal and external, that it must address to realize its dreams. In short, the association's leadership and staff probably know more about the organization at this moment than has been identified in years, if ever. And if ever there was a case of knowledge being power, this is it! Armed with the knowledge gained to this point, those engaged in the planning exercise can quite literally create the future of this association.

First, of course, must come the next essential and once again sequential steps in tactical planning.

III. Identification of Key Audiences

Audiences in our context may also be thought of as publics, markets, and targets. In brief, these are the buyers, nonmembers, potential members, legislators, funders, and consumers of products, services, benefits, and programs that the association wants and needs to reach.

On a global scale, listing the audiences includes virtually everyone with whom the association wants or needs to interact. For a specific, single-purpose campaign, the list would be narrowed to those audiences relevant to the purpose or goal at hand.

The author has regularly been surprised at how narrowly many associations define their universe. When asked how many media would be on a key audiences or target list for a public information program, they will respond with six or eight; a minimal list could include more than 20, and the author has seen successful and ambitious media lists with 40 separate kinds of media targets. Similarly, a membership recruitment and retention campaign target list might yield half a dozen different types of audiences. However, there are so many different audiences involved in a proactive campaign that any good list should extend well into double digits.

The same point could be extended to lists of audiences for fund-raising campaigns, legislative and governmental initiatives, conference and meeting development plans, and more. Far too many associations allow their grasp to exceed their reach. Here is another place where blue-sky thinking on the part of all involved can produce surprising results. And only when an association defines all its possible audiences for any given outreach can it achieve the full potential envisioned in its campaign. No one has ever erred in identifying too many potential buyers.

Okay, then, the association has identified all possible audiences, buyers, consumers, publics, targets, and markets for its intended purposes. Now, how does it go about reaching them? That would be step four, logically enough.

IV. Identification and Development of Vehicles and Tactics

In our tactical-planning context, the ideas of vehicles and tactics are almost interchangeable. Once an association has defined all of its audiences, it must define and determine the best ways, the best vehicles and approaches, for reaching them. And as with audience definition, on a global tactical plan the association must list every possible, conceivable method of reaching the targets in its plan. Newsletters, meetings, workshops, e-mail, fax, blogs, podcasting, testimony, letters, speeches, trade press coverage, general interest media, annual conferences, and so on ad infinitum must be listed. Even if an approach or vehicle isn't being used currently, it should nonetheless be listed; it is something to be aspired to and may eventually prove to be a key element in achieving success.

On a cautionary note, the same concern expressed in step three pertains in step four. Namely, associations regularly underestimate the number, breadth, and range of vehicles and tactics for reaching their intended audiences. If a list of audiences can extend well into double digits for any given tactical campaign, the methods, tactics, and vehicles possible for reaching these publics should, at the minimum, match it. Too often the author has asked an association to list the vehicles it needs to reach a given audience, say, the media. After consideration, staff will list perhaps six vehicles. With a little prodding and some free thinking, the list expands to 26 or 28 different vehicles and approaches.

The only limits here are self-imposed. There are those who could argue quite successfully that there are literally no limits when it comes to reaching essential publics. Doing so will certainly increase the margins of success.

To this point, the association has set goals, objectives, and strategies. It has analyzed its current status and defined its problems. It knows its audiences and the vehicles and tactics it must use to reach them. This is very powerful information indeed. Now, put it all together.

V. Creating the Tactical Plan: "A Matrix of Opportunities"

Flush with all the knowledge gained to this point, you will discover that the rest is simplicity itself. Actually, it is all mechanistic from here on.

If an association has set its goals and objectives, knows what it has to overcome, has identified its audiences and the vehicles needed to reach them, it need only match column A with column B, calendar the activities, and put a cost line on the enterprise.

Let's look at three brief examples of single-purpose tactical campaign planning. It is important to bear in mind that if we were looking at a global, organization-wide plan, the audiences and vehicles would be integrated in their respective steps, or columns, and that all activities would be intertwined synergistically. This, of course, would produce the aforementioned multiplier effect: When one or two elements in audiences and vehicles are cross-linked with others, they become worth four or five times their value alone.

Example One

The Ozone Society decides it wants to create a tactical membership recruitment/ retention plan. It has conducted all the preliminary steps outlined to this point. In items three and four, it identified its key audiences and the vehicles/tactics required to reach them as:

Step III *Audiences/Publics*	Step IV *Vehicles/Tactics*
• potential members • former members • students • affiliated organizations • those ineligible, but, none-theless interested • corporations • foundations • auxiliary members • retired members • inactive members	• personal letters to best prospects • direct mail letters to remainder of list • telephone calls to best prospects • telemarketing to remainder of list • member-get-a-member and other campaigns • personal visits • special offers • inducements • incentives • discounts for joining in conjunction with book purchases, workshops, and annual meeting attendance • special campaign-only rates • World Wide Web information/target messages

Example Two

The American Ethereal Association wants to design and mount a major fundraising/endowment building campaign. It successfully navigated all steps to this point and has identified its targets and methods as:

Step III *Audiences/Publics*	Step IV *Vehicles/Tactics*
• all members • foundations • corporations • potential donors • former donors • known benefactors • most likely individual contributors • medium-to-least-likely contributors • program sponsors for annual meetings or workshops	• individualized letters • direct marketing • funding proposals • grant proposals • telemarketing • campaign and collateral theme • personal visits • participation/contributions, gifts, and/or acknowledgments • formal recognition programs • electronic campaign information and targeting

Example Three

The National Sea Shells League (NSSL) wants to pump attendance at its annual conference. It has identified its key publics and tactical methods as:

Step III *Audiences/Publics*	Step IV *Vehicles/Tactics*
• current members • interested nonmembers • those who always attend • those medium-to-least likely to attend • NSSL book and periodicals buyers and subscribers • all workshop attendees • current exhibitors • potential exhibitors • former exhibitors • members of affinity organizations • members of affiliated organizations • general public • press • students • spouses	• meeting program promotions and brochures • letters • magazines • newsletters • telemarketing • home page, Internet, member bulletin board systems • state and chapter newsletters • press releases • media wires • feature articles targeted to interested publications • postage-meter cancellations/indicias • buck slips • stuffers/flyers for book orders • blow-ins and tip-ins for NSSL publications • stationery legends/logos

At this point, tactical planners would simply draw synergy lines between the audiences, targets, and publics identified in Step III with the vehicles, tactics, and methods needed to reach them as listed in Step IV. For ease of purpose, it can be helpful to create a "Matrix of Opportunities" with audiences listed on one axis and vehicles on the other; contacts and activities would then fall into the grid of the matrix. In Step IV, it is important to remember that some vehicles will reach only one public; others will reach all. Similarly, some audiences are continuously key, while others have value only once or twice. Identifying who is to be targeted and when, and with what vehicle, can produce the earlier referenced multiplier effect, where multiple vehicle hits with various target publics can produce excellent results with modest efforts.

Technological Tactics

The astute reader will recognize that in the three examples given, there were few references to electronic vehicles and tactics. The Internet has changed the playing field dramatically in tactical planning and association growth opportunities, and it is evolving faster than almost anyone's ability to keep pace. It is quite possible for a medium sized or even a small association to have a worldwide portal and presence, reaching audiences not even conceived of a mere decade ago. It is almost comically whimsical to remember even a handful of years past when a Web site was considered cutting edge. Now new methodologies and vehicles are emerging almost instantaneously, only to be replaced in a blink by still newer ways to reach key audiences.

At this writing, the latest high-utility tactics for reaching vast publics include viral marketing, blogs, and message boards, social networking through sites such as MySpace and LinkedIn, and podcasting. Before the ink dries here, there will be still newer, better, faster, farther reaching technologies to reach key markets. The wise planner will try to keep an eye one or two clicks above the horizon and see which of these new methods, these singularly valuable vehicles, will be most beneficial in reaching what audiences to achieve specific goals.

VI. Scheduling the Plan

The difficult part of the planning is now complete. Not incidentally, the association is probably armed with more useful knowledge about itself, its audiences, and how to reach them than it has known for years.

Having identified the who, what, where, and how, the planning association need only identify the when. In years past, strategic planning—along with the tactics needed to support it—could be thought of in multiyear terms, with typical plans stretching out four or five years and beyond. That is no longer practical or wise today. Events simply move too rapidly. A good tactical plan will be in the 24-month range, with a top-end max of 36 months.

Many associations use the "NASA" approach to tactical plan calendaring—identifying the goal and then working backward on the steps it will take to get there. In real terms, if an association wants to increase membership attendance at its August annual meeting, it needs to identify its target audiences several months earlier, perhaps in October or November of the preceding year, and then begin applying its tactical steps and employing its vehicles at calendared intervals in January, March, May, and so on.

A Handy Shortcut

For those new to the tactical planning process, creating a matrix of opportunities and linking various vehicles with numerous audiences may be a bit daunting. It gets easier with each plan created. If the reader feels somewhat stymied at this step, there is an easy shortcut to creating the plan and moving forward in Step VI.

Simply look over the list of vehicles identified in Step IV and prioritize them numerically in Step V. What will yield the greatest return from the most beneficial publics quickly? The most successful plans the author has been involved with developing have always identified the "low-hanging fruit" first, targeted them, and reaped the benefits to go on and finance later activities in the plan. For example, radically increasing annual meeting or workshop attendance will provide the monies to greatly increase essential publications and other revenue-producing information services. Also, high yields from those activities will then finance, perhaps, new technologies that will in turn help recruit new members and retain existing ones. Every part of the plan inter-locks with others and yields additional benefits and returns in still other listed activities and goals.

So, continue numbering the vehicles in Step IV, from highest return to most modest, until the entire list is prioritized. You now have the next step in your tactical plan. If you have taken this shortcut approach just noted, simply start creating your schedule and your tactical plan calendar with those first-identified high yield vehicles, and keep sequencing them in until all vehicles are allotted specific time periods for accomplishment and the calendar is complete.

There is a very important consideration in the calendaring step. All tactical plans should contain a lot of air. Do not think of any tactical plan as a finished document. Rather, with ongoing evaluation, the plan will be continuously tweaked. Certain vehicles will be dropped while others are being added, and new or additional target audiences will replace existing ones. Most important, with sufficient malleability or air built into the plan, it will be possible to add and maximize opportunities not thought of or included in the plan during its design phase.

VII. Budgeting to the Plan

In the not-too-distant past, tactical and strategic plans were stand-alone enterprises, almost entities unto themselves, whose implementation—though demanding the seri-ous commitment of staff, volunteer, and financial resources—simply wasn't viewed in economic terms.

Fortunately, that is no longer the case today.

In fact, in the current climate, everything is thought of in economic terms, includ-ing and especially planning. And that is precisely the way it should be. So, to add the validity a serious tactical plan will require, a column should be added to the right of the matrix of opportunity, and in every place where an action is being calendared—where a vehicle or tactic is being used to reach a targeted audience—its economic impact must be indicated. On a happy note, not every reference connotes cost. Rather, when the tactical plan is being used to generate greater meeting attendance, hype book sales, promote membership, or whatever, its positive economic consequences should be listed as well.

Not only will you have an accurate idea of what your effort will cost in human and financial resources, you will also be able to show the benefit to be derived. And that promotes buy-in by all the stakeholders in the plan, including other staff, boards, lead-ership, and interested volunteers.

A final benefit of budgeting to the plan is that it forces the planner(s) to focus and prioritize. When costs are added to the wish lists, those involved usually become a little more serious and begin to look at such things as return on investment before expending precious association resources.

VIII. Evaluation

Evaluation is the *sine qua non* of tactical planning. It separates the professionals from the amateurs. It is the essential step. Everything to this point would be, in fact, pointless if some measure of the plan's progress weren't used.

In prior days, evaluation checkpoints could be built into a plan at longer intervals. In today's rapidly evolving climate, opportunities present themselves at a moment's notice, and the longest possible interval between evaluation points should be six months, and preferably three months or less for 12- to 18-month plans.

In brief, evaluation is a snapshot of your progress at a given moment. It tells you where you've been, where you are, and where you appear to be going. It can tell you what to add, what to drop, what needs additional reworking, and where some tuning would help. It allows you to prevent failure and to measure success.

Most important, periodic evaluation guarantees that your tactical plans won't suffer the fate of most strategic and/or tactical plans: growing dust on a shelf. As noted at the outset, many associations think it is quite enough just to create the plan; somehow, implementation will take care of itself. By evaluating the plan at specific intervals and making the changes required to ensure its success, you also ensure that the plan becomes a living, working blueprint for accomplishments. You institutionalize accountability, and that is a powerful motivator.

Well, all of this sounds fine and good. A matrix of opportunity. Budgeting to plan. Vehicles and audiences. Accountability.

But does it all work? The author has working, personal experience with either the planning just described or derivative variations of it and can respond with an emphatic yes! In one association, such planning increased net revenues on member professional development from $150,000 to $800,000 in a three-year period and more than doubled annual meeting attendance—from 4,500 to 9,700—in the same window. In another association, it produced a 10 percent increase in membership that costs three figures each year, and in still another association, generated a 6 percent increase in membership that costs four figures a year. A fourth association quadrupled its non-periodical publishing output and income within a four-year period, while tripling its advertising revenues. The list goes on, but the point is already made.

Everyone can plan *strategically,* and many quite frequently do. It is those association professionals who knowledgeably back up their strategic plans with *tactical planning* who guarantee achievement. In a nutshell, high-yield tactical planning is the engine that can drive an association's success. And everybody wins: the planners, the association, its members, volunteers, and leaders. Very few other association activities can make that claim.

So go forth, do some tactical planning, and prosper!

Crisis Management

It would be nice to believe that strategic and/or tactical planning would obviate the need for all other plan development. It would be nice, but it would be foolish. Regardless of how well an association professionalizes its planning, structures its messages, and achieves its objectives, crises will occur. Witness the rash of crises that have affected entire industries and professions in the past several years and, ultimately, the associations and societies representing them. In every case, associations became the focal point for information and response to the issue.

It is a wise association that presumes sometime in its future it will face a major crisis, with all its attendant scrutiny.

There are probably as many crisis management strategies as there are crises. All will see an association through a rough period of forced response.

It is recommended that an association use the most simple, effective formula for dealing with a crisis, and that it insist on strict compliance with the crisis policy for all involved leadership, members, and staff. Following is a three-phase process that should help any association deal with any crisis.

Phase I: Pre-crisis

• Plan for crisis
  – Assume that at some future point a crisis will occur.
  – Identify possible or probable crises and how membership will be affected.
  – Identify essential vehicles for reaching critical publics during a crisis.

• Establish policy
  – Determine spokesperson(s).
  – Determine essential message-clearance procedures.
  – Inform those concerned—especially all staff—about clearance procedures and designated spokesperson(s).
  – Develop **fact** sheets on the assumption of crises, tailored to specific need.

• Establish a crisis information function (typically in the communications or public affairs offices)
  – Ensure that all inquiries and information will be directed to and from this office.
  – Ensure that staff is knowledgeable and has access to essential contact numbers for clearances and spokesperson(s).
  – Keep this function current at all times; crises have a way of occurring when least expected.

Phase II: The Crisis

• Define the crisis
  – Assemble every knowable fact about the crisis.
  – Determine which members, if not all, are affected.
  – Determine which publics are affected.
  – Determine whether the crisis is national, local, or regional.
  – Determine whether the crisis is of short or long duration.
  – Determine what other associations, industries, or professions are involved.
  – Can and should they be allied with for response(s)?

Continued on next page

- Access existing crisis plan
  - Determine if it is adequate to meet the crisis or if it will more likely have to be modified.
  - Determine if all key personnel are alerted and know their roles. Are response policies in place and adequate? Is the response procedure, including clearances, functional and ready?
- Respond professionally
  - Prepare a feet sheet about the crisis with all information verified and essential clearances obtained and distribute it to all concerned publics—particularly the media.
  - Do not speculate about the crisis, at any point or with any public; stick to the facts at all times.
  - Be accessible to the media.
  - Schedule regular briefings as appropriate, and stick to the schedule.
  - Document every aspect of the crisis while it is in progress, including statements, fact sheets, legal reviews and clearances, interviews, media coverage, public response, and final resolution, if possible.

Phase III: Post Crisis

- Review the association's crisis performance
  - Did the generic precrisis planning help?
  - Did spokesperson(s) and clearance procedures function properly?
  - Did the internal mechanisms, especially the crisis information, function correctly?
  - Was the association blindsided by any aspect of the crisis?
- Plan for the next crisis
  - Use information and experience gained during the process to build an even more successful response procedure for the next occurrence.

The following tips should help both knowledgeable and inexperienced association professionals when confronting media during a crisis.

- Never say "no comment." It is an admission of guilt to contemporary publics.

- Do not be afraid to say that not all the facts are available, and a response can only be forthcoming when they are. Media are always on deadline, and will try to force a speculative response. The only safe response is possible when all knowable facts are available.

- Never go "off the record" with the media during a crisis. There is no such thing to a deadline-oriented press in a crisis situation. Even if direct attribution is not made, careless remarks can and will easily be traced back to their source.

- Anticipate a media ambush. It is a sad but true fact of life in the Information Age that media will go to great and not so attractive lengths to get stories during a crisis. There is an old but accurate adage in professional communications: "The only kind of visibility you will get without proper planning is the kind you don't want."

The underlying theme, the most common word, is planning. Planning is not the ultimate panacea. It is not the miracle cure. It is the only way professional management can take place in an association. Indeed, planning separates the amateurs from the professionals. When activity is professionally planned, everyone—members, publics, the industry or profession, and the association—profits. It is an exercise well worth the effort.

About the Author

John B. Cox, CAE, is principal and CEO of Association Growth and Income Builders, LLC, an international and national consultancy that helps associations maximize their potential. He has three decades of experience working with, consulting to, and/or evaluating not-for-profit, member-based organizations, and NGOs ranging from trade associations through professional societies.

Review Questions

1. Do you feel that you really understand the principle involved in that crucial step five of tactical planning? Do you really know how to create a matrix of opportunities, with audiences on one side of the grid, vehicles on another, and a wealth of opportunities, made more so by the "multiplier effect" in the field area?

2. Can you envision using one tactical planning exercise to cover two or more seemingly unrelated activities, thus achieving still better returns and rewards? For example, how could you pair a goal of doubling annual meeting attendance with, perhaps, generating double-digit increases in membership?

3. How would you go about creating a high-yield tactical plan that encompasses the entire organization, interlinking every program, product, benefit, and service into one, major organic planning document to produce enormous returns in every area?

13

Budget and Finance

Kathie Berry, CAE

SSOCIATIONS ARE UNDER EVER-INCREASING scrutiny from Congress, the Internal Revenue Service, other regulatory bodies, and the public. Association executives must understand what financial statements say about the performance of the organization and must make sure their elected leaders understand these statements as well. They and their staff must know how budgets are prepared and be able to explain variances between actual performance and budgeted performance. They must feel comfortable with the financial implications of the organization's strategic plan. They must be satisfied that proper safeguards are in place to protect the association's assets and that adequate external reviews of their operations and performance are undertaken. Providing timely, accurate, and complete financial information to internal and external users is a requirement for competent association executives.

Budgeting

In broad terms, the budget is the organization's strategic plan in financial terms. In operational terms, it is the best estimate of the future performance of programs and services. Although three-year, five-year and 10-year budgets may be prepared to anticipate long-range activities, most association executives will be concerned with preparing detailed annual budgets. The proposed annual budget is usually prepared by staff with input from elected leaders and committees, and it is presented to the board for approval prior to the beginning of the fiscal year.

Associations prepare annual budgets consistent with their fiscal years, whether a calendar year or some other 12-month period. Within that budget, the timing of revenue and expenses may be consistent over the 12 months or may be based on esti-mates of when revenue will be earned and expenses will be incurred. In the budgeting process, it is wise to spread revenue and expenses over the appropriate time periods. An association's complete budget consists of an *operating budget*, a *capital budget*, and a *cash budget*.

Operating Budget

Every program or service offered by the association should support its strategic plan. If there are programs utilizing the association's resources but not supporting its plan, they should be discontinued or redefined to mesh with the goals and mission of the association.

Each program or service area has its own detailed budget. The combined net revenue and expense from each of these program and service areas will produce the net revenue for the association for the upcoming fiscal year. The association may wish to produce a budget with a certain net revenue (excess of revenue or over expenses). This may be considered a contribution to reserves and may be a set dollar amount, a certain amount per member, a percentage of expenses, or some other amount set by the board.

For some programs, a *zero-based budget* may be appropriate. Zero-based budget-ing assumes that a project starts with no income and no expense, and every source of revenue and every expenditure are computed in detail. A new program or meeting, for example, would require zero-based budgeting. Many associations will look at each of their programs through the zero-based lens to make sure that budgeted expenses are not increased without due consideration being given to the reason for an increase. *Incremental budgeting* assumes that a certain percentage increase or decrease will be added to stable programs. Salary budgets are frequently budgeted incrementally. It is dangerous to take the current budget for any program and repeat it for the next year without considering how closely actual results in the current year are conforming to the budget.

Although associations are exempt from tax on most activities, they are subject to tax on unrelated business income generated from a trade or business that is regularly carried on that is not related to the exempt purpose of the organization. Tax expense on unrelated business income, such as advertising in a periodical, needs to be budgeted.

There are many sources of information available for formulating a budget. Year-to-date and prior year's performance will certainly be a starting point. The impact of trends, both internal and external, should be taken into account. Member needs sur-veys can give an idea of how new programs may perform. Operating ratios reports and salary surveys from ASAE & The Center or other organizations can help guide budgeting, as can an analysis of the trends of internal programs during the past sev-eral years. Publications and information used and drawn from chapter members can identify trends that may affect them and their financial contribution to the association, whether via dues or in support of events and programs. In short, budget preparation must consider the impact of economic and environmental factors on the association.

The association must decide if it wishes to assign only direct costs to each of its programs or if it wishes to allocate indirect costs to each program. Indirect costs would include overhead such as facilities and management salaries. The rationale for assigning only direct costs to each program area is that the budget manager has control over these costs. The rationale for assigning indirect costs is that each program or service offered to members bears some of the expenses of the entire organization and to include those gives a "true" cost of the program.

Capital Budget

The association should have a capitalization limit and depreciation policy for the purchase of fixed assets (assets that will last longer than one year). If the capitalization limit is $1,000, any purchase of a fixed asset greater than $1,000 will be capitalized. Anticipated capital purchases should be included in the capital budget. A depreciation policy will determine the number of years over which the cost of a capital asset will be expensed. If a fixed asset was purchased for $1,200 and was to be depreciated over a period of 5 years, then $240 per year ($20 per month) would be expensed. The capital budget sets out what fixed assets will be purchased or leased and when they will be acquired. This budget feeds into the operating budget for determining depreciation expense and any maintenance or interest expense associated with the asset. It also feeds into the cash budget.

Cash Budget

The cash budget anticipates the flow of cash. It pulls in information from the operating budget to determine when revenue will be received and expenses incurred. It pulls in information from the capital budget to determine when cash will be used to purchase fixed assets, and incorporates principal payments on leases and mortgages. Since depreciation does not use cash, the cash budget does not include depreciation or other non-cash expense items. Once the flow of cash for the year is determined, investment income can be budgeted.

Implementing and Monitoring the Budget

Each staff member responsible for preparing a program or service budget should also be responsible for implementing and monitoring that budget throughout the year. Budget managers inform their supervisors of the progress of implementation and of any variances from the budget. The association's chief staff executive should make sure that he or she understands the status of all programs and should be able to present cogently to the elected leadership the reasons for all significant variances from budget.

The leadership—both staff and elected—must be able to understand the budget and variances from the budget, take steps to correct shortfalls, or take advantage of significant surpluses. Since the budget is the financial presentation of the current year's strategic plan, constant evaluation by staff and leadership is necessary to ensure that the association's resources are working efficiently towards achieving the plan.

Financial Reporting

Association executives must be aware of the financial position of their associations at all times. Association boards have fiduciary responsibility for the assets of the association, and the executive must keep them informed in a timely, accurate, and transparent manner.

Using the accrual basis rather than the cash basis of accounting gives a clearer picture of the operations of the association because accrual accounting recognizes revenue when earned and expenses when incurred. Cash basis accounting, on the other hand, recognizes revenue when received and expenses when paid.

The statement of activities (income statement) may significantly overstate or understate net revenue using cash-basis accounting. For example, if expenses related to a profitable program or meeting are paid before any revenue for that event is recorded, that event will show a loss, which would not be mitigated until revenue had been received. If revenue is received before expenses are recorded, the net for that event would be significantly overstated. Accrual accounting helps to alleviate potentially significant month-to-month variances and allows staff and leadership to evaluate performance more consistently.

At a minimum, the association's *balance sheet* and *statement of activities* should be available on a monthly or quarterly basis. A *statement of cash flow* is a required report in the audit of nonprofit organizations and can be presented to the board along with the other two reports. The association's leadership needs to decide on which format of these statements gives them the most meaningful and useful information and presents the association's financial position in a transparent manner.

Balance Sheet. The balance sheet presents the financial condition of the organization at a given point in time. It sets out the assets (what the association owns, what others owe the association, and what the association has paid for future events), liabilities (what the association owes and what the association has received from others for future events), and net assets (the accumulated earnings of the association since inception). The term "net assets" is comparable to "equity" in a for-profit environment.

The balance sheet is prepared as of a certain date (usually the last day of the month). It is a snapshot of the organization at that date. The executive would pay particular attention to cash and investments as well as to amounts receivable by the organization or payable to others. Subsidiary schedules showing the aging of receivables and payables would give a good idea of how quickly the association is collecting its accounts or paying its bills. The change in net assets from the prior year-end balance to the date being presented would equal the net revenue of the association from the beginning of the year to the date on the balance sheet. Donor-restricted and board-designated funds are segregated on the balance sheet from undesignated and unrestricted funds. A useful comparative tool is to include on the balance sheet several columns showing current information as of the date on the balance sheet, the balances at the same date of the prior year, and the balances at the end of the prior year.

Statement of Activities. This report shows activity for a certain period of time, usually the beginning of the fiscal year through the same date that is shown on the balance sheet. It is comparable to a statement of net income or statement of revenue and expenses. The statement of activities shows all sources of revenue and of expenses. These may be presented either by showing each major source of revenue comprising total revenue and then each major expense category comprising total expense. Revenue less expenses equals net revenue. Another way to present the statement of activities is by program area. Each revenue-producing program is shown with its revenue and expense, and a net figure for that program is given. Those activities that have no revenue are shown by program area.

A statement of activities for a specific period is enhanced if the year-to-date budget and the variance from budget are given, the annual budget is shown, and the prior year-to-date and prior full-year activities are presented. Doing so assists readers of the statements in identifying areas that may need their attention. The association executive should be prepared to address major variances from budget and significant differences from the prior year. The statement of activity with these variance and comparative analyses are very useful in identifying negative trends that need to be addressed or positive variances that may offer opportunities for new or increased investment by the association.

Cash Flow Statement. This statement shows the use and flow of cash over the period covered by the statement of activities. It begins with the net revenue from the statement of activities and then makes adjustments for cash used or not used in producing this net revenue. For example, it adjusts for revenue recognized but not received and expenses incurred but not paid, for non-cash expenses such as depreciation, for principal payments on leases and mortgages, and for money derived from the sale of investments or used to purchase investments.

There are many factors which may affect the amount of cash available to the association at any point. If dues are collected on an annual basis, cash may be high at the beginning of the year, and the association must make sure that cash is managed

---

Tools for Analysis

The association may wish to study certain ratios that show how well it is performing:

• *Liquidity and current ratios* measure the organization's ability to pay its short-term obligations. A liquidity ratio is cash and marketable securities not held for the long-term divided by current liabilities. A current ratio is current assets divided by current liabilities. A liquid or current ratio higher than 1 is desired.

• *Profitability ratios* show how well the organization performed relative to its sales, assets, or net assets. It is calculated on net revenue divided by the appropriate amount.

• *Activity ratios* measure how quickly the association converts its receivables into cash.

These tools are useful in identifying trends and in comparing the association with others of similar size and composition.

sufficiently well to ensure that expenses through the end of the year will be covered. Cash may be high as registrations for a meeting are received, but will dip as meeting expenses are paid. The purchase of capital equipment and payments on capital lease obligations are not operating expenses but will use cash. Depreciation and amortization are operating expenses that do not use cash. The association must consider all such factors and ensure that adequate cash will be available to meet its disbursement needs.

Controls, Oversight, and Independent Evaluations

Associations are not private enterprises owned by individuals, but are custodians and managers of funds given by others. Whether the association's resources come from member dues, contributions, or grants, it is incumbent on the association to have reliable internal controls and external oversight in place.

Internal financial controls are intended to provide assurance that members' assets are properly accounted for and reported. Good internal controls

- Safeguard association assets from fraud, misuse, and waste;
- Ensure that financial records and reports are accurate and reliable;
- Promote operational efficiency and effectiveness in accordance with management's objectives;
- Provide means for identifying possible avenues for fraud and instituting deterrents; and
- Provide comfort to the volunteer leadership that the members' investment in the organization is being handled properly.

Written policies should be in place covering the receipt and recording of cash, authorization of disbursements, payment of bills, payroll preparation, account reconciliation, investments, and journal entries. There are four segments of every financial transaction:

- **Initiation**—request to purchase or pay, receipt of money, payroll preparation, journal entry preparation
- **Authorization**—budget manager, board decision, senior management
- **Custody**—verifying that all assets shown on the books are in the possession of the association (reconciliations of cash and investments, inventory, deposits, and prepaid expenses)
- **Recording**—ensuring that every cash and non-cash item has been recorded to the correct account.

Ideally, a different person is responsible for each segment. If this is not possible, oversight by someone outside the finance operations (staff or volunteer) should be instituted. Internal control policies should include clear lines of authority, a clear definition of responsibility and assurance that responsibility has been accepted, authority commensurate with the responsibility assumed, and proper training.

The "American Competitiveness and Corporate Accountability Act of 2002," commonly known as the *Sarbanes-Oxley Act*, requires nonprofit organizations to adopt policies protecting informants ("whistleblowers") from retaliation and not allowing employees to obstruct justice by destroying documents. The board should adopt both a whistleblower protection policy and a document destruction policy, and staff should be made familiar with these policies.

Independent evaluation of financial information is performed by an outside firm. When engaging an independent accounting firm, make sure the firm is familiar with the regulations and reporting requirements affecting nonprofit organizations, and that it has performed audit and tax work for other nonprofit organizations. The auditor may provide 1 of 3 levels of reporting on the financial statements:

- An *audit* performed by an independent CPA firm uses specific auditing procedures to provide assurance that the financial statements "present fairly, in all material respects, the financial position" of the association. The financial statements are the responsibility of the association's management, and the auditor's responsibility is to express an opinion on those statements.

- A *review* is limited in scope and offers less assurance. A review is designed to uncover any "material misstatements" on the association's financial statements.

- A *compilation* is simply the consolidation of the association's financial information by the independent firm and does not offer independent assurance of the information presented on the financial statements.

If possible, it is prudent to engage an independent accounting firm to perform an annual audit. If doing so is beyond the resources of the association, a review would be advisable. Having a review or audit performed annually offers the most comfort. Good management practice dictates that an audit or review be performed at least once every three years.

Accounting for the association's finances may be performed by internal staff or may be outsourced. Whether internal or external, the finance staff should be familiar with the association's internal controls and with standard accounting procedures for nonprofit organizations. If the accounting function is outsourced, gain assurance that the provider understands nonprofit accounting and reporting. Whether the accounting function is outsourced or is performed internally, the chief staff officer must be sure that he or she fully understands the statements and is comfortable with the information they contain.

Reserves

An association is a business and must be viewed as having a life extending beyond the current year. A healthy balance in reserves affords comfort that the association will be able to weather a downturn, allows the association to seize opportunities that arise that may be outside the operating budget, and provides funds for capital improvements or investments.

Establishing and monitoring reserves is not a casual process. The association should decide and record in its minutes such components of reserves as

- *Definition:* Reserves may be defined as net assets, as long-term investments, or as some other figure that the association feels would meet its requirements if reserves were tapped.

- *Goal:* Establishing this goal will require analysis and discussion on the part of the executive and the board. Is the goal a certain percentage of operating expenses (and if so, what is included in operating expenses)? Is the goal to have enough to cover association activities for a specified period of time? Will the goal be composed of diverse elements, such as a certain amount to cover a downturn, a certain amount to provide for unbudgeted opportunities that may arise, a certain amount to purchase equipment or buildings, a certain amount for start-up programs? In considering how much to set aside to cover a downturn, how severe would a downturn be and how long would it last?

- *Annual contributions:* The association may decide to set aside a specific dollar amount, a specific amount per member, or a specific percent of net revenue. Whatever amount is decided upon should be included as part of the budget.

- *Time frame to meet the goal:* The association should establish a reasonable time frame to meet the goal. If the reserves goal is significantly larger than the current balance in reserves, the amount of time needed to reach the goal may be as long as several years. Annual updates on the progress of reaching the goal should be presented to the leadership to validate the time frame.

- *What happens when the goal is met?* Does the amount that has been set aside for reserves in prior years then become available for programs and services?

- *When and how can reserves be tapped?* Is this the decision of the full board or of the executive committee? Would a simple majority suffice, or is a super-majority or unanimity required?

- *How often is the goal for reserves to be revisited?* It is wise for the board to validate periodically the amount of reserves that the association needs and to record the outcome of these discussions in its minutes.

The board should establish and regularly review a reserve policy addressing all of these goals.

Investments

Associations must not only monitor their cash flow to ensure they have adequate funds to meet their disbursement needs, they must also provide for prudent investment of funds that are not needed for current operations. A board-approved investment policy should be reviewed periodically and updated as needed. The policy would address such topics as

- *The various components of cash.* There may be operating cash, undesignated funds to be used incrementally and only as the board authorizes, designated funds that may be used in future time periods, donor-restricted funds that may be accessed on a known periodic basis, or building funds that may be tapped at a known time in the future. Each component might require specific investment guidelines.

- *The projected timeline for use of funds.* If funds are to be used for specific programs in future years, the anticipated timing of using such funds should be included. For example, an association may be investing funds for a building to be constructed in five years. The investment policy would include the goal for that building fund at a certain date in the future, and the investment vehicles used to achieve this goal would consider that timeline. If funds are set aside to cover downturns or take advantage of unbudgeted opportunities, the investment mix for such money might well be more liquid.

- *Investment vehicles to be used.* Will funds be invested in equities? If so, what should be the ratio of equities to fixed income instruments? Are fixed income investments limited to government securities, or can there be corporate bonds? What other investment vehicles are to be considered or excluded?

- *The expected return on investments over time.* Should it keep pace with inflation, with an index, or with a return of a certain percent above inflation or a selected index?

- *Will the funds be managed by association staff or by an investment manager?*

- *Who authorizes the sale or purchase of securities?*

- *Who is responsible for engaging and reviewing the performance of the investment manager?*

If the association does not have an investment policy, it may wish to work with an investment manager to design a policy that would address these and other areas of interest. The association executive must feel comfortable with the role that an investment manager plays in terms of the results of the investment portfolio compared to similar portfolios, the level of involvement of the manager, and the timeliness and clarity of reports from the manager.

Affiliated and Subsidiary Organizations

Many associations have affiliated or subsidiary organizations such as foundations, service corporations, educational affiliates, and publishing arms, to mention a few. It is wise to review periodically the bylaws of each organization for consistency and current practice and to determine that the roles of the parent and the subsidiary organizations are identified.

Annual agreements for service provided by one to the other should be signed by the chief staff and chief elected officer of each. These agreements should be arms-length transactions. For example, if a subsidiary organization leases office space from the association, rent should be computed at fair market value. Hours that an employee of one organization spends on the other's work should be recorded contemporaneously. Expenses that one pays for another should be recognized either as a receivable on the books of one and a payable on the other, or as a contribution given and received. An organization may offer reduced rent or complimentary services or staff, but the value of these needs to be recognized by each organization and recorded on the organization's Form 990.

Each organization's policies and procedures manuals should address the ways in which the finances and business operations are conducted and contain policies for assuring that each organization is accurately reporting its involvement with the other. The association executive must be comfortable that all inter-organization transactions are recorded correctly on the books of each. The annual service agreements should address who has oversight for the operations of the subsidiary corporation. There should be a clear understanding of who is responsible for engaging auditors and investment managers and reviewing their reports and performance.

Conclusion

Knowing what resources the association owns, what it owes, how it receives money, and what programs and services this money provides is key to an association executive's success. Ensuring that proper internal controls are in place to safeguard the association's assets and that independent periodic evaluation of its financial statements is being conducted will bring comfort to the executive and credibility to the association.

About the Author

Kathie Berry, CAE, is vice president of finance and administration for Associated Builders and Contractors, Arlington, Virginia. Kathie oversees the finance, human resources, and facilities management areas of ABC. She is an ASAE Fellow and has served as chairman of ASAE & The Center's Finance and Administration Section Council and chairman of the ASAE Ethics Committee. Active in ASAE & The Center, she has been a frequent presenter at programs for both organizations. She is a graduate of Mary Washington College and has received a CPA certification.

Review Questions

1. Discuss the three major financial statements for an association, addressing the information that is contained in each and the ways in which association executives would most effectively use each to manage and report on their associations' financial condition.

2. Why should an association have a reserve policy? How would an association executive establish such a policy, and what components would be addressed in the policy?

3. Discuss the value of internal controls and external oversight of an association's finances. What questions and considerations should an association executive address when determining whether such controls and oversight are sufficient?

Human Resource Management

Michael R. Losey, SPHR, CAE

OR-PROFIT CORPORATIONS MAY HAVE a competitive advantage because of their technology, a superior manufacturing process, or unique products and services protected by patents and trademarks. In trade and professional associations, however, success is primarily determined by how well members' needs and interests are met. Given the decreasing availability of volunteers and the increasing demands on their time, it often falls to association staff to identify and fulfill membership needs.

Such an organizational setting requires not only effective governance but also efficient, knowledgeable, and motivated personnel who are involved in the development, administration, and maintenance of member programs and services. The idea that employees are an association's most important resource is not mere rhetoric: The better the organization manages its human resources, the more competitive and successful an association can be in meeting members' needs.

Larger associations may have one or more HR professionals. This luxury, however, isn't enjoyed by most associations, according to *Policies and Procedures in Association Management 2006,* a study conducted by the ASAE and The Center for Association Leadership.[1] In fact, the median number of full-time employees in this survey was only 10, with 33 percent of respondents reporting only five full-time staff members or fewer. Only slightly more than one out of every four associations reported having a full-time human resource representative on staff.

---

[1] This survey includes responses ranging from approximately 600 to 1,000 associations, depending on the issue.

The professional demands and employment related risks and consequences associated with human resource management have also contributed to greater outsourcing of the various human resource management functions, especially in associations with a modest number of full-time employees.

Most Frequently Outsourced HR Functions

Function	Percent Outsourced
Payroll Administration	83%
Retirement Plan Administration	67%
Benefits Administration	40%

Source: ASAE Policies and Procedures in Association Management 2006

Instead, as in any small business, the association chief staff officer (CSO), office manager, or finance director typically has the responsibility for human resource management.

Few things will derail the career of a CSO, or other senior manager, faster than failing to create a work environment that promotes teamwork, communication, and effective use of staff resources. This chapter covers the key elements of a human resources program that can contribute to a favorable and productive work environment in associations.

Recruitment

As noted in the diagram, right, effective human resource management begins with recruiting the right people. And recruitment actually begins by carefully defining the duties and requirements of the position needing to be filled and making sure that interviewers can answer general questions about the association and specific employment requirements. A standard approach to employee recruitment is recommended to help ensure consistency in the evaluation of candidates. The people who will be interviewing candidates should formulate questions that focus on job-related

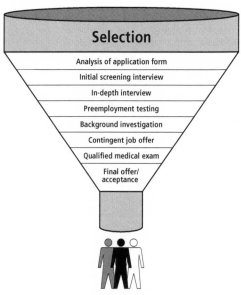

Selection
- Analysis of application form
- Initial screening interview
- In-depth interview
- Preemployment testing
- Background investigation
- Contingent job offer
- Qualified medical exam
- Final offer/ acceptance

Source: Society for Human Resource Management 2006 Learning System

requirements, determine the order in which they'll ask the questions, and review the candidate's resume or application for employment before the interview begins.

Most organizations have a formal employment application that collects consistent data from all candidates. A person's resume can be attached as a supplement to—rather than a substitute for—the employment application. Most employment applications ask for the following information:

- Personal data (name, address, telephone numbers)
- Education and training
- Special skills the applicant possesses
- Work history (in order of latest to first)
- Authorization to check references
- Employment and other waivers
- Equal employment and affirmative action statements
- Applicant's signature

Before turning to outside sources to fill vacancies, it is almost always a good practice to first determine who on your current staff may be interested and qualified for available positions. Customarily a department head would promote an individual within his or her department, usually consistent with individual development plans, without seeking candidates from elsewhere in the association. If no suitable candidates are available within the department, then the availability of the position opening is usually communicated by either *job posting or job bidding.*

Job posting is when the position that is available is "posted" or otherwise communicated to employees at the time the position is available. The advantage to this approach is that all employees are informed at the same time when the position is actually available and under current circumstances. The disadvantage is that the posting requirements can delay the selection process slightly, especially if it is anticipated that the internal posting procedure may not yield a qualified candidate and external recruitment will be required.

Job bidding is when employees are encouraged to consider their future promotional interests and apply at any time for one or more positions, should they become available. The advantage to this approach is that it encourages employees to think about their own careers and once their interests are known, if they have the potential, the association can provide additional guidance. For instance, there may be opportunities for a candidate to obtain the position's specific educational requirements, training, or developmental experiences (Example: Temporarily serving as vacation replacements so they can actually "test" the job). Of course, having a predetermined list of who is interested in the position helps speed the selection process.

The primary disadvantage to the job bidding process is that employees either do not take advantage of the process to identify their interests, or they never thought of a particular position until it became available.

The dominant practice is job posting.

Neither job posting or bidding should be utilized for management positions. Good candidates may not apply and/or may even resent the fact that their performance and career aspirations are not clearly enough known by key management. It is management's job to identify, select, and train future management.

Recruiting outside the association can be accomplished by:

- Alerting your current employees in the event they know and can recommend others who may have an interest in the position.[2]
- Running advertisements online or in newspapers, association journals, or magazines.
- Posting on national or specialty job boards, or on your own website.
- Reviewing resumes of individuals, including those who may have applied previously when the position was not available.[3]
- Retaining an executive search firm for senior positions.

Most organizations want to ensure their recruitment efforts reach candidates who reflect the diversity inherent in the workforce and community. Aside from the legal aspects of equal employment opportunity, experience has shown that the more diverse the organization, the better its opportunities for excellence.

Efforts to achieve diversity may be disadvantaged, and legal risks incurred unintentionally. For instance, alerting current employees to a vacancy in an attempt to solicit referrals could be discriminatory if all or most of your employees are white and might be expected to refer mostly white acquaintances or family members.[4] In such cases, special affirmative efforts must be taken to attract applicants from minorities, older workers, disabled workers, veterans, women, and other protected classes.

Interviewing

Once as many candidates as needed have been obtained, the field from which to make the final selection will need to be narrowed. The first step is reviewing all employment applications or resumes. Those who appear to have the necessary qualifications must be screened and reduced to an even smaller number of candidates who can be interviewed.

Telephone screening can be an effective way to confirm that candidates have not only the necessary qualifications and experience but are still available, willing to relocate (if necessary), understand the nature of the position, and have a reasonable level of

---

[2] Although this is normally a good procedure since current employees will rarely nominate someone for employment who is unlikely to perform well, ASAE & The Center for Association Leadership reports that only 11 percent of associations follow this practice with most being associations of greater than 100 employees.

[3] This requires some type of efficient process for inventorying resumes and applications for employment so that they can be retrieved when a particular position becomes available.

[4] As highlighted later in this chapter, the technical term for unintended but actual discrimination is *disparate impact* versus *disparate treatment,* which would be intentional discrimination.

interest. Failure to meet any one of these "knock-out" requirements may justify immediate termination of interest by either or both parties.

The actual interview represents the candidate's introduction to the association. Depending on how the interview goes, it may affect the candidate's willingness to continue discussions or accept employment, if offered. Applicants might also be current or potential members or people who are otherwise influential within the association and other industries. To conduct a good interview as well as maintain the association's professional standing, follow these interviewing guidelines:

- **Create a list of job-related interview questions.** By ensuring that all applicants for the same position are asked the same basic questions, you'll bring consistency to the interview process, which is practically and legally desirable.

- **Ask open-ended questions,** which prompt behavioral descriptions rather than a simple yes or no answer. For example, rather than asking, "Did you like your last job?" say, "Tell me what you liked about your last job."

- **Let the interviewee do most of the talking.** After an appropriate welcome and introduction to put the candidate at ease, move to questions you need answered. Listen carefully to the responses, take notes when appropriate, and provide verbal ("Yes, I understand" or "Good") and nonverbal reinforcement (such as nodding the head) to encourage the person to continue.

- **Avoid questions that might suggest discrimination.** Under Equal Employment Opportunity Commission (EEOC) and other guidelines, certain questions should not be asked. Also, under the Americans with Disabilities Act (ADA), employers with 15 or more employees must ensure that employment-related actions, terms, and conditions do not discriminate against any individual who has or could be perceived as having a disability. Also, a preemployment physical examination can only be conducted after the applicant for employment has been given a contingent job offer.

- **Stay focused on the job and its requirements,** not preconceived assumptions about what an applicant can or cannot do. For instance, someone who comes across well may have had many jobs and a lot of practice interviewing but isn't necessarily the best person for the job.

- **Balance "selling" the organization with keeping expectations realistic.** Although you want to position the association in the best possible light, avoid overstating or making promises that, if unfulfilled, may lead to employee dissatisfaction and turnover.

- **Obtain background information** to use during the reference checking process. Ask, for example, if the applicant had full accountability for developing a new membership development program or if he or she had only a contributory role. Have the applicant complete a reference checking authorization, if one doesn't appear on the employment application. Specifically, verify educational credentials required for the position (the most frequent applicant misrepresentation).

- **End on a cordial note.** If possible, inform the candidate of the next step and the expected timing. While the interview is still fresh in your mind, complete an evaluation form on the candidate.

Note: See sample forms at the end of this chapter that will assist in the interviewing process.

It is also important to know what questions can and cannot be asked during an employment interview.

Although federal EEO laws do not specifically prohibit any preemployment questions, the EEOC does look with "extreme disfavor" on questions about age, color, disability, national origin, race, religion, gender, or veteran status. Many state fair employment laws do expressly forbid certain types of questions. Following is a representative list of unacceptable and acceptable questions. It is NOT all-inclusive.

Topic	Unacceptable	Acceptable
Reliability and Attendance	• Number of children? • Who is going to baby-sit? • What religion are you? • Do you have pre-school age children at home? • Do you have a car?	• What hours and days can you work? • Are there specific times that you cannot work? • Do you have responsibilities other than work that will interfere with specific job requirements such as traveling? • Do you have a way to get to work?
Citizenship/ National Origin	• What is your national origin? • Where are your parents from? • What is your maiden name?	• Are you legally eligible for employment in the United States? • None • Have you ever worked under a different name?
For Reference Checking	• What is your father's surname? • What are the names of your relatives?	• None • None
Arrest and Conviction	• Have you ever been arrested?	• Have you ever been convicted of a crime? If so, when, where and what was the disposition of the case?
Disabilities	• Do you have any job disabilities?	• Can you perform the duties of the job you are applying for?
Emergency	• What is the name and address of the relative to be notified in case of an emergency?	• What is the name and address of the person to be notified in case of an emergency? (Request only after the individual has been employed.)

Topic	Unacceptable	Acceptable
Credit Record	• Do you own your own home? • Have your wages ever been garnished? • Have you ever declared bankruptcy?	• None • Credit references may be used if in compliance with the Fair Credit Reporting Act of 1970 and the Consumer Credit Reporting Reform Act of 1996. • None
Military Record	• What type of discharge did you receive?	• What type of education, training, and work experience did you receive while in the military?
Language	• What is your native language? Inquiry into use of how applicant acquired ability to read, write, or speak a foreign language.	• Inquiry into languages applicant speaks and writes fluently (if the job requires additional languages).
Organizations	• List all clubs, societies, and lodges to which you belong.	• Inquiry into applicant's membership in organizations which the applicant considers relevant to his or her ability to perform job.
Race or Color	• Complexion or color of skin. Coloring.	• None
Worker's Compensation	• Have you ever filed for worker's compensation? • Have you had any prior work injuries?	• None • None
Religion or Creed	• Inquiry into applicant's religious denomination, religious affiliations, church, parish, pastor, or religious holidays observed.	• None
Gender	• Do you wish to be addressed as Mr.?, Mrs.?, Miss?, or Ms.?	• None
Addresses	• What was your previous address? • How long did you reside there? • How long have you lived at your current address? • Do you own your own home?	• None • None • None • None
Education	• When did you graduate from high school or college?	• Do you have a high school diploma or equivalent? • Do you have a university or college degree?
Personal	• What color are your eyes, hair? • What is your weight?	• Only permissible if there is a bona fide occupational qualification.

Source: Society for Human Resource Management Information Center, 2006

Summary for Interviewing Persons with Disabilities

Do	Don't
Do ensure that the interview facility is accessible to people with disabilities.	Don't assume the person is able to shake your hand in greeting.
Do inform the applicant of any special parking available.	Don't lean on an applicant's wheelchair.
Do allow the applicant at least a full day to prepare for your interview.	Don't shout or raise your voice to a person who is hearing impaired.
Do identify the essential functions of the job.	Don't touch or talk to a seeing-eye dog.
Do make eye contact with the person.	Don't ask about a person's disability history.
Do talk directly to the person with the disability—not to an interpreter.	Don't ask about prior workers' compensation claims.
Do, after the initial greeting, sit down so that a person who uses a wheelchair can easily make eye contact.	Don't ask how the person became disabled.
Do ask about the person's ability to perform the job.	Don't ask how a person is going to get to work.

Source: Society for Human Resource Management, 2006

Checking References

The most common error made in the employment decision is hiring people based on what you "think" they can do versus what they have proven they have done. This is why checking prior employment experience is very important. As noted below, many associations do employment reference and background checking but with most checking limited to prior employment.

Does Your Organization Require Background Checks?

Type of Reference	Percent
Professional	73%
Educational	34%
Criminal	24%
Credit	12%
Other	6%

Source: ASAE Policies and Procedures in Association Management 2006

Unfortunately, some employers, usually upon the advice of their own legal counsel, hesitate to provide references on prior employees or limit their comments to verification of employment dates and position title. This position is usually unrelated to the merit and ability of an employer to defend against a claim of slander or libel and, instead, is usually based on avoiding any claim whatsoever and the cost of any defense, even if successful.

Reference checking, however, is receiving renewed attention given concerns about possible negligent hiring claims and the increasing number of cases where professional and managerial candidates have "fudged" their credentials, especially education. Also, to respond to these needs, many states have passed laws to protect employers from legal action if they give a truthful reference.

When giving references on former employees, "truth" is usually considered an absolute defense. However, to mitigate the opportunity for any former employee to make a claim, specify who and how references will be provided in order to promote consistent and balanced treatment. (Note: If a candidate is not provided employment because of a purchased reference or credit report, consistent with the Fair Credit Reporting Act, the employer must give the applicant notice of such a determination and the opportunity to review the report and make corrections, if applicable.)

Some employers, usually during the exit interview, will review the organization's policy on giving references with the terminating employee. Some even summarize what the employer will confirm about the position held, time employed, nature of termination, and performance.

Note: See sample forms at the end of this chapter.

Making the Offer

Thorough interviewing and reference checking assist in making a fair and unbiased employment decision. To reinforce a sincere interest in the candidate, make the job offer in person and follow up with a confirmation letter that includes employment-at-will rights.

An employment-at-will statement tells the candidate that his or her employment may be terminated at any time, by either party, for any reason. The notice might read as follows:

"Just as you retain the right to resign from your employment with XYZ Association without notice or cause, XYZ Association may elect to terminate your employment without notice or cause. Your employment is for no definite term, regardless of any other oral or written statement by any XYZ Association officer or representative, with the exception of an express written employment contract signed by the President."

The job offer should also indicate the date by which the employer expects a response.

Note: See sample forms at the end of this chapter.

Employment Orientation

Once the new employee has accepted the position and reports to work it is critical that the new employee be effectively welcomed and provided an orientation to the association that emphasizes his or her employment responsibility. Some suggest one of the most difficult things in every person's life is the first day on a new job. Understand the new employee's anxiousness and that "first impressions" do make a difference. Therefore, take the necessary time to do the job orientation professionally. In fact, the best approach is to spread the orientation out over several sessions, providing important reinforcement, rather than attempting to "cram" everything into one day.

Often overlooked or performed marginally, the orientation process should consist of two steps:

1. A *general orientation* provided by the human resource department or the manager who maintains employment records.

2. An *orientation checklist* used by supervisors to welcome the employee into the department and explain relationships to other departments, work hours, breaks, meal times, equipment, job description, safety and emergency procedures, and so forth.

Note: See sample forms at the end of this chapter.

Employee Performance

ASAE & The Center for Association Leadership reports in the latest edition of *Policies and Procedures in Association Management* that virtually all organizations with five or more full-time equivalents (FTEs) conduct formal job performance evaluations with most (82 percent) completing the evaluation annually.

An employee's worst nightmare—and a major contributor to an association's failure of full employee utilization—is the lack of clearly identified performance expectations. Factors typically included are expectations of quality and quantity of work, interpersonal skills, reliability, and other performance issues.

The job description can provide a good starting point for establishing job requirements.[5]

However, based on current operational plans or initiatives, more specific requirements may be identified for a particular year. Assuming the association has a strategic or operational plan, it is usually best to discuss that overall plan with all employees first and then establish departmental and individual goals that support the organization's goals.

It is important to identify such items at the beginning of a performance year so they can serve as a basis for performance evaluation throughout the year. This enables

---

[5] And ASAE & The Center for Association Leadership reports that 85 percent of associations have written job descriptions for all full-time positions.

managers to provide continuous feedback as opposed to evaluating an employee's performance only during his or her annual review. Supervisors can do this by regularly noting specific job-related behaviors (both positive and negative), providing reinforcement immediately, and making note of major issues and examples for future reference.

Performance Appraisals

Most organizations maintain a formal performance appraisal process. Almost universally, such reviews are conducted once a year. Some associations schedule formal reviews on the employee's employment anniversary date. Although this may tend to "spread out" the performance review requirements for supervision, this approach makes it almost impossible to relate employee reviews to annual departmental or organizational objectives.

Others schedule the performance review 12 months from the date of the last salary increase. This has the same advantages and disadvantage as the first method, plus it may also suggest all compensation adjustments will be on a 12-month basis when a shorter or longer interval may be justified.

The preferred option is to conduct all performance reviews after the close of the organization's fiscal or program year. This approach requires that all reviews be done during the same period. Although time-intensive, it offers the advantage of consistency in establishing the relative rankings of employees and permits better linking of performance to specific departmental and organizational goals. Also, as more associations continue to add employee incentive compensation programs, it is critical that any incentive or bonus payments be effectively linked to the association's performance.

Regardless of when the review is conducted, the important point is that it *is* conducted. Failure to conduct a performance review after making a commitment to do so is one of the most significant sources of employee dissatisfaction. Simply stated, most employees do a good job and appreciate being told so. If the association does not ensure that appropriate and timely performance reviews occur, employees may assume that future compensation adjustments will be delayed or otherwise affected.

The critical steps in conducting an effective performance appraisal are:

- Be prepared. Know the objectives and goals of the meeting.
- Have records of instances demonstrating both high and low performance.
- Pick an appropriate time and place—preferably a quiet, private spot.
- Make the employee feel at ease, and create a positive environment.
- Give balanced feedback, both positive and negative—but start with the positive.
- Ask questions and allow the employee to provide feedback.
- When discussing areas for improvement, talk about specific methods and objectives.

Writing Job Descriptions

Although the formats of job descriptions vary, they typically include the following components:

- **Summary**—a brief description that summarizes the overall purpose and objectives of the position, the results the worker is expected to accomplish, and the degree of freedom to act.
- **Essential functions**—the tasks, duties, and responsibilities of the position that are most important to get the job done.
- **Nonessential functions**—the desirable, but not necessary, aspects of the job.
- **Knowledge, skills, and abilities**—the specific minimum competencies required for job performance.
- **Supervisory responsibilities**—the scope of the person's authority, including a list of jobs that report to the incumbent.
- **Working conditions**—the environment in which the job is performed, especially any unique conditions outside a normal office environment.
- **Minimum qualifications**—the least amount of education and experience required to perform the job.
- **Success factors**—personal characteristics that contribute to an individual's ability to excel on the job.

Source: Society for Human Resource Management, 2006

- Discuss the employee's aspirations regarding future employment opportunities within the organization and, if possible, necessary actions that might be taken to help prepare him or her for such opportunities.
- After the performance appraisal, follow up with the employee to see how plans for the next year are proceeding within the given time frame.

Accurate performance appraisals are the cornerstone to the establishment of the relative ranking of employee performance; they assist in determining how employees are paid.

Determining a Compensation Policy

It is critical to link employee contribution and performance to compensation. Compensation differences among employees that are not supported by performance can be a greater source of dissatisfaction than an individual's perception that his or her compensation is not competitive when compared to the market.

Most associations are prepared to pay employees competitively, that is, the market value for similar positions. Accurate compensation and benefits information for the market also helps explain the association's compensation plan to the board of directors, especially when the association market differs from the trade or profession represented.

As reported in *Policies and Procedures in Association Management*, 40 percent of associations have a formal salary administration plan. Formal plans are more common in associations with greater than 100 employees. Nine out of ten associations (93 percent) with a staff of 100 or more maintain a formal salary administration plan.

When defining a compensation policy, start with the job description of each position. An accurate position description ensures that there is an understanding of the educational background, work experience, special skills, and other requirements related to the position. Such a description is not only helpful in recruitment but also helps to determine the relative worth of each position compared to all other positions within the association. Individual positions are then placed in different salary grades: A position in a higher-ranking grade has a higher relative value to the organization and the market than lower-rated positions. Positions within that same level or grade have the same relative value.

Within a particular grade there is customarily a range of salary rates (thus the name "rate range"). The mid-point of each range is usually the *market* rate. To establish the minimum or starting point of the range for employees meeting the minimum requirements of the position, the market rate is usually reduced by 20 percent. The maximum is also usually 20 percent greater than the mid-point. The range, therefore, can have as much as a 50 percent difference between the minimum and the maximum (120 - 80 = 40/80 = 50%). This provides for appropriate salary positioning in the range for the newly hired employee, the progressing employee, the fully qualified employee, and the employee who consistently performs above the requirements of the position.

Once positions are grouped into the necessary grades, representative *benchmark* positions are selected to determine their actual competitive relationship to the market. Benchmark positions are those that, for purposes of comparison in salary surveys, can also be found in other organizations. Examples might be receptionist, secretary, meetings and conference manager, publications director, financial director, and executive director. It is important, however, not to rely simply on titles. Instead, ensure comparability of these positions in terms of such organizational issues as size of budget, number of members and employees, and other factors reflecting overall accountability.

Determining the market to be surveyed depends on where your association would normally recruit for such a position. For instance, secretarial, administrative, and lower level exempt positions would be found in a local market—so that market is surveyed to create the salary range. Since the local market customarily supplies not-for-profit as well as for-profit organizations, compensation for such positions in for-profit organizations should also be included in the survey. Higher-level management positions would usually be recruited from a national market; therefore, national market data should be used.

Rather than burdening themselves with establishing such position relationships and conducting their own surveys, many associations use a consulting firm that has already invested in a job-evaluation process and perhaps conducted association-related compensation surveys. A consultant may be able to more cost effectively benchmark the association's positions with jobs in an existing survey, plus provide credibility to employees, management, and the board of directors.

Consultants and/or ASAE & The Center for Association Leadership's Salary and Benefits Survey can also provide guidance on compensation policy. For instance, if the survey of the market indicates that the association pays 5 percent below the market in relation to similar positions in other associations, the consultant would need to determine if that positioning is appropriate or should be adjusted. Some organizations, either because of their inability to pay or a stated compensation policy, intentionally operate at a level below the established market. Others may establish a compensation policy to pay 5 percent or 10 percent above the market in order to assist in employee recruitment and retention.

When appropriately administered, a compensation policy not only confirms that the association has a predetermined formal compensation program but also how it balances the shared needs of the company and the employees.

At a minimum a good compensation program should confirm to employees that they have approximately the same compensation opportunity within their current association as they could reasonably expect to find in other associations or firms in their market (local or national).

When the *pay practice* (the amount employees are actually paid) materially exceeds the policy (the amount the association wants to pay), corrective action may be required. The remedy is usually reducing future merit increase budgets until the proper position is re-established. If the pay practice is less than the compensation policy, the customary remedy is to petition the organization's board of directors for an *equity increase*—a one-time adjustment to make up for the differences between the stated policy and actual compensation practices. Such adjustments require a specific and continuing cost increase without assurances of improved or sustained association performance. However, some organizations may, therefore, provide a necessary equity increase but not all at once, instead spreading the adjustment(s) over several years or making them contingent upon the association's meeting selected operating objectives.

Salary Planning

Once the association has determined its compensation policy and compared it to actual practices, it is in a position to establish an annual compensation plan. Customarily, salary planning occurs along with or just before the association's annual budget process. In this way, the projected increase in salaries can be incorporated into the next year's overall operating plan. The rate ranges must also be adjusted depending on how the association's current compensation policy relates to the current market. In other words, if the current policy is to be equal to the current market and the market is anticipated to move 4.5 percent, then your association's policy line (rate ranges) would also move 4.5 percent. If, however, your policy line was already 3 percent greater than the market and the market was anticipated to move 4.5 percent; the rate ranges would be increased only 1.5 percent (4.5 percent minus 3 percent) so they would more closely approximate the market.

The overall salary allocation is subsequently distributed to departments and individuals based on their relative positioning within their rate range. A merit type of compensation program typically exists, under which an employee may receive more or less than other employees based on his or her position in the range and level of performance. A good practice is to allocate available monies by department, then by supervisor, and ultimately to individual employees, making certain that performance differences are recognized and the supervisor stays within the budgetary guidelines.

The actual increase would normally be scheduled for a subsequent date during the actual budget year based on the time since the last increase, employee performance, and relative positioning in the rate range. For instance, if an employee is at or below the minimum in a range, accelerated increases may be justified. Normal increases would be at a 12-month interval. Employees who might be paid above the mid-point but are contributing only at the mid-point in terms of performance may exceed 12 months in order to correct pay relationships over a reasonable period of time.

An alternative practice is to establish and actually grant all employee increases in various percentages but to grant all increases at the same time. Although the opportunity to differentiate between employees via the time period between increases is lost, supervisors and employees increasingly prefer such an approach.

Incentive Compensation

According to *Policies and Procedures in Association Management,* approximately 49 percent of associations have a incentive or cash bonus system, up from 18 percent reported ten years ago, in 1996. Also, 76 percent apply the program to all staff, up also from 66 percent in 1996.

Part of the justification for the growth of association incentive systems is the desire to link key staff's compensation to association performance. In addition, the board of directors may want to adopt a "corporate model" for association management or may be more accustomed to incentive-compensation programs linked to organizational performance.

Nonprofit organizations do not offer long-term incentive-compensation programs such as stock options.[6] The all-cash orientation for nonprofits is another justification for some organizations to seriously consider incentive compensation opportunities for at least key employees.

Incentive opportunities can be effectively used instead of an equity increase when the organization's compensation practice lags behind its compensation policy. In this way, the association can commit to increased compensation opportunities but link

---

[6] Frequently not-for-profit board positions are held by for-profit executives accustomed to for-profit incentive programs, which do not exist or are severely restricted in the not-for-profit sector. It is, therefore, important to ensure that the board, or at least the compensation committee of the board, is aware of these major compensation differences. Essential not-for-profit compensation is "all cash" with little or no deferral or long-term incentive opportunities.

them to specific performance objectives. For instance, if the executive compensation of key managers lags the market by 10 percent, that amount could be established as the *incentive target,* with more or less being paid based on specific performance criteria. If, however, the compensation practice is already close to or exceeds the market, an association wishing to establish an incentive program would need to decrease future base compensation increases in order to ensure total compensation (base plus bonus) is not excessive in relationship to the market for other associations that also provide an incentive opportunity.

If considering establishing some type of incentive compensation system or reviewing the effectiveness of existing systems, the following issues should be considered.

What "target" bonus will you offer? In other words what is the expected level of accomplishment in order to pay out some type of bonus, and will the target be the same for everyone?

For instance, consider if your target is only 5 percent, then is this enough to make a person or team work each day on dedicated objectives? This is especially the case for key executives. (Remember, "If you hold the stick too high, the dog will not jump.")

And is the same percentage incentive bonus for everyone the right target? Should the target not be greater for senior management and professionals for instance? This is normally the case and less for others—if your plan is ever extended to other employees, including non-exempt employees. This is not a status issue. It simply recognizes that non-supervisory employees are not usually considered for inclusion in such incentive bonus programs given their lesser opportunity to contribute substantially greater than their normal and more clearly defined job requirements.

On the other hand, senior managers and supervisors can sometimes contribute much more given their roles and management accountability. Therefore, should they not be more at risk and more of their compensation dependent on individual performance?

Usually what happens is that an association may have a "target" bonus opportunity of, for instance, 25 percent for the Chief Staff Officer of the association, possibly 15 percent for the directors, 8 percent for exempt managers and professionals and only 2 or 3 percent for the non-exempt employees.

Then you must have the metrics to pay the bonus. For instance, if the bonus is linked to growth in membership (as one of the criteria), what is the planned growth? Is it 5 percent, and what happens if only 4 percent is reached, or the goal is exceeded by gaining 7 percent? Usually some bonus is paid for substantial progress towards the objective—possibly 80 percent of this 5 percent goal. If staff achieved a 4 percent membership growth versus the full 5 percent objective, they would still get 80 percent of the target bonus. But since the membership piece is but a part of the total bonus, that has to be factored in also.

For instance, if the overall bonus target for the CSO was 25 percent—and there were several payout goals—you must determine how each goal is weighted. Almost never are they all the same level of importance/weighting.

For instance, consider the following example:

Incentive Plan Bonus Elements
1. Net Financial Performance
2. Net Cash Generation
3. New Member Recruitment
4. Membership Retention Rate
5. Member Satisfaction Survey

Here the association would be "paying out" based on these five objectives. But again, all are not necessarily "equal." In other words, 100 percent of the bonus objective is not divided by 5 to get 20 percent each. You can and should weight them.

Again, using the above example possibly the weightings could be as follows:

Bonus Weighting

Net Financial Performance	20%
Net Cash Generation	15%
New Member Recruitment	30%
Membership Retention Rate	20%
Membership Satisfaction Survey	15%
Total	**100%**

Then you must allocate these weightings to the allocation per class of participating employee. In the case of the CSO—who has in our example a 25 percent bonus target, the bonus payout at target would be:

Bonus Payout at Target

Net Financial Performance	20% x 25% target = 5% of base salary
Net Cash Generation	15% x 25% target = 3.75%
New Member Recruitment	30% x 25% target = 7.5%
Membership Retention Rate	20% x 25% target = 5%
Membership Satisfaction Survey	15% x 25% target = 3.75%
Total	**25% of base salary%**

So now you know that the membership gain piece is worth 7.5 percent of pay. If the CSO meets only 80 percent of that objective, and if the plan provides for a "threshold" benefit, then 80% x 7.75 = 4.8%.

So if the CSO is making $100,000 a year, this part of the bonus would equate to 4.8 percent of $100,000 or $4,800. Of course, if the association exceeded the membership growth plan of, for instance, 5 percent and made 6 percent then a larger bonus would be paid—20 percent greater since 6 percent versus 5 percent is 20 percent better than the plan. In that case the membership piece would be 120 percent of the plan, or 120 percent of the 7.5 percent target or 9 percent or $9,000 versus the $7,500 target for this factor.

You would then complete this same process for the remainder of the bonus objectives.

Again, you should check what is actually paid (Base salary plus bonus = total compensation). How does it compare to the market? For instance, you cannot say you will give a 10 percent bonus and then discount your salary rate range/salaries 10 percent expecting your people to get to the market rate by earning a bonus. A bonus is for achievement beyond normal requirements. This is not to say you cannot build in some discount, and most bonus paying companies do. For instance, position yourself for the 95 percentile of the market with a 10 percent bonus opportunity. Assuming that the people will make at least 5 percent bonus and possibly 10 percent, therefore, consistent with their performance, be paid slightly above the market. If they knock the socks off of the bonus and earn 15 percent they will be 10 percent above the market. And don't forget if the bonus is also linked to financial performance, then the bonus is frequently self funding.

These steps are usually preferred so that the bonus is not just an "on or off" thing, e.g. you get it or you don't! Making associations work well can be multifaceted and can be influenced by conditions beyond employee effort and motivation, so judgment must also be incorporated into the evaluation process. But evaluations must also track performance, or they are just another way to provide cash and are hard to defend to a board of directors or the membership.

Executive Compensation Issues

Nonprofit organizations are subject to special regulations that, for instance, do not make available the customary nonqualified retirement options that exist in the private sector. Under the current tax code, there is a limitation of $220,000[7] in program compensation that can be used for the determination of any pension. Executives and other members of management who earn more than $220,000—or are projected to earn that much by retirement age—may therefore be disadvantaged in terms of protecting a targeted income replacement ratio[8] unless other arrangements are created. The terms are typically spelled out in an employment contract.

Key elements of employment contracts may include:

- Term of employment (beginning and ending contract dates, renewal provisions).
- Salary, incentive compensation, benefits, special conditions, "perks."
- Duties of the position.
- Executive to devote full time to organization; any noted exceptions.
- Confidentiality of proprietary information.
- Reimbursement of expenses, memberships, and so forth.

---

[7] These amounts are customarily changed by the IRS each year.

[8] A targeted income replacement ratio is that percentage of final pay that an association, by policy, would attempt to provide an employee through the association's pension plan, including anticipated Social Security benefits.

- Termination of employment (for cause, without cause, indemnities, notice, and so forth).
- Executive not to engage in specified competitive activities.

Employee Benefits

The average cost of employee benefits in most organizations can easily exceed 30 percent of payroll. This, of course, is not an insignificant cost and must be effectively managed.

Effective benefit management begins with reviewing all benefits provided employees to determine their competitive positioning. As with salary planning, is the association policy to position its benefit program approximately at, above, or lower than other associations? In addition, accurate cost accounting must be accomplished to fully appreciate the cost of the various benefits (retirement, health insurance, dental, life insurance, time off, and so forth).

As in compensation planning, many associations lack the professional expertise to address such issues. For instance, an association's policy to provide fully paid health insurance for employees' dependents may put the association at a disadvantage compared to another employer that requires a premium contribution from the employee. Where the association requires no premium, and a spouse's plan requires a premium contribution, it invites the employee's spouse and dependents to elect the association plan, thus increasing employee and dependent participation and utilization of the plan and invariably greater cost.

Many associations are finding health care costs materially affecting their total employee costs, especially with direct wage costs possibly increasing at a rate of 4 percent or less, and their health care costs increasing at more than 10 percent a year.

This has required many associations to either discontinue health insurance coverage or to seek ways to decrease the employer's cost burden. Most frequently utilized practices are to "shift" some of the cost to employees, hoping to make them "better consumers." Examples are:

- Employee contributions towards the premium costs
  - Higher subsidies for employees
  - Lower subsidies or no coverage for dependents
- Higher deductibles
- Substituting "non-duplication" of benefits for "coordination of benefits"[9]
- Co-payments linked to a maximum "out-of-pocket" employee cost per individual covered
- Use of generic drugs and/or purchasing via mail order

---

[9] Non-duplication of benefits differs from COB in that the covered employee or dependent only receives reimbursement up to what the secondary employer would have paid and not total out-of-pocket employee costs.

- *Case management* for major illnesses and disabilities[10]
- Incorporating a defined contribution element into employees' group health care plans. This defined contribution element is usually represented by one or more of the following:
  - Flexible spending accounts (FSAs)
  - Health care reimbursement arrangements (HRAs)
  - Health savings accounts (HSAs)
    - When an employer adds a defined contribution element to a group health plan, it achieves two objectives:
      1. Limiting the employer's liability for that portion of the plan to the amount of the employer's annual contribution to the defined contribution element.
      2. Shifting to the plan participant the responsibility for appropriately using the defined contribution funds for health care goods and services.

To date, few employers have converted their active employee group health plans entirely into defined contribution plans. Most employers modify their existing plans to increase deductibles and co-payments and include a defined contribution element to offset those increases. This combination reduces the employer's overall liability for the group health plan while still providing comprehensive health care coverage for employees and their families.

Another costly benefit is providing employees with pensions. Until the last 15 years, the traditional method was a defined benefit plan under which the employer promises a retirement benefit, usually a function of employee length of service and earnings. It is called a defined benefit because the employer promises to pay the benefit at retirement and assumes responsibility for the funding of the future pension.[11]

However, if the employer investments of the money set aside in the employee retirement trust fail to meet expectations and/or earnings assumptions upon which funding is planned, then the company must make up any financial short-fall.

To avoid the uncertainty of such long-term pension costs, many companies have installed or changed existing plans to a "defined contribution plan" (401(k) and related plans). Under this approach, employees decide what percentage of their salary goes into the plan, subject to the association's plan limitations and IRS regulations. The employee's eventual benefit depends on how their investments perform.

---

[10] Case management is the practice of affirmative intervention by the insurance administrator to provide necessary medical treatment in a fashion that is not only consistent with the patient's needs but also the personal needs and life requirements. For instance, consider a stroke patient who would prefer to be at home but needs a hospital bed, enlarged bathroom door, special toilet, and other special facilities. The health plan may cover such costs related to equipment and remodeling in order to provide better care and at the same time do so at much less cost than maintaining the patient within a hospital.

[11] Such plans customarily do not require an employee contribution.

Customarily, employers encourage employee participation in the plan by offering to also make a contribution to the employee's account on some type of matching basis.

Legislation passed in August 1996 (effective for plan years beginning after December 31, 1996) allows employers to set up "Savings Incentive Match Plans for Employees" (SIMPLE plans), including 401(k) plans. Under the "simple" plan, employers are required to match employee contributions on a dollar-for-dollar basis for the first 3 percent of an employee's compensation.

Because of the complex administrative requirements, including determining what investment options will be offered, transfers between funds, regular reporting, discrimination testing, and fiduciary requirements, most associations choose to have 401(k) plans administered by an outside consultant.

HR Policy

In addition to establishing terms and conditions of employment, such as compensation and benefits, every association should take time to articulate its HR policy towards employees. This is not just a manual of policies and procedures but rather the overall approach to employee relations. At a minimum, HR policy should represent a sincere definition of how management intends to define employee relationships and their role in advancing the interest of the association. This can range from broad policies that establish a supportive employee culture to specific policies or procedures where supervisory guidance is necessary to promote consistency of application, fair treatment, and, in some cases, compliance.

Customarily, specific policies exist for such areas as working hours and attendance, paid and unpaid time off, corrective disciplinary procedures, employees' rights of appeal, and health and safety regulations. Sample policies are available from a number of sources. Also, some software programs provide sample policies that can be modified to suit an organization's particular requirements.

Corrective Discipline

The word *discipline* actually comes from the root word "disciple," which means, "to teach." Discipline, therefore, is a "teaching and counseling" attempt to correct inappropriate behavior or poor job performance. The hope is that most situations can be corrected by promptly bringing the area of needed improvement to the employee's attention.

Lack of improvement generally results in the escalation of disciplinary action, thus reinforcing the seriousness of the performance issue. Sanctions could include extending initial verbal counseling or reprimands to a more formal level of documentation. If the employee cannot make the necessary corrections or remains indifferent to the need for improvement, discharge is usually justified. Immediate discharge can also be justified if the employee commits a severe breach of employment policy.

Again, an employer should always protect the right to terminate an employee by establishing and maintaining an Employment At Will Policy. Use the following check-list to investigate situations before taking corrective disciplinary action:

- Thoroughly investigate and review the facts.
- Find and obtain statements from witnesses, if applicable.
- Talk with the employee to get his or her perspective on the situation.
- Obtain related, current, and prior documentation, if applicable.
- Summarize and outline the facts of the most recent situation.
- Examine the employee's previous disciplinary history and work record.
- Examine records of employees with similar infractions and compare the discipline imposed in those situations.
- Allow adequate time for all parties to review the details of the offense.
- Determine if the employee is in a protected class. If so, determine if disparate treatment or disparate impact has occurred.
- If appropriate, review the facts of the investigation with an objective third person.
- Pinpoint the basis for corrective action or termination.
- Determine if the discharge violates any federal or state laws: employment at will, unfair dismissal, equal employment opportunity, disabilities, and veterans' protection rights.
- Discuss your decision with an HR professional, employment attorney, corporate association counsel, or a professional society with human resource expertise before implementing the final decision.
- Determine the best time and place to conduct the disciplinary interview.
- Carry out the corrective discipline or discharge in a calm but direct and compassionate manner. Consider including a witness in this meeting, if appropriate.
- Document what was said and actions taken during the disciplinary interview.
- If the employee was terminated, arrange for the employee to obtain personal belongings, return company property, and leave the property promptly, without creating an awkward and embarrassing situation.

Employee Development

Employees' ultimate opinion of their association as a good and productive place to work rests not only by how they are treated daily but also whether their employer demonstrates a sincere interest in their continued training and development. The best way to accomplish this is to train employees to not only do their current job but also meet the future requirements of positions for which they may be considered. Training of employees should normally be done on an individual basis, recognizing the wide range of individual development needs. Examples of individual development programs might be giving effective presentations or improving communication and interpersonal skills. When an association-wide common developmental need exists, training can be delivered to all staff in a more structured and cost effective way. Examples of more generalized training topics include effective report writing, sexual harassment and diversity training, or understanding the association's finances.

Managerial training is especially critical because employees' satisfaction with their jobs frequently reflects little more than the treatment they receive from their immediate supervisor. Such training includes a complete understanding of the association's policies and procedures, especially as they relate to its human resource management policies. Emphasis should also be given to consistency of treatment, recognizing that frequently it is not how generous a policy is but how fairly it is applied that determines employee satisfaction. Effective communication and interpersonal skills are also important characteristics that contribute to effective leadership.

Most supervisory and employee development, however, occurs on the job, not in the classroom. Therefore, managers should learn to carefully identify the individual development needs of each subordinate and tailor a plan to meet those needs. The most effective development tool is to identify on-the-job projects and responsibilities through which the employee can develop new skills and gain important experience.

Feedback Mechanisms

Providing association members with good customer service requires a total team effort to ensure that departments are not operating independently. In turn, each member of the team must understand how his or her work fits into the total package of products and services offered to the membership.

Employee feedback can enhance individual contributions and foster teamwork. It's best obtained through *effective supervision*—especially when the supervisor has a good appreciation of how employees feel about their work and the association. A more formalized approach to feedback uses an *employee attitude survey,* particularly effective when the association can benchmark its results against those obtained by similar organizations. In addition, when done at regular intervals, surveys can be benchmarked against the association's employee responses as gathered over time. A note of caution: Attitude surveys require substantial follow-up and should not be attempted unless top management has a sincere commitment to pursue the issues that employees indicate need attention.

State of the society (or association) meetings, if conducted regularly, can help employees deepen their understanding of their employer's activities and operations. For example, employees may have a poor understanding of the interests and nature of the membership, the association's revenue and expenses, or the role of unrelated business income. One large association typically holds such meetings immediately after its board of directors meetings using much of the CSO's board presentation. This discipline serves to not only promptly update employees on the status of major organizational objectives but also summarizes actions taken by the board.

Another mechanism is for the CEO to regularly conduct informal *koffee klatch* meetings with a small group of selected employees. Such meetings typically include a brief update by the CEO, followed by an opportunity to actively solicit employee questions and suggestions. Over time, such informal meetings build the expectation that the association's top management is not aloof and is willing to share information and seek direct employee input and feedback.

Similarly, *skip level interviews* are an effective technique for "staying in touch" with departmental employees who do not report directly to the department head. Under this approach managers informally meet with subordinates two levels below their direct level of supervision to solicit direct feedback.

Emerging Trends

The following trends have emerged in human resource management and bear watching:

- **Workplace Diversity.** As more women and people of many ethnic groups enter the workforce, employers are making an effort to value the unique contributions that diverse individuals and groups have to offer. Respect for individual differences enriches the work environment and brings with it new ideas and ways of working.

  Employers who focus on diversity believe that differences among people can contribute to the success of the business and that all employees, regardless of their differences, have the same opportunities to contribute. Employers who are cognizant of the changing workforce take steps to not only ensure diversity as an objective in recruitment and promotion but also to build an awareness of diversity issues into their workplaces. This includes offering diversity-training programs that promote respect and teamwork among staff members.

- **Telecommuting.** As the range of computer and communications options grows, employers find that some employees can accomplish their tasks away from the traditional workplace. Using a personal computer and high-speed networks, employees can access files remotely and assist members and customers from a home or satellite office. Many of these employees, for various family and personal reasons, prefer to work from home, at least part of the time. Disadvantages to telecommuting include the costs of setting up equipment in employees' homes; difficulty in assessing employee performance when managers do not see day-to-day operations; and difficulty in determining the hours actually worked by an employee. Too, if an employee is injured while working at home, it may be difficult to ascertain whether the employee is entitled to workers' compensation. Employees may feel neglected and "out of the loop" and find it difficult to establish boundaries between working and other tasks at home.

  Still, telecommuting employees can save on transportation, parking, and clothing costs; decrease their stress levels; and assist with family care needs.

Telecommuting may allow employees more flexibility and control over their work and lives. For employers, it can help retain talented employees while reducing expenses for office space and parking.

- **Flextime.** This practice allows employees to vary their schedules within limits established by the association. Most employers set a "core" time when all employees must be at work, for example, between 10 a.m. and 3 p.m. Outside the core hours, employees may choose to work from 7 a.m. to 4 p.m., or from 9 a.m. to 6 p.m. Usually employers ask staff to set a definite schedule but allow occasional changes.

  Some employers allow employees to work four 10-hour days and have one day off each week—or work nine days for 80 hours in a two-week period, with a day off every two weeks. This variation on flextime is usually called a compressed workweek.

  Flextime, if matched to the association's culture and business needs and managed well, can give employees more scheduling freedom and allow employers to experience increased productivity and coverage without increased costs.

- **Employee Privacy.** Employees have become increasingly concerned about their right to privacy, as employers have developed the means to collect more information. Electronic mail messages, for example, may appear to be private correspondence between employees yet are often read by management or MIS employees in the course of their duties. Such messages can also be retrieved even after being deleted and have been used as evidence in court.

  Employees should not expect privacy in the normal course of business. E-mail, voice mail, desk space, locker space, and the like, are property of the organization, not of the individual. Special efforts, however, should be taken to keep personnel records private, available only to management on a need-to-know basis and available for review by employees on request. Medical records should always be kept private—and separate—from other files.

- **Independent Contractors.** An independent contractor is someone hired to do a particular task, according to his or her own methods, and not subject to employer control except for the result. Employers do not pay Social Security taxes, unemployment taxes, health benefits, and so forth, for independent contractors.

  Determining whether an individual is an employee or an independent contractor is critical for an employer's tax reporting and withholding obligations.

The Internal Revenue Service makes specific distinctions between employees and independent contractors. Factors to consider when testing whether a person is an independent contractor are: extent of control of employer over the details of the work; whether the person is engaged in a distinct occupation or business; the kind of work to be performed; the skill required for the work; whether the employer supplies the tools and location; the length of time the person is employed; the method of payment (hourly or by the job); whether the work is a regular part of the employer's business;

Federal Labor Laws By Number of Employees

1-14 Employees
- Civil Rights Act of 1964 and Civil Rights Act of 1991, Title VII (for employment agencies and labor organizations). See 15-19 for other employers.
- Consumer Credit Protection Act of 1968
- Employee Polygraph Protection Act (1988)
- Employee Retirement Income Security Act (ERISA) of 1974 (if company offers benefits)
- Equal Pay Act of 1963
- Fair Credit Reporting Act (1970)
- Fair Labor Standards Act (FLSA) (1938)
- Federal Insurance Contributions Act of 1935 (FICA) (Social Security)
- Health Insurance Portability and Accountability Act (HIPAA) of 1996 (if company offers benefits)
- Immigration Reform & Control Act (IRCA) (1986)
- Labor-Management Relations Act (Taft-Hartley) of 1947
- National Labor Relations Act (NLRA) of 1935
- Uniform Guidelines of Employee Selection Procedures (1978)
- Uniformed Services Employment & Re-employment Rights Act of 1994

11-14, add
- Occupational Safety & Health Act (OSHA) (1970) (maintain record of job related injuries and illnesses)

15-19, add
- Civil Rights Act of 1964 Title VII, Civil Rights Act of 1991
- Title I, Americans with Disabilities Act of 1990 (ADA)

20-49, add
- Age Discrimination in Employment Act (ADEA) (1967)
- Consolidated Omnibus Budget Reconciliation Act of 1985 (COBRA)

50 or more, add
- Family and Medical Leave Act of 1993 (FMLA)
- EEO-1 Report filed annually w/EEOC if organization is a federal contractor

100 or more, add
- Worker Adjustment & Retraining Notification Act of 1988 (WARN)
- EEO-1 Report filed annually w/EEOC if organization is not a federal contractor

Federal Contractors, add
- Executive Orders 11246 (1965), 11375 (1967), 11478 (1969)
- Vocational Rehabilitation Act of 1973
- Drug Free Workplace Act of 1988
- Vietnam-Era Veterans Readjustment Act of 1974
- Davis Bacon Act of 1931
- Copeland Act of 1934
- Walsh-Healy Act of 1936
- Service Contract Act (1965)

Source: Society for Human Resource Management, 2006

the intent of the parties; the opportunity for profit or loss; and whether the employer is in a distinct business. By classifying individuals correctly, the employer can avoid fines, penalties, and additional taxes.

Federal Labor Laws

All organizations are expected to operate within the law. The breadth and scope of employment-related legislation may create a situation where organizations, especially small ones, find it difficult to fully understand and comply with current laws. Outlined below are the basic requirements of the laws that affect an overwhelming majority of small businesses and associations. (Please recognize that organizations must also be aware of municipal and state laws that may regulate terms and conditions of employment, discrimination, workers' compensation, family medical leave provisions, and so forth.)

Labor Law Summaries

Consumer Credit Protection Act (1 or more employees)

The Consumer Credit Protection Act prohibits employees from being terminated for garnishments for any one indebtedness. Although two or more garnishments from separate organizations allow an employer to terminate, exercise care to prevent disparate impact if the employees being terminated are mostly women and minorities. Also some states may have additional limitations on an employer's opportunity to discipline an employee with a history of garnishments.

Penalties for non-compliance: fine of up to $1,000, one-year imprisonment, or both.

Employers who have a legitimate business need to evaluate and monitor employee credit problems, and who use credit reports to do so, should also be aware of the Fair Credit Reporting Act. The FCRA requires employers who deny employment on the basis of a credit report to so notify the applicant and to provide the name and address of the consumer reporting agency used.

Penalties for non-compliance: actual damages, punitive damages, and attorneys' fees.

Americans with Disabilities Act (15 or more employees)

ADA is a federal anti-discrimination law that prohibits private employers, state and local governments, employment agencies, and labor unions from discriminating against qualified individuals with disabilities in job application procedures, hiring, firing, advancement, compensation, job training and other terms, conditions and privileges of employment.

This law is designed to remove barriers that prevent qualified individuals with disabilities from enjoying the same employment opportunities available to people without disabilities. When a qualified applicant's disability creates a barrier to employment opportunities, the ADA requires employers to consider whether a "reasonable accommodation" could remove the barrier.

An individual has a disability under ADA when he or she:

- Has a physical or mental impairment that substantially limits one or more major life activities.
- Has a record of such an impairment or is regarded as having such an impairment.

Someone who currently uses illegal drugs does *not* have a disability under the ADA. Tests for drug screening are the only pre-employment medical tests allowed under the ADA. Addiction to illegal substances *in the past* is a covered disability as long as the person is not a current illegal drug user.

A qualified individual is one who, with or without a reasonable accommodation, can perform the essential functions of a job. A reasonable accommodation is a modification that will allow a person with a disability to perform the job's essential functions. A reasonable accommodation may include but is not limited to:

- Making facilities used by employees readily accessible and usable by persons with disabilities
- Job restructuring
- Modifying work schedules
- Reassignment to a vacant position
- Acquiring or modifying equipment or devices
- Adjusting or modifying examinations, training materials, or policies
- Providing qualified sign language interpreters

A reasonable accommodation does *not* include lower production or quality standards. Also, the employer need not provide an accommodation that would impose an "undue hardship" upon it.

Penalties for non-compliance: The Equal Employment Opportunity Commission enforces ADA, and the penalties are the same as for violations of Title VII of the Civil Rights Act, with maximum amounts for intentional discrimination mandated by the Civil Rights Act of 1991.

For more information: Call the Job Accommodation Network at (800) 526-7234.

Federal Insurance Contributions Act of 1935 (1 or more employees)

Virtually all employers and employees are covered by FICA—otherwise known as Social Security. It provides employees with retirement income, as well as income security in the event of disability for surviving members of deceased workers. It also provides hospital insurance for disabled and retired persons (age 65 or over) and, for those who elect additional coverage, also medical and prescription coverage.

Social Security benefits are financed by employee and employer contributions made at rates set by the IRS and the Social Security Administration. Mandatory employee contributions are withheld from wages; employer contributions are deposited on a regular schedule of payments. All monies deposited with the IRS are held in a Social Security Administrative Trust Fund from which all benefit payments to eligible retirees and others are drawn. All wages up to the "taxable wage base" (set each year) are subject to withholding.

For more information: Call the IRS at (800) TAX-FORM or the Social Security Administration at (800) 772-1213.

Fair Labor Standards Act (1938) (1 or more employees)

Most employers are covered by the Fair Labor Standards Act (FLSA), which applies to public agencies and businesses engaging in interstate commerce or providing goods and services for commerce. The FLSA provides guidelines on employment status, child labor, minimum wage, overtime pay, and record-keeping requirements. It determines which employees are exempt from the act (not covered by it) and which are non-exempt (covered by the act).

Penalties for non-compliance: The U.S. Department of Labor administers FLSA. Employers who willfully or repeatedly violate the act may be penalized up to $1,000 per violation. Plaintiffs can recover back pay and liquidated damages if the violation was willful. The Secretary of Labor may sue to enjoin the interstate shipment of goods of an employer who violates the act. Penalties are higher for child labor violations.

Specific provisions include the following:

The Minimum Wage

This act establishes the least amount of pay, or minimum hourly compensation, that an employer pay an employee. The minimum wage is subject to review by Congress and may change from time to time. The Department of Labor's website at http://www.dol.gov/esa/whd/flsa lists the current federal wage requirements. (Note: Many states have higher minimum wage provisions that supersede the FLSA.)

Overtime

Employees covered by the Fair Labor Standards Act must be paid at least one-and-one-half times their regular rate for all hours worked in excess of 40 in a week (seven consecutive days). The regular rate of pay must be determined to calculate overtime pay; it includes the base rate, bonuses, commissions, piece rates, incentives, shift differentials, and training pay.

The regular rate of pay excludes: pay for time not worked (vacation, sick time, holidays); contributions to pension and insurance plans; gifts or employer discretionary bonuses; distributions from profit-sharing plans that meet Wage and Hour regulations; contributions to bona fide thrift and savings plans; and longevity pay. Tests for Exemption from the overtime provisions of the FLSA follow.

Effective August 24, 2004, the Wage and Hour Division of the Department of Labor issued new rules. Under these new rules overtime protection is ensured to any employee with a quoted salary of less than $23,600 per year or $455 per week.

In addition, the separate long and short tests based on employee's weekly wages were eliminated.

New exemption rules, where the employer has no obligation to pay overtime, were also issued. Under those rules much of the determination as to whether a job is exempt or non-exempt depends on what is called the "primary duty" of the position. A primary duty is the most important duty of the job. Generally the primary duty must require the exercise of discretion and independent judgment in matters of significance. Matters of significance refer to the level of importance or consequence of the work performed.

For purposes of the "Executive Exemption" the executive must:
- Manage an enterprise or a department or subdivision.
  - Direct the work of at least two or more full-time employees.
  - Have authority to hire and fire.
  - Affect promotion decisions.

For purposes of the "Administrative Exemption" the employee must:
- Have a primary duty involving performance of office or nonmanual work directly related to the management or general business operations of the employer or the employer's customers.

For purposes of the "Professional Exemption Type 1" or "Learned Professionals" the employee:
- Have a primary duty that requires advanced knowledge that is in a field of science or learning and is acquired by prolonged instruction.
  - Work is intellectual in nature and requires exercise of discretion and judgment.

For purposes of the "Professional Exemption Type 2" or "Creative Professionals" the employee must:
- Meet minimum salary requirements.
- Have a primary duty performing work that requires invention, imagination, originality, or talent.
- Perform in a recognized field of creative or artistic development.

There is also a "highly compensated employee" exemption. Under this provision an employee must:
- Make a salary of $100,000 or more.
- Perform one of the job duties of an exempt administrative, executive, or professional.

Computer employees can also be exempt if:
- They meet the salary minimum with a salary of $455 per week or $27.63 per hour.
- Employees are not subject to deductions inconsistent with salary basis requirements.
- Primary duties fall within a specified list.

Outside sales personnel must:
- Have a primary duty involving making sales or obtaining orders and contracts.
- Be customarily and regularly engaged away from the employer's place of business.

Improper Deductions:
- Employers who make improper deductions may lose the exemption if they did not intend to pay on a salary basis. Example: An exempt employee is normally not subject to deductions for illness in less than full-day increments although for purposes of complying with FMLA an exception may occur.
- Blue Collar workers remain nonexempt no matter how highly they are compensated if they perform work involving repetitive operations with their hands, physical skill, and energy.

Employee Record Requirements

FLSA requires employers to maintain the following employee records. *(Note: State requirements may be more strict):*

- Name, address, date of birth if under 19
- Day and hour on which the work week begins
- Number of hours worked each day and total number of hours worked each week
- Inclusions and exclusions from regular rate of pay
- Total daily or weekly straight time earnings
- Total overtime earnings
- Total deductions from earnings
- Total wage each period
- Date of payment, amount, and period included in payment
- **Hours of Work:** All time spent in an employee's principal duties and all essential ancillary activities must be counted as work time. Principal duties include productive tasks. Work time is compensable if expended for the employer's benefit, if controlled by the employer, or if allowed by the employer. Activities that occur before or after an employee's principal duties need not be counted as work time. Some examples:
  - *Clothes changing and washing:* Not compensated unless done at the workplace at the employer's request or because of the nature of the principal duties, such as handling toxic chemicals.
  - *Travel time:* Travel to and from work is not generally compensable. Travel in the course of the day, such as from one job site to another, is compensable work time. Travel out of town may be compensable, depending on when it occurs (occurs during the time the employee would have worked) and whether the trip is overnight.
  - *Meal periods and breaks:* Meal periods are not compensable if they last for more than half an hour; if the employee is relieved of all duties; and if the

employee is free to leave the workstation. Breaks of 15 minutes or less are considered work time and are compensable.

– *Training time:* Training is not considered work time if all these conditions are met: It is outside of regular work hours; attendance is voluntary; no productive work is performed there; and the training is not directed toward making the employee more proficient in his or her current job.

• **Child Labor:** The FLSA prohibits the employment of oppressive child labor and regulates the hours that children may permissibly work. The requirements become more strict as the age decreases. Children are divided into three groups for regulatory purposes: 16- and 17-year-olds, 14- and 15-year-olds, and all younger children. The hours that they may work and the occupations at which they may work vary from group to group.

Anyone under the age of 18 is considered a child. States frequently regulate the employment of minors; the requirements vary.

Consolidated Omnibus Budget Reconciliation Act of 1985 (20 or more employees)

COBRA mandates that employers (with more than 20 employees on 50 percent of the business days of the previous year) continue healthcare coverage for employees enrolled in their healthcare plan for a certain number of months (usually 18) after the employees have lost healthcare benefits—usually through termination of employment, a reduction in hours, or a life event (such as a divorce) that makes an employee or dependent ineligible for the benefit plan.

All people covered by a plan, including spouses and children, are eligible for COBRA. Healthcare continuation coverage premiums are generally paid in full by the employee, and the employer may charge the employee 2 percent of the premium for administrative costs. The American Recovery and Reinvestment Act (ARRA) of 2009 established a short-term, employer-provided subsidy for employees who involuntarily lost their job. COBRA mandates the length of time employees have to elect COBRA benefits, response time for employers, and what notices must be provided.

Penalties for non-compliance: Under ERISA, for failure to provide notice, the penalty is $100 per day per violation until notice is provided to employees or beneficiaries. Under the Internal Revenue Code, excise tax of $100 is charged per day per violation for each qualified beneficiary during the non-compliance period. A qualified beneficiary who did not receive coverage can bring a lawsuit against the employer.

Equal Pay Act (1 or more employees)

This amendment to the Fair Labor Standards Act prohibits employers from discriminating between men and women by paying one gender more than the other "for equal work on jobs the performance of which requires equal skill, effort, and responsibility, and which are performed under similar working conditions."

Penalties for non-compliance: Back pay for up to two years (or three years if the violation was willful) and liquidated damages in an amount equal to back pay.

Employee Retirement Income Security Act of 1974 (1 or more employees)

ERISA sets requirements for the provision and administration of employee benefit plans such as healthcare, profit sharing, and pension plans. ERISA was passed to protect the interests of participants and their beneficiaries in employee benefit plans by establishing standards of conduct, responsibility, and obligations for plan fiduciaries.

ERISA does not force employers to create employee benefit plans. It does set standards in the areas of participation, vesting of benefits, and funding for existing and new plans. ERISA requires companies that meet certain criteria to file a form (Form 5500) annually with the Internal Revenue Service that discloses basic information about each benefit plan, such as expenses, income, assets, and liabilities. ERISA also requires employers to submit a Summary Annual Report to plan participants and beneficiaries.

Penalties for non-compliance: The IRS and the Department of Labor jointly enforce ERISA requirements. Willful violations result in criminal and civil penalties.

Age Discrimination in Employment Act (20 or more employees)

The Age Discrimination in Employment Act of 1967 (ADEA) prohibits discrimination against workers aged 40 and over in any employment or employment-related decision. One of the act's main provisions is that employers, with few exceptions, cannot force an employee to retire. Voluntary retirements are allowed; however, specific conditions must be met to avoid violation of the act.

Penalties for non-compliance: Employees may be awarded back pay, reinstatement, retroactive seniority, and attorney's fees. Liquidated damages equal to the amount of back pay may be awarded if the violation is willful.

Family and Medical Leave Act (50 or more employees)

FMLA allows employees who have met minimum service requirements (12 months employed by the company with 1,250 hours of service in the preceding 12 months) to take up to 12 weeks of unpaid leave for either:

- A serious health condition
- To care for a family member with a serious health condition (26 weeks if the family member is a member of the Armed Forces)
- The birth of a child
- The placement of a child for adoption or foster care

Although there is no complete list of serious health conditions, six categories must be evaluated to determine if an employee (or their family member) has such a condition. The determination is made by the employee's (or family member's) doctor on the "Certification of Health Care Provider" form. Those categories are: hospital care, absence plus treatment, pregnancy, chronic conditions requiring treatments, permanent or long-term conditions requiring supervision, and multiple treatments (non-chronic conditions).

FMLA requires employers to allow their eligible employees to take up to 12 weeks of unpaid leave for the above circumstances; provide continued health benefits during leave on the same basis the individual enjoyed while actively employed; restore employees to the same position upon return from leave (or to a position with the same pay, benefits, and terms and conditions of employment); and appropriately notify employees of their rights and responsibilities under the act.

Scheduling: Employees can take 12 weeks of leave in one block of time, in smaller blocks as needed (intermittent leave), or on a reduced work schedule (for example, part time for 24 weeks). Managers may need to rearrange the duties of other workers or hire a temporary to cover the responsibilities of a worker on FMLA leave. With few exceptions, it is important not to interfere with an employee's right to use FMLA leave and be reinstated upon its completion. The employer, however, can expect reasonable notice and may exercise some control in cases of intermittent or reduced work schedule leave.

Recording FMLA Leave: It is the employer's responsibility to designate leave as FMLA leave, whether the employee mentions FMLA or not. The employee must be promptly notified that leave will be counted as FMLA leave in order to limit the total amount of time the employee can be away from work. The employee has the responsibility to notify the employer of the need for leave and to provide enough information so the employer can determine if the leave qualifies under FMLA.

Penalties for Non-compliance: Employees may recover back pay and benefits with interest, as well as reinstatement or promotion. Attorney's fees and costs may also be awarded. Where FMLA, state family and medical leave laws, and state temporary disability requirements do not apply, small organizations have several options. They can provide no paid leave or guarantee of reinstatement following absence for family or medical reasons; provide paid leave for medically necessary absences only (pregnancy must be treated like any other medical absence); or provide some combination of the above.

Immigration Reform and Control Act (1 or more employees)

IRCA prohibits the employment of individuals who are not legally authorized to work in the United States or in an employment classification that they are not authorized to fill. The act requires employers to certify (using the I-9 form) within three days of employment the identity and eligibility to work of all employees hired. I-9 forms must be retained for three years following employment or one year following termination. Acceptable proof of the eligibility to work is one of these documents:

- An original Social Security Number Card
- A birth certificate issued by a state, county, or municipality
- An unexpired INS Employment Authorization Specify form

This act also prohibits discrimination in employment-related matters on the basis of national origin or citizenship. Discriminatory actions include, but are not limited to, requesting additional documents beyond those required, refusing to accept valid documents or consider an applicant who is suspected of being an illegal alien, and harassing or retaliating against employees for exercising their rights under the law.

Penalties for non-compliance: Civil fines of $100 to $10,000 per violation for record-keeping and employment violations. Back pay/front pay and attorneys' fees for discriminatory actions. Criminal penalties may be imposed for repeated violations.

National Labor Relations Act (1 or more employees)

The National Labor Relations Act (NLRA), passed in 1935, provides that all employees have the right to form, join, and assist labor organizations and to bargain collectively with their employers. The National Labor Relations Board enforces the act, and the body of decisions and regulations from the NLRB forms an extensive set of standards for electing and decertifying unions, for negotiating bargaining agreements, and for defining activities as fair or unfair labor practices.

Penalties for non-compliance: Violations of the act are addressed by the National Labor Relations Board. A wide variety of penalties may be applied, depending on the type of violation.

Occupational Safety and Health Act (11 or more employees)

The Occupational Safety and Health Act of 1970 (OSHA) includes a "general duty clause," which requires employers to maintain a workplace free from recognized hazards that would cause injury or death to employees. Most employers must comply with OSHA safety and health standards that apply to their workplaces. OSHA requires employers to maintain a log of certain injuries and illnesses (Form 300), report certain deaths and multiple hospitalizations, and post supplementary records on an annual basis.

Employers may not discharge employees who refuse to do a job that, by their reasonable apprehension, places them at risk of injury or exposes them to a hazardous workplace condition. The standards are voluminous and may be obtained from the Government Printing Office.

Penalties for non-compliance: Civil penalties up to $1,000 for individual violations; up to $10,000 for repeated and willful violations; back pay and reinstatement for employees who suffered discrimination.

Title VII (15 or more employees)

Title VII is a provision of the Civil Rights Act of 1964 that prohibits discrimination in virtually every employment circumstance on the basis of race, color, religion, gender, pregnancy, or national origin. The purpose of Title VII protections is to "level the playing field" by forcing employers to consider only objective, job-related criteria in making employment decisions.

The above classes of individuals are considered "protected" under Title VII because of the history of unequal treatment identified in each class. Title VII must be considered when reviewing applications or resumes (for example, by not eliminating candidates on the basis of a "foreign" last name), when interviewing candidates (by not eliminating candidates on the basis of sex or race), when testing job applicants (by treating all candidates the same and ensuring that tests are not unfairly weighted against any group of people), and when considering employees for promotions, transfers, or any other employment-related benefit or condition.

See also The Pregnancy Discrimination Act of 1978 below. (See also the Family and Medical Leave Act.)

Penalties for non-compliance: For intentional discrimination, employees may seek a jury trial, with compensatory and punitive damages up to the maximum limitations established by the Civil Rights Act of 1991 according to the employer's number of employees:

- 15-100 employees, a maximum of $50,000
- 101-200 employees, a maximum of $100,000
- 201-500 employees, a maximum of $200,000
- More than 500 employees, a maximum of $300,000

Remedies of back pay, reinstatement, and retroactive seniority are available for all types of discrimination, whether intentional or disparate impact.

Pregnancy Discrimination Act of 1978

The Pregnancy Discrimination Act of 1978 amended Title VII to provide that pregnant women are treated the same as other employees who are disabled. The employer's policies for taking leave, health benefits during leave, and reinstatement after leave apply equally to pregnant women and other employees. (See also the Family and Medical Leave Act.)

Sexual Harassment (15 or more employees)

Since 1980 Title VII of the Civil Rights Act has prohibited sexual harassment. Unwelcome sexual advances, requests for sexual favors, and other verbal or physical conduct of a sexual nature constitute sexual harassment when either of these applies:

- Submission to such conduct is made either explicitly or implicitly a term or condition of an individual's employment.
- Submission to or rejection of such conduct by an individual is used as the basis for employment decisions affecting an individual.
- Such conduct has the purpose or effect of unreasonably interfering with an individual's work performance or creating an intimidating, hostile, or offensive work environment.

Whenever sexual harassment is claimed or suspected in the workplace, it should be promptly and thoroughly investigated. Ignorance of its occurrence within the workplace only serves to increase the organization's possible liability. Sexual harassment has the same penalties for non-compliance as the Civil Rights Act.

Uniform Guidelines on Employee Selection Procedures (1 or more employees)

These address the use of interviewing, testing, training, and other employee selection tools and their effect on discrimination based on race, color, religion, sex, or national origin. Specifically addressed is "adverse impact," measured by the 80 percent test or 4/5ths rule. Tested is if a selection practice yields less than 80 percent of a protected group as compared to the most frequently selected group. If this occurs there may be evidence of discrimination.

The guidelines also require employers to maintain records, for an unspecified period of time, on their selection procedures and any adverse impact noted, as well as records of the employer's workforce broken down by race and ethnic groups.

Uniformed Services Employment and Reemployment Rights Act (1 or more employees)

The Uniformed Services Employment and Reemployment Rights Act (USERRA), which replaced the Veterans' Reemployment Rights Act, broadly prohibits employers from discriminating against individuals because of past, present, or future membership in a uniformed service (including periods of voluntary training and service). The act:

1. Prohibits discrimination in employment, job retention, and advancement.
2. Requires employers to provide retraining opportunities.
3. Requires healthcare and pension benefits to continue during leave.
4. Allows an employee to take military leave up to five years.
5. Provides additional protection for disabled veterans.
6. Requires employees to provide notice of their need for leave.
7. Requires service members to notify their employers of their intention to return to work.

Individuals reemployed after a period of military service are generally required to be allowed to return to work and receive all the benefits and seniority they would have, had they remained continuously employed.

Penalties for non-compliance: Back pay and benefits and liquidated damages (if conduct was willful).

Federal Reporting Requirements

The following summarizes the general requirements for employers to file reports with various government agencies.

Function	Reporting Requirements	Forms
Payroll	Income Taxes, Federal Unemployment Taxes, Social Security Taxes	Forms 940, 941,942, 943, 1099, W-2, W-4
Benefits	Employee Retirement Income Security Act (ERISA) requires employers to file summary plan descriptions and annual reports on employee benefits offered.	Form 5500 Series, 990 series, PBGC forms and others
EEO	Under Title VII, employers must file the appropriate EEO-1 form indicating employment by covered categories; EEO-1 is due Sept 30 for the current year.	EEO-1 or similar form based on type of organization covered; VETS-100 for federal contractor; AAP for federal contractors with more than 50 employees and more than $50,000 in annual federal contracts
Labor Relations	The Landrum-Griffin Labor Management Reporting and Disclosure Act (LMRDA) requires unions to file reports on the union's constitution, bylaws, status, and finances. Union officials have additional reporting requirements.	LM-1, LM-2, LM-3, LM-4, LM-15, LM-15A, LM-16, LM-30 and others

Source: Society for Human Resource Management 2006

Compliance Calendar

Pension Plan Documents: Summary Plan Description (SPD)	• Provide to new participants no later than 90 days after the person first becomes covered. • Provide to participant within 30 days of request for copy. • Provide to participants SPD's for a new plan within 120 days after it is adopted. • Furnish copy to DOL upon request. Civil penalties will be assessed for failure to do so.
Summary of Material Modifications (SMM)	• Provide copy within 210 days after end of plan year in which amendments are adopted. • Provide at least every 5 years to plan participants when plan has been updated.
Summary Annual Report (SAR)	Provide within 9 months after close of plan year (additional 2 months if extension is granted).
Form 5500	Annually. File by the last day of the 7th month following the end of the plan year (July 31 for calendar year plans). One time extension of 2 1/2 months may be granted upon submission of extension request form.
Federal Contractor Requirements: VETS-100 Form	September 30
Payroll/Taxes: Federal Unemployment Tax Return	January 31 for previous year. Additionally, if state contribution is paid in full by that date, employer can take a credit of 5.4% of the unemployment taxes paid. If paid after that date, credit is 90% of regular credit.
COBRA	Effective January 1, 2005 calendar year health plans are required to amend their SPD's to include the plan's procedures for when participants are required to notify the plan administrator of a qualifying event. These procedures include identifying the parties to whom notice must be given, describing the items that must be included in the notice, and describing the means by which notice must be sent.
Equal Employment: EEO-1 Report	September 30 for the payroll period selected in the current year.
OSHA: Form 300 and 300A	Maintain OSHA 300 Log of Work-related Injuries and Illnesses Maintain a calendar year record of all reportable injuries and illnesses incurred during the year. Used to prepare OSHA 300A for posting on February 1 through April 30 of each year.

Source: Society for Human Resource Management, 2006

References

ASAE & The Center for Association Leadership, *Policies and Procedures in Association Management,* Washington, D.C., 2006.

Allison, Loren K., *Employee Selection: A Legal Perspective,* Society for Human Resource Management, Alexandria, Virginia, 1996.

American Compensation Association, *Building Blocks in Compensation* (series), Scottsdale, Arizona.

Bacarro, Joseph P., *Getting Started in Human Resource Management,* Society for Human Resource Management, Alexandria, Virginia, 1996.

Beam, Burton T., and John J. McFadden, *Employee Benefits,* 3rd ed., Dearborn Financial Publishing, Dearborn, 1992.

Dixon, R. Brian, *The Federal Wage and Hour Laws,* Society for Human Resource Management, Alexandria, Virginia, 1994.

Isler Dare Ray & Radcliffe, P.C. "Sample Offer Letter," Vienna, Virginia, 2007.

Johnson, Richard E., *Flexible Benefits: A How-To Guide,* International Foundation of Employee Benefit Plans, Brookfield, Wisconsin, 1992.

Mathis, Robert L., and John H. Jackson, *Human Resource Management,* 8th ed., West Publishing, St. Paul, Minnesota, 1997.

Nelson, Bob, *1001 Ways to Reward Employees,* Workman Publishing, New York, 1993.

Rock, Milton L., and Lance A. Berger, eds., *The Compensation Handbook: A State-of-the-Art Guide to Compensation Strategy and Design,* McGraw-Hill, New York, 1991.

The Society for Human Resource Management Information Center and Library, Alexandria, Virginia.

About the Author

Michael R. Losey, SPHR,CAE is the retired president and chief executive officer of the Society for Human Resource Management, Alexandria, Virginia and is currently President of MikeLosey.com, specializing in HR and association management consulting, writing, and speaking.

Review Questions

General

1. If your organization does not have a human resource professional staff person, what resource is the association using to ensure tools, practices, compliance, employee relations, etc. are competitive and appropriate and oversight is maintained on a regular basis?

Recruitment and Selection

2. Does the association's recruitment and selection program:

- Consider current employees first?
- Have a clearly defined recruitment and selection procedure?

- Use related technology (such as the Internet)?
- Provide sufficient candidates (recruitment) to make good selections?
- Are all tests and interview questions job related?
- Are managers and supervisors trained on what questions can and cannot be asked in an employment interview?
- Include background and other reference checking?

Employee Performance

3. Do job descriptions exist and are they up-to-date and include the *"essential"* requirements of the job for ADA purposes?

- Is individual employee performance reviewed formally, at least annually?
- Are supervisors trained on how to conduct performance reviews and relate performance to job requirements without unintended bias? (Halo effect, horn effect, personal issues, etc.)
- Are employee aspirations and related development needs known and acted upon?
- Is there a clearly defined approach to employee discipline?
- Is there a clearly defined employee appeal process?
- What employee feedback mechanisms exist (attitude surveys, state of the association or other employee meetings, skip-level interviews, etc.)?

Compensation and Benefits

4. How does the association stand in terms of providing competitive compensation and benefits when compared to other employers (not just associations) in your labor market?

- Do employees understand how compensation and benefit programs are determined and administered?
- What association employee healthcare changes could be made to help reduce the association's cost but still provide meaningful employee protection?
- Is there any opportunity for incentive or bonus based compensation, and if so, what performance/goal-based methods will be used?

Emerging Issues

5. What is the association's experience or plans in regards to:

- Flextime?
- Telecommuting?
- Diversity?
- Compressed workweeks?
- Employee privacy?
- Employee security (Workplace violence, terrorism, etc.)?

Candidate Evaluation Form

Name of Applicant _____

Position _____ Department _____

Answer the following questions as they pertain to the requirements of the job:

Education
☐ excellent   ☐ meets job requirements
☐ does not meet job requirements   ☐ not applicable for this position
Comments _____
_____

Relevant Job Experience
☐ excellent   ☐ meets job requirements
☐ does not meet job requirements   ☐ not applicable for this position
Comments _____
_____

Supervisory Experience
☐ excellent   ☐ meets job requirements
☐ does not meet job requirements   ☐ not applicable for this position
Comments _____
_____

Technical Skills
☐ excellent   ☐ meets job requirements
☐ does not meet job requirements   ☐ not applicable for this position
Comments _____
_____

Interpersonal Skills
☐ excellent   ☐ meets job requirements
☐ does not meet job requirements   ☐ not applicable for this position
Comments _____
_____

Motivation
☐ excellent   ☐ meets job requirements
☐ does not meet job requirements   ☐ not applicable for this position
Comments _____

Strengths _____
Comments _____
Weaknesses _____
Comments _____

Overall Ranking
☐ excellent   ☐ meets job requirements
☐ does not meet job requirements   ☐ not applicable for this position
Comments _____
_____

Salary Expectations:_____   Date Candidate Available to Begin Work _____

Interviewer _____   Date of Interview _____

Source: Society for Human Resource Management, 2006

Reference Checking Form

(Verify that the applicant has provided permission before conducting reference checks.)

Candidate Name _____

Reference Name _____

Company Name _____

Dates of Employment: From: _____ To: _____

Position(s) Held _____

Salary History _____

Reason for Leaving _____

Explain the reason for your call and verify the above information with the supervisor (including the reason for leaving).

1. Please describe the type of work for which the candidate was responsible.

_____

_____

2. How would you describe the applicant's relationships with coworkers, subordinates (if applicable), and with superiors?

_____

_____

3. Did the candidate have a positive or negative work attitude? Please elaborate.

_____

_____

4. How would you describe the quantity and quality of output generated by the former employee?

_____

_____

5. What were his/her strengths on the job?

_____

_____

6. What were his/her weaknesses on the job?

_____

_____

7. What is your overall assessment of the candidate?

_____

_____

8. Would you recommend him/her for this position? Why or why not?

_____

_____

9. Would this individual be eligible for rehire? Why or why not?

_____

_____

Other comments?

_____

_____

Source: Society for Human Resource Management, 2006

Sample Offer Letter

Name
Address
City, State ZIP

Dear _____:

On behalf of ABC Company, I am pleased to offer you a position as _____. As we discussed, in this position your starting compensation will be $_____ week/hour, which is equivalent to an annual amount of $_____. This position is considered an [exempt/non-exempt] position for purposes of federal wage-hour law, which means that you [will not/will] be eligible for overtime time pay for hours actually worked in excess of 40 in a given workweek. You will be eligible for annual performance reviews which might lead to increases in your compensation.

In addition to your compensation, you will be eligible to receive the benefits which are offered to all ABC Company employees. These benefits are described in the enclosed materials. We also have enclosed a copy of the employee handbook, which describes the Company's policies and procedures that will govern certain aspects of your employment. Please be sure to review the handbook and sign and return the acknowledgement of receipt page at the end of the handbook.

This offer of employment, if not previously accepted by you, will expire seven days from the date of this letter, although additional time for consideration of the offer can be made available if you find it necessary. If you wish to accept the offer, please sign in the place provided below and return it to me within the prescribed time.

We greatly look forward to having you join our Company and become a member of our team. However, we recognize that you retain the option, as does the Company, of ending your employment with the Company at any time, with or without notice and with or without cause. As such, your employment with the Company is at-will and neither this letter nor any other oral or written representations may be considered a contract for any specific period of time.

Should you have any questions about starting with the Company, please do not hesitate to contact me or a representative from the Human Resources Department.

Sincerely,
[Signature of Company Official]

I agree to the terms of the employment set forth above.

_____   _____
Signature   Date

Source: Isler Dare Ray & Radcliffe, P.C., Vienna, VA

Orientation Checklist—Human Resources

Name: _____

Department: _____

Hire Date: _____

Introduction to the Company
☐ Organization and its function
☐ Corporate Culture
☐ Company Mission
☐ Corporate Literature/Video

New Employee Paperwork
☐ W-4 and State Tax Forms
☐ I-9
☐ Health, Life & Disability Insurance Enrollment Forms
☐ Copy of Employee Handbook

Benefits and Compensation
☐ Health, Life, Disability Insurance
☐ Retirement Benefits
☐ Educational Assistance
☐ Credit Union
☐ Stock Purchase Plan
☐ Employee Assistance Program
☐ Child Care
☐ Pay Procedures
☐ Salary Increase/Performance Review Process
☐ Incentive/Bonus Programs
☐ Paid and Unpaid Leave

Training Scheduled and/or Completed
☐ Computer System
☐ Log on
☐ E-mail
☐ Software
☐ Telephone System
☐ Voice Mail
☐ Long-Distance Calls

Other Items
☐ _____
☐ _____
☐ _____
☐ _____

Date Completed:_____ By:_____

To be filed in employee's personnel file upon completion.

Source: Society for Human Resource Management, 2006

Orientation
Orientation Checklist for Supervisors

- ☐ Welcome New Employee
  - ☐ Introduction to work group
  - ☐ Tour Department and Important Places: Restrooms, Coffee Area, Cafeteria, Coat Area
- ☐ Introduction to the Organization (may be handled on a separate day)
  - ☐ History
  - ☐ Product(s)/Service(s)
  - ☐ Resources for Company Information
  - ☐ Tour of Company
- ☐ Introduction to the Department
  - ☐ Purpose
  - ☐ Relation to other departments
  - ☐ Organization of department
  - ☐ Procedures for leave, overtime, etc.
- ☐ Introduction to the Job
  - ☐ Work space
  - ☐ Work hours, breaks, mealtimes and other rules
  - ☐ Equipment
  - ☐ Telephone number
  - ☐ Copier
  - ☐ Mail
  - ☐ Fax machine
  - ☐ Tools
  - ☐ Job Description
  - ☐ Duties, Responsibilities, Purpose
  - ☐ Handling Confidential Information
  - ☐ Performance Expectations/Goals
  - ☐ Promotions/Transfers
  - ☐ Safety/Emergency Procedures
  - ☐ Emergency Exits
  - ☐ Injury Prevention
  - ☐ Reporting Injuries
- ☐ Introduction to Mentor, Coach or Buddy

- ☐ Training
  - ☐ Computer System
  - ☐ Log on
  - ☐ E-mail
  - ☐ Software
  - ☐ Telephone System
  - ☐ Voice Mail
  - ☐ Long-Distance Calls
  - ☐ Training Opportunities
- ☐ General
  - ☐ Time sheet/Time card, if applicable
  - ☐ Parking
  - ☐ ID Card
  - ☐ Credit Card(s)
  - ☐ Bulletin Board and Newsletter
  - ☐ Places to Dine

Source: Society for Human Resource Management, 2006

Job Description Worksheet

Job Title: _____

Salary Range: _____   Department _____

Reports to: _____

Position Summary: _____

_____

Essential Functions/Percentage of Time Spent on Each:

Percentage:

1. _____   _____

   _____

2. _____   _____

   _____

3. _____   _____

   _____

4. _____   _____

   _____

Other Functions:

1. _____

   _____

2. _____

   _____

3. _____

   _____

Minimum Job Requirements:

Education: _____

_____

Experience: _____

_____

Specific Skills: _____

_____

Specialized Knowledge, Licenses, etc. _____

_____

Supervisory Responsibility, if any: _____

_____

_____

Source: Society for Human Resource Management, 2006

Monthly Absenteeism Tracking Form

Record staff absences/reasons as follows:

V = vacation   S = sick   B = bereavement   P = personal   M = military   J = jury   F = FMLA   H = holiday

Month: _____

Employee	1	2	3	4	5	6	7	8	9	10	11	12	13	14	15	16	17	18	19	20	21	22	23	24	25	26	27	28	29	30	31

Source: Society for Human Resource Management, 2006

Fundraising

James P. Gelatt

W HY UNDERTAKE A FUNDRAISING program in your association? The most obvious reason is to pursue new funding streams by raising additional revenue beyond member dues, convention income, and the like. Although a fundraising program can indeed be a source of additional income, the sources for that additional income are likely to come from individuals and organizations with whom the association is already familiar.

Think of it as concentric circles. Funding for associations tends to come from association leadership, association membership, companies that provide products and services to the membership—or would like to—and public members who have an interest in the profession or trade represented by the association, including the family and friends of association members.

The circle rarely extends beyond this. A few, but only a few, associations, through their related foundations, have secured funds from unrelated major corporations and grant-making foundations. The reason why the fundraising potential for associations is contained is simple: Associations exist to serve their members. Potential funders—a grant-making foundation, for example—recognize the self-serving nature of associations. If the association wants to launch a new program that will be primarily aimed at its members or their profession or trade, the general sentiment is that those most affected by it should support it.

Although fundraising is a fundamental part of most nonprofit organizations, it is not basic to the operations of most associations. The reasons for this are clear:

- Associations exist to serve members. Nonprofits exist to advance a charitable cause.

- Associations rely primarily on member dues and the support of companies with a vested interest in the association. Nonprofit organizations as a rule do not have members and rely on support from donors in order to survive.

As a result, it is probably safe to say that most association executives have less familiarity with fundraising than they do with other more central functions of running an association. This chapter provides an overview to fundraising by addressing six points:

1. The fundraising program needs to be reflective of and integrated into the association's strategic planning.
2. Effective fundraising follows marketing principles.
3. Fundraising is all about motivation.
4. There are several ways to raise funds; each has its pros and cons.
5. It may be necessary to establish a separate entity within the association in order to undertake a fundraising program.
6. There are challenges to establishing a fundraising program that should be anticipated.

3. Fundraising is all about motivation.

One of the key ways that fundraising applies marketing principles is by understanding motivation. The process of contributing involves an *exchange*. Although the donor does not receive a tangible product or service for his or her contribution, that donor does get something in return. Baumeister (1991) identified seven donor types based on what motivates them to contribute. The following table summarizes Baumeister's classification of donors.

Donor Types	Profile
The communitarian	Mostly business people; committed to their community; feel a strong sense to give back.
The devout	Believe it is God's will for them to help others and give out of a sense of moral obligation.
The investor	Want to maximize their support by giving wisely.
The socialite	Drawn to the organization in part because they identify with the people who comprise it; tend to enjoy creative ways to give (e.g., special events).
The altruist	Give in order to grow spiritually; evaluate the organization on who runs it; like recognition of their gifts.
The repayer	May have benefited from the association (e.g., scholarship recipient) and look to give back.
The dynast	Believe that philanthropy is everyone's responsibility regardless of wealth; want to build strong relationships with persons within the organization.

As with any such classification, there is a tendency to oversimplify. Most of us have characteristics of more than one of the donor types noted above, and we may even move between types depending on the situation. I may be the "repayer" for some organizations that I support (e.g., my college alma mater), and an altruist for others. It's also important to recognize that despite type in general people tend to contribute for one or more of the following reasons:

- Belief in the mission and wanting to make a difference;
- Regard for the volunteer leadership and staff leadership (obviously an important factor for association fundraising);
- Respect for the organization;
- Fiscal responsibility of the organization;
- Service in a volunteer capacity;
- Interest in a particular project; or
- The persuasiveness of the person making the ask.

4. There are several ways to raise funds; each has its pros and cons.

Assuming that the association has decided to undertake a fundraising program, with expressed support of the board, the next step is to develop a strategic marketing (fundraising) plan. Your association's fundraising plan might address several elements:

- **Goals.** Set modest goals at first. Better to under-promise and over-deliver. Don't make a dollar amount the principal goal, especially in the beginning. The goals should be matched by stated outcomes so that there is concurrence on how success will be measured.

- **Case Statement.** The case statement is a written document that makes the case for why the organization is worthy of donor support. It can be as brief as a few pages or as lengthy as a business plan. The case statement has several uses:
  - It provides common language with which to refer to the fundraising effort.
  - It clarifies what the effort is all about and is thus a way of making sure that everyone involved is in agreement on the goals of the fundraising effort.
  - Excerpts from it can be used for fundraising letters, business cards, and blurbs about the fundraising in association publications.

- **Infrastructure.** How will the fundraising program be staffed and to whom should the staff report? What role will volunteer leadership play? What internal support systems (e.g., public relations, finance) need to be in place? Would it make sense to retain fundraising counsel?

- **Communications.** Who needs to know about this new venture? Who needs to buy in? Who are the gatekeepers who can kill the project if they are not on board?

- **Implementation plan.** What will the fundraising program undertake in its first year, second year, and third year?

In addition to addressing these areas, you will need an operating plan that reflects an informed decision on which fundraising mechanisms should be pursued. The table on the next page lists the pros and cons of the various options.

Fundraising Methods	Pro	Con
Direct Mail	• Built-in source of potential contributors in membership. • Most scientific of all fundraising. • Can be a way of identifying donors at a relatively low cost.	• Tendency to be satisfied with small donations; may be letting some donors off too easy. • Intense competition.
Corporations	• Fairly easy to approach. • Doesn't require extensive research or lengthy proposal. • Can be a source of in-kind contributions (e.g., equipment).	• Companies are in the business of business, not charity. Need to ask: What's in it for them, and be prepared to deliver. • May be relatively modest gifts. • Prefer to give for specific projects and won't give for endowments.
Special Events	• Can increase visibility of the fundraising. • May provide an entry to persons whom you might not interest in the organization.	• Labor-intensive: the same amount of time might be better spent with a major donor. • Potential for public failure.
Major Gifts	• High return on investment. • Follows the 80/20 fundraising axiom: spend 80 percent of your effort on the 20 percent of the donors who can contribute 80 percent of the dollars.	• Strings tied to donation, such as having some control over how the money is spent. • Takes time to cultivate major donors out of average donors.
Planned Giving	• Offers additional opportunities for existing donors, especially those who want to be remembered in perpetuity. • Can be fairly easily launched by including appropriate language in association publications.	• Need to understand planned giving instruments or retain counsel who does. • Requires sensitivity and tact; no one wants to think about his or her demise.
Memorial and In Honor	• An easy way for members to recognize persons who have passed away or to honor leaders in the association. • May be the entry to donors who can then be cultivated for ongoing or larger gifts.	• Can be time intensive; both the donor and the person being honored (or his or her family) need to be contacted. • Usually results in fairly small donations.
Check-off on Dues Notice	• Probably the least costly of all association fundraising methods. • May be a way of acquiring donors who can be upgraded.	• Usually results in relatively small dollar amounts. • If the average member resents having to pay his or her dues, may be the wrong place to interest people in contributing.

Source: Based on J. P. Gelatt, *Managing nonprofit organizations in the 21st century.* Phoenix: Oryx Press, 1992.

5. It may be necessary to establish a separate entity within the association in order to undertake a fundraising program.

In order to accept tax-deductible contributions from individuals, as well as grants from private grant-making foundations, it is necessary to have 501(c)(3) tax status. According to the IRS, "to be tax-exempt as an organization described in IRC Section 501(c)(3) of the Code, an organization must be organized and operated exclusively for one or more of the purposes set forth in IRC Section 501(c)(3) and none of the earnings of the organization may inure to any private shareholder or individual. In addition, it may not attempt to influence legislation as a substantial part of its activities and it may not participate at all in campaign activity for or against political candidates." To be eligible for 501(c)(3) status, the association foundation must have been created for purposes including "charitable, religious, educational, scientific, literary, testing for public safety, fostering national or international amateur sports competition, and the prevention of cruelty to children or animals."

Most association foundations are also separately incorporated in a state or the District of Columbia. Becoming incorporated requires that the entity have its own board (often called a board of trustees, which distinguishes it from the association's governing body). The process of applying for 501(c)(3) status need not be onerous. The IRS provides considerable guidance in its publications and on its Web site on how to apply, including model proposal language. In addition, a Web search will yield the

---

More on Affliliate Nonprofits

For additional information on establishing a nonprofit organization affiliated with your association, you may want to explore one or more of the following:

BoardSource
www.boardsource.org

Council on Foundations
www.cof.org

Establishing a Nonprofit Organization
www.fdncenter.org/learn/classroom/establish/index.html

Free Complete Toolkit for Boards
www.managementhelp.org/boards/boards.htm

501(c)(3): To Be or Not To Be?
www.tgci.com/publications/96summer/tobeor.htm

Info Central: How to Start a Nonprofit Organization
www.mncn.org/info_start.htm

Nonprofit Law Resource Library
www.hurwitassociates.com/l_start_forming.html

Starting a Nonprofit Organization
www.snpo.org

---

names of several organizations that walk the applicant through the process. To be sure that the application meets requirements prior to submitting it to IRS, it may be prudent to retain legal counsel familiar with nonprofit law. For additional information on applying for 501(c)(3) status, visit www.irs.gov/charities.

Creating an entity within the association that is capable of, and focused on, fundraising, should not be undertaken without giving consideration to what it will mean to have, in effect, two organizations under the same roof, both of which will have their own governing boards. Associations considering such a move might want to address:

- How will the fundraising entity be comprised? Should its board be made up entirely of association members, or would it be advantageous to have public members on the board who have access to sources of funds? How will its board members be selected?
- How should the entity be staffed? And to whom should the staff report?
- What will be the purposes of this new entity, and how will its purposes complement and hopefully advance the purposes of the association?

6. There are challenges to establishing a fundraising program that should be anticipated.

Setting up a fundraising program can offer real benefits to the association, but doing so is not a panacea. The program needs to be integrated into the way that the association operates and not be seen as a separate add-on. The program will require start-up funding; without such support, the program may be set up to fail. At the same time, it's also important to recognize that fundraising is a different kind of activity. It requires a different kind of accounting and records keeping, and the staff hired to manage this area are more likely to come from fundraising rather than association backgrounds.

The fundraising program should be part of the association's overall strategic intent to secure nondues revenue. If it is planned well, using proven marketing techniques, the fundraising program can become a significant revenue stream.

Reference

Baumeister, R. F. (1991). *The meaning of life*. New York: Guilford.

About the Author

James P. Gelatt is a collegiate professor at the Graduate School of Management & Technology, University of Maryland University College, Adelphi, Maryland. He was the founder of the Association Foundation Group and has provided fundraising and strategic planning consultation to numerous associations.

Review Questions

1. Why isn't fundraising basic to the operations of most associations?

2. What are the characteristics of communitarian, socialite, and repayer donors?

3. How are marketing principles applied to fundraising?

4. What are the pros and cons of at least two fundraising methods that might be used in your association?

CHAPTER
16

Supplier Relations

Stacey Riska

L ET'S FACE IT. LIFE in associations means you're going to wear many hats. Juggling those hats would make a professional juggler proud, but most association professionals can't be experts in everything. Today, many associations are finding that focusing on their core competencies and outsourcing other activities helps to make them more productive, efficient, and effective. This chapter addresses

- The benefits, implications, feasibility, and advisability of outsourcing association functions;
- The procedures for the appropriate utilization and evaluation of requests for proposals (RFPs); and
- The procedures and criteria for reviewing the performance of partners, suppliers, and consultants.

Benefits of Outsourcing

The debate as to whether outsourcing is an important management tool is long over. To argue that an organization should not be actively seeking ways to use outsourcing to improve its operations would be like arguing that it should not be using technology. What's more, the management systems needed to make outsourcing some functions work are well-documented, and, in fact, the very future shape of business is being redefined through outsourcing.

Simply put, no organization, regardless of its size or sophistication, can possibly hope to be "best in world" in every aspect of its operation, yet none can afford to be anything less. This means that every organization must surround itself with a network of specialized providers who are themselves best in world at what they do. Through outsourcing of non-core activities, cost savings in the 15 percent range are common, with comparable increases in quality and throughput, according to the Outsourcing Institute, an association of professionals dedicated to outsourcing.

Outsourcing provides your association with both tangible and intangible benefits, including

- Allowing staff to focus on the bigger picture;
- Allowing staff to focus on the project at hand without conflict with other staff about who is responsible;
- Improving efficiency and the bottom line;
- Providing flexibility—outsource what you need to, when you need to;
- Saving office space; and
- Allowing the development of compensation on a shared-risk, shared-reward basis.

The most notable benefit of outsourcing is that it allows staff to focus their time and resources on revenue-generating activities and core competencies.

Areas to Consider When Outsourcing

The first thing to consider before outsourcing is what your staff's core strengths and competencies are. Next, match those strengths and competencies to the activities and functions of your association. Once those are identified, the remaining functions or peripheral activities are candidates for outsourcing.

Your members, customers, other providers, and board of directors must also be considered. An outside firm, in many instances, will have to interface with them. You obviously want to work with a supplier with whom you're confident and comfortable and who will provide excellent service to both internal and external customers.

Another consideration is the way your association conducts its business. Your association probably has a set culture for how things should be handled from a process perspective. Perhaps some of your processes and procedures haven't been reviewed or changed in years "because we've always done it that way." Outsourcing will probably entail change. Your supplier may recommend changes in current procedures to improve efficiency or save costs. The point of outsourcing is to take advantage of best-in-class abilities. While cost savings and increased quality are the anticipated outcomes of outsourcing, this may not always be the case in every area of your organization because each organization's culture and circumstances are varied. Each time you identify candidates for outsourcing, weigh the potential advantages and disadvantages of doing so versus the pros and cons of fulfilling functions in-house.

Before an outsourcing agreement begins, be very clear in the contract about who is responsible for what, what your expectations are, how disputes will be resolved, and what happens if the relationship does not work. Set specific expectations, standards, and responsibilities.

Soliciting Requests for Proposals

The first stage in implementing an outsourcing strategy is to determine whether outsourcing can help your association become successful. This process involves soliciting proposals from prospective suppliers by sending out a request for proposal (RFP). The objective of the RFP is to identify a group of suppliers that can best support your association's needs. You should be able to take your RFP to the outsourcing marketplace and say, "Who can do this for me, and what will it cost?" The process discussed below explains how to develop an effective RFP so that the responses you receive will be on target.

Taking the time to develop a thorough RFP will help you when you're ready to develop the final outsourcing agreement. Bidders need to know at this stage exactly what your requirements are. In addition, developing a thorough RFP forces you to decide what you're looking for in specific products, services, or abilities. If you do not know exactly what you want or need, consider hiring a consultant to help you develop the RFP. Whether you decide to go through the RFP process alone or with outside help, you should remember that the RFP's purpose isn't necessarily to note what you have now; it's to define what you want going forward. Once the RFP is developed, it can be incorporated into your contract describing what you expect from your supplier and what the company agrees to provide.

Putting Together Your RFP

RFP's provide valuable background information about your organization to prospective suppliers, enabling them to submit a proposal detailing how they can best provide a solution to your challenge(s). Your RFP should include the following information:

- **Introduction**
  - Provide background information about your association—who your members are, your organization's structure, and your project goals.

- **Responsibilities**
  - Describe what you expect from the supplier. Try to express responsibilities in terms of *what you want the outcome to be.* Say *what* not *how.*

- **Quality of service expected**
  - Let prospective suppliers know what minimum level of quality is required.

- **Budget**
  - It is important to let your providers know what resources you will commit to the relationship and for how long. Knowing that an association only has so many dollars to work with lets the provider decide whether it can provide a cost-efficient solution and what those solutions may be.

- **Supporting information**
  - In this section, include sample applications, brochures, forms, and other relevant materials that the selected supplier would be working on.

- **Response format**
  - You need to be able to adequately compare proposals when they are returned. Let prospects know how you want the proposal formatted. Note the specific sections that should be addressed, define your evaluation criteria, and give a deadline for the submission of the proposal.

Making the Decision

When you begin reviewing the proposals, you will realize how critical it is to define the criteria for selecting a provider before you send out the RFP. You may receive some beautiful, impressive-looking proposals from suppliers, but the decision to outsource should be based on the proposal's content and substance.

The goal is to define success before you begin an outsourcing relationship. What is outsourcing success? Meeting deadlines? Meeting or exceeding accuracy standards? The number of new members recruited? Revenue increased? Expenses reduced? You need to identify the criteria and values for each goal.

Sample Supplier Assessment Form

Description Of	Weight	Supplier1				Supplier2			
Assessment Criteria		Pass/ Fail	Rate	Score	Comment	Pass/ Fail	Rate	Score	Comment
	(W)	(P/F)	(R)	WxR		(P/F)	(R)	WxR	
Association experience	30								
Specific work experience in this area	15								
References	10								
Pricing structure	10								
Understanding of needs	10								
Culture match	5								
Size of business	5								
Location	5								
Tools and technology	5								
Behavior	5								
Totals	100								

Association experience = *Does vendor have association experience with similar organizations of similar scope?*

Experience = *Is the vendor well experienced in supply of this type of service?*

References = *Does the vendor receive good references from their existing and previous customers?*

Pricing structure = *Does the pricing structure provide value-added to your association within your budget?*

Understanding of needs = *Does the vendor have a good understanding of the project's scope?*

Culture match = *Does the vendor's business have a good fit for your own over the term you are considering?*

Size of business = *Will you be a large or small customer, able to influence your supplier or of small significance?*

Location(s) = *Is the provider operating in the location(s) where you require the service?*

Tools and Technology = *Is the supplier well equipped with the tools, processes, and technology skills to provide the service?*

Behavior = *How has the supplier behaved during the process so far?*

This can be set up on a simple spreadsheet so that all criteria can be equally compared among competing prospects. The purpose of the spreadsheet is not to tell you which prospect can provide the services at the lowest cost, but which one can bring the greatest value to the organization and deliver the best end product to your customer(s).

Essentially, a winning proposal should satisfactorily answer the four questions:

1. How will the supplier integrate operations?
2. How will the supplier master change?
3. How will the supplier provide cutting-edge business solutions for particular problems?
4. How will the supplier share risks and rewards?

In some instances, associations may decide not to outsource a core function after completing their review of proposals. Participating in the RFP process often serves to further clarify what resources the association actually has available to fulfill a function through current staff. If, however, the association opts to move forward with outsourcing, significant steps must be taken to establish a successful working relationship with the chosen provider.

Managing the Outsourcing Relationship

Beginning a successful outsourcing relationship is not like handing over the keys to your beach house and saying, "Here you go. Have a wonderful time." During the transition and in the beginning stages of the outsourcing relationship, you need to ensure your members and prospects continue to be served well. In addition, you don't want to get into the beginning stages of the relationship only to learn that projects are falling through the cracks because each side thought the other side was going to take care of it.

Outsourcing is a process that involves people. Because of this, communication is critical to its overall success. Many people resist change, especially when they don't know what's going on. The more you communicate about the outsourcing to employees, the more willing they will be to accept it. Companies that successfully implement

Ten Tips for Developing a Win-Win Relationship with Your Outsourcing Partner

1. **Find a match for you, the organization, and the project.**
   You have to feel comfortable with the company because you will probably be involved in a long-term relationship with it. Look for suppliers that provide value-added ideas, suggestions, and initiatives that can improve current processes.

2. **Look for the qualities of integrity, dependability, a strong work ethic, responsiveness, and an understanding of your organization's culture and values.**
   To identify the right outsourcing partner, you must identify the qualities you are looking for at the start of your search. Determine ahead of time what's most important to you and your association (i.e., deadlines, communication skills, creativity, etc).

3. **Be clear and realistic about your expectations.**
   Let the outsourcer know the history of the function you want to outsource, good or bad. Why are you outsourcing, and specifically what results do you expect? The more specific you can be in your expectations and goals with your outsourcing partner, the more the outsourcer can help you reach your association's goals.

4. **Agree on the goals of the program/project from the beginning. Set objective measurements, determine deadlines, and establish a realistic budget.**
   Define success before you begin. Whatever your definition of success is, you need to let your outsourcing partner know before any project begins.

5. **Identify a key staff liaison to the outsource provider.**
   This staff person acts as a facilitator. He or she is in charge of holding the outsourcing company accountable and administrating updates and progress reports.

6. **Let the outsource provider meet the staff liaison.**
   To encourage a good, effective working relationship and make both parties feel more comfortable, it is important to have your staff liaison and your outsourcer's liaison meet face to face. All concerns should be filtered through these two individuals to reduce miscommunication.

7. **Inform staff of the outsource arrangement.**
   To effectively implement an outsourcing program, it is a good idea to have staff involved in the decision. Inform staff each step of the way, let them know why you are outsourcing, and have them involved in the development of the outsourcing relationship.

8. **View the outsource company as an extension of your staff.**
   Outsourcers need to know the organizational changes, issues, and decisions. If you change your applications, they need to know. If you change your database, they should be involved. By keeping them involved in these changes, they may be able to provide critical insight.

9. **Learn/take advantage of all services a company offers.**
   Your outsource provider may have expertise in other areas that could be helpful to your organization and may be able to provide you with ideas and services to streamline your processes, increase revenues, and/or decrease expenses.

10. **Communication is crucial.**
    With communication, it seems there's never enough of it, it's not timely, it doesn't reach the right people, or it's not what they really wanted to know anyway. If you want a successful outsourcing relationship, repeat this motto over and over, "Communicate a lot; communicate often."

outsourcing programs inform employees about the process leading up to an outsourcing announcement. They communicate early and often.

There are three goals for a successful transition management program:

1. Ensure your association continues to run smoothly.
2. Establish a timeline for when responsibilities will be turned over to the supplier.
3. Ensure the transition is smooth and orderly.

This beginning transition sets the tone that gets the outsourcing relationship off to either a great or rocky start. It is important to take the time to discuss transition management with your outsourcing partner so that all responsibilities are transferred and a realistic timeframe is established.

As the customer you need to define your minimum expectations for the supplier and note that they may change at any time to reflect the association's priorities. Those expectations may come in three forms and should be evaluated throughout the term of the contract:

- **Target goals**—what you're trying to achieve (for example, 100 percent accuracy). This goal may be difficult to reach, but allows both sides to know what they're working together to achieve.

- **Minimum standards**—the minimum point at which service levels become unacceptable and consequences may occur. The provider should be notified immediately of any decrease in standards and, together, a plan of action should be developed that defines what improvements are required and when. You should negotiate increasing consequences into your outsourcing contract for each time performance drops below minimum standards.

- **Unacceptable standards**—performance is unacceptable and is in breach of contract. At this point, the association can usually terminate the contract without recourse or termination penalties. Your association will need to weigh the costs and benefits of providing a recourse period in which the supplier is allowed the opportunity to show measurable improvement.

Legal Issues to Consider

"Outsourcers aren't the bad guys. Bad agreements are the bad guys."

There are many legal issues surrounding outsourcing that are cropping up as more and more organizations turn to outsourcing as a business strategy. The association and the supplier need to create a structure that allows for early identification of issues, their escalation, and their resolution. It is critical that before associations outsource functions, they consider some of the legal issues.

The contract must include

- A detailed description of the roles and responsibilities of each party;
- The products and services to be provided;

- A description of what will not be provided;
- The scope and boundaries of the activities to be performed;
- Cost structures;
- A service-level agreement that defines the performance characteristics for the provision of services, which creates success on the part of both parties;
- The process to be followed for issues such as problem escalation, issue resolution, penalties and rewards, and terms of disengagement; and
- Some type of service-level reporting or review process to track actual performance versus the service-level agreement defined in the contract.

Below is a list of legal issues your association needs to contemplate and discuss with your outsourcing partner before a contract is signed:

- Duration
- Cancellation clauses
- Roles and responsibilities, including subcontracting
- Compensation
- Physical property
- Intellectual property
- Human capital
- Jurisdiction

Each of these items needs to be defined explicitly in the contract. As with any type of contract, legal counsel should be consulted and given the opportunity to review the contract before it is signed.

Outsourcing is meant to be a win-win-win situation (a win for your association, a win for the supplier, and a win for your members). Remember both your association and your outsourcing partner will be expending a lot of time, energy, and money to ensure success. Both organizations will have a certain level of dependency on each other. This means there will have to be a certain level of trust right from the beginning that will continue to be built over time. The attitude of both parties should be, "We need them to be successful just as they need us to be successful."

About the Author

Stacey Riska is president of DataMax Solutions, Inc., Gaithersburg, Maryland.

Review Questions

1. What does your organization do in-house that may be better handled by a professional outsourcing provider?

2. What benefits would your organization achieve by outsourcing some of these activities?

3. What criteria should you use to evaluate potential outsourcing providers?

Research and Statistics

Michael Sherman, CAE

A MAJOR BENEFIT OF MEMBERSHIP in an association is the information collected for the mutual benefit of all members. An association provides a legal way for competitors to share information that helps them compete more effectively and efficiently. Unlike government statistics, which are usually broad rather than deep because they must meet the needs of many audiences, information gathered by an association can be as detailed and targeted as the industry or profession requires. Associations can change data-reporting systems much faster than government agencies; this is especially important in high-tech industries or emerging professional specialties in which information needs are dynamic.

Individual membership organizations offer a variety of surveys and research products, including:

- Individual salary and compensation
- Member demographics
- Individual fringe benefits
- Education and training requirements of the profession
- Trends in the profession (careers, education, and so forth)
- Operating ratios for a professional office
- Public opinion polls of the profession
- Benchmarking
- Best Practices

In their surveys, trade associations generally emphasize business statistics or information about markets, employees, and products. Typical areas include:

- Salary and executive compensation

- Wages
- Fringe benefits
- Business conditions (monthly, quarterly, annually)
- Business trends and forecasts
- Operating ratios
- Industry practices (related to advertising, use of technology, and so forth)
- Factory safety analyses
- Benchmarking
- Best Practices

Regulatory hearings and legal proceedings often require supporting documentation that associations can gather by sponsoring surveys related to product safety, measurements of compliance with regulations (for example, EPA and OSHA), background and education of professionals, economic damages suffered by an industry or profession, and measurement of participation in voluntary programs (such as standards-setting and credentialing programs).

External and Internal Research

These surveys and studies, conducted to gather data that members and other interested parties can use to make business or professional decisions, are considered external research. In other words, members and others outside the association use the information and statistics for their own benefit. On the other hand, *internal research* is used by staff and leaders for making decisions about the association itself. The results of internal research are not necessarily distributed to members or other constituencies.

Internal research gathers data about members, nonmembers, and related industries or professions. This information is used to define or segment markets by individual characteristics such as age, gender, length of experience, and education, and business characteristics such as size, location, type of business, and scope of products or services.

A common type of internal research conducted by associations is the *needs assessment* or *general membership survey.* Its primary objectives are to determine the characteristics or background of members; evaluate familiarity, importance, and satisfaction with association services and programs; uncover needs; and identify new products and services that will help members meet their needs.

Internal research is also used for:

- **Issues management.** To effectively represent members, the association must determine the governmental, environmental, and economic issues that will have the greatest impact on the industry or profession. Asking members what is important to them will identify the legislative and regulatory priorities that, in turn, will shape the government relations program.

- **Strategic planning.** A key component of the planning process is determining member needs and interests, as well as feelings and perceptions about the future of the industry or profession.

- **Meetings and trade shows.** Many organizations survey attendees and exhibitors and use the evaluations to ensure that these events meet the needs and expectations of all parties.

- **Member satisfaction.** A diagnostic tool known as the member satisfaction survey, patterned after the customer satisfaction models used by many corporations, monitors how members feel about the association in a general or overall sense. By determining the mood of members, such surveys can help associations pinpoint and correct problems before they negatively affect retention.

Primary and Secondary Research

Research can be either primary or secondary. In spite of its name, *secondary research* should be considered the first step in any research project because it refers to information that already exists. As a result, you spend far less time and money locating it than initiating research to gather new data.

A good source of secondary research is your association's archives. You may have research already on the shelf, as well as a large amount of data about your members just sitting in the membership database. Another source is related associations that may have conducted research on your primary or associate members.

The vast amount of information available on the Web makes Internet search an essential tool for finding and sourcing secondary research.

Trade publications offer a wealth of information about a profession or industry, ranging from subscriber demographics to specialized studies. Many U.S. government agencies gather information or fund outside research. The Bureau of Health Professions in the Department of Health and Human Services, for example, tracks education and human resource levels in many health-related professions. The U.S. Bureau of the Census provides statistics about industries and retail and wholesale markets, while the Bureau of Labor Statistics covers not only labor markets but also regional and local inflation rates.

Colleges and universities also are excellent sources of research—especially schools that concentrate on a particular industry or profession—as are commercial enterprises that develop and sell research products and services.

If you cannot locate the desired information from existing sources, the association must establish a process for gathering and analyzing data. This is known as *primary research*. Careful planning will yield the specific information you need, but it will cost more and take longer to complete than relying on secondary research. Most external research, for example, is primary and usually involves collecting data from members and nonmembers alike.

Planning Research

Whether for internal or external use, all research projects must be well-planned and focused. You must identify your research objectives and understand how the information obtained will be used.

Several considerations underlie a good research plan. Why is the research being done? Is it a management decision to learn about specific products or markets, or is it a reaction to a committee or board request to "see if we're doing a good job" or to "find out what the members want"? As you delineate your objectives, you should visualize the desired research product—statistical tables, data, conclusions—as they will appear after the project is completed. During the planning stage, emphasize the "answers" you need more than the "questions" that will be designed to get them.

Your research plan should describe sampling methodology (who and how many will be surveyed), how the questionnaire will be developed, when the project will take place, and who will approve the research program. Approval and buy-in by a committee or the board at the early stages will help you develop a realistic timetable. However, asking an entire committee to approve a survey instrument, for example, can add many weeks to a project. A realistic budget is essential because financial and staff resources will affect what information you are able to gather and how you will accomplish the task.

Having specific objectives keeps the research focused and manageable. It is hard to resist the temptation of asking members for additional information when they already have a questionnaire in front of them. For example, some associations request salary information in the middle of an opinion survey. This mixes confidential data—personal compensation, which many members don't wish to share with the association—with general opinions that they don't mind sharing. Asking for information that is not targeted to your overall purpose or that is highly sensitive can lower your overall response rate.

Adding questions designed to educate or inform rather than elicit information also dilutes a survey's effectiveness. Take, for example, this question: "Did you know that new IRS regulations will increase the likelihood that individuals in our profession will be audited next year?" Avoid this type of question as it is not consistent with research objectives. Communicate and educate in other, more effective ways.

When planning external research, determine whether your members have access to the data you're requesting; if they do, will they share it with the association? Some data are proprietary and highly confidential. In some cases, data such as price levels should not be collected or distributed due to antitrust laws and other legal considerations.

Survey Research Methods

There are four basic methodologies for collecting data:

1. **Quantitative Surveys** (written questionnaire). This type of survey, which can be facilitated on numerous platforms (mail, fax, Web-based), is based on a survey instrument that asks questions that are quantifiable and measurable. This format accommodates complex questions and is especially useful when asking respondents to compare options. Also, a written survey gives respondents a high level of anonymity, which is especially important when encouraging frank opinions that might be critical of the association, its products, or its policies.

If the instrument appears complicated or time-consuming, you risk losing the respondent's interest. The best "hook" is a cover letter that discusses the overall objectives of the survey and why participation is important to the respondent and the association. Emphasize the member's involvement and commitment.

For the survey itself, start with questions that are easy to read and answer, such as background demographics (respondent's location, age, gender, education, and so forth). Questions should graduate from simple to more complex and from general to specific. Objective response mechanisms—check boxes, yes/no questions, and rating scales—further ease the burden on the respondent and simplify data entry. Conversely, open-ended questions require more of the respondent's time and are hard to code and analyze. Whenever possible, anticipate likely answers to open-ended questions and provide respondents with a checklist; they'll have an idea of what type of information you're looking for and will spend less time contemplating each question.

Incentives may improve the response rate, but be careful about the impression you create. For instance, including a dollar bill in a mailed survey might be viewed as wasteful for a nonprofit organization. A discount on association publications or an optional check box of charities to which a small amount will be donated may accomplish more.

2. **Telephone interviews.** When based on carefully scripted questions and handled by experienced interviewers, telephone interviews can be completed quickly and, with appropriate call-backs, achieve a high response rate. They can be one of the fastest ways to obtain quantitative data. On a per-respondent basis, however, telephone surveys cost more than quantitative surveys.

Telephone surveys require a high level of training and supervision, and sometimes interviewer "bias," which can come from interpretation, can be a problem. Associations sometimes propose using staff members to conduct telephone surveys to save money. A poorly designed and inadequately executed telephone survey, however, will not produce reliable, accurate, or representative data.

3. **Individual interviews.** Person-to-person surveys accommodate the most complex of questions and allow the interviewer to ensure that the respondent understands the question and gives a reasonable response, which is difficult to do with a quantitative

survey. The interviewer can also ask for clarification or refinement of a respondent's opinions or beliefs.

Interviewing requires a lot of time to cover a truly representative group of respondents. It is also expensive because of the time needed to acquire the data and analyze the transcripts. Of all the survey techniques, interviews are most likely to be affected by interviewer bias and subjectivity.

4. **Focus groups.** Focus groups are best-suited for brainstorming sessions or where interaction among respondents is desired. This type of qualitative research is especially useful when asking simple questions, such as, "What do you, as a member, want from our association?" Many people limit their thinking to what is already available, but in a focus group they typically go beyond that barrier when discussing ideas and interacting with peers.

Focus groups are moderately expensive and require more logistical support than other survey techniques. To properly conduct a focus group, you need a trained moderator and a research plan known as a moderator's guide. Also, facilities are required that are centrally located and conducive to discussion. Depending on the type of respondents desired, you might need some assistance in recruiting a representative group of people.

Focus groups can be conducted at association meetings, but be mindful of the bias that might result because members who do not attend meetings are not included in this group. Online focus groups are also being used to gather data.

No matter how representative a focus group is, a sample of just eight to ten people— or even samples from six different groups—is far too small to project out to a large or even moderate-sized group. A focus group can provide invaluable insights, but the results must be quantified by some other research technique in order to draw reliable inferences about the entire membership.

Comparison of Popular Survey Techniques

	Mail	Web Based	Fax	Telephone Interviews	Individual Interviews	Focus Groups
Relative cost	High	Moderate	Low	Moderate	High	Moderate
Length of Time	Long	Short	Short	Short	Long	Short
Response Rate	Moderate	Moderate	Moderate	High	Moderate	High
Respondent Confidentiality	High	Moderate	Moderate	Low	None	None
Validity of Sample	High	Low	Moderate	High	High	Moderate
Complexity of Questions	Moderate	Moderate	Moderate	Low	High	High
Potential for Interviewer Bias	Low	Low	Low	Moderate	High	Moderate

Data Collection Techniques

There are many ways to collect quantitative data, and many techniques are evolving due to changes in technology.

- **Mail surveys.** The most basic technique is sending questionnaires through the Postal Service. The main advantage of mail surveys is the ability to generate a sample that is representative of the entire membership, not just those who have e-mail addresses, for example. With the proliferation of e-mail traffic, legitimate and otherwise, a mailed survey just might get more notice on a member's desk than an e-mailed survey in a crowded computer inbox.

  There are two major disadvantages of a mailed-out survey: 1) the long time it takes to mail and receive a written questionnaire, and 2) the high cost of printing and postage.

- **Fax surveys.** If a written survey is faxed to a carefully designed sample, it has the same characteristics as a mail survey—plus a few advantages. Distribution of the questionnaire is faster, and a fax may draw more notice from the respondent. Surveys that are either mailed or faxed can both be faxed back by the respondent.

  Be wary of the "fax back" survey that is dropped into the middle of a publication or newsletter. Although inexpensive, this approach does not have a designed sample, and it presumes—erroneously—that everyone reads the publication or all parts of it. Therefore, the results can easily be biased.

- **Web-based surveys.** Typically, the Web-based survey is accessible through a link on the association's Web site or in an e-mailed letter to the member. It is easy to access the survey with a browser as no special software is required.

  The key advantages of this method are the speed at which members can be contacted, the instantaneous capture of data, and the confidentiality afforded respondents. Drawbacks include a lower response rate than mailed surveys and biased samples since all members don't have or don't provide their e-mail addresses to the association, as well as e-mails that bounce due to bad addresses or erratic connections.

- **E-mail (Internet) polling.** Questionnaires, as a document or PDF attachment, can be distributed by e-mail. Sampling techniques, of course, should be used to ensure valid and reliable responses. The questionnaire can be completed and e-mailed back to the association. This method is less effective than Web-based since there may be a software requirement on the part of the respondent, questionnaires returned by e-mail can bounce, and data processing is more cumbersome.

- **Interactive surveys.** Computer-assisted surveys (distributed on diskette or via the Internet) tailor questions to the initial responses. For example, a regular member might see certain questions while an associate member might see others. As a further refinement, a large company might be asked about different issues than a smaller one.

- **Instant-response units.** Freestanding boxes or kiosks represent another means of computer-assisted data collection. They can be used at a meeting or trade show to gather on-the-spot evaluations and information. The major drawback of such devices is that respondents are self-selected and might not necessarily be representative of all meeting attendees.

- **Mixed mode.** One technique offers the advantages of Web-based surveys with fewer of the disadvantages. Mixed mode surveys combine Web-based, mail, and even fax techniques. As an example, if you drew a sample of association members, a link to the Web-based survey would be e-mailed to members with good e-mail addresses. Members whose e-mail bounced or who didn't have an e-mail address would be sent a fax survey. Finally, remaining members would receive a copy of the survey by mail. This adds time and money, but ensures that all members have an equal chance of participating.

Some of the newer approaches offer convenience or cost savings to the association, some lower the burden on respondents, and almost all promise expediency. The overriding question to answer is whether the data collection method will help your association achieve its research objectives within a given budget.

Survey Sampling

After you have established a research plan, you must determine how many people to survey. In many associations, the first inclination is to survey all of the members. Depending on the size of the organization, however, doing so could prove very expensive and time consuming.

It's usually appropriate and more efficient to survey a specially selected subgroup of members. There is a scientific basis for determining how large a sample is required to provide a statistically significant representation of the entire group. If you have a large membership or list of names, a probability sample can be constructed that will produce statistically reliable estimates of the attitudes and opinions of the entire association. For example, 400 randomly selected responses from an association with 10,000 members will produce statistics that are within 5 percentage points of the statistics for the entire group, 95 percent of the time. This is a standard of reliability that is customarily expected of association surveys.

Using a sample enables you to save on printing and postage (for a written survey) and on data entry and tabulation fees. A smaller sample is easier to manage and follow up, especially if a telephone survey is being conducted. By using sampling procedures, you can determine the precision of the statistical estimates derived from the sample—the level of confidence and level of sampling error.

In general, the total number of questionnaires received is less important than the percentage of people who responded. Consider a trade association with 2,000 corporate members. If you mailed a questionnaire to all members and 500 of them returned it, you would have a reasonably large database on which to conduct statistical analysis. However, 500 out of 2,000 is only a 25 percent response rate; you have *not* heard from 75 percent of your members, after giving everyone a chance to respond.

For comparison, suppose you sent a questionnaire to every other member, a sample of 1,000. Furthermore, you sent a follow-up mailing of the questionnaire to the same group. Your total out-of-pocket costs are the same as the first example, a mailing of 2,000. If you again receive 500 responses, your response rate is 50 percent (500 out of 1,000 names) and your statistics are based on one-half rather than one-fourth of all members. There is a greater likelihood that the second group of respondents (based on a 50-percent return) is more representative than the first scenario in which the response rate was only 25 percent.

The science of sampling is well-established, and much of the information we are exposed to every day is based on sampling. Political polls, for example, are based on relatively small samples of voters (less than 2,000) and usually provide accurate estimates of how the larger group will vote. Government and businesses frequently use sampling techniques to provide information for decision making while minimizing the cost of research and reducing the time it takes to collect data.

Sampling Terminology

The total group you would like to gather information about is referred to as *the population*. This could be all of your members or, more likely, everyone in your profession or industry—both members and nonmembers. The *sampling frame* is the actual source of names used to select the sample. While the *universe* (another term for population) might be all people in your profession, your only source of nonmembers might be the subscription list of a professional journal. This list, therefore, becomes the *sampling frame*.

A *probability sample* is a group of people selected or drawn so that everyone in the population has a known probability of being included. Combining the probability of being selected with known characteristics of the population—such as age, location, and gender—allows you to develop a sample that, in fact, represents the population. The reliability of information obtained from a probability sample can be computed with the help of statistical theory.

A sample in which each person in the population has an equal chance of being selected is known as a *simple random sample*. Statistical measures exist to indicate how reliable the data from a random sample will be. Many associations have sophisticated membership databases that can select a random sample of any given size. (Remember to print or make additional copies of the list for reference because you usually cannot reproduce a random sample at a later date.)

A practical approach to obtaining a probability sample is the *systematic* or *nth name* sample. This is useful if you don't have the capability of drawing a random sample or if the sampling frame is only available as hard copy, such as membership directories or mailing labels. To obtain a systematic sample, first determine the size sample you need.

(Remember, if you want opinions from 400 respondents, but you expect a 50 percent response rate, you need 800 people in your sample. When half of the 800 respond, you will have sufficient data for your analysis.)

The proportion of the sample size to the sample frame is expressed as a fraction, such as "one-fourth" or "one twenty-fifth" or "one nth." Finally, sample units are chosen by determining a random statistical starting point and then choosing every "nth" name from the sampling frame. For example, if you need 800 names from a mailing list of 3,200, you would determine a random starting point between 1 and 2,400 (using a random number table, computer programs, or even a calculator), and select every fourth name thereafter (800 divided by 3,200 = one fourth). If you want the sample to be representative geographically, use a mailing list in zip code order. This procedure will work with a limited list of names or a list in a spreadsheet.

Associations often want to make sure their sample is representative of various subgroups or "strata." *Stratified sampling* requires you to divide the population into smaller groups of people with similar characteristics—strata—and draw a separate sample from each group.

For example, if 20 percent of your membership is female, a random sample of the entire membership might not generate enough questionnaires from females to do any reasonable analysis. You can obtain a larger number of females with a stratified random sample. First, treat male members as one strata or group, and select a random sample of all males; next, select a separate random sample of females. The size of each sample can be adjusted or weighted so that you end up with a total group of respondents that is representative of the entire sampling universe.

A *non-probability sample* simply means everyone in the group does not have an equal chance of being selected. A frequently used non-probability sample is the *convenience sample,* which includes people who can be contacted easily—such as those attending a convention or members of a committee. Frequently, however, those groups are not representative of the entire association membership.

An inexpensive means of sampling, especially for personal interviews or telephone calls, is *quota sampling.* With this technique, the interviewer selects people until a predetermined quota is reached. For example, a personal interview (intercept) at a trade show might require the interviewer to talk to the first 20 men and the first 35 women he or she encounters and then stop after each quota is reached. Here again, you have no way of ensuring that these interviewees are representative of the larger universe of trade show attendees.

Accuracy and Precision of Results

There is no guarantee that the sample used for a survey is actually representative of the entire population. You can, however, measure the *sampling error* associated with the results to determine the precision of the survey's findings. Precision is measured by two values: the *confidence level* and the *margin of error.*

The confidence level is a measure of how representative the sample is of the total population. Many random samples can be drawn, but since you will only conduct the survey once, you use the first random sample drawn. The question then arises whether the first sample drawn is, in fact, representative of the entire population. You can design a sample—determine how large it should be relative to the population—so that if you drew 100 different random samples, 95 of them would be very representative of the population. The other five samples might be a little biased. This is an example of a 95 percent confidence level.

The other ingredient in the precision of survey results, the *margin of error*, refers to the variation in responses between the sample and the entire population. Expressed as a plus-or-minus figure (+/- 5 percent is typical for association membership surveys), it gives you the projected range of responses had you surveyed the entire population. With a +/- 5 percent level of error, for example, if 75 percent of respondents answered "Yes" to a certain question, you could assume that between 70 and 80 percent of the entire population would answer the same way.

First decide the acceptable level of error for your survey. Then, by referring to the statistical table, you can determine how large a sample you need (number of questionnaires returned, not mailed out) for any given population. The table contains sample sizes required for finite populations, given a 95 percent confidence level for a given maximum sampling error. It gives the highest sampling error and, consequently, the most conservative estimate of the sample size needed to obtain the desired sampling error.

To use the table, look up the size of the population you want to survey—say, 4,800 members—and the sampling error you are willing to accept (5 percent). The value at the intersection in the table (rounding off the size of the population to 5,000) is 357

Sample Sizes Required for Finite Populations
95% Confidence Level
Percent in population assumed to be 50%*

Size of Population	±3%	±4%	±5%
1,000	**	375	278
2,000	696	462	322
3,000	787	500	341
4,000	842	522	350
5,000	879	536	357
10,000	964	566	370
20,000	1,013	583	377
50,000	1,045	593	381
100,000	1,056	597	383
>500,000	1,065	600	384

* Use this table when unable or unwilling to estimate a maximum or minimum percentage value to be expected. Using 50 percent, while conservative, will result in a larger sample size than if an estimate other than 50 percent is used.

** In these cases, more than 50 percent of the population is required in the sample.

Source: Adapted from tables in H.P. Hill, J.L. Roth, and H. Akin, *Sampling in Auditing*, The Ronald Press, New York, 1962.

individuals. The survey results estimated in a sample of 357 will be within 5 percentage points of the actual value of the entire membership of 4,800. Remember, to get 357 responses, you will have to sample a larger group since it's unlikely you will achieve a 100 percent response rate. For most associations, a random sample of 1,000 members would produce a response of at least 350, a 35 percent response rate.

Special Considerations

Association surveys are voluntary—you can't force members to participate. You can, however, restrict the results of a survey to participants, thereby providing a tangible incentive for members to submit data.

With a large membership, the same sampling considerations apply to external research surveys as to internal ones. This is appropriate when you are estimating values that are typical of a whole class of individuals or organizations, such as salaries, operating ratios, and so forth. If the objective of the survey is to project a total value for a group, such as industry shipments or the aggregate revenue of a group of professionals, other sampling approaches are appropriate.

The U.S. Bureau of the Census uses special sampling methodologies, such as trying to achieve very high participation rates for the largest companies but accepting lower participation rates for smaller companies. This is the well-known 80-20 rule or Paretos Law: You obtain about 80 percent of the total units from the largest 20 percent of the companies. Also, if you must make estimates for some missing companies, those for smaller companies will have a much smaller effect on the overall value you wish to quantify.

Some trade association research programs aim to estimate the total size of the industry. Since participation is voluntary and nonmembers might be excluded, there are always some companies that do not submit shipments or sales data. The data from the association's sample of participants can be extrapolated or projected up to an industry total by two methods.

The first method uses association data to estimate periodic changes, such as month to month, which are benchmarked to independent estimates of the industry total. This is known as the *link-relative method*—literally linking one period of time with an earlier period. You can obtain the independent estimate from government reports, such as the Annual Survey of Manufacturers published by the Bureau of the Census. Some associations even hire consultants to conduct their own annual census of all known companies, using the resulting information to benchmark periodic surveys.

The second technique used to generate an industry estimate is known as *load factoring*. This procedure requires you to identify all companies in the industry that do not participate in the association survey. Members who participate in the association's program are then asked to estimate the size of each non-participating company. These independent estimates are analyzed, and a composite estimate of each non-participant is factored into the association's periodic survey to produce an estimate for the entire industry.

Survey Logistics

Some associations with comprehensive statistical research programs rely on full-time specialists or a department to handle all aspects of a project internally. Staff responsibilities will vary from association to association, but may include committee liaison, data collection, statistical tabulations, and report preparation and distribution.

The scope of in-house research activities can be broad, ranging from surveys of members and nonmembers to surveys of constituents such as the general public, industry customers, or industry suppliers. Some associations allow their research departments to sell reports and conduct custom research for outside organizations.

Another alternative is to outsource the entire research function to an outside supplier or consultant. Suppliers can serve as an extension of the association's staff, not only collecting and tabulating data but also communicating directly with members and even serving on the research committee. It's also possible to combine the two approaches, so that the association's staff collaborates with a provider, and each performs some elements of the research function.

Contracted Research

If the association staff lacks experience in conducting survey research, research firms, consultants, or specialists should be engaged. Comprehensive or ongoing research projects require a lot of planning and outside counsel is often beneficial.

When looking for providers, search for firms or individuals with experience in conducting research for associations. Also check the firm's credentials, such as membership in the trade groups such as Council of American Survey Research Organization or the Marketing Research Association.

Competitive bids are important but, because research is often hard to pin down in advance, prepare a request for proposal so that all of the bids you receive are comparable.

The RFP should include your research objectives, the size of the population to be surveyed, the desired completion date, the importance of experience in your industry or profession, and what the basis will be for selecting a partner.

Associations with formal research programs usually rely on a committee for guidance and policy setting, and implementation is handled by staff or consultants. The statistics or research committee is typically charged with defining the products, services, job descriptions, and so forth that are measured by the research program. It also monitors the accuracy and reliability of the data being generated. Committees can be standing or ad hoc and may have budget authority. However configured, the statistics or research committee is the members' voice in gathering useful and valuable information.

Information Reporting

An important role of the association is to be the clearinghouse of information for the industry or profession. As such, external research for the association not only gathers data, it must also disseminate that information. Just as there are numerous methods for collecting data, there are many techniques for reporting information back to stakeholders:

1. **Written Reports.** Can be printed and mailed, or, increasingly, delivered as PDF attachments via e-mail. Reports can also be posted to the association's Web site.

2. **Data tables.** Tabular data can be displayed in spreadsheets and mailed, e-mailed, or posted to a Web site. The advantage to the user is that ubiquitous spreadsheets are easy to use, eliminate the re-keying of data from written reports, and are easily stored. Spreadsheets can also be designed to show member data next to composite or aggregate data from the association.

3. **Interactive Database.** Custom programs can be designed, implemented, and posted online to offer members and users instant access to data. These systems can also accommodate the continuous updating of member data, such as monthly sales, and the continuous updating of industry-wide results.

Legal Issues

Although associations can gather and disseminate data, even from and to competitors, they must not run afoul of antitrust laws in the process. The association may not use its research to fix prices, allocate markets, or reduce competition in general.

Based on legal opinions and interpretations of federal guidelines issued by the Federal Trade Commission and the U.S. Department of Justice, observe the following guidelines when conducting association research:

1. Participation in the program must be voluntary.

2. Clarify that the program's intent is to collect and furnish useful business information and not to affect any agreement or understanding between competitors with respect to business activities.

3. Data received should involve historical or past transactions.

4. Preserve the confidentiality of an individual participant's data.

5. Present information in a composite or summarized form.

6. Do not show data supplied by one participant to any other participant.

7. Ensure that published reports do not contain comments that may be interpreted as advising or recommending to participants that they take any sort of joint or concerted actions.

8. Make results of association statistical programs available to nonmembers, including customers and suppliers of members, if they have a legitimate business need for such information.

9. You may charge nonmembers a higher price for the results than members—but the price charged may not be so high as to compel membership.

10. The results of a survey may be restricted to participants, but neither nonparticipating members nor nonmembers may have access to the results.

References

American Society of Association Executives, *Attracting, Organizing & Keeping Members,* Washington, D.C.,1989.

American Society of Association Executives, *Conducting Marketing and Industry Research,* Washington, D.C., 1998.

American Society of Association Executives, *Policies and Procedures,* Volume 6 PR/Publications/Marketing/Research, Washington, D.C., 2006.

American Society of Association Executives, *Principles of Association Management,* 3rd ed., Washington, D.C., 1996.

Carey, Stephen, ed., *Marketing the Nonprofit Association,* The Greater Washington Society of Association Executives Foundation, Washington, D.C., 1991.

Foundation of the American Society of Association Executives, *How to Conduct Association Surveys,* Washington, D.C., 1976.

Jacobs, Jerald A., *Association Law Handbook,* 3rd ed., American Society of Association Executives, Washington, D.C., 1996.

Kotler, Philip, *Strategic Marketing for Nonprofit Organizations,* 5th ed., Prentice-Hall, Englewood Cliffs, New Jersey, 1996.

Rea, Louis M. and Richard A. Parker, *Designing and Conducting Survey Research: A Comprehensive Guide*, 2nd edition, Jossey-Bass Inc., 1997.

Salant, Priscilla and Don A. Dillman, *How to Conduct Your Own Survey,* John Wiley & Sons Inc., 1994.

Sirkin, Arlene Farber and Michael McDermott, *Keeping Members: The Myths and Realities,* ASAE Press, 1995.

Webster, George D., *The Law of Associations,* Mathew Bender, New York, 1975.

Zotta, Leann, *1,000 Ideas for Membership Professionals,* Berkshire Press, 1998.

About the Author

Michael Sherman, CAE, is president of Association Research, Inc., an independent research firm that specializes in conducting surveys for associations. Before founding ARI in 1984, Sherman served on the staff of the National Association of Furniture Manufacturers for 10 years, the last three as executive vice-president.

Review Questions

As the membership director of a national professional association with 10,000 members, you are asked by the president to prepare a plan to conduct research to find out what current and future members want.

1. What staff or volunteers would you include in planning or overseeing the project?

2. Outline the basic steps in planning and completing the survey.

3. What types of surveys (mail, fax, web-based) would get the highest response rate from your members?

4. What staff resources are available, and what outside resources (research firms, consultants, or experts) will be required?

5. How will the results of the survey be used to evaluate or improve your association's products or services?

18

Managing
Information Technology

Maynard H. Benjamin, CAE

W HEN I LOOK BACK at almost 30 years of advising association executives about the management of information technology, it is amazing
to see how far we have come in such a short period of time. When
Professional Practices in Association Management was put together in
1997, we were in the middle of an explosion of knowledge in our understanding of the
Internet and what it could do for us as association managers.

Today, the Internet is a mature technology, and we are comfortable in our work with
this important communications channel. Most of us probably feel that we could not
operate an association without a Web page. We communicate everything via e-mail
today, and many association management publications are as available on the Web as
they are in hard copy. We have created a diverse communications system that requires
a different set of information management skills as well as overlaying association management skills.

We call ourselves information technology managers; we're not systems managers
anymore. Most of the computer technology we work with centers around desktop
computers linked to a server. In today's environment, we are seldom without access
to our information network. We are connected via our personal digital communication devices, e-mail coupled with cellular telephones, or our "Blackberry." We cannot
function well without broadband access, and it seems all of us are working more hours
because we are interacting so closely with our membership via the technology we use.
So how do we manage this information?

Getting Comfortable with the Information Management

When I first wrote this chapter, I told you that the most important aspect was the technology. Now, I am telling you that it is the information you have that is unique to your organization and your profession. In today's environment, everything is accessible. By simply going to www.google.com, you can find out just about anything on anyone. You can find out where your members live, what sort of a house they live in, what type of community, and more information than you ever wanted to know. If it is on your association's Web site, then chances are you have been or you will be "googled." So how do you deal with this information explosion, and how do you build a unique environment for your organization in which you can thrive in this world of knowing everything about everyone? Here are some rules to master before you go forward:

- **Information has value.** Your advantage as a trade association or professional society is that you have the corner on the information that relates to your trade or profession. If you don't, your members are going elsewhere so the information that you have, the "content" of your trade or profession, is the real asset that you have to manage today. We start with the understanding that information has value in this new association marketplace.

- **All information is time sensitive.** All of the content you collect has a short shelf life, so you have to develop a system of processes that keeps your information base updated continuously. This is where costs come in because keeping member profiles updated, member purchases updated, and just the changes in the member data updated requires a great deal of information maintenance time, so you have to acquire technology that assists you in the maintenance function.

- **Privacy is an issue.** The privacy of the personal information that you store in your association's database must be guarded against intrusion. Many associations have not given very much thought at all to the information that they keep on members, what that information involves, and how they are going to protect that information. Yet, we as an industry are just as vulnerable as other industries because we gather and retain this information. Home addresses, private telephone numbers, e-mail addresses, and the like are just the type of information that Web-based advertisers would like to have, so how are you going to protect yourself?

- **Information security is the issue for the next decade.** All of us went through exercises to update our information systems to check them during the changeover to the current millennium, and I am sure that everyone is now thinking "why did we do that." September 11 caused us to rethink backup systems and offsite security. For example, many associations have designated another association to serve as a backup site if something happened to their offices. If you are in a major metropolitan area and you don't have an information backup processing and security plan, you need to think about this quickly.

So we operate in a much broader information environment today, and we have to analyze our needs for information much differently than ever before. Association management processes are no longer linear; they are nonlinear and that means we work with information bases that can arrange information in a wide variety of different ways. We just have to worry about the source information; the rest is created for us via the relational databases that power many modern association information systems. So now that we have got this concept of information management rather than systems management locked in our thinking, it is important to talk about what functions we manage and the process we use to manage those functions.

Managing Common Functions with Information Technology

Association management, at its essence, is a relationship management business. The most common functions that are supported by technology are the following:

- **Membership Management and Activity Tracking.** The most successful and effective associations have the ability to create a unique relationship between themselves and their members. Some know this process as customer relationship management, and others call it member relationship management. Whatever you call it, it is important to understand that personal relationships count in this Internet-driven communications world. How many associations do you know that send out e-mail blast after e-mail blast and wonder why their members do not respond? Given the quantity of e-mails that most members receive today, if it is not immediately relevant or known, it gets deleted. So your association systems solution must give you the capability to uniquely target offers of products or services to individuals, not just to companies or families of members. That means you must collect as much information as you can on member purchases, event attendance, and preferences.

  Larger associations have an even more difficult problem in this regard because their data collection and management tasks are magnified by the volume of their members. Finding new ways to gather data is important. For larger associations it may involve bar coding publications so that the barcode is lifted when the publication is sold, and you can track sales to an individual and then a company. It is also important to keep in mind that the value of members is far beyond the dues they pay. It is their asset value to your association. That asset value is the sum of their dues, purchases, money spent at meetings, and some sense of the value of time they spend with your organization. I often argue that when you are developing a membership retention plan, start with the shifts in asset values first. A member who suddenly stops purchasing products or attending events is at risk for leaving, and you need to spend time with that member. A well-structured information system can assist you in gathering this information.

- **Donor Management.** If your association has a foundation that is a related business entity or if you are a 501(c)(3), then donor management is a critical software function. Donors are as critical as members in terms of their management and preferences. Donors provide resources because they identify with the cause or issue that is in need of support. It is the value proposition you offer that is critical to their desire to give and keep giving to your organization. So donor management is a great deal like membership management. It involves collecting data on preferences and interests and linking the offer with the interests of the donor. Too many organizations act like once a donor has given they will never give again. This is one of the most critical mistakes you will ever make in a donor management program.

  Many donors will give time and again if they feel that the organization they are giving to uses their resources wisely and continues to make progress on issues for which they provided their money in the first place. So that system must give you information about key data for donors: when they gave, why they gave, and what they gave for. This information will help you link them to other donors and campaigns. I learned a long time ago that one never stops raising money; it is a continuous process of linking donors and opportunities to give. The truly effective fundraisers are able to raise a great deal of money from relatively few donors and then link those donors to others to raise even more money. Statistically, most donor-based organizations find that 40 percent of donors are providing 80 percent of the money donated. Fundraising campaigns fail because they lose their linkage with the reasons that people gave to the organization in the first place. Systems that support that process are critical. Donors are often members, too. They have a link with the association and an enthusiasm that must be nurtured and supported.

- **Committee and Chapter Management.** Volunteerism is under attack from a host of forces today. Corporations are wary of having their executives participate in professional societies or trade associations because it is just one other thing that takes time away from work. Publicly owned corporations are even more sensitive today because shareholder activism is at an all time high, and sometimes association involvement is considered a perk rather than something that is important in which to participate. This means that managing involvement and targeting involvement on those members most likely to find that involvement meaningful is critically important to the future of an association. It is much easier to spot a potential problem through a system that monitors member involvement than if you are just using anecdotal data.

  Many companies want reports on what their company volunteers are doing, and having a system that supports this process is important to continuing their involvement. For professional organizations or trade associations that have chapters, systems that support chapter activities help to support staff productivity. Many of these chapter management modules also interrelate with education and certification management software. The most important thing to keep in mind is the interrelationship that must exist between the functions that are supported by your information system. Chapter management must be a subset of the membership management system; it must use the same membership file. Committee management is also the same; remember it is all about the time and dollars that a member spends with your organization. If it does not all fit together, you do not have a complete picture.

- **Education and Certification Management.** Associations assist in the knowledge management process through their educational and certification processes. There must be an interrelationship between those processes that manage a member's information and those that provide access to learning opportunities. Remember, it is all about creating customer value and a relationship with a member.

- **Meeting and Events Management.** Part of any standard association system should be a meeting and events management system that pulls from the membership database and also arrays event statistics, points of contact, manages counts, interfaces with cash and receivables management processes, and otherwise supports the executive in conducting education programs and other events.

- **Marketing and Marketing Campaign Management.** Sometimes these modules are part of a member relationship management system or a donor management system. These modules will help track a given promotion in terms of who responds to that promotion. Too many associations just send out e-mail blasts and hope for the best. A marketing or marketing campaign management module helps the executive manage the information flow from a marketing effort. Would it not be nice to know who responded to your email or direct mail and why?

- **Web Content Management and E-commerce Activities.** Most associations have Web sites today that present more than just static information. We have staff called Web masters who are responsible for the placement of the content that we generate on the Web or interface with other Web sites to present that content. Information has a short shelf life, so Web content has to constantly be updated. Some association management systems are designed to work with the member-only areas of a Web site, while many others are stand alone. This preference is really up to the executive as the challenge to the association is information security. What seems most efficient to do can create even more information management challenges. Just be mindful that there is software that can work with your word processing system, your electronic spreadsheet, and presentation software and translate these files into files that will be displayable on your Web page. This feature is simply called an HTML conversion utility, and most popular office management software packages have this utility.

- **Order and Inventory Management.** If you sell publications, offer educational opportunities, or sell other materials, an order and inventory management module is a must for your association management system. You need to quickly be able to determine inventory levels, the number of people attending an event as related to the capacity of that event, easily send a confirmation, print a shipping label, and send a transaction record to accounting for billing. Without an order and inventory management module, you will be doing a great deal of hard work that your system could better accomplish.

- **Billing and Accounts Receivable.** One of the final key components of an association management system is a billing and accounts receivable module. This allows you to receive transactions from order entries, combine them with membership data, and send out a manual or electronic invoice. Most associations that sell on the Web accept credit cards, and these modules also account for credit card transactions in process, saving you a great deal of reconciliation in the long run. Managing your receivables is critical to management of the association's cash flow. Your accountant will love it if you have a system to do so rather than manual effort. Remember, every bill is also an opportunity to sell. Use your billing system as a marketing opportunity.

- **Accounting.** Most association management systems readily interface with standard off-the-shelf accounting packages. Try not to buy a package that is customized into the association management system you are considering. It is best to let your accountant or auditor do the shopping for you in this area because it will make your life easier.

- **Reporting.** If you put it in, it means you have to be able to get it out, so arranging information in files is a critical feature of most good association management systems. The ability to extract information from your database and present that information in reports should be a straight forward process to even the CEO. So make sure that the reporting applications are simple, straightforward, and produce the results that you want them to produce.

Assessing, Upgrading, or Acquiring Information Management Systems

The process of assessing and acquiring an information system is a great deal simpler than it used to be. Most information systems are networks of personal computers, and yes, you can easily integrate an Apple Mac into most networks today. So the first thing to keep in mind is that it is not complicated. Below is a 10-step process that has been used time and time again when associations take a look at their information support management.

Step 1: Form a Team. The best way to look at whether you need to upgrade or change the information system you use is to form a cross-departmental team to do the research. Use people that are actually accomplishing the work instead of a management team. You will get a better result. If you have an information technology manager or director, put that person in charge, but don't give that person the sole vote. The group needs to decide the factors that need to be reviewed.

Step 2: Follow an organized process. If you want an external and independent view, hire a consultant to help you. It is cheap insurance to ensure that your team has covered all the angles. However, as a long-time consultant, I do not believe that hiring a consultant abdicates the need for the team. Remember, at the end of the process, everyone has to be reasonably satisfied. You need to go through department by department and examine what the information system is supposed to provide and what it is not currently providing. Document these inconsistencies and find out why it is not doing what you want it to do. Is it the capability of the system or just the structure of the information? ASAE & The Center have a great deal of information that you can use that shows you the process to follow. It is just a matter of documenting steps, needs, and capabilities.

Step 3: Determine if you need an upgrade or a completely new system. Most association management software packages have been in the market for a long time, so there are multiple versions of each system. In many cases you will not have to throw out your system, but merely purchase the next generation of that system. However, if you have custom-developed software built from a relational database system that is no longer in the market, get prepared to spend some money. If you always stick with the standard packages that other associations use, you should be able to upgrade with ease. Hardware is the same way. Personal computers are so cheap today that it is easier just to purchase a new one than fix the old one. At my association, we fully depreciate our desktops every three years and replace them. We do the same with Notebook computers every four and with printers a maximum of every five years. We upgrade our servers every eight years maximum. Why does a small association do this? Because we have found that you have fewer problems in the long run if you catch the problems earlier.

Step 4: Think about distance learning. Many associations that are in the process of acquiring or upgrading information technology or a new Web solution completely forget about the importance of distance learning. In this broadband-driven world of today, content and people can be separated by more than the distance of a classroom. ASAE & The Center have great resources on distance learning, but I have also found that your local university has terrific resources and a system that you just might be able to leverage. Many universities offer classes on the Web, so what is stopping us? There is a skill to distance learning and procedures that have to be followed, so don't just jump in. Learn before you commit your organization to the wrong solution, but distance learning should be part of any consideration of an information technology upgrade or acquisition.

Step 5: Remember that communications and computing are interrelated today. How much thought have you given to going wireless or getting wired? How fast is your wire? If you are going to offer education across the Web, you cannot do it well on 100-based T wire. Wireless technology has come a long way; and if you have members that are constantly visiting and using your network, wireless may come in handy.

Remember that buildings are made out of all sorts of materials, so keep that in mind if you are thinking about a wireless network.

Hire a competent information systems wiring professional. Don't let your local electrician do the job unless he or she has experience. All wiring jobs are priced by drop, so get several bids, not just one; and go with someone who can wire the telephone system and the network. Make sure they are dependable by asking for references. You don't want to be waiting forever when moving into a new office because the wiring guy does not show. If it means paying a little extra to get a good person, do it. You should not be cutting the essentials.

Many associations now have telephone systems that integrate with their local area network. When you pull up a member record, it should be easy with one mouse click to dial that member's number via your telephone system. For larger associations that have a diverse membership this helps greatly in keeping a personalized relationship with members. Smaller associations may want to think twice because these systems are not cheap. It does help somewhat if your information system is integrated with your Web server, but remember to consider the security of the total system. Most hackers are a great deal more technically competent than your information technology manager, so distance and separation do not necessarily make the information system stronger.

Step 6: Don't forget backup and security. September 11 has taught all of us that we need backup for our information systems. Make sure that your systems development plan clearly outlines how you will be operational in the event of a catastrophic failure. Fires do happen and destroy association records, so keep backup tapes in a fire-proof container and also maintain a set offsite. Have another association with a system like yours serve as backup and vice versa. Data security is the issue of the next decade. If you are keeping credit card and personal information on members, you need to have a data protection plan. People do come in and steal desktop units, passwords are easily overcome, and now you have a problem. The best action that you can take is to have your system's security assessed by a competent professional. Again, ASAE & The Center have listings of these individuals, or your auditor can provide you with some names.

Step 7: Make sure you understand the technology; it should not mesmerize you. Too many association executives when faced with a system purchase or upgrade decision say, "I don't want to know." That is not a good approach nor is it healthy for your career. You have to know today because information management is association management. If you don't know how your system works and why, find out. If you don't understand the terms, get someone to define them. Ask questions and more questions until you are sure you know. This is not something that a CEO can delegate to a subordinate without some vague understanding of what is going on. Too many associations make big mistakes in this area because information management becomes a non-priority when it is delegated to lower level staff in the organization. Stay involved, ask questions, and make sure you understand.

Step 8: Put it in writing with contracts. Never sign an information technology acquisition agreement without understanding the terms of that agreement. Never pay more than 50 percent up front and never pay everything until you are totally satisfied or your staff is satisfied with what you received. That goes for Web development services, system development services, and hardware and software development. It is always best to let counsel see everything and never get pressured into signing for a good deal. Remember, they never loved you as much as they did before you signed their contract. Keep it professional, understand the terms, and you will avoid being disappointed.

Step 9: Hire good people. We were most fortunate at my association to have a staff person who started as a membership coordinator and later became our systems manager and "Web goddess." It takes people that have a good set of analytical skills to figure out how something operates and how it can be changed, but they do exist. And you don't have to hire them from a large computer consulting company. Given the simpler nature of many Web-based applications, mere mortals can become pretty good Web masters. Accountants and membership staff can be trained to maintain an information system. Just make sure that whomever you hire is dependable, patient, willing to be trained, and willing to train others. Never put all your eggs into a single basket; always have a backup person that is cross-trained. ASAE & The Center also have terrific resources and job banks in which to locate people, as do your accountant and fellow association executives. Use the network of people in ASAE & The Center. It works.

Step 10: Use the resources available to you. Every year *Associations Now* publishes *A Guide to Technology Solutions*. It is a great reference with much useful information, including software reviews, articles evaluating Web site development activities, and a provider directory.

If your association is like ours, your e-mail inbox is full of offers to attend Webinars sponsored by software companies, consultants, and hardware providers. Use some care in what you go to, and don't be afraid to state up front that you're not buying, just learning. Webinars offered by ASAE & The Center, as well as their onsite education programs, are all pretty good.

You can pull up almost anything about association management and computing by going to Google, the popular Web-search utility. You can also go to www.netscape.com, www.yahoo.com, or even use the search utilities in Microsoft Explorer. There is no end to the information that is available to you today. It just takes a little time to search.

In closing, I hope that I have helped to demystify the process of upgrading an information technology system for you. Just remember the functions that need to be there and the steps to follow, and you will do just fine. There are many people through ASAE & The Center who will gladly provide you with information and advice. Use these resources, don't be afraid to ask questions, and remember that there is a little "geek" in all of us.

About the Author

Maynard H. Benjamin, CAE, is president and CEO of the Envelope Manufacturers Association, Alexandria, Virginia.

Review Questions

1. How involved should the chief staff executive be in information management?

2. What are two primary issues associations must address in relation to how member data is obtained and stored?

3. What are the major challenges in information management?

19

Knowledge Management

Richard V. Lawson

S O WHAT EXACTLY IS knowledge management? Knowledge management is something that all of us do. Specifically, we all use knowledge management systems, whether that knowledge simply resides in your brain, in a paper filing system, or in a multimillion dollar software system. Knowledge management happens continuously throughout our everyday lives. What makes this a tantalizing question—which incidentally seems to reinvent itself as a hot IT fad every other year—is that the ultimate premise remains the same, "How can I attain, organize, store, and retrieve information that is critical—mission critical if you prefer over-used IT metaphors?" When you boil it down to those essential requirements for knowledge management, the pictures clears significantly.

Knowledge Management (KM) can be further defined by three primary elements:

- How organizations gather, manage, and use knowledge. This is the 50,000 foot definition of KM.

- More specifically, KM refers to how an organization looks to improve outcomes and institutional learning by introducing specific practices and processes to identify know-how, best practices, expertise, and other intellectual capital for reuse in the organization.

- The key outcome of KM is knowledge transfer. How do you develop knowledge workers and is your organization committed to being a learning organization? A learning organization is simply one that has committed itself to a state of continuous adaptation and improvement.

As with many technologies, or technology-centric initiatives, KM shouldn't be undertaken without a clear strategic plan and certainly not out of tactical urgency. The underpinnings of KM require great consideration. It's often the easiest thing in the world to undertake an initiative such as KM simply because it's sexy. Unfortunately, it can also be the worst reason to do so and the initiative will likely fail and prove extraordinarily costly. The decision to implement a consolidated KM system should be driven by a clear vision of how knowledge can be gathered and reused and what the tangible benefit is.

In many cases, the vision is online communities of practice. Communities of practice usually consist of content areas on the Web site users go to leverage best practices and institutional knowledge. A tangible example of this type of KM could be a meeting topic database. Such a database might consist of keyword tagged historical program information detailing each session by topic with information about participation and financial performance. It could also have the related speakers list that would allow users to drive through the data by topic, venue, region, or speakers. Both staff and planning committees could leverage this kind of data to make more informed go, no-go decisions on current meeting proposals.

Other examples of motivations that often lead organizations to KM include the desire to

- Gain competitive advantage;
- Have greater innovation;
- Provide better customer experiences;
- Maintain consistency in best practices;
- Provide knowledge access for global organizations;
- Create a network effect between employees to increase the quality of shared information;
- Facilitate organizational learning; and
- Manage intellectual capital.

Once the organization has a vision on KM and its reuse, the next step is to decide what knowledge is mission critical and how the organization can gain a quantifiable benefit from its reuse. Aligning KM assets typically involves an analysis of existing knowledge repositories—scholarly journals, financial systems, meeting content—and the creation of new knowledge generating activities. Priorities need to be assigned and driven by measurable high-level organizational goals and vision. Knowledge can exist in paper and electronic forms, and proper attention needs to given to the costs associated with the digitization of paper assets and integration of electronic assets. Once an organizational commitment has been made and knowledge assets have been identified and prioritized, management can begin to assess what form a KM system might take.

It's probably prudent to speak briefly about these early KM steps and whether they should be undertaken solely by staff. Obviously there's a lot at stake, and nonprofit organizations vary considerably in size, structure, and staff expertise. In most cases, it's probably wise to engage a consultant specializing in KM to assist in the strategic and tactical discovery and decision making. Many of the interfacing areas could require special expertise, so you might need another consultant well versed in taxonomy, for example, to assist with the very rigorous exercises of developing your KM architecture. And even though you're likely to rely on outside expertise, it's important for executives to understand the high-level principles and the process. Also, many KM tasks can be staff driven and reduce cost, and it's always a good idea to have a dedicated project manager on staff to interface with the consultants and drive major milestones and deliverables.

The KM study and planning engagement will commence with a discovery phase where the consultant will look for answers to the following questions:

- **Is there a taxonomy or keyword system in place that can help organize and describe the knowledge assets?**
  This crucial first step is to assess/develop the organization's taxonomy. Taxonomy is simply a hierarchical classification system that defines an organization's information, disciplines, and activities that it undertakes as part of its routine business. Without an understanding of the business knowledge assets and how they can be organized and classified, knowledge chaos ensues. Put more simply, don't put the cart before the horse.

- **What are the paper-based knowledge sources?**
  This includes sources such as archives of journals and other publications that are considered relevant to the current market. It could also be meeting minutes, election results, financial statements, or any myriad of historical information.

- **What are the electronic-based knowledge sources?**
  Web site content is obvious. How about other electronic applications such as financial systems, journal manuscript and submitted paper systems, listservers, and membership directories. Also, consider emerging technologies that rapidly become knowledge repositories on their own, such as social networks, podcast archives, Wiki's, and intra-society information networks.

- **Is there an organizational mandate to become a learning organization?**
  Is the organization serious about leveraging knowledge to make meaningful business decisions and changes? Without the will to do so, it's not worth doing.

- **Are there any significant cultural hurdles?**
  To accomplish the needed outcomes, does the culture of the organization need to change? Who are the change agents within? Communication throughout the planning process will be essential to breaking down stovepipes and moving the organization forward effectively.

- **How will knowledge be reused, and how will knowledge transfer be facilitated?**
  What are the knowledge deliverables? How are they disseminated? What are the technology requirements and costs?

All executives need to concern themselves with what information/data is critical to strategic and tactical decision making in our organizations. How do we store this information such that it can be easily retrieved? Of key importance in today's high-flux technology environment overloaded with data is how knowledge can searched. Once your knowledge management environment or architecture is established, search technologies become just as important as the base system that stores the knowledge in the first place.

Knowledge management enablers, or repositories, come in some familiar names. Organizations leverage expert systems, knowledge bases, help desk tools, and document management software to organize and distribute knowledge. More recently, these enablers have increased in number to include such evolving technologies as e-learning, web conferencing, collaboration, content management, directories, Wiki's, and blogs. Implicit to all the systems is an enterprise search and, often times, a portal application that ties in the search and various knowledge sources into an easy-to-use computer interface. Managing a proliferation of data and information in increasingly complex operating environments and still allowing users efficient access remains KM's most challenging call.

The most typical reuse of knowledge is top-down. For example, an individual or small group of individuals working on a business objective evaluate knowledge assets to make their effort more efficient and productive. Using search information or information portals, users like these search across knowledge assets to access and retrieve relevant data. There are evolving efforts to make the collection and distribution of knowledge more organic, using a bottom-up approach, but in practice one typically finds the top-down strategy far more common.

To facilitate the capture and reuse of knowledge assets, many larger organizations now have a Knowledge Management Office (KMO) and even a Chief Knowledge Officer (CKO). The purpose, obviously, is maintaining a high commitment level to the practice of KM and a competitive advantage as a learning organization. It is doubtful that many associations could establish resources dedicated solely to the practice of KM. Often, successful KM initiatives are undertaken within a more limited scope, focusing on customer service or human resources where success is more easily quantified.

This leads one to the inevitable question, "Is knowledge management relevant to nonprofit organizations?" For the sake of discussion, a nonprofit organization should be viewed no differently than any other enterprise that survives by making smart strategic business decisions and leveraging historical experience in the context of salient market information. What's important to realize is that every enterprise must be agile when it retrieves information, analyzes it, and then makes smart business decisions. In the case of the nonprofit organization, this could be any number of decisions from a program outsourcing decision to marketing and member retention to finance. And the challenge in most of our organizations will be bringing the growing disparate information systems together into one useful knowledge repository.

What remain the nonprofit organization's greatest challenges are the financial resources and human assets to undertake and then make successful a KM practice. In other words, the desire may be there, but the resources may not. It's advisable to take smaller steps, maximizing your return on investment by leveraging KM in areas where the outcomes are measurable. For most nonprofit organizations these activities center on member services. Executives should look to sources of information that exist, such as places where members are already using electronic tools to facilitate the creation of content within their disciplines. Look to e-learning and your Web site, Web conferences, and collaboration. Extend existing information systems in logical ways to enrich content. For example, many nonprofit organizations have membership directories. Such directories can become invaluable sources of knowledge if the members are allowed to enhance their listings beyond the typical point-of-contact information. Look for the low hanging fruit. Identifying existing, valuable electronic assets and then putting a search interface on top of them remains the quickest and most cost-effective approach to reaping the rewards of knowledge collection and reuse.

Case Studies

At the time of this writing, the American Association of Pharmaceutical Scientists (AAPS) had undertaken several innovative, online, knowledge-generating initiatives. Two of these projects will be examined here to illustrate how AAPS is attempting to facilitate the capture and reuse of the knowledge. In both cases, the goal is to facilitate professional advancement for its member scientists and to give staff the opportunity to leverage the knowledge contained therein for business intelligence.

Case Study—AAPS MemberNet

In 2005, the American Association of Pharmaceutical Scientists replaced its membership directory with a social networking application named AAPS MemberNet. The intent was to leverage the high-level of use of the existing online directory to achieve an electronic facsimile of the face-to-face professional networking that remains a major benefit of membership. Since its inception, AAPS members have relied heavily upon meetings and conferences to connect with their colleagues to exchange innovative scientific ideas and enhance their professional development.

Online social networking software attempts to replicate this through extensive personal and professional profile pages that are then used by members to search for other members. Search criteria extend to personal interests, professional disciplines, educational experience, and so forth. As more members complete profiles, the data within the system becomes richer. The system mimics face-to-face networking, as it requires members who aren't acquainted to be "introduced" by a common friend, often referred to as a "connection". So, as members search and connect, a tiered network results…a friend of a friend, if you will. What develops over time is an incredibly rich set of data about your members.

Data, or in this case knowledge, can then be mined for expertise and other data by both staff and other members. Access to this type of knowledge can also be repurposed and combined with other electronic applications on the Web to create communities of practice. For example, users tracking a topic in a traditional bulletin-board thread could click on member profiles to understand more fully the background of the major contributors. They could also connect with them and ground their contacts by theme to facilitate a future working group around the topic. Perhaps they could leverage the expertise in the form of a publication or journal article. The possibilities are nearly endless.

However, after a successful launch, the "care and feeding" of the system remains a challenge. The early adopters are actively using the system, but the ultimate value of the system relies on a high percentage of usage. Without a critical mass of profiles, the networking effect doesn't occur. Like many Web-based community building initiatives, the AAPS MemberNet will require a commitment to marketing and product awareness. Its use is never in question, as it now serves as the online member directory. Staff effort will revolve around encouraging member adoption of the enhanced features and developing novel ways to utilize the knowledge contained within.

Case Study—AAPS Career Network

AAPS has also embarked upon a forward-looking initiative to partner with sister societies to enhance employment opportunities for the community as a whole. Member organizations typically service a vertical segment of a greater market. However, job opportunities don't necessarily fit so neatly within those silos. Put another way, scientists in related fields—members of related societies—can be equally qualified for those jobs. AAPS is spearheading an integration of association job boards to enhance member benefit and maximize employer value by networking job openings across all relevant societies. In effect, a multi-organization network is being created. Through open Web-based computer protocols, information is being shared across organizations to the benefit of all participants. This doesn't just extend to job advertisements, but also to job seeker profiles, professional development resources, and hiring company information.

The Career Network is also a network of hiring events with each participant hosting a network job fair at their annual conference. The outcome is a scientific hiring "road show" collaboratively promoted by the partners. Technology provides an information-systems backbone to run scheduling software and resume searching, but the end result is an opportunity for members to participate in a live, in-person event with the leading companies in the industry. The event is enhanced with professional development training seminars and receptions.

The KM applications to the network are fascinating. Not only is there an obvious and tangible benefit to the job seekers and hiring companies, but also to the society participants. Business rules will dictate what information is exposed to protect the privacy of the individuals, but there are robust prospects for understanding the hiring environment and industry trends at a much higher level than previously realized. Another obvious outcome could be to understand the impact colleague curricula is having on the pool of job candidates. Are colleagues teaching the right skills to make these graduate scientists employable? This is the true essence of business intelligence—the ability to gather, retain, and reuse critical information to benefit the programs and services offered.

The Career Network currently has four participants and is growing. The primary challenge has been in integrating commercial software providers. Commercial vendors don't have a stake in the project and aren't driven by the same member service imperative. In the worst case, the partner supports the network through face-to-face hiring events and promotional outreach, but in doing so, fails to realize the maximum potential for their organization. The network as a whole is being positioned as a strong nonprofit competitor to leading for-profit job boards, with the major differentiator being that the revenues are being captured and reinvested in the community as a whole. It's an innovative association business concept that is reaping valuable KM rewards.

Conclusion

In summary, knowledge management is a constantly evolving discipline. From its strictest definition, there's value to be gained from capturing, storing, and re-purposing knowledge to make more agile, strategic changes to your products and services. Big KM systems don't easily fit into the nonprofit world, and the organizational overhead of maintaining them is burdensome. Smart association executives will understand the basic premise of KM and the impact it can have in creating a learning organization. As is true with most things, targeted, limited scope implementations have the greatest chance of success and reap the maximum return on investment. Understand the sources of knowledge within your organization and more importantly how to access and leverage them. Monetary and staff assets should be aimed at planning a KM strategy and deploying the best search/portal technology to put the information in the hands of the end user. Lastly, don't underestimate the cultural and technology barriers to enhancing organizational learning and do so only under a clear objective and strategy.

About the Author

Richard V. Lawson is the technology director of the American Association of Pharmaceutical Scientists, Arlington, Virginia. He currently directs the association's Internet and career services strategies and had previously served as a technology strategist and consultant in the for-profit and government sectors.

Review Questions

1. What is Knowledge Management (KM), and what is a key benefit or outcome?

2. What is the name of the classification system that is commonly used to organize knowledge assets?

3. List some common knowledge repositories that exist within most organizations.

Facilities Management

Wayne E. Leroy, CAE

OW AN ASSOCIATION DESIGNS, furnishes, and equips its offices can greatly affect staff productivity and satisfaction. In addition, the association's physical environment contributes to the perception members have of the overall organization. Association office space is usually obtained in one of three ways:

- **Renting** is primarily for temporary or short-term arrangements, approximately two years or less. Associations often rent space during a transitional phase—such as when preparing to relocate or searching for different space requirements—or when they have a small staff and little capital to invest in property. In general, renting is the most expensive of the three options.

- **Leasing** is the method used by most associations. Lease arrangements usually are negotiated for three, five, or even ten years. Unlike renting, leasing gives the association greater control of occupancy expenses and the ability to negotiate leaseholder improvements to the space.

- **Owning** space or an entire building is the choice of associations that want permanency in a particular area or location. Like all forms of space occupancy, ownership has its pros and cons. Some of the positive aspects include the ability to budget for long-term expenditures, tax advantages (primarily in the area of depreciation), and more flexibility and control of space. On the downside are the responsibilities of maintaining and operating the facility.

No matter how space is obtained, consult experts in the fields of real estate, contracts, and property management before making your decision.

Occupancy Satisfaction

The people who use and visit the office space ultimately determine its efficiency, effectiveness, and appropriateness. Their satisfaction will depend upon how well the space and facilities perform in these four categories:

1. **Heating, ventilating, and air conditioning (HVAC) systems.** Occupants expect heat when the outside temperature is cold and cool air indoors when the outside temperature is hot. A well-designed system will perform these functions satisfactorily, while at the same time providing an appropriate mix of fresh outside air in exchange for exhausting inside air.

2. **Lighting.** Adequate, non-glare lighting is important for all employees, particularly those who spend much of their time in front of computer screens. Most office environments now use energy-efficient fluorescent lights with electronic ballasts. When designing appropriate lighting configurations, it is recommended that a minimum of 75 foot candles be provided in all work areas.

A Checklist for Productivity

Office space should be designed to allow optimum use and efficiency. Here are some general guidelines for office layout and furniture arrangement:

1. Plan each room with a purpose. Decide what the room will be used for and by whom. Consider noise and how it may affect surrounding work areas.
2. Keep furniture within the scale of the room.
3. Provide space for traffic by keeping doorways and major traffic lanes unobstructed. To redirect traffic, turn a sofa, a desk, or chairs toward the room and at right angles to the door, leaving a passageway.
4. Arrange furnishings to give the room a sense of equilibrium. For instance, balance high and low, angular and rounded furniture. If all furniture is low, create a feeling of height by incorporating shelves, mirrors, or pictures in a grouping.
5. Consider architectural and mechanical features. Nothing should interfere with the opening of windows or doors or with the operation of heating or air conditioning devices.
6. Don't overcrowd a room. It is always better to under furnish than over furnish.
7. In general, place large pieces of furniture parallel to the walls.
8. Avoid pushing large pieces tightly into a corner or close against floor-to-ceiling windows where a passageway should be allowed.
9. In rooms with slanted ceilings, arrange the heaviest furniture grouping along the highest wall.
10. For each employee—including his or her desk, chair space, and share of the aisle—calculate 50 to 75 square feet of working space.
11. A minimum of 9 feet by 12 feet is a standard size for small private offices.
12. Standard widths for main circulating aisles vary from 5 feet to 8 feet. Less important aisles vary from 3 feet to 5 feet.
13. Allow for at least one phone jack and two ethernet connections in every office or workspace to accommodate a telephone and high-speed electronic services such as ISDN, DSL, and T-1 lines for your computer.

---

3. **Facilities services.** These are the "little things" that go far in determining satisfaction or dissatisfaction with the space. They include custodial services (people expect their trash baskets to be emptied along with an occasional dusting of the furniture and vacuuming of the carpet) and parking (in reasonable proximity to the office and elevators). Other amenities that might be important to staff are eating areas for breaks and lunch and the availability of coffee, soft drinks, or snack items.

   Many cities and municipalities mandate recycling for certain items, such as office/white paper, glass, plastic, aluminum cans, newsprint, and cardboard. Recycling efforts are usually accomplished with the cooperation of the facility's custodial or housekeeping services; this may include providing specially designated containers in the office environment to encourage recycling initiatives.

4. **Aesthetics.** This is the intangible "feel" an office evokes—possibly through plants or greenery in the lobby, through framed photographs depicting the trade or profession the association represents, or through a display of the association's award-winning magazines and books. Whatever the furnishings chosen, they should reflect that people enjoy working in the environment and prompt visiting members to say, "I belong to a first-class association."

Health and Safety

Many factors control the health, safety, and well-being of association staff and visitors. Three areas require special attention:

- **Environmental health and safety**—The Occupational Safety and Health Administration (OSHA), www.osha.gov, of The U.S. Department of Labor, which oversees the Occupational Safety and Health Act of 1970, can provide volumes of materials on safeguarding the well-being of office occupants. The Environmental Protection Agency, www.epa.gov, also has a wealth of information on protecting one's health and environment. Because this area is the responsibility of managers and supervisors, it should appear in their job descriptions. Supervisors and managers are then more likely to treat the subject seriously by periodically holding safety discussions. During a staff meeting, for example, employees might talk about burn prevention in the kitchen or the use of handrails when going up and down stairs.

   Although common sense, along with wise and prudent judgment, will go a long way toward preventing office accidents, it's still helpful to provide health and safety training to employees. Appropriate training may be as simple as reviewing instructions for properly lifting or moving heavy items, such as boxes of materials being prepared for shipment to the annual meeting.

   Ergonomics is another key area that OSHA oversees. As employers, associations have an obligation to keep their workplaces free from recognized serious hazards, including ergonomic hazards. OSHA encourages employers where necessary to implement effective programs or other measures to reduce ergonomic hazards and associated muscular skeletal disorders. A great deal of information is currently available from OSHA and various industry and labor organizations on how to establish an effective ergonomics program, and OSHA urges employers to avail themselves of these resources.

Through its Alliance Program established in 2002, OSHA works with groups, including many trade and professional organizations, to leverage resources and expertise in developing compliance resources and sharing information with employers and employees to help prevent injuries, illnesses, and fatalities in the workplace.

- **Building security**—The goal is to protect the occupants of an office as well as its contents. For optimum security, only staff or other designated personnel typically have entry access to office space. Visitors' access may be controlled by staff at a receptionist area or some other type of security system (sign-in sheet, visitors' badges, employee escort, and so forth).

  Other security concerns include adequate lighting in outside areas such as parking areas and courtyards.

- **Emergency preparedness and fire protection**—The local jurisdiction in which the office is located will determine emergency requirements, which vary from one area to the next. Four common building requirements are:

  1. Fire alarms and smoke detectors.
  2. Sprinkler systems. All facilities require some type of fire-suppressant device—if not a full-fledged sprinkler system, then at least numerous fire extinguishers. Note that fire extinguishers require periodic inspection to ensure they will function when needed.
  3. Emergency lighting. If the building's electrical systems are designed to automatically shut off when an emergency system is activated, emergency lighting is necessary to guide office occupants to the nearest exits.
  4. An emergency plan. In addition to discussing emergency operations for office evacuations at staff meetings, an association should develop an emergency plan and distribute it to all staff members.

ADA Compliance

The Americans with Disabilities Act (ADA) became effective in the early 1990s. The original ADA regulations were divided into two categories:

1. **Existing facilities.** The basic provisions in the regulations indicated that existing buildings had to be made accessible to people with disabilities as long as making the required modifications did not constitute an undue financial burden of the facility owner.
2. **New construction.** New facilities were required to meet more extensive specifications for ensuring accessibility, which were contained in a document known as the ADA Accessibility Guidelines (ADAAG).

At its inception, two federal agencies were responsible for administering provisions of the ADA. The Department of Justice, Civil Rights Division, handled public accommodations regulations, while the Architectural and Transportation Barriers Board (Access Board) reviewed accessibility guidelines for both existing and new facilities. Today several federal agencies and departments have involvement with ADA.

ADA has multiple areas of compliance. The ones having the greatest effect on association facilities can be grouped into these four areas:

- **Detectable warnings.** This category includes warnings for such areas as curb ramps, hazardous vehicular areas, reflecting pools, platform edges, and so forth.
- **Employee work areas.** Current regulations for employee-only work areas require that a person be able to "approach, enter, and exit" the area.
- **Toilet rooms.** Toilet rooms must be accessible with appropriate door widths, wall clearance, handrails, and fixture heights.
- **Elevators.** Elevators should be equipped with audible systems, reachable control pads, touch identification, and an emergency telephone.

Because finding the correct information in a bewildering array of agencies can be daunting even for those experienced in dealing with ADA issues, it is recommended that the reader begin any search on matters involving ADA compliance by contacting:

United States Access Board
1331 F Street NW
Suite 1000
Washington, DC 20004-1111
www.access-board.gov

In an Emergency

To ensure the health and safety of staff, your association should have an emergency plan. Although the details will vary depending on the type of facility, a plan should address these four types of emergencies:

- Natural element—any unusual natural occurrence that has the potential to disrupt normal activities. Examples include earthquakes, floods, high winds, snow, and tornadoes.
- Civil disorder—actions by a person or people that have the potential to cause bodily harm. Examples are demonstrations, domestic disturbances, looting/robbery, and suicide.
- Structural—any emergency related to the building or facility, such as a bomb threat, fire, explosion, or other structural failure.
- Utility—problems associated with operation and functioning of the building. Examples include loss of electricity, loss of water, natural gas or steam leaks, and general loss of communications equipment (telephones and computers).

Emergency plans should be included as part of new staff orientation as well as periodically reinforced during staff meetings and drills, which should be held to practice for each type of emergency. In addition, post the telephone numbers of emergency agencies and emphasize the calling of 911 for emergency situations.

Facilities Resources

If you are looking for office space, furnishings, layout ideas, and so forth, here are just a few of the associations that can provide assistance.

- American Institute of Architects—www.AIA.org
- American Society of Heating, Refrigerating, and Air Conditioning Engineers—www.ashrae.org
- APPA: The Association of Higher Education Facilities Officers—www.appa.org
- Association of Energy Engineers—www.aeecenter.org
- Association for Facilities Engineering—www.afe.org
- Building Owners and Managers Association, International—www.boma.org
- Business and Institutional Furniture Manufacturers Association International—www.bifma.com
- Illuminating Engineering Society of North America—www.iesna.org
- International Facilities Management Organization—www.ifma.org
- Society for Occupational and Environmental Health—www.soeh.org

About the Author

Wayne E. Leroy, CAE, is president and CEO of W & N, LLC, a consulting company for nonprofit associations and organizations. Prior to that, he was executive vice president of the Association of Higher Education Facilities Officers.

Review Questions

1. What are the three primary ways that associations usually obtain office space?

2. What are the advantages and disadvantages of each?

3. To ensure the safety of staff and visitors, what areas require special attention?

4. How should emergency plans be developed and implemented?

Government Relations

Janis L. Tabor, CAE

L IKE GOVERNMENTS, ASSOCIATIONS FORM for the purpose of achieving common goals. Government relations activities conducted by associations give members a greater voice in government decisions: Collective action stands a better chance of getting results. In addition, the public benefits from sound laws and regulations.

Although some associations form for the purpose of advocating for their members in the government arena, many more have added a government relations function as laws and regulations increasingly affect individual, professional, and business interests. For associations whose members are highly regulated, a government relations program is likely to be a necessity, not an option.

Increased Activity

Associations interact with government at the federal, state, county, city, and international levels. Government relations at the federal level have steadily increased since the mid-1970s, when regulatory growth and reach began to accelerate. Congress opened committee processes for greater public information and involvement. Formation of the Federal Election Commission opened the door for political action committees (PACs). The Freedom of Information Act provided the option of accessing executive branch information, and the Office of Management and Budget assumed an expanded role in regulatory matters.

Increased opportunities for public interaction with government have led to a proliferation of interest groups on all sides of the issues. Collectively, government relations professionals became known as "the third house" of the legislature or "the fourth branch of government." The opinion pendulum swings back and forth; terms such as "special interest groups" and "lobbyists" have at times seemed like less than positive connotations.

Since the mid-1990s, for instance, Congress has tightened rules for lobbyists, eliminated the tax deductibility of association dues applied to lobbying activities for some tax-exempt categories, tightened disclosure rules, and proposed campaign-finance reforms.

In the states, government relations activities have increased in the move to shift power from the federal to the state and local levels. And as business and professional practices have become more global, many associations have done likewise by becoming involved in international government relations activities. These associations may form alliances with international counterpart organizations to develop a presence before multinational or regional government entities and to become involved in matters associated with government-to-government policy making.

Each locale and level of government has certain rules and requirements. Although the details may differ, the basic principles apply to all levels. For the sake of simplicity, the discussion below focuses on domestic federal government relations.

Associations' Role

Associations have a right and a responsibility to educate legislators and other government officials about issues affecting members' businesses and professions. When properly managed and conducted, a government relations program benefits both association members and the public at large. Its goal may be simply to make information available; in other instances, the goal may be to achieve a specific outcome on a bill or regulation.

The role of associations in government relations is to communicate the perspectives and views of members to officials in the legislative and/or executive branches of government. These views should be based on the members' expertise and technical or professional knowledge.

Few government officials have a working knowledge of the activities and expertise in which association members are involved. Associations are especially well-equipped to provide accurate, timely information about their areas of interest. The most successful government relations programs couch issues in the context of the overall business and professional community and society in general—the framework in which government decisions are made. When laws and regulations are well-thought out and properly applied, they can stimulate growth and improve services to the public. Conversely, the actions of uninformed lawmakers and regulators can adversely affect an industry or profession, thus denying services to society.

Legal Issues

An association's tax-exempt category provides the legal parameters for its government relations activities. Key issues include the amount of lobbying and political activity allowed, as defined by the Internal Revenue Service. The following chart outlines in general terms the nature and extent of lobbying and political activity currently allowed for charitable, social welfare, and trade associations.

Tax Status/ Description	Lobbying	Political Activity	Qualifiers
50l(c)(3) charitable scientific, educational, religious	Limited*	Prohibited	• (c)(3) criterion: "exclusively" devoted to public benefit activities * "Insubstantial" lobbying only
50l(c)(4) social welfare	Unlimited (if for social welfare)	Limited*	• (c)(4) criterion: "primarily" devoted to social welfare * Political activity must be less than half of total activity
50l(c)(6) business league trade	Unlimited	Yes*	• (c)(6) criterion: "primarily" devoted to common business interests of members * Political activities not restricted by IRS, but may be subject to other laws (e.g., FEC)

Most associations rely on legal counsel to ensure their government relations activities comply with tax, lobbying disclosure, and government ethics laws. Legal experts can also explain current interpretations of terms such as "exclusively," "primarily," and "insubstantial."

Many charitable associations erroneously believe their tax status prevents them from conducting a government relations program. Although it is true that 501(c)(3) organizations must limit and control the nature and extent of their government relations activities, they are not precluded from lobbying as an "insubstantial" portion of their overall activities. However, exceeding the "insubstantial" limit or participating in political activities puts the charitable association at risk of losing its exemption from federal income taxation.

Issues associated with the association's tax status and its ability to lobby should not be confused with registration requirements for lobbyists.

Plans and Procedures

Government relations involves putting forth the association's name and members in a potentially high-profile public arena. Consequently, high-level commitment to this activity is essential and is preferably articulated within the strategic plan.

Government relations goals—for programs as well as issues—need to be established and updated at least annually with broad-based input from association leaders and

Showing Value to the Board

Despite the benefits of a government relations program for many associations—and for society as a whole—selling the board of directors on the activity can be difficult. Some people are uncomfortable with government interaction and reticent to get involved unless a clear and imminent threat is evident. Others find the concept of lobbying unappealing.

Boards need to understand the concept of the association as a resource and a good citizen with useful knowledge to share; the educational nature of government relations; the acceptability of association lobbying under the law; and the need to develop relationships with policy makers before a crisis occurs.

The first step in establishing the value of government relations to the association is to engage the board in assessing the public policy priorities of the business or profession. Once a government relations program is underway, the board should be kept informed of progress on those priorities and asked for feedback on how the effort is proceeding.

Board members also need to understand that clear cut victories are the exception rather than the rule. Successes on issues are most often characterized by slow and incremental progress taking years. Achievements are best couched in terms of how the association is participating in shaping the issues and how the issues are evolving. Often, a government action not taken is considered a victory.

Quantitative metrics are not especially useful in government relations—the number of meetings held or statements issued does not show that objectives are being met. What is meaningful is that the association helps members have a voice in shaping the outcome of selected issues.

Government relations activities are better understood by board members who have firsthand experience. It is good practice to give association leaders opportunities to interact with key government officials, and encouraging "leader-to-leader" interactions can be an excellent way of advancing the association's goals and values.

members. Some associations determine their goals by surveying association leaders. Others conduct focus groups or annual retreats to identify issues and evaluate ongoing efforts. Association staff play an important role in this process by educating leaders on the external environment, issues outlook, and potential effects on members, as well as by recommending strategies.

The association's public policy issue priorities should be concisely stated and approved by the association's board of directors. They must reflect the needs and interests of the association and its members and take into account government agendas. Because there are usually more issues than resources to address them, getting consensus on the issues of greatest importance to the association helps to focus efforts—and staff resources. Associations that do not establish agendas often find their efforts fragmented by individual member concerns that take a lot of time and yield little benefit for the association as a whole.

Each association also needs board-approved policies or procedures for conducting the government relations function. The culture of the organization will determine if a simple policy or a detailed set of procedures is needed. Key items to address include the review and approval process for position statements, determining who has the authority to speak for the organization, and how the board is to be kept informed of actions taken on behalf of the organization.

Such policies or procedures should clarify the respective roles of members and staff. In some organizations, for example, staff represent and speak for the organization both informally and formally. In others, staff serve more as government relations advisers and facilitators.

Once procedures are in place, the board of directors can delegate responsibility for the government relations function to a separate standing committee. This committee should have a reporting path to the governing board as well as responsibility for recommending changes to the government relations policies and procedures, as needed. The role of the government relations committee varies widely, providing basic program oversight in some associations while preparing and presenting the organization's views in others. Some associations establish separate committees or subcommittees for federal, state and local, and international government relations activities. Criteria used in selecting government relations committee members might include links with other key programs of the association, geographic location, government affairs experience, and political contacts.

Types of Programs

Government relations programs can be *informational, reactive, proactive,* or a *mix.* Some associations do not take positions or make specific recommendations on legislation or regulations but do interact with policy makers and provide information about their members' profession or business. They also alert association members to relevant legislative and regulatory developments.

An *informational* activity could include providing information on the status of a certain technology, a best practice, or even statistics on employment levels.

Because many associations become involved in government relations to respond to a threatening situation, government relations programs are frequently *reactive:* They respond to legislation that has already been introduced; they mobilize grassroots volunteers when a bill is approaching final action or to comment on published regulations. Threatening situations can develop because government itself tends to operate in a crisis mode.

Reactive efforts do not necessarily mean the end of the line for an issue. Even after legislation has been introduced, an association may have opportunities to provide input to lawmakers, especially those on the committees or subcommittees that work on fine-tuning bills. In fact, some organizations intensively work issues at this stage, strategically involving association members from the districts of legislators who serve on the relevant committees. By the time a bill goes to the full legislative body for deliberation and voting, however, changes are hard to make. At this point many associations go for the numbers and mobilize their full membership or grassroots network. It is best to remember that the earlier in the legislative process, the easier it is to make suggested changes and have an impact.

With the collective views of their members—and a body of knowledge in the form of statistics, standards, and other information—associations are in a unique position to identify legislative and regulatory needs for industries or professions. They can take a *proactive* approach to government relations by initiating legislation and providing input for laws and regulations as they are written.

Proactive government relations requires internal collaboration between government relations and technical groups within the association to identify members' needs and concerns; it also requires external communications with decision makers to help them understand and act on issues. Associations and coalitions will often identify a legislative or other official as a "champion" who shares knowledge or legislative goals with them. That champion will serve as the point of contact for input to the legislation and the process. These activities can be costly from the standpoint of staff and volunteer time, but the return on investment can be great in terms of the association's influence on the public policy process.

Program Components

All types of government relations programs have one vital component: ongoing education of government. Organizations may educate policy makers directly through written information and briefings or indirectly through publicity or public service activities that enhance understanding of the business, profession, or other interests represented by the association. Through these efforts, the association gains a credibility and visibility that can increase its opportunities to participate in the public policy process.

The Internet and World Wide Web have afforded new ways for associations to communicate, and experimentation with these communication technologies is continuously evolving. Associations' Web sites can be updated in a real time basis that can provide almost instantaneous communication with members and the public. One of the newest techniques is the "blog," which allows members to provide comments back to associations.

Government relations programs typically include some or all of these activities:

- **Issues identification and analysis.** Spotting issues of potential interest or concern—and providing expert analysis of their potential effect on the association, its members, and the public—is usually a reactive activity that involves monitoring hearings, bills, and proposed regulations. It can also mean working within the association to determine areas of need for legislative or regulatory action that the association might promote.

  In either case, the legislative calendar and regulatory process drive issues management. Most legislative initiatives are spawned early in the legislative session (and most sessions in the United States begin early in the calendar year). The regulatory process is year-round, with prescribed review steps and timetables.

- **Position statements.** The views conveyed to government on behalf of the association must be based on written position statements that have been approved for public release in accordance with the association's policies and procedures. Because government timetables are geared to internal schedules and priorities, the time frame for preparing position papers is often tight. As a result, association procedures need to have built-in flexibility to shorten the approval process in urgent circumstances.

Some associations empower their chief elected officer to approve statements in special circumstances. Others have two levels of statements with different approval chains: one for the organization as a whole and one for subordinate groups within the organization. Subordinate group statements are useful in larger organizations that have a diversity of expertise and interests. For example, technical divisions in a large professional society will have expert knowledge about specific topics that other divisions may not have. Rather than committing the whole organization to a position on a topic not all understand, authorship may be attributed to the technical division that prepared the statement.

- **Government interaction.** Although most associations must work diligently to develop and maintain contacts, government decision makers do seek and are receptive to the views of associations. Successful programs recognize that government officials have many urgent and complex problems to address: They provide information that will help government officials solve these problems but do not expect the officials to become fully conversant with the members' business or profession.

   Like most people, government decision makers endeavor to do well and appreciate support. The best rule for maintaining good relations with them is to observe the Golden Rule. Legislators and government officials are likely to respond favorably when approached positively and given due credit for their efforts. In addition, legislators and other government officials rely heavily on their staff for advice and counsel. Association members should recognize that these staff are often vital links in the decision-making process and should be treated accordingly.

   Interactions with government officials must be thoughtful, brief, to the point, and technically accurate. Under no circumstances should the interaction become adversarial in tone. Interaction may be through letters (mailed, faxed, or e-mailed); telephone calls; face-to-face meetings with legislators, their staff, or executive branch officials; or formal testimony on legislative or regulatory proposals. A constructive, considerate approach and a reputation for reliability, follow-through, and a willingness to go the extra mile are the keys to successful relations with government officials. Because of security concerns, mailed letters to federal officials will often take two to three weeks until received. E-mails and faxes are becoming more the norm and well received. Mass mailings—whether e-mail, fax, or snail mail—that appear to be the products of large-scale, targeted, and organized campaigns and often include the use of "form" scripts or recommended language, are not as effective as individually composed communications from constituents.

It is also important to recognize that after legislation is voted up or approved, appropriate thank you letters will continue to build on important relationships and are much appreciated by government officials.

- **Testimony.** Oral testimony is an important and formal method for communicating the association's views to government. It is usually based on an approved position statement, which can subsequently serve as the source document for an entire legislative campaign. Associations often have an edge in gaining the opportunity to present oral testimony because they represent constituencies of people who are knowledgeable about the issues. In addition, testimony can be submitted "for the record" if an oral testimony cannot be given.

  In the oral testimony, a witness will present a statement at a hearing convened by a government entity, such as a Congressional committee or a regulatory agency. The witness may be the chief elected officer; the chief staff executive; or an association member, staff person, or consultant who is particularly knowledgeable about the subject. Although most testimony is submitted in writing, the oral presentation is usually a shortened version of the written testimony and the proceeding is recorded and transcribed to serve as the official record of the hearing. That's why it is important for witnesses to possess excellent public speaking skills.

  In addition, a witness should be thoroughly briefed on the issue, the purpose of the hearing, the presiding officials, and other practical matters (such as forms of address, where to sit, and the likely sequence of events). The opposition's case needs to be thoroughly studied so the witness can be prepared to fairly respond to the opponent's arguments. Even the most experienced witness is likely to benefit from rehearsing the testimony and a mock question-and-answer period. Using a videotape for rehearsal can greatly improve the witness' performance and comfort level.

  Witnesses need to possess all the facts on the issue at hand and be prepared to answer difficult questions. They also should be instructed to acknowledge when they do not have the answers and to offer to gather the information requested. Finally, an association staff person should accompany the witness and provide assistance as needed.

- **Regulatory government relations.** Executive branch personnel—from City Hall to the White House—far outnumber those of the legislative branch. Their actions (or inactions), interpretations of the law, and rule making can greatly affect association members. Some association government relations programs deal primarily with the regulatory process and often provide input as regulations are being drafted.

  Associations also provide comments when a regulatory agency publishes proposed regulations and solicits public comments. These comments are themselves an association position statement and need to be approved in accordance with established procedures. Regulatory comments are submitted in writing and also may be presented orally at hearings.

- **Member involvement.** Although the collective voice of the association works most effectively for some government interactions, individual legislators want to hear from their own constituents. Members can benefit from and advance the association's government relations agenda by interacting with their own elected officials.

   Associations can facilitate this one-on-one interaction by establishing a grass-roots network of members. A network may be selective (for example, participants might have an existing relationship with legislators) but is always voluntary—some members don't have the time, don't want to interact with their legislators, or are limited by their employment in doing so. Member networks utilizing the Web and other communications technologies can provide a means for high-volume communications, which can be particularly effective when an issue is coming up for final consideration by Congress or the President.

   Ongoing communication with participants is essential to a network's success. Some associations regularly convey information and suggestions for framing a clear and concise message, including issue updates that call to participants for action, requests for feedback on contacts with legislators, and reports about the outcome of issues addressed by the network. An often used technique for interaction at the federal level is to hold a meeting of the government affairs committee that could include visits to meet with the appropriate officials. This can begin an important relationship with these officials and their staff.

   Some associations encourage their members to develop relationships with their elected representatives at the local level. A particularly good technique is the "site visit," when a member invites government officials to tour a plant, laboratory, or other facility as a means of increasing understanding of the industry, business, problems, and importance to the community. Inviting local media to these events provides both the association member and the legislator with publicity while advancing the public's understanding of the association's interests.

- **Coalitions.** Associations can find strength in their advocacy by aligning with others who share their views and positions. These could include other associations, industry, academic institutions, or individuals. The most effective government relations programs include networking with others on common issues for a variety of purposes, from information sharing to collaborative action.

   Coalitions range from formal, dues-supported organizations with paid staff to ad hoc groups where one member organization serves as the volunteer secretariat. Associations that participate in coalitions need to specify the nature and extent to which their organization's name is used in coalition activities. (See chapter 24.)

- **Public relations.** Communicating the association's views can be as simple as issuing a news release that announces a public policy position or action taken. Guest editorials and letters to the editor can educate the broader public about the association's perspective, while large advertisements—a more costly option—can capture the attention of both the public at large and government officials.

The association's tax status may affect its choice of a communication vehicle (see the discussion of grassroots lobbying below). But whatever the vehicle selected, the content should be based on the association's approved position statements.

- **Informing members.** Information about laws, regulations, and legislation may be the most visible benefit of the government relations function for most association members. Government relations information typically includes updates on the status of legislative or regulatory issues, in-depth analyses of major issues, interviews with or articles by government officials, positions adopted by the association, and summaries of the actions taken to promote those positions.

  In addition to providing timely information on pending and proposed actions, some associations distribute in-depth information on enacted laws and regulations along with instructions on how to comply with them. Although costly to compile in terms of staff time and legal services, such information may be a primary reason for belonging to the association.

  Electronic options have greatly enhanced the timeliness and usefulness of government relations communications. Although weekly, biweekly, or monthly newsletters are a mainstay, updates via fax and e-mail can supplement or replace print communications. Computer bulletin boards on government relations topics not only give members an opportunity to comment on or debate issues but also provide government relations committees and staff with insights into members' priorities and perspectives. Government relations-related archival and reference material can be made available through the association's home page on the Web site.

- **Speakers, briefings, and trainings.** Associations provide information to their members via training in government relations techniques; seminars, conferences, or roundtables on specific issues; and presentations by high-level speakers.

  For example, many associations conduct annual or biennial government affairs conferences to help inform their members about current issues and, at the same time, help legislators better understand their concerns. Typically, such conferences assemble association members and involve officials from the legislative and executive branches of government for speeches, question-and-answer sessions, and person-to-person contact. The conference may also feature group visits by association members to legislative offices. Detailed planning and thorough preparation of members are essential to the success of these visits.

- **Candidate events.** All associations—even 501(c)(3)s—can interact with candidates and political parties, but IRS rules that apply to the association must be clearly understood. In addition, associations that can participate in political activities sometimes find it risky, in terms of internal politics, to take a position on a candidate. A safe option is to create forums or other mechanisms, such as questionnaires, to sound out the field of candidates on issues important to association members.

- **Political action committees (PACs).** These are vehicles that enable associations—except 501(c)(3)s—to participate in the election process. While associations are forbidden from contributing to candidates, they can establish PACs to raise and contribute funds to political campaigns. PACs must be registered with the Federal Election Commission and comply with applicable laws. Funds may be solicited only from association members and staff. Members who participate in a PAC typically increase their political awareness and interest in the issues.

  PACs are subject to stringent federal, state, and local regulations. Before establishing a PAC, an association should look at the legal issues, its objectives for the PAC, the funding expectations that legislators may have, and its ability to raise sufficient funds to meet those expectations.

Management and Administration

Because government relations is a function of representation, the association's Chief Staff Executive (CSE) usually has an important role in the government relations program. When additional resources are needed, two options exist: hire in-house staff or contract with a consultant or outside lobbyist.

Contracting with a consultant or lobbyist may be the best option when association staff lack expertise in an area, when the issue is of limited duration and does not warrant internal staffing, or when additional help is needed on critical issues. If no conflict of interest exists, it may be feasible for associations with limited government relations needs to team up and jointly retain a government relations professional.

With regard to in-house staff, some associations combine government relations with another function, such as public relations. Others establish a separate government relations department with multiple staff members, whose responsibilities may be divided by federal, state and local, or international levels; by legislative or regulatory affairs; or by topic or issue.

Whether in-house staff or outside consultant, government relations professionals serve as representatives of the association. They must be familiar with the association's priorities and procedures, know legislative and regulatory processes as well as the primary "players" in the association's area of interest, be comfortable working with high-level officials, and have excellent oral and written communications skills. High ethical standards, honesty, integrity, and credibility are also essential traits in the sensitive world of government relations and advocacy. Any action that smacks of deception or manipulation can mortally wound relationships the association has spent years building.

Because so much is at stake, a high degree of trust in government relations professionals is required. For in-house staff, a close reporting relationship between the top government relations staff executive and the CSE helps build that trust. To help keep contractors and outside lobbyists in tune with the association's priorities, build checks and balances into the working relationship.

Additional Areas

Other areas that require attention include:

- **Lobbying rules and taxation.** Multiple definitions of lobbying and an array of record-keeping requirements for nonprofit organizations have emerged from changes in federal laws that govern the tax treatment of association dues applied to lobbying, the registration of lobbyists and disclosure of lobbying activities, and ethics rules for legislators and other government officials. It is imperative that an association know the current applicable laws and regulations and operate within their limits.

  For example, lobbyist restrictions and reporting requirements vary from place to place and are subject to periodic review. And, although there is no limitation on grassroots activities within the association's membership, advocacy efforts that involve the public at large will have tax implications for some associations. Associations often use the term "grassroots" to refer to their own members, but the IRS defines "grassroots" as the broader public. Associations must find out what rules apply before they take action. Information on lobbying rules is readily available from the IRS, Congress, the Office of Government Ethics, the Federal Election Commission, and state legislative services offices, as well as from the association management community.

- **Political activities.** In addition to PACs—which require separate governance, registration, record keeping, and reporting—associations must monitor and control all political-related activities to ensure they comply with the law. All members must be informed of the rules and restrictions that apply to the association. At the same time, they should be encouraged to fully exercise their rights and responsibilities as individual citizens.

- **Government ethics.** Ethics rules related to entertaining and gift-giving are common for legislative and executive branch officials and staff. For example, certain officials may not be able to accept a complimentary meal or to travel to an event under some circumstances. Being aware of the rules will ensure the association avoids embarrassment and rule violations. In recent years, these rules can change on a regular basis. Be sure to double-check that your association is in compliance with the latest changes.

Trends in Government Relations

Government relations will continue to be a dynamic and demanding area for associations. To survive and prosper, associations must exert leadership in developing and executing effective government relations and advocacy programs on behalf of their members at all levels of government.

Association member issues are not the only public policy concerns of associations, however. Government has increased its scrutiny of business and tax matters, including those pertaining to associations. The specific issues under discussion range from non-profit postal rates to unrelated business income tax, from taxation of lobbying activities to tort law reform. Even when the association does not wish to undertake a government relations program to address member interests, the CEO must stay on top of issues that could affect the association's ability to fulfill its mission in the future.

References

Ernstthal, Henry, *Principles of Association Management, 2nd edition,* American Society of Association Executives, Washington, D.C., 1988.

Jacobs, Jerald A., *Association Law Handbook,* Bureau of National Affairs, Washington, D.C., 1986.

Butler, Wilford A, ed., *Attracting, Organizing & Keeping Members,* American Society of Association Executives, Washington, D.C., 1989.

Expert editorial contributions to this chapter were provided by Timothy F. Burns of the Chemical Manufacturers Association, Washington, D.C., and Kathleen A. Ream of the American Chemical Society, Washington, D.C.

About the Author

Janis L. Tabor, CAE, is the director, external relations, for the Council for Chemical Research. She has more than 25 years of experience in government relations, including seven years on Capitol Hill, seven years as president of a public policy consulting firm, and 11 years in association management.

Deborah Rudolph *reviewed and edited the updated version of this chapter. She has managed the technology policy activities at IEEE-USA for fifteen years. Rudolph has led a congressional visits activity for the engineering and scientific community that brings more than 200 scientists and engineers to Washington, D.C., each year. Previously she handled public affairs with Ogilvy Mather PR in New York and for an economic consulting firm. Her career in government relations started as a Hill Staffer and later included positions at the Office of Management and Budget and the U.S. Department of Transportation. She has a B.A. in government relations from American University.*

Review Questions

1. Are quantitative metrics useful in establishing the value of a government relations program?
2. What activities does an association's government relations program typically include?
3. What provides the parameters for an association's government relations activities?

Public Relations

─────── **Barbara Hyde, CAE** ───────

D EFINITIONS OF THE TERM *public relations* abound. Some of these as noted by the Public Relations Society of America include "the art of reputation management," "the planned effort to influence opinion through good character and responsible performance, based upon mutually satisfactory two-way communication," and "the management function which provides the professional skills necessary to communicate truth effectively to concerned publics." Simply put, public relations is the management of communication between an organization and its publics. This definition implies a two-way process—not only do public relations practitioners send out messages to their public, they also actively monitor and respond to the messages these publics are sending back, either directly or through the media.

Public relations is a management function. Public relations guides the organization in carrying out sound policy decisions and responsible practices. In the association world, public relations helps secure the resources—financial and otherwise, volunteers, and public and government support—to help organizations achieve their missions.

Among associations, public relations is likely to be branded as communications. Another term, public affairs, is sometimes used to refer to this function, but in general this term implies communications with government representatives and other officials to influence public policy. PR is sometimes used in a pejorative sense as synonymous with "spin" or "cover-up." In response to these negative connotations, associations seem to use the term communications more often than public relations.

Another concept becoming increasingly popular in the corporate and association worlds is *integrated marketing communications*. Within this type of structure, public relations may be integrated with advertising, sales promotion, direct marketing, membership, and other types of communications. Both marketing and communications require similar skill sets and share audiences. An integrated structure ideally avoids duplication, produces coordinated messages, and achieves cost savings. However, communicators and marketers may not share the same goals or missions. Centralizing these functions may not be appropriate for all organizations. Nevertheless, as associations face increasing pressures for improved financial results and doing more with less, collaboration between these two functional areas will become more important. In addition, these areas may be combined in smaller associations that do not have the budget or staff to maintain separate departments.

Regardless of its various names and structures, the goal of an association's public relations program is to shape public opinion as well as the organization's response to public opinion. A successful PR program will devote attention to four key areas: overall

---

Coming to Terms

Public relations is connected with a number of other organizational communication activities, especially those defined below:

Publicity is an uncontrollable part of public relations. It disseminates information through selected media based on the information's news value and without payment. In the extreme, publicity becomes press agentry, with the sole purpose of getting the client's name in the media.

Advertising is paid, one-directional communication, based largely on appeals to the emotions. Public relations uses both intellectual and emotional appeals. Advertising is totally controlled: The association selects the media, timing, placement, frequency of repetition, and so forth.

Marketing is also a one-way communication process. It motivates publics to purchase goods, services, or ideas, based on a quid pro quo exchange with the marketing organization (For example, I provide you with a car; you give me money or sign a financing agreement.)

Promotion includes special events and activities designed to create interest in a person, product, organization, or cause.

Public affairs is the government's name for public relations. When applied to corporations, it concerns corporate citizenship and public policy issues.

Government relations concerns dealings and communications with all three branches of government.

Community relations communicates with the citizens and groups within an organization's area of operation.

Media relations deals with the press. It involves obtaining media coverage for the association and its agenda and facilitating access of the press to the group's sources of information.

Industry relations focuses on communicating with other companies within the industrial sector of the organization.

Lobbying directly attempts to influence legislative and regulatory decisions of government.

– William J. Wilson, CAE
Reprinted from the 1st edition of *Professional Practices in Association Management*

---

planning, presence on the Web, relationships with the media, and preparation for crisis situations.

Public Relations Plans

Public relations in associations is not only reactive, such as responding to media inquiries, but is proactive as well in projecting a positive image of the association and achieving its objectives. Two types of public relations planning are relevant to association communicators. One, the strategic public relations plan, is broader and more general than the plan for a specific campaign. The strategic public relations plan should stem from the association's mission statement and the association's strategic plan and be modeled on these documents. An examination of many strategic plans reveals that their goals, objectives, and tactics often involve communications.

Elements of the strategic communications plan may include the following information:

- The mission of the public relations/communications function
- Key messages of the association
- Target audiences
- Vehicles for message delivery
- Communication strategies
- Evaluation mechanisms

The strategic plan should be framed in broad terms to allow flexibility in implementing it with specific projects. Once the strategic directions have been set, specific campaigns and programs can be developed to fulfill the organization's strategic communications objectives. Planning for a specific campaign will necessarily be more detailed than the strategic public relations plan.

Of these elements, evaluation is probably the most ignored part of a public relations plan. There are two major aspects to evaluation: 1) did the message reach its target audience? and 2) did it achieve the desired outcome? Most associations do not have the resources to undertake formal research on behavior and attitude change as a result of exposure to an association's message. However, at a basic level, it's relatively easy and inexpensive to track what the media and others are saying about your association in print and online. Some services, such as Google News, will track mentions of your association or subject of interest as they occur. The disadvantage of such free services is they do not have an archival function, so you can't search for mentions outside the current day.

Several commercial press clipping services will track media and online coverage of your association on a per-clip fee. These services can now deliver electronic copies of press clippings. A clipping service can provide some simple evaluations, such as what news releases get picked up, where they are run, what kind of audience sees them, and, most importantly, what others are saying about your organization. Analyzing media placements provides a rough measure of the effectiveness of public relations efforts, and some type of media monitoring should be part of every public relations program.

Other ways to examine how your association is perceived and how effective your messages are include focus group research and e-mail surveys. Some national public opinion research firms conduct national surveys that allow you to insert a specific question on a fee-per-question basis. The results are a representative, statistically valid sample of the U.S. population. (As an additional benefit, survey responses frequently make good hooks for news releases.) Some universities also offer research services similar in quality to those offered by commercial firms but generally for a lower cost.

Nine Steps in Conducting a Public Relations Campaign

1. State the objective.
2. Analyze the situation.
   a. Internal factors
   b. External factors
3. Define the program goal.
4. Identify target audiences.
5. Define program objectives for each audience.
6. Determine communication strategies.
   a. Message strategies
   b. Media strategies
7. Implement the program.
   a. Assign responsibilities.
   b. Determine budget.
   c. Develop schedule.
8. Evaluate results.
9. Modify program as necessary.

Media Relations

Relationships with media are the heart of most public relations programs. Although the electronic era may have changed the specifics somewhat, the core of the adage is still true: "Never get into a pissing contest with someone who buys ink by the barrel." The media look to public relations practitioners for two things: information and access. Providing reliable, interesting, and useful information and prompt access to your experts will give you a solid footing with the media.

The basic tool of public relations is the press release. Virtually all press releases are now sent via e-mail. The sending organization should be clearly indicated with the subject line serving as the headline to attract a reporter's attention. In the message section, put the contact information at the top, followed by a headline and the body of the release. The first paragraph should be the essence of your story—the who, what, when, where, why, and sometimes, how. Other than the headline, it is your only chance to capture a reporter's interest. The second paragraph is often a quote from an association official or a brief so-what explanation about the significance of what you've said in the first paragraph. Releases should be brief, no more than four to six short paragraphs, with links to your Web site for additional information.

For a fee, commercial services such as U.S. Newswire will distribute your releases. Media directories are also available from which you can compile your own distribution list. When sending information to multiple reporters, include all the addresses in the message as blind copies. In addition, there are two big no-no's to avoid when sending out press releases:

1. Don't ever send an attachment with your e-mail news release (link instead to your Web site if necessary or add something like "photo available").

2. Don't follow up with a call asking, "Did you get my release?" If you do follow up with a phone call, pitch the story briefly and offer to send more information.

When calling reporters, either to pitch stories or return requests for information, be aware of deadlines and avoid calling at that time. Daily newspaper deadlines are usually at 6 p.m. Television evening news deadlines are usually around 3 p.m. Radio stations are busiest during morning drive time, 6 a.m. to 10 a.m., and the evening drive period, 4 p.m. to 6 p.m.

The media advisory is another tool that announces an upcoming event or press conference. It is simpler than the press release. After the headline and contact information, put the five W's in bulleted form. The Associated Press, along with other wire services, maintains a "daybook" in major cities that lists upcoming events of interest to the media. Contact the daybook about a week before your event to get listed.

In our wired society, in-person press conferences must compete with many other sources of information. Time-strapped and information-overloaded reporters are becoming less likely to venture out to these events. Your news and your speakers must be compelling before you arrange an onsite press conference.

Every organization needs a designated spokesperson that is both reliable and comfortable in speaking with the media. In associations this is often the president or executive director. Various issues that require differing expertise may have their own spokespersons in your organization. Your association should also have a policy in place outlining who is authorized to speak to the media on its behalf.

All spokespersons should have media training before interacting with the press. If the budget allows, consider hiring a professional media trainer for a half day or full day session. An outsider may have different perspectives than those who are closer to the issues and thus may be more likely to pose questions that may be asked in actual interviews.

Media training should focus on delivery of no more than three simple messages in simple language. Think sound bytes. The simpler the message, the more likely it is to be remembered. Role-play and practice interviews. Videotaping practice interviews is extremely helpful in reinforcing media training guidelines. The key to your spokesperson's feeling competent and comfortable is practice and rehearsal. In your rehearsal, identify the questions from hell that might faze your speaker, then formulate and practice the answers. With good preparation, there should be very few surprises in media interviews.

Ten Commandments of Media Interviews

1. **You have the right to know who is interviewing you**—who the audience is and what the reporter's angle is on the story.

2. **Respond in a timely fashion and ask what the reporter's deadline is.** This question shows you care and helps establish rapport. The sooner you respond, the more likely it is that your key points will appear in the story.

3. **Have three major points you want to make.** Write them down and refer to them if you need to during the interview. If you don't select your key points, the reporter will.

4. **"Off the record"—There is no such thing.** If you don't want to read it or hear it attributed to you, don't say it. Establish ground rules for the interview before you start. If a reporter asks you to speak "on background," make sure you both agree on what this means.

5. **"No comment" implies guilt.** Never say these words, and never lie, misrepresent, or make other comments to the media that will undermine your credibility.

6. **Silence is ok.** Many people will jump in to fill the gap. You don't need to fall into the "dead-air" trap.

7. **Saying "I don't know" is not a sin.** Offer to find out the information for the reporter or refer to someone who might know.

8. **Don't answer "what if" questions.** It's hard to stop, and speculative answers rarely include your key points.

9. **Accentuate the positive.** Do not repeat the negative in your answers, e.g., "I am not a crook."

10. **Remain in control through *bridging* and *flagging*:** Bridging: "That's an interesting aspect, but the real issue is…" Flagging: "The most important thing to remember is…"

Web Sites

"The introduction of online networks is the single most significant change to the environment in which communicators do their work," according to Shel Holtz, prominent Internet communications consultant. It has changed the communication process from few-to-many to many-to-many, and for public relations professionals, this means you can communicate directly with your public, without going through a media filter. It also provides an opportunity for members and the public to communicate quickly and directly with your association.

Your Web site is the public face of your association. It should have an area for media information and background on the association, as well as PR contacts. Association

Web sites almost always serve multiple purposes—as an information resource for members and others, a meeting registration vehicle, a sales and marketing mechanism, and a public education site, among others. Too often associations build their Web sites based on the structure of the association, which is generally not how users, including members, approach the site to find information. Don't neglect the value of white space in Web design, and simplify the text. People tend to scan text on Web sites rather than read it word for word. Web tracking software is helpful in evaluating your communications efforts if you can afford it. Such software tallies not just the number of hits to your site but where the hits come from, how people navigate through your site, how long they spend on different pages, and similar measures.

Crisis Communications

The challenge in crisis communications planning is always attempting to predict what the crisis will be. Granted, the nature of the crisis will drive the nature of the response. However, every association can and should have in place a structure or procedure to follow if a crisis occurs that can be adapted quickly to deal with a particular situation.

Assemble a crisis management team that will develop a written document, including emergency checklists. The team should include the chief staff officer, the head of communications, other senior staff, top-level volunteer leadership, and legal counsel. Assign responsibilities to each. Designate one, and only one, trained spokesperson for the association. This might be the chief elected officer, the executive director, or the head of communications. A staff person may be the best choice, especially if the chief volunteer officer is not geographically located at association headquarters. This will smooth and speed the communications process, reduce the likelihood of errors, and make staff resources immediately available to deal with the crisis. The volunteer leadership should of course participate in developing messages and should have knowledge of all public statements. All association staff as well as the membership should also be continually updated about the situation and steps being taken and should be instructed to refer all inquiries to the designated spokesperson. It is vitally important in these situations that the association speaks with one voice and remains "on message." Your Web site can be one of your most valuable communication tools in a crisis, so make sure it figures in your planning.

Together, the crisis management team should examine possible crisis scenarios and the questions that they may pose. For associations, the crisis may concern damages or accidents at the headquarters building; various sources of business disruptions; events surrounding meetings that threaten continuity or legal liability; financial, legal, or personnel problems; and reputation problems. For each type of scenario, determine the target audiences for crisis communications and other key individuals to contact during an emergency. Specify the chain of command and the chain of communication, including 24-hour contact information. Beware of trying to anticipate all permutations of a particular crisis situation. Getting bogged down in details can hamper your planning

Do's and Don'ts in Crisis Communications

Do...
1. Select one spokesperson for the association.
2. Get the facts before making public statements.
3. Be proactive in contacting press.
4. Issue statements in writing if possible.
5. Monitor media coverage and correct any errors immediately.
6. Express regret for the situation as well as compassion and sympathy for any victims.
7. Admit it when information is not known; then commit to finding out.
8. Report on what is being done to prevent similar situations.

Don't...
1. Say "no comment."
2. Guess or speculate, even if asked.
3. Ever comment "off the record."
4. Mislead, cover up, or lie.
5. Place blame somewhere else.
6. Repeat negative or inaccurate statements in answering questions.
7. Show media favoritism; provide the same information to everyone.

and could impede your response if a crisis strikes. Developing some broad guidelines for dealing with a few types of situations, such as those mentioned above, will give you a solid framework for responding to particular situations.

Once the plan is developed, take it for a test drive. Go through the procedures you've developed, look for any flaws, and make the appropriate changes. Don't wait until a crisis arises to discover any shortcomings in the plan. Revisit your plan at specified intervals to ensure that it is up to date.

The former head of a major international public relations firm always advised his clients to "tell it all and tell it fast." Shine a light on your own problem before someone else does. By being first to deliver bad news about your organization, you have the opportunity to frame the issue. Once you get it all out there, there may be very little additional fodder for the press or others, and something else may become the focus of the next news cycle. Your organization can almost always survive a body blow, but it may not be able to take repeated public pummeling.

"No comment" is never an acceptable response. It makes you look a) guilty and b) like you're hiding something. Be proactive in both your public statements and in monitoring how the situation is being covered in the media. If you as a spokesperson for the organization are asked a question for which you don't know the answer, say you don't know but that you will find out and report back; then do it.

Acknowledge the association's accountability and accept responsibility. Offer an apology and express sympathy and concern for any victims. Describe what steps you are taking to ensure against a similar crisis in the future and report on their implementation. Be accountable, take action, and commit to change.

When you have successfully weathered the crisis (because you had a good crisis communication plan in place), evaluate your plan, response, and outcome.

Two case studies have become classics in the public relations field as illustrative of positive and negative responses to crisis. Johnson & Johnson has been universally acclaimed for it public relations management following the deaths of seven people in 1982 who took Tylenol injected with cyanide. The company immediately recalled 31 million bottles of Tylenol, set up an 800-number for concerned consumers, and its president made extensive media appearances. The company then took the lead in establishing new tamper-proof packaging that became standard throughout the industry. Six months later Tylenol's market share was close to what it was right before the crisis.

At the other end of the spectrum is the case of the Exxon Valdez, which in 1989 hit a reef in Alaska's Prince William Sound, spilling over 10 million gallons of oil, the largest spill in American history. The company's CEO assigned a deputy to handle public relations and was rarely seen in the media. The company's public responses were clothed in legalese, while the media featured repeated footage of oil-soaked birds and shorelines and angry residents whose lives had been severely disrupted. Exxon was the target of public attacks and ridicule and became symbolic of the sins of corporate America.

Outsourcing the Public Relations Function

There are several reasons for outsourcing the public relations function. Your organization may not have a public relations or communications staff, your project is more than you can do in-house with existing personnel, or you may need special PR expertise not otherwise available. Either with or without a PR staff, you may also wish to develop a relationship with a PR agency on a retainer basis.

The right fit is crucial to a successful relationship with a PR consultant or agency. If you are a small-budget association, don't go to a large, multinational PR firm. First, you won't be able to afford it, and second, even if you can, the facts of life in large agencies are that big potatoes get favored over small ones. Get recommendations from colleagues for smaller, local firms or individual consultants. You can also find firms and consultants who specialize in dealing with associations.

When hiring outside PR help, ask for work samples in project areas similar to your own and work done for other clients of similar size. Don't be afraid to ask for a ballpark figure on what a particular project costs. When negotiating, be clear about how much you will spend, and be certain that the scope of work as proposed fits in with your budget guidelines. Note that you will be buying time only. Costs for other materials and services, often called out-of-pocket costs, will be billed to you at a percentage mark-up over the agency's actual costs. Most agencies have a standard mark-up percentage for items such as postage, delivery services, and materials. Find out what this percentage is and explore how you might save money if you take responsibility for these goods and services and pay for them directly.

If you opt for a retainer arrangement, you will pay a monthly fee for the agency to be on-call for you and perform work for you up to an agreed-upon number of hours. Again, you will be buying time only and will still have to cover the out-of-pocket costs. Rebates are generally not available if the agency does not work the full complement of hours, although the unused hours may be applied to another month. In all cases in dealing with an agency, get a periodic accounting of the hours devoted to your project and the associated costs. These issues and others should be specifically delineated in the contract you sign with a PR consultant on a project or retainer basis.

Your PR agency is an extension of your staff. You need to feel comfortable with the agency personnel who are actually handling your account and provide the information they need in a timely manner. You are partners in developing strategy and should agree on goals and tactics. Agencies are experts in public relations matters, but you know your association better than anyone else.

Most importantly, you must maintain realistic expectations about what a PR agency can do for you. You must have a solid, compelling story to tell that is appealing to your target audiences. The best PR agency in the world cannot get you on the cover of *Vogue* if the emperor has no clothes.

Summary

This chapter has provided a brief overview of the basics in establishing a public relations program. A strategic public relations plan should be linked to and support your organization's strategic plan, as should specific public relations projects. Evaluation is an essential part of the plan, and there are several relatively inexpensive ways to monitor outcomes. Good relationships with the media are necessary in achieving your objectives. Following a few professional practices can ensure that your media relationships are mutually beneficial and not adversarial. The first place someone will go for information about your association is your Web site. Make sure it contains helpful material and is easy to navigate. Every association should have a crisis communications plan in place to deal with critical situations, and it should be tested before it's needed.

Finally, outside PR expertise can be an asset to your organization in some situations, especially when first establishing a PR program.

References

American Society of Association Executives, *Crisis Management for Associations*, Washington, D.C., 2002.

Bonk, Kathy, Griggs, Henry, and Tynes, Emily, *The Jossey-Bass Guide to Strategic Communications for Nonprofits*, Jossey-Bass, San Francisco, 1999.

Cutlip, Scott M., Center, Allen H. and Broom, Glen M., *Effective Public Relations*, 8th ed., Prentice-Hall, Inc., Upper Saddle River, New Jersey, 2000.

Fitch, Brad, *Media Relations Handbook*, TheCapitol.Net, Alexandria, Virginia, 2004.

Grunig, James E. (ed), *Excellence in Public Relations and Communication Management*, Lawrence Erlbaum Associates, Hillsdale, New Jersey, 1992.

Holtz, Shel, *Public Relations on the Net*, 2nd ed., American Management Association, New York, 2002.

About the Author

Barbara Hyde, CAE, is director of communications for the American Society for Microbiology. She has career experience as a reporter, editor, and public relations executive and is the recipient of a Silver Anvil Award, the highest recognition from the Public Relations Society of America.

Review Questions

1. If you are an executive at a small association with a budget of less than $2 million, what steps would you take to establish a public relations program? Would you hire an outside public relations agency or consultant?

2. What are some relatively inexpensive ways to evaluate the success of your public relations efforts and the perception of your association among the public?

3. What are the two words you should never be quoted as saying?

CHAPTER

23

Diversity

-------- **Velma R. Hart, CAE** --------

A SSOCIATIONS REFLECT THE LARGER society in which they operate and exist. Thus, diversity is now one of the governing realities in the existence of all membership organizations—whether their volunteer and staff leaders choose to believe so or not. A decade ago, diversity was considered important to association executives. In the 21st century, it plays (or should play) a vital part in every association operation and activity, from hiring to customer service to community awareness and involvement. Several astute associations have changed their very business models in recognition of diverse societal imperatives, and they will be the stronger for it. Additionally, with an eye on diversity, some associations are striving to become "third place" in their members' lives, after home and work in first and second place, respectively. And with a strong enough offering of diverse programs, benefits, and services to an increasingly diverse membership in an equally diverse society, they have a high probability for success in their efforts.

To effectively lead and manage the organizations they represent, all association executives and volunteer leaders must grasp the meaning of diversity and inclusiveness and the place and importance of those concepts in the context of their organizations' offerings. Further, leaders are responsible for recognizing and fostering the hallmarks of a climate and operating philosophy that genuinely embrace and advance the inclusion of diverse people and perspectives not only because doing so is right but because their organizations will be better and more appealing as a result. After all, as ASAE President and CEO John H. Graham IV, CAE, said in his February 2007 column in *Associations Now* magazine, it is vitally important that membership organizations and their leaders view ideas and issues through a variety of eyes. The inclusion of diverse perspectives, opinions, experiences, cultures, and beliefs will ensure that "the dialogue will be that much richer and the decisions that much more well-informed."

Defining Diversity

When we think of diversity, typically a number of images come to mind. Most of them revolve around what we can see—at least until we start peeling back the layers to appreciate the richer meaning and its implications. Simply put, *diversity* means "differences or variety," and being inclusive means genuinely welcoming diverse people and perspectives into our organizations.

If we view diversity and inclusiveness only through the lens of race and ethnicity, we and our organizations will limit ourselves to only a small glimpse of what their appreciation really means, or can mean. I like this definition, which I discovered on the Web at http://gladstone.uoregon.edu/~asuomca/diversityinit/definition.html. Similar versions appear on other sites as well:

> *The concept of diversity encompasses acceptance and respect. It means understanding that each individual is unique, and recognizing our individual differences. These can be along the dimensions of race, ethnicity, gender, sexual orientation, socio-economic status, age, physical abilities, religious beliefs, political beliefs, or other ideologies. It is the exploration of these differences in a safe, positive, and nurturing environment. It is about understanding each other and moving beyond simple tolerance to embracing and celebrating the rich dimensions of diversity contained within each individual.*

Another way of looking at the richness in the meaning of diversity and inclusiveness is represented by the "Four Layers of Diversity" wheel in the accompanying diagram. The ASAE & The Center for Association Leadership Diversity Committee relies on the wheel as one way of illustrating that diversity goes well beyond race and ethnicity. While not fully inclusive, the wheel gives a clear picture of the vast number of opportunities that we have to welcome variety and make a difference in the lives of our members, our constituency, our communities, and our world.

Take a moment to consider the definitions discussed here and their implications for associations and other organizations.

- How would you define diversity and inclusiveness? What would you add to the definitions previously described?

- How present are these ideas, and to what extent are they applied, in your organizational culture?

- What does embracing these definitions as they apply to business do for your ability to attract the best and brightest in your membership and employment recruitment efforts? For your organization's transparency?

Today diversity and inclusiveness have much broader and more relevant meanings. As the demographics of the United States and the world shift in response to migrating

Four Layers of Diversity

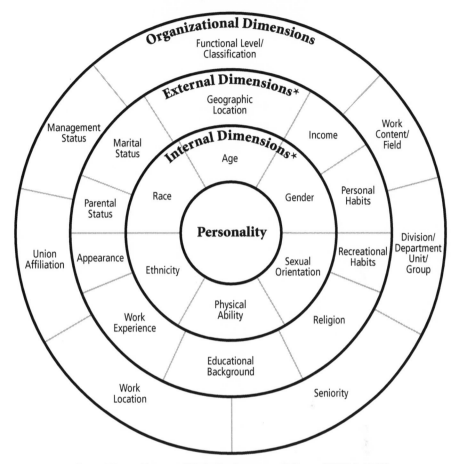

From *Diverse Teams at Work,* Gardenswartz & Rowe (SHRM, 2003)

* Internal Dimensions and External Dimensions are adapted from
Marilyn Loden & Judy Rosener, *Workforce America!* (Business One Irwin, 1991)

cultures and transitioning populations, understanding and appreciating the value that more inclusive thoughts and representation of differences can make for us, our planning, and the value proposition for our businesses should be integral to our strategic planning. This planning should be a major consideration for leaders defining and guiding the future of the organizations they represent.

Being diverse and inclusive can, in fact, open new doors of opportunity in your audiences, prospects, products, and services, as well as increase the relevance of your products and services to markets that may have never been considered. Associations and other organizations that live and breathe inclusiveness may also realize an increase in loyalty among their members and a rising interest in taking a more active part in organizational planning. These results are not guaranteed, nor should they be the sole motivation for a leader's actions. Nonetheless, they are outcomes that often accrue to organizations that actively embrace diversity as a part of their operating philosophies.

Why Leaders Should Care

If you see a problem it's yours. If you think somebody should do something about it, remember, you're as much a somebody as anybody.
– Center for Zen Buddhism

I like that statement for the impetus it puts on ownership. Embracing and fostering diversity and inclusiveness comprise an issue that "somebody" in the organization should own, and that issue is something for which everyone is responsible. An association's leadership does not have to be as philosophical as this statement implies, but it is imperative that key messages be established on the issue of diversity and widely used. The implementation of initiatives in one association may be completely different from that of another. Organizational environment and culture contribute to process, as does the desire of those charged with leading the initiatives. If these efforts are viewed as priorities by the association chief executive, they tend to move forward. And they move forward even more aggressively when both the association staff and the volunteer leadership are in harmony and sync on the priority of these initiatives.

Effective execution begins with motivation. Why should leaders care and be motivated to make the inclusion of diverse people and perspectives a cultural imperative? Here are three key reasons:

1. It makes business sense. In 2001 the ASAE Diversity Committee created a resource called the "Business Case for Diversity," designed to help the leadership of organizations understand the importance of diversity from a business standpoint. It clearly and concisely laid out reasons, objectives, action steps, and positive outcomes that can come from organized efforts around the issue of diversity. The document put diversity initiatives in the context of a changing environment—one to which business must respond. For instance, the resource noted trends such as these: 1) By 2010 Hispanics will number 41 million and their purchasing power will triple to $965 billion. 2)During the next 15 years, the aggregate income of people with disabilities will top $1 trillion. The document stated, "Trends show that our pool of future members, customers, staff, and our members' customers and staff will primarily be those who are now underrepresented in our society. Organizations that are able to relate to these audiences will have larger labor pools and member/customer bases."

Another solid example of articulating the business case for diversity comes from the Department of Transportation. The DOT materials in its "Toolkits" section (http://dothr.ost.dot.gov/Toolkit/index.html) acknowledge changing customer bases and the benefits of a workforce that reflects the makeup of that customer base. Further, DOT emphasizes the positive impact different perspectives can have on generating new opportunities for an organization.

What can you do? Plans and action steps that take into account the differences and that respect those differences as part of an organization's planning process are more likely to garner wider grassroots support and acceptance. For example, would a mentoring program pairing people with similar experiences and backgrounds work for your organization? Do you consciously ensure that your communication messages contain a diversity theme? How will we know when we are successful?

2. Change happened. As noted earlier in this chapter, demographic, cultural, and environmental change is all around us. The sooner organizations make it a priority to reach out to underserved and underrepresented groups, the greater their competitive advantage. The face of an organization, both tangible and intangible, does make a difference. People come to a place where they are comfortable and get involved where they feel invited and welcome. From an outward perspective, this also lends itself in ways such as increased relevancy that is always good for business.

3. It's the way of the world. To be in step with the world—and able to be both competitive and able to attract human resources and customers—leaders and organizations must acknowledge that up-and-coming generations are growing up embracing diversity. Here is an example of a group that is helping engrain that mindset in our youth and future leaders, members, and customers. In my research I found a program called CREDE, which stands for the Center for Research on Education, Diversity and Excellence. The program is operated out of the University of California at Santa Cruz, and while it is not an association but university setting, it represents an example of a very efficient but detailed program for embracing and teaching diversity at the university. CREDE, a federally funded program, focuses on improving education for students whose ability to reach their potential is challenged by language or cultural barriers, race, geographic location, or poverty. The belief is that if CREDE reaches students—children—and helps frame their thinking, acceptance, and appreciation of diversity early, they will help to positively shape the world to embrace our differences. In some ways, this program has abandoned the idea of changing the minds of adults by deciding to focus on students and children as a way of framing the future. This strategy indeed takes time for the results, particularly the positive domino effect the program is hoping to create, to be recognized. However, if successful, this approach would make a major dent in the fight for tolerance and appreciation of differences.

Creating the Climate

Part and parcel of a culture that actively values difference are (1) a common, organizationwide understanding of diversity and inclusiveness and (2) the motivation, which can take numerous forms, not least that of representing a value proposition to business. At least two other qualities, though, must be in place for the cultural imperative to become real. One is authenticity. That is, efforts in this area must be genuine. Insincere efforts are discovered quickly and can undermine not only the diversity initiative but also an organization's overall image and how it is perceived. The second is made up of buy-in and accountability, which comes from the top, both in the form of staff and volunteer leadership. Without these factors, efforts to create a culture that values difference will fail.

To be sure, the climate that embraces diversity—one that respects and includes differences and that recognizes and invites the unique contributions of those differences— produces tangible, measurable results. It takes commitment and work, though. The strategy for any organization's diversity efforts must be as thoughtfully planned as a segmented membership marketing campaign or an organization's advocacy priorities. As said earlier, top leadership must demonstrate a clear focus and commitment to go the extra mile in outreach efforts to underserved groups and perspectives. Some of the ways in which organizations and their leadership can extend this reach and demonstrate organizational commitment to diversity follow:

- Consider images in your print materials and visual images from a diversity standpoint. Do your print materials convey your reach to audiences you serve or represent and more importantly those you want to serve or represent? What does your Web image convey? Could it be more inclusive and/or diverse?

- Who is in your leadership, and are all your constituencies represented? Are the groups you want to attract represented?

- In the leadership structure of your organization, do you have all like-minded members on your committees and boards, or does diversity of thought ensure rich planning processes?

- Are business decisions concerning your organization made in an open and transparent manner, using the leadership structures as they are intended and involving the key stakeholders, or are the formal board and committee meetings used as a rubber stamping formality?

- Do you perform surveys, focus groups, or other methods of information gathering to involve members and constituents who otherwise would not have a voice in the organization's planning?

- While most of us focus on our external image, what does our internal message convey? What steps do you take to ensure that you are attracting the best and brightest staff that represents your cultural and philosophical vision? What training is available to ensure understanding, appreciation, and sensitivity to diversity, inclusiveness, and the supporting initiatives?

- Do your mission and vision statements convey your diversity perspective, and do you live it in every facet of your business?

- What are the measures of accountability and responsibility to your organization's objectives, and how are they executed?

- Regarding organizational culture, does your organization have an environment in which all know that every thought and suggestion is valuable?

Implementing Diversity Initiatives

The specifics of diversity initiatives take many forms. Many actions are unique to a given organization. However, some do's and don'ts are useful considerations.

Do's

- **Conduct your research.** Don't assume you know the answers. View the findings as opportunities.

- **Recognize cultural differences.** Consider offering language translation to members and/or constituents and employing bilingual staff to respond to the changing demographics.

- **Make reasonable accommodations.** Don't forget about staff with disabilities and their valuable contributions.

- **Train and retrain.** Some staff and leaders bring sensitivity to diversity issues with them; however, the majority will need regular training.

- **Model leadership in diversity.** In addition to ensuring that the people who comprise your leadership reflect cultural, global, experiential, environmental, and other factors, diversity must be seen as serious business and therefore a core part of your business planning.

Don'ts

- **Use stereotypes.** A book really should not be judged by its cover, so when it comes to assumptions on your members, constituents, or the community you serve, just say, "No."

- **Follow trends.** Some trends are worth following. Others are not. Don't assume that everything will work in your environment. Make assessments and do what you think will work best for your organization.

- **Develop perfunctory mentoring programs.** Only do them if they are sincere attempts to bring rising leaders along or as way of demonstrating organizational value or even bring a real and meaningful experience to those who would otherwise not have the experience.

Remember that creating a culture and climate that embraces and values diversity is serious business and must represent real and genuine efforts that promote inclusiveness.

These are just a few of the questions that should be asked, not only during the initial planning stages of a diversity imperative but on a regular basis in an environment that embraces diversity as a way of life and a fundamental business principle. It is not a process that happens overnight, but if the initiatives are genuine and constant, the long-term benefits to your organization and this world are immeasurable. Further, the thought processes will not have to be taught. They will become as natural as breathing to your business practices.

Weaving the Message

Adopting a diversity statement as policy is just the beginning. The vital work comes in the actions and in weaving the message throughout your organization and all that it does. Thoughtful consideration about what you want to accomplish in your communication effort is critical to the overall success and certainly to measuring success long term. Remember that the point of a diversity initiative, like many initiatives, is to slowly work the initiative out of a job—that is, that the conscious effort will at some point become subconscious operation. To that end, the major work starts once the message or statement is finalized. It is a process of care, nurturing, cultivating, and feeding that is much like the care of a tiny seed planted in the ground. If that seed is not cared for, protected (especially while it is new and young), and cultivated to a directed outcome, how then can it be expected to thrive? This too is true of the diversity initiative you start. An education process must be clear and far-reaching, an evaluation process must take into account that this is indeed a process, a reward/recognition program must confirm the value and importance of the effort, and the constant support and guidance from the top of your organization are required to make it all real.

The key to weaving your diversity message into your association's culture is making sure the message is well-researched and, once determined, consistently applied. Equity is also a consideration when weaving your diversity or inclusiveness message, and that message must be clear. What are your staff directives related to diversity, and are they consistently evaluated? Also, like all other projects and initiatives, staff and leadership should have direct responsibility and ownership of diversity initiatives. Without ownership, accountability is non-existent.

Coordinate your communications message across all departments and function areas. Ensure that efforts and new visions are communicated in a timely manner and that new opportunities are seized as quickly as possible. Ensure that your message is not just lip service, but that it can be demonstrated and measured when challenged.

Diversity in all the communication vehicles of your organization is critical. A well-researched and honed message regarding this area cannot be faked or done with a partial commitment. The themes must be part of your organization's key messages in both written and verbal form. The messages must also be regularly reviewed to keep them fresh and alive.

Measuring Success

The specific metrics by which each organization will evaluate its performance on diversity initiatives are unique. They are defined by the vision that drives them and should be fluid and flexible. They should pass that ever-popular but simple SWOT (strengths, weaknesses, opportunities, and threats) test as well as be based on realistic and achievable goals and objectives. Strict timelines are optional, but timelines should be in place that will keep all involved on point as far as expectations.

While ultimately, the success measures are unique, the answers to questions such as the following will suggest whether a diversity effort is making progress:

- Is membership on the rise, and does its makeup comprise a range of characteristics and perspectives?
- Is the work recognized in formal ways?

- Do leaders talk about the value of differences to the organization when they talk about what will make it valued and successful?
- Is the diversity initiative part of the budget? To what extent is it funded?

These questions and their answers certainly do not provide all-inclusive clues about whether a diversity initiative is succeeding. Again, the specific success metrics should be based on your individual goals and objectives and little else. Once those measures and timelines are set, your organization must be committed to staying the course to fully evaluate the goals and objectives set for your diversity initiatives.

Are There Risks?

Always. There are cautions that must be executed in any matter of a sensitive nature such as those connected to diversity initiatives. To many, the issues that are addressed in the layers that the diversity wheel included earlier in this chapter are very personal and intimate qualities. But to counter the questions, you must ask what is compromised by not embracing diversity. Relevancy, responsiveness, inclusiveness, outreach, and visibility are a few of the organizational qualities that can be deeply compromised when diversity initiatives are not viewed as a valuable business proposition. You will have to make the choice. Organization leaders are responsible for choosing wisely.

About the Author

Velma R. Hart, CAE, is the national finance director and chief financial officer of AMVETS National Headquarters. She is responsible for all aspects of the financial operations for the national headquarters and review of the six subsidiary operations. She has served in various volunteer capacities, including as a member and chair of ASAE & The Center's Finance and Administration Section Council as well as a member and chair of the ASAE Diversity Committee. Currently, she serves on the executive committee of ASAE's Board of Directors as well as on the Nurses Organization of Veterans Affairs Foundation Board of Directors and the board of the National Blood Foundation Research and Education Trust. She is a 2005 ASAE Fellow.

Resources

Here is just a sampling. Many other useful resources exist via the Web and elsewhere.

Books:

Generational Synergy: An Excerpt from Exploring the Future: Seven Strategic Conversations That Could Transform Your Association. Washington: ASAE, 2001.
http://www.asaecenter.org/Marketplace/BookstoreDetail.cfm?ItemNumber=15202

Inclusivity: An Excerpt from Exploring the Future: Seven Strategic Conversations That Could Transform Your Association. Washington: ASAE, 2001
http://www.asaecenter.org/Marketplace/BookstoreDetail.cfm?ItemNumber=15201

Articles:

Bartrum, Norma. "Diversity for All," *Association Management*, July 2003, pp. 57-61.
http://www.asaecenter.org/PublicationsResources/AMMagArticleDetail.cfm?ItemNumber=1519

Digh, Patricia. "Developing a Diversity Statement," *Association Management*, February 1999, pp. 53-55. http://www.asaecenter.org/PublicationsResources/AMMagArticleDetail.cfm?ItemNumber=4956

"Engineering Diversity," *Association Management*, April 2005, pp. 62-63.
http://www.asaecenter.org/PublicationsResources/AMMagArticleDetail.cfm?ItemNumber=11368

"Inclusivity is Imperative," *Association Management*, April 2005, p. 58.
http://www.asaecenter.org/PublicationsResources/AMMagArticleDetail.cfm?ItemNumber=11370

Kaminsky, Laraine. "Leveraging Diversity: The Business Case," *Dollars & Cents*, July 2005.
http://www.asaecenter.org/PublicationsResources/EnewsletterArticleDetail.cfm?ItemNumber=11914

Motley, Apryl. "Dare to Diversify," *Association Management*, April 2005, pp. 56-58, 60, 62-64. http://www.asaecenter.org/PublicationsResources/AMMagArticleDetail.cfm?ItemNumber= 11006

Romano, Gerry. "Including All," *Association Management*, June 2000, pp. 30-37. http://www.asaecenter.org/PublicationsResources/AMMagArticleDetail.cfm?ItemNumber= 4654

Soutar, Sami. "Beyond the Rainbow," *Association Management*, April 2004, pp. 27-33. http://www.asaecenter.org/PublicationsResources/AMMagArticleDetail.cfm?ItemNumber= 2240

Tennant, Melvin. "The Practical Aspects of Implementing an Effective Policy of Inclusion," *Executive Idealink*, April 2006. http://www.asaecenter.org/PublicationsResources/ EnewsletterArticleDetail.cfm?ItemNumber=18442

Tsurutani, Paula. "Getting a Place at the Table," *Association Management*, Dec. 2002, pp. 56-61. http://www.asaecenter.org/PublicationsResources/AMMagArticleDetail.cfm?ItemNumber= 11969

ASAE & The Center for Association Leadership . . . . www.asaecenter.org

Society for Human Resource Management (SHRM) . . . . . . www.shrm.org

Diversity Initiatives. . . . . www.diversityinitatives.com

Center for Research on Education, Diversity and Excellence . www.cal.org/crede

National Extension Diversity Center . . . . www.ediversitycenter.net

Diversity Radio . . . . www.diversity-radio.net

Diversity Resources. . . . . www.diversityresources.com

Review Questions

1. Has your understanding of diversity changed, and if so, how?

2. Do you think that understanding and appreciating diversity matters for business today and will continue to be a factor for business in the future? Will its importance increase, decrease, or remain constant?

3. How does inclusiveness relate to diversity, or are they the same?

4. Why should we care to increase our understanding of diversity?

5. What contributions can you make to enhance the understanding of diversity within your organization and/or the advancement of diversity initiatives now?

6. Do you think diversity is about race as a primary issue of concern?

7. What message will you take away from this reading that will change your professional and personal actions regarding diversity and inclusiveness?

8. Based on our changing world, do you think this issue will be important for organizational effectiveness?

Coalition Building

John J. Mahlmann

Since the 1980s, associations with public policy goals have become increasingly vigorous in pursuing their agendas; they seek to head off or reinforce emerging trends—or to create new ones. Association staffers with "public affairs" duties in their job descriptions have become commonplace.

In policy-related areas, the usual approach to creating change is through lobbying—a focused effort that provides legislators and other decision makers with information and arguments aimed at persuading them to vote one way, while pointing out the consequences of voting the other way.

Lobbying efforts tend to be highly targeted and narrowly defined by the specific interests of the organization doing the lobbying. A lobbyist's goals are typically short-term: *this* piece of legislation must be defeated, *that* vote must be speeded up, or *another* set of talking points must be delivered to a key legislator.

In the give-and-take of the policy-making process, an effective tool for advocacy is often overlooked—the coalition. The coalition strategy itself is certainly not new. Samuel Gompers employed it effectively early in the 20th century when he redefined the narrow interests of many craft and building trades (for example, plumbers, carpenters, and garment workers) to create the American Federation of Labor. He saw that these trade groups would each benefit more if they defined themselves as members of a single force—skilled workers—above and beyond their identity as practitioners of a specific craft.

The fundamental proposition undergirding all coalitions is simple: People who share a common purpose and perspective can accomplish more when they collaborate than when they pursue narrower interests on their own. Of course, associations themselves are coalitions—members joining together to do more than they can independently. Yet associations often neglect to take their "base coalition"—their members—to what can be a more productive level.

Associations that form coalitions commonly bring together people in the same business or profession. It is fairly easy to identify the common interest of different organizations in the various art forms or even among some manufacturers in industries as divergent as medical equipment and machine tools. But the possibilities for leverage on issues—and more important, for developing new perspectives on issues that cut across constituencies—are necessarily limited.

A Shared Vision

Coalitions can broaden their self-definitions and their reach by including organizations with interests that *run parallel with* their own or that *converge* in some areas. That was the case with the formation of the National Coalition of Music Education (NCME) in 1990, which included three very different associations:

- Music Educators National Conference (MENC), Reston, Virginia, the *education* association for the nation's public school music teachers. Its mission is to achieve better music instruction in the schools.

- National Association of Music Merchants (NAMM), Carlsbad, California, a national *trade* association comprising local music store owners, music instrument manufacturers (including electronic music), and music publishers. NAMM focuses on helping its members operate successful and profitable businesses.

- National Academy of Recording Arts & Sciences, Inc. (NARAS), Santa Monica, California—the Grammy® Award people—an *industry* association made up of performing artists, music producers, and recording industry craftspersons. The mission of NARAS is to preserve the cultural and financial health of the American recording industry.

As different as their missions are, the three coalition partners agreed on one simple point: The future of all three associations depends significantly on healthy and widespread programs of school music. Without those, music teachers would be out of work; band instrument rentals and instrument sales in local music stores would plummet, with a ripple effect on manufacturers, music publishers, and those who do instrument maintenance; and future audiences of recording artists (buyers of compact discs, videos, and concert tickets) would decrease.

A persistent, nationwide erosion of music education, characterized by cuts in both funding and instructional support for school music programs, provided the impetus for the coalition. Increasingly, arts programs operating in financially strapped districts were viewed as expensive "extras." NAMM spotted and identified this development as a future threat to its members and recognized the threat to others as well. Therefore, NAMM joined with the other two associations. From its founding in 1990 until the partners moved on because their priorities had changed, the coalition succeeded in getting its message before the public and attracting more support for its objectives.

Making It Work

These activities apply to associations considering a coalition strategy:

- **Redefine core issues in terms that appeal to new (and perhaps unlikely) allies.** This is the organizational equivalent of "thinking outside the box." Instead of identifying allies from among fellow travelers on familiar paths, look off to the side of the road. In the music coalition, for example, NAMM members had never before viewed educators or entertainers as their natural allies; while NAMM focused on helping members in their businesses, music teachers were not businesspeople nor was their association profit-oriented.

  For its part, MENC's natural allies were other educators and their associations, who communicated well in "schoolspeak." They saw the decline in school music as a professional and cultural disaster, not an economic problem. As for NARAS, because of its constituency's strong concern about royalties, copyright issues, and the role of music in the entertainment business, it had more in common with people in book publishing and the movie industry than with educators, instrument manufacturers, or store owners.

  Whatever the predictable interests of their constituencies, the three associations all had a vital stake in creating more music makers. This was the redefining proposition that made it possible to see many issues as part of the same issue. In other words, the redefinition created a new set of stakeholders.

  Once MENC could see the future of music education in terms of creating music makers—not just espousing the importance of music education or the

---

Unique Contributions

Based on their members and missions, the three associations that formed the National Coalition for Music Education each contributed something different to the joint effort.

MENC
- Strong content expertise in music education
- Respect of educators' experience
- Entree to other allies in education

NAMM
- Business sense
- Strong focus on outcomes; bottom-line orientation
- Involvement in music beyond the schools

NARAS
- High public visibility
- National public relations capabilities
- Market orientation

---

professional development of teachers—new advocacy possibilities opened up immediately. Once NARAS could see beyond promoting the recording industry and acknowledge that building and strengthening a musical infrastructure was necessary for tomorrow's audiences, it could envision a new role for many of its members—especially nationally known performers who could serve as spokespersons for music education. And once NAMM could think in terms of creating the next generation of its members' customers—not just selling to the current generation—local music store owners became catalysts for coalition building at the community and school levels.

- **Create an immediate focus.** Both to generate energy and sustain involvement, coalitions need an action focus. For NCME, that focus came in the form of a 60-member National Commission on Music Education. Its purpose was to define issues, make contact with decision makers, issue a national report, and attract public attention.

MENC recruited presidents and CEOs of about a dozen leading education associations, both within and outside the arts, to serve as commission members. NAMM brought in leading members (both individuals and companies) from the music products business, and NARAS persuaded more than a score of famous recording artists to join the commission and serve as advocates in a publicity campaign. Five members of Congress and a U.S. senator, all known for a personal commitment to the arts, signed on as well, as did a number of luminaries from the nation's cultural and higher education communities.

The commission sponsored regional meetings in Los Angeles, Chicago, and Nashville, with appropriate press coverage and local radio interviews, to hear testimony from parents, teachers, students, school administrators, music store owners, performers, university professors, and politicians on the state of music education and its prospects. The commission's final report, *Growing Up Complete: The Imperative for Music Education,* was released nationally and presented at a 1991 conference titled "America's Culture at Risk."

From that point forward, the commission's recommendations became the programmatic floor beneath the coalition's agenda, in the form of three broad goals:

1. Every child in every school should receive a balanced, sequential, high-quality program of music taught by certified music teachers.
2. Every school should receive what it is entitled to: the full support of local musicians, music organizations, indeed, the entire music community, in its efforts to provide high-quality music education.
3. Every community should have in place policies and strategies to ensure that music education in the schools is integrated with significant opportunities for music experiences, through such community resources as music groups, vocal and instrumental concerts, and theaters.

The motto devised for the report and later adopted by the coalition succinctly summed up the goals: "Just as there can be no music without education, no education is complete without music. Music makes the difference."

Of course, creating a "National Commission on Our Problem" is not a strategy open to all coalitions, nor is it necessarily the most effective in getting people's attention. Coalitions forming around different issues and goals might register equal success with a press campaign, a video campaign, the creative use of an Internet home page, or a well-orchestrated and highly-publicized event.

Because what was happening to music education was part of the larger education-reform picture, the coalition next linked its efforts to the work of the arts education community across the United States. As with any coalition, the strategic concern was finding the right issue to hang the argument on. For NCME, that issue arose when the arts were omitted from the list of core academic subjects in the National Education Goals.

That omission became the coalition's "soapbox." An education in music and the other arts, the coalition insisted again and again, is not an "extra"; it is essential to what it means to be an educated human being. The skills that an education in the arts teaches directly—for example, problem-posing and problem-solving, self-discipline, and cooperation—are valuable workplace skills.

As the coalition built its own network of advocacy for music education around these points, it attracted new allies in its campaigns to have the arts included in the National Education Goals and, later, to develop the National Standards for Arts Education.

• **Build from the bottom up, not the top down.** For all its importance in initiating action, the national commission was short-lived: Its job was to make recommendations for other people to carry out, period. The real work was left to the coalition itself.

Even as the national commission was holding its hearings, NCME had begun building a network of state and local coalitions to focus on these five goals:

1. Rescuing music programs in trouble.
2. Building parent advocacy networks for school music programs.
3. Building pressure for including music and the other arts in the National Education Goals and the Goals 2000 legislation.
4. Creating a favorable climate for adoption of the National Standards for Arts Education.
5. Publicizing state and local efforts.

By the end of 1994, coalitions had been established in 40 states. Materials available to them included an Action Kit for Music Education; an organizing manual; three videos; a host of feature articles placed in local newspapers and magazines; brochures, fact sheets, and leaflets; a monthly national newsletter; and a speakers bureau featuring coalition leaders.

The most important resource in any local political campaign is shoe leather—people talking to people they know, telling others what's at stake, describing why it's in their interest to act, and enlisting their support. The grassroots efforts of coalition members rippled outward until the ripples intersected and created waves at the state and national levels.

- **Maintain visibility.** Although a "behind-the-scenes" strategy is sometimes called for, visibility is important when public pressure is a key to success. After its initial splash, a coalition has to stay visible if it is to remain effective. NCME accomplished this in a dramatic way on the night of the 1992 Grammy Awards, when the NARAS president gave the customary welcoming speech. With approximately 1 billion TV viewers tuned in, he reminded the audience of the importance of an education in music and the other arts. In part, he said, "If current trends persist, music will no longer be a universal entitlement, but one of the markers future historians point to as the beginning of a cultural caste system tied to personal and class economics.... [I]f a child has never been inspired by a poem, if a kid has never been moved to tears by a great symphonic work....why on earth should we believe that our future generations could even be bothered by the banning of records or the burning of books?"

A week later, the coalition's local organizing efforts paid off when a choral music teacher in Maryville, Tennessee, opened her students' spring concert with an empty stage. She commented to the audience and local newspapers that, "If the arts are not included as part of Goals 2000, then maybe by the year 2000, there will be no honors course in chorus"—and created an auditorium of concerned parents. Then-Secretary of Education Lamar Alexander (a Maryville native and piano player) immediately reopened the policy discussion about core subjects by launching a "National Arts Education Partnership." That eventually led, on Secretary Richard Riley's watch, to the addition of the arts to the list of core subject areas in the Clinton Administration's *Goals 2000: Educate America Act of 1994*.

Not every coalition will have access to a platform like the Grammy Awards for its message. But local venues of one kind or another are within every coalition's reach. The lesson of visibility applies at any organizational level.

- **Never stop organizing.** All planning and activity must be jointly executed, which requires some form of central coordination to keep everyone's efforts on point and moving toward the agreed-upon goals and objectives. Some sort of "coalition central" must be empowered to act on behalf of the partners in carrying out activities that advance the group's goals.

Associations unaccustomed to anything but "lone-eagle" status may find this the most difficult part of coalition building. After all, most groups do not relish a process that may put their good name at risk or place their resources into the hands of people who have until only recently been relative strangers.

NCME approached these issues from three directions. First, a great deal of time was spent up front in defining the nature of the association's commitment, stating clear goals, and deciding who would be in charge of what. As discussions continued, the trust level rose, partly because the commitment level was so high. Each partner wanted to make the coalition work.

Second, the CEOs and boards of the three associations were all highly committed to the coalition. That commitment was strengthened as each CEO repeatedly defined the coalition effort for his or her own members through journal articles, letters to members, and speeches. Frequent strategy sessions, memos, and e-mail messages kept all decision makers current and served as an early-warning system about potential disagreements.

Third, the coalition was well-staffed. NAMM "loaned" its director of market development and an administrative assistant; they worked almost exclusively on coalition matters. This staff also had access to resources and personnel at each of the three organizations. As needs arose, "borrowed" MENC and NARAS staff worked on everything from organizing conferences and meetings, to creating PSAs, to preparing the coalition newsletter, to writing press releases. As part of their job descriptions, staff also took responsibility for making sure all partners were involved in all important decisions.

- **Figure out financing.** Although the financing pattern adopted by NCME may not be universally applicable, it bears consideration. The partners contributed staff time, space, and office overhead. A separate office housing the coalition effort was not necessary, nor was a separate budget. Each coalition partner simply created one or more line items within its budget.

  In the case of NCME, running a National Commission on Music Education and its hearings, mounting two national conferences, producing several videos, sustaining a continuing publications effort, and supporting coast-to-coast travel were not a low-budget exercise. But even though the time and monetary contributions of the partners were sometimes unequal, the differences never caused anyone to pull rank. From the outset, all the partners recognized that creating a new organizational bureaucracy and budget could become counterproductive. Instead, they determined to make NCME a priority for each association's mission and to support it from within their own organizations.

- **Learn to laugh.** The wall of pride surrounding each organization was broken through early on, as all three partners realized that the true gift of partnership is greater flexibility and its true grace is laughter. These truths became evident with the first conference sponsored by the National Commission on Music Education. Not only did a keynote speaker—an international music personality—fail to show, but the hotel's lunch turned out to be a disaster. And 20,000 reports came back from the printer on the morning of an important conference with an error and had to be replaced that day. With that conference behind it, the coalition knew it could survive.

- **Stay focused on the issues.** Early successes were followed by others, particularly a National Summit on Music Education, which NCME held in 1994 together with a new partner, the American Music Conference. It brought together more than 100 association presidents and executives and business leaders to develop strategies for building on gains already made in professional development, teacher preparation, curriculum, opportunity to learn, and partnerships for advocacy.

And, in 1996, NCME orchestrated special screenings of *Mr. Holland's Opus,* a feature film that focuses on music education. Leading decision makers, educators, community leaders, and representatives from the arts community were invited to attend the premieres, which were used both as information sessions and to recruit these individuals to the cause.

Moving On

The National Coalition of Music Education made great strides in strengthening the place of music education during its decade or so of effort. NCME endured because of its emphasis on "kid issues" (learning about and experiencing music and the other arts) rather than "grown-up issues" (teachers' jobs, a music store's profit, or protecting organizational and academic turf). But even the best of coalitions doesn't last forever. Since that time, NCME has evolved; two of the three organizations—MENC and NAMM—have formed closer bonds and the third organization, NARAS, has changed its priorities. However, the three associations are still sympathetic to the original goals, and they all still participate in a few school-based programs. MENC and NAMM may work together, but their participation no longer involves the original triumvirate created by the coalition because of the change in priorities that NARAS has adopted.

In 2002, MENC and NAMM again joined forces and shared resources, revitalizing their coalition as a public service initiative that could develop support for music education at the grassroots level in local communities around the United States. This advocacy effort, known as the SupportMusic Coalition, is a clearinghouse for communication among more than 120 affiliated arts, music, and parent and civic organizations. The critical need addressed by MENC and NAMM was to generate a higher level of dialogue and active collaboration between grassroots and national leadership, specifically by engaging parents of music students. In 2003, the coalition launched a Web site (www.supportmusic.com), making advocacy tools and resources available to citizen advocates and community stakeholders.

The SupportMusic Coalition recognizes that effective advocacy requires targeted goals, strategies, solutions, and participation for long-term success. In 2006, the coalition held a National Affiliate Summit, with more than 100 leaders from participating organizations, to pinpoint goals and strategies, explore advocacy opportunities on state and local levels, plan for action during the upcoming reauthorization period of the No Child Left Behind Act, and develop an action plan for the future.

Because of these successful experiences, partnerships have become part of the strategic plan for MENC and other organizations. We've developed the habit of being in coalition to achieve common goals. If organizations align themselves together with their various agendas, while not giving up particular interest areas within their organizations, they can bring a critical mass to achieving some major goals—in our case, for music education.

Lessons Learned

Coalitions are, more often than not, good, effective, and successful. Coalitions can and do change. It's like a neighborhood where residents come and go, but some issues still remain (leaves, garbage, safety).

As someone once said, "No one is as smart as everyone." Together, we are stronger and more able to achieve common goals and objectives than we ever could alone.

References

Bovet, Sara Fry, "Leading Companies Turn to Trade Associations for Lobbying," *Public Relations Journal*, Vol. 50, No. 7 (August 1995).

Bruhn, Karl, "Advocacy: Getting to How-To," in Bruce O. Boston, ed., *Perspectives on Implementation: Arts Education Standards for America's Students,* Music Educators National Conference, Reston, Virginia, 1994.

Ornstein, Norman J., *Interest Groups, Lobbying, and Policymaking.*

Wilson, James Q. *Political Organizations.*

About the Author

John J. Mahlmann is executive director of MENC: The National Association for Music Education, Reston, Virginia.

Review Questions

1. How is participation in a coalition beneficial to the associations that form it?

2. What are some of the key issues that need to be addressed for a coalition to be successful?

3. Why do coalitions sometimes fail?

Community Service

⸺⸺ Randolph R. Schools, CAE ⸺⸺

THE NEEDS OF YOUR association and society go hand in hand: If society is better, your association will be better. Given the pervasiveness of the problems affecting society, neither government, nor business, nor the nonprofit sector on its own can make the world a better place. Yet if all the sectors become involved, each bringing its own management style and creativity to the table, the team can effectively address the problems.

The American Red Cross and the Salvation Army are just two of the well-known nonprofit organizations dedicated to serving people in need. More than 1 million other organizations exist throughout the United States, addressing issues that range from child abuse to homelessness, from education to disaster relief, and many others.

Trade associations and professional societies have a special responsibility to their philanthropic "sister" organizations—their members often have the expertise, resources, and contacts that community-based groups need to survive and grow. By getting involved in these organizations—whether by serving on the board or volunteering at an event—association staff and members can bring a valuable business orientation. In return, they'll be personally enriched by the experience of helping others, have opportunities to develop their leadership skills, and will become more capable citizens.

The association itself benefits through enhanced visibility within the community, improved morale and camaraderie among volunteers and staff, and the development of an internal value system that puts a premium on giving something back to the community. Too, the association will become stronger because volunteers and staff will have faced the challenges associated with developing new skills and having new experiences.

Some associations provide direct financial support to philanthropic organizations, either by matching employee contributions or providing in-kind services such as public relations or legal advice. Other in-kind services might include assisting with printing costs or handling newsletter design and production.

Doing Good

Many members of the corporate community have developed long-term relationships with nonprofit organizations—for instance, General Electric and Mobil have sponsored many series on public television, while Coca-Cola and Kodak have given continued support to the Olympics. Associations may not have the same name recognition, but the projects they support are equally important. Here are just a few examples:

- The Civil Air Patrol reached out to help the victims of Hurricanes Katrina and Rita. The CAP national headquarters established an around-the-clock command post to coordinate flight crews and search teams with Federal, state, and local requests for aerial reconnaissance and rescue.

  Volunteers came from all over the United States to help in this effort. The CAP volunteers were able to provide digital photos of the damages from the storms. These volunteers also went through the disaster areas to help find trapped victims.

  In the end, the CAP volunteers had surveyed 4,266 homes and made 8,524 contacts with people affected by the hurricanes. They flew more than 1,848 hours and contributed 35,495 man hours of assistance to the effort.

- The American Dental Association developed the first annual "Give Kids a Smile" National Children's Dental Access Day to provide oral health care for disadvantaged children. Too many children are affected daily with untreated oral health conditions.

  This program was developed with volunteers around the nation to treat low-income children for free. Different surveys indicated one million children were treated at more than 5,000 sites around the country. In addition, more than $100 million in free dental care was provided.

- In October 2005, the National Restaurant Association developed "Dine for America." This campaign had 17,000 restaurants participate to support families whose lives were affected by Hurricanes Katrina and Rita.

  "Dine for America" raised more than $10 million dollars for the Red Cross, with help from restaurants in every state. All types of restaurants from around the United States showed their support and played an important role for a great cause.

- The Boy Scouts of America National Council launched "Food Turn for America." Boy Scouts of America joined with The Salvation Army, American Red Cross, and

A Broad Base of Needs

Here are just a few of the many community groups with which associations could get involved:

1. Youth
   - Boys and Girls Clubs
   - Big Brothers and Big Sisters
   - Child Welfare League
   - Boy Scouts and Girl Scouts
   - Junior Achievement
   - YMCA and YWCA

2. Arts
   - Arts councils
   - Theater groups
   - Community theaters
   - Opera company
   - Youth in the arts programs

3. Senior Citizens
   - Meals on Wheels
   - Nursing homes
   - Senior partnership programs

4. Environment
   - Wilderness protection groups
   - Zoo programs
   - Recycling campaigns

5. Society at Large
   - Homeless shelters
   - Shelters for victims of domestic abuse
   - Habitat for Humanity
   - Free clinics

Habitat for Humanity to provide opportunities for youth and volunteers to fight hunger and homelessness and teach the habits of healthy living.

Their efforts from January 1, 2004 through April 30, 2005, resulted in more than 1,248,790 service hours being performed.

- The National Education Association created "Read Across America Day" to celebrate the importance of reading. The program uses media outreach, events, and Web materials to increase visibility. Many athletes, celebrities, and political leaders participate. The program began with 25 million participants and has risen each year to an estimated 45 million participants.

Getting Involved

"To help assist society with its needs" is not a phrase that appears in many association mission statements. Therefore, whatever an association undertakes is done out of responsibility to the local community and society at large. Here are some suggestions for launching a community service program:

- **Appoint a leader.** Look for a staff member or volunteer who is talented, creative, and ripe for leadership responsibility. Choose someone who will expect, and therefore foster, success. He or she typically works with a committee of staff or volunteers.

- **Select committee members.** Committees are an excellent training ground for future leaders within the organization. Members should make a commitment to developing a long-range strategy that will allow the association to be known for its innovation in solving problems.

- **Involve the leadership.** Staff leaders, as well as the executive committee and board of directors, should support the concept of community service and be willing to devote the labor and financial resources to initiating a project.

- **Select a project.** The committee should investigate numerous possibilities before deciding who and how the association can assist. Some types of projects may prove too controversial to consider, while others might offer a natural fit. A group of professional communicators, for instance, might address literacy issues; an association representing foodservice establishments might get involved with food banks.

  For ideas, the community service committee could check with the local United Way or volunteer clearinghouse to find out which groups have the most significant needs for volunteers. The community service committee should meet two or three times to discuss possibilities before selecting a project and setting up a timetable for its implementation. Some associations work with the same nonprofit or for the same cause year after year, while others designate a new project each year or two.

  The committee should also consider whether assistance will be ongoing or a one-time effort. Some associations, for example, sponsor a volunteerism-oriented "work day" in conjunction with their annual meeting; during the rest of the year, these groups encourage staff and members to become involved on their own.

- **Be flexible**. Community service volunteers may have a definite idea of how they'd like to be involved—which may not match what the philanthropic or social service organization really needs. Be prepared to assist with these types of activities:
  - Addressing envelopes, creating posters, and typing information.
  - Marketing the organization through telephone calls to possible members.
  - Providing direct service, such as cooking or serving food or being a companion.
  - Offering operational and financial expertise, especially in the area of fundraising.
  - Publicizing the nonprofit by contacting local television, radio, and newspaper reporters.
  - Planning special events, which might range from a black-tie dinner and dance to a chili cook-off. A silent auction, a popular fund-raising effort, can benefit greatly from an association's contacts with local businesses and suppliers.

- **Publicize the commitment.** Not only members want to know the good that their association has done. Word should also reach the local community and the association community through traditional public relations vehicles.

- **Evaluate your efforts.** By gathering information on the strengths and weaknesses of a community service program, you'll be able to make better decisions regarding continuation or modification. In addition, the board of directors may be interested in the return on the association's investment of time and possibly resources. True, benefits can be difficult to measure in dollars and cents, but focus on results such as skills development, public relations, and volunteers' satisfaction levels.

When considering whether to change or adjust a community service program, other questions to answer are:

- Was the environment safe for participants and staff?
- Was the length and timing of the program appropriate?
- Did the program attract and maintain people's interest?
- Were enough financial resources allocated to the program so that it could reach its goals?
- How can the committee be designed better for next year?

Use of the Internet

There is no question that the Internet has transformed the way volunteers are managed and recruited. Many cities have programs such as DC Cares, which matches up volunteers with social service needs. However, it is also important to be mindful of remaining high touch. Many people volunteer to connect to their community in a more personal way, and electronic communications, while efficient, should not be a substitute for personal interaction. Programs such as volunteer match are helpful. Also, your organization having an electronic newsletter allows the volunteer and organization to bond. The Web site also enhances volunteers' understanding of charitable giving, as well as educating them about the mission of the organization.

Community Service

Community Service is also a great way to interact with your local city or county. Many have volunteer leaders. Many colleges and universities as well as high schools offer programs where the students become involved in the nonprofit community. They want to learn and are a wonderful resource for the social service sector.

About the Author

Randolph R. Schools, CAE, is president and CEO of the Recreation & Welfare Association, Bethesda, Maryland. He is the co-founder of three nonprofit organizations: Special Love–Camp Fantastic, Friends of the Clinical Center, and Children's Inn at NIH, and currently serves as president of the Employee Service Management Foundation in Chicago and is past president of the Bethesda-Chevy Chase Chamber of Commerce.

Review Questions

1. What are the benefits of association staff and members getting involved with community-based groups?

2. What are some of the steps an association needs to take when launching a community service program?

3. How can the Internet be useful in facilitating community service efforts?

Education Programs

Ralph J. Nappi, CAE & Deborah B. Vieder

T HE VERY PURPOSE OF an association—enabling people to achieve common goals, meet common needs, and solve common problems—is realized by sharing information, networking, or joining together for a common good. In many associations, education programs help achieve these goals. These training programs help members better understand complex issues, learn about the latest information shaping their business or profession, hear about developing trends, and provide a ready resource for the continuous learning necessary to keep pace with today's rapid rate of change.

Adult Learning

Researcher and scientist Malcolm Knowles believed that adults and children should be taught differently because of their different approaches to learning. He identified the adult approach as *andragogy,* which directly involves the *student* in the design, implementation, and evaluation of the learning experience. *Pedagogy,* the approach used for children, emphasizes the role of the *teacher* in designing, delivering, and evaluating the educational process.

Additional research by Knowles identified these distinctions between the way children and adults process learning:

1. **The need to know**—When adults set about learning something, they have a desire to know what they will gain by learning the new knowledge.

2. **The learner's self-concept**—Adults are more intentional in their learning.

3. **The role of experience**—Adults bring a wealth of experience to the learning event, whether from a life experience, career advancement, or professional development.

4. **Readiness to learn**—At a particular moment, a unique set of factors converges to create an environment that prepares adults to learn.

5. **Orientation of learning**—Children's education is subject-centered, whereas adults approach a learning event seeking solutions to problems they've experienced and answers to questions they have.

6. **Motivation**—Adults are personally motivated to learn based on varying aspects of their respective environments.

The term *education* refers to the system and process by which learning takes place or the format of learning. In an association, education can range from conferences and seminars, to workshops and expositions, to online training and interactive webinars. From a marketing standpoint, associations have an advantage in being able to provide knowledge and skills training specific to an industry or profession, which may not be met through other resources such as on-the-job training, schools, home-study courses, or existing computer-based studies.

Another advantage for associations is that members learn alongside their peers, who share the same profession or industry and have similar expertise and backgrounds.

Needs Assessment

There's a difference between what your members want and what they *need*—an important distinction when determining the type of education programs your association should offer, and also when, where, and in what format. Industry trends, the sophistication level of participants, and environmental forces can help determine the difference. You will need to factor them in when analyzing and interpreting your needs assessment data.

The most common way to assess educational needs is to conduct a mail or online survey. Whether developed internally or outsourced, the survey instrument should contain questions that are free of response bias. Other survey methods include focus groups, personal interviews, and telephone interviews (for more information on conducting research, see chapter 17).

Consider using a combination of approaches, as no single method of data collection is as credible as a mix. Also, when selecting a sample size, favor a larger and more varied sample; the more responses you have, the more ways you can divide the data for analysis and discussion.

Demographic data gathered may include type of member (or nonmember), job function, number of years in the trade or profession, number of employees, geographic location, and other associations in which respondents are currently involved. This type of data may help in determining inconsistencies or similarities among the sample group. Also, questions relating to logistics, budget, and education delivery are helpful in determining how, and in what format, the association should provide the program. Consider having survey participants prioritize their needs so that you'll know what programs offer the best chance for success.

While it is important to acknowledge the opinions of non-members or inactive members (those with low participation history), placing the same weight on their responses as active members will skew the data used for decisionmaking.

When analyzing your needs assessment results, you may discover that respondents aren't necessarily aware of trends in their field or know how to prepare for the future. Then you must interpret the results and offer programs that will fulfill those unanticipated needs.

Program Design and Development

This step challenges you to:

- Select a program topic that meets the needs identified by the member assessment.
- Create measurable learning objectives and outcomes.
- Select an appropriate delivery system. Education and training can be provided through seminars, workshops, conferences, short courses, symposiums, computer-based learning, institutes, teleconferences, webinars, and forums.
- Determine instructional strategies. A variety of instructional techniques can be employed, including lectures, role playing, demonstrations, and case studies. You'll also have a choice of instructors, ranging from speakers and facilitators to consultants and skill trainers. If "motivation" is a program objective, consider hiring a professional speaker; if "relaying information germane to the industry or profession" is the primary objective, members can serve as speakers.
- Design a program that also accounts for such factors as budget, logistics, site, and format. In designing a program, remember that you are dealing with adult learners who have varying degrees of expectations depending on their background, experience, type of employer, and personal objectives. Adult learners comprehend and retain information better when it is gained through informal and experiential-based learning.

Budgeting

Before finalizing any aspects of an education program, the association must determine if it will be a subsidized, break-even, or profitable activity. The financial framework for this decisionmaking consists of fixed costs and variable costs.

Fixed costs include items such as room rental, audiovisual equipment rental, speaker honoraria, travel expenses for speakers and staff, and promotional materials. *Variable costs,* which depend upon the number of participants, are primarily related to food and

Assisting Speakers

Even if he or she is an expert in the subject area to be addressed, a speaker isn't necessarily familiar with the target audience. By providing speakers with the following information, you can ensure their presentations will match attendees' needs:

- **General background on the industry or profession.** Describe current challenges and opportunities, specific terminology or buzzwords, and any audience sensitivities, such as topics to avoid. Also, provide historical background about the association. An excellent way to familiarize speakers with the association and the field it represents is to have them talk with several members in preparation for their presentation.

- **Context of the presentation.** Describe the meeting's or program's theme, purpose, and objectives. Mention other speakers and their topics, specific objectives the speaker should meet, and how the program was promoted.

- **Audience profile.** Provide information about members' education level, experience, average age, gender, and job titles. Also, anticipate the size of the audience, along with any special guests who may attend and thereby affect the speaker's message (for instance, media representatives or government officials).

To increase the audience's retention of information, encourage speakers to reinforce their messages with handout materials and audiovisual aids—such as PowerPoint presentations for larger groups, videotapes for smaller groups, or flip charts for interactive sessions. For larger meetings, the availability of "ready rooms" allows speakers to prepare and review their audiovisual components and notes before the actual presentation.

---

beverage expenditures and handouts, such as conference proceedings and copies of presentation visuals.

Speaker fees can represent a substantial portion of the overall fixed costs. However, a presenter (especially the sole speaker for a workshop, seminar, video-conference, audio-taped program or webinar) who is also involved in marketing the program may be interested in negotiating a tiered honoraria schedule based on the number of actual participants.

Marketing and Promotion

Early in the program development phase, focus on the marketing and promotion component. The needs assessment will identify the audience and choice of delivery system and provide insight into how the program is packaged and priced—all integral parts of the marketing plan.

In the past, many associations enjoyed the position of being the only, or primary, source for their industry's or profession's adult education. Today, a more competitive marketplace exists, which requires a proactive approach for getting members to attend programs.

Although brochures and direct mail remain the core of most education marketing and promotion plans, e-marketing, telemarketing, and direct sales have grown in importance. In an effort to control the escalating costs of developing and offering educational programming, some organizations use beta sites (test markets) to try out new speakers, topics, and approaches.

Targeted database marketing can be effective for associations because they already have specific demographic information about their members and customers. Associations also have the advantage of a high level of credibility among members, who have already demonstrated a commitment to the organization by paying dues.

Implementation and Management

All of the best planning, needs analysis, and marketing can be negated if attention to details and on-site logistics are not properly handled. Many associations employ professional meeting planners to concentrate on this area, which encompasses: site selection, room set-up, registration, air and ground transportation, shipping, food and beverage functions, and audiovisual contracts. It also includes instructor orientation and training and contracting with hotels, convention centers, or other meeting facilities.

Room set-up, like the meeting location, will vary depending upon the objective of the meeting and the number of participants. For larger and more formal meetings, classroom and auditorium-style arrangements work well; smaller or interactive groups usually prefer a roundtable, U-shaped, or conference-style set-up. (For specific information on meeting planning, see chapter 32.)

The person charged with planning meetings must be detail-oriented, adaptable, and have the physical and mental stamina necessary to deal with the last-minute changes—such as medical emergencies, speaker no-shows, inclement weather, technological glitches, and transportation difficulties—that inevitably arise during education programs. Extensive planning makes a program successful, but even the best-laid plans are susceptible to adjustments and changes.

ADA Requirements

Although individuals with disabilities may experience limitations in some areas, they are not limited as learners. Their needs are as important as those of any other learner. In fact, under the Americans with Disabilities Act (ADA), the association has the responsibility to make "reasonable accommodations" for participants with disabilities.

Reasonable accommodations may include sign language interpretation, Braille handouts, special meals, and aides for the hearing impaired, to name a few. The meeting planner is required to make a reasonable attempt to provide such accommodations. The person with the disability has the responsibility to provide adequate notice so that the necessary arrangements can be made. Most associations request that attendees highlight such needs on their registration materials.

Evaluation and Review

It's easy to breathe a sigh of relief once the program has concluded and you've packed your bags to head home, but a key activity still remains: evaluating and reviewing the educational program.

The evaluation process identifies, collects, interprets, and provides information for the purpose of judging the effectiveness and future of the program. Questionnaires and surveys tend to be the most popular vehicles for gathering feedback, but interviews and focus groups also provide useful results. Evaluations can also be done with written examinations, performance tests, and general observation.

Whatever the format, the evaluation instrument should ask how well the program objectives were met, ask about the presenter's level of competence, and solicit suggestions for program improvement. More specifically, here are ten key components of an educational program to evaluate:

1. Program content
2. Instructional methods
3. Handout materials
4. Instructor/speaker knowledge
5. Instructor/speaker presentation
6. Location and facility
7. Program agenda
8. Knowledge gained
9. Attitude and behavior changes of the participant
10. Effect on the participant's organization

In general, there are two types of evaluations: *summative* and *formative*. A *summative* evaluation focuses on the program's overall effectiveness. It enables you to document program accomplishments, determine the degree to which program objectives and member needs were met, justify the allocation of staff and financial resources, judge the opportunities provided for membership participation, identify program weaknesses and strengths, and have a benchmark for future programming decisions. A *formative* evaluation deals with program improvements, particularly during the event itself.

In addition, evaluation takes place at four different levels. *Level 1* involves participants' reactions—how well did they like the program? This is generally where most associations stop. *Level 2* addresses the knowledge gained; it assesses what principles, facts, and techniques were learned. *Level 3* analyzes behavioral changes; it documents changes in participants' behavior resulting from the program. *Level 4* examines the organizational consequences (to the business or employer) by studying the tangible benefits of the participants' involvement in the program.

Although evaluations can occur before, during, or after a program, many associations find that on-site evaluations at the end of the program provide the highest return. However, this method may involve a greater level of subjective responses compared to those from a post-program mailed or online evaluation. On-site participants tend to be affected by the "motivational high" that occurs immediately following a speaker's closing. A post-program survey allows participants time to reflect on the program and might render more realistic evaluations.

Evaluation results provide a basis for continuing, adjusting, or eliminating a program. Although program evaluation is the final phase of the education cycle, it is not complete until the data has been compiled and the program enhancements are determined. Many associations provide the results to the staff, leaders, and attendees as a courtesy and to promote further discussion for future programs.

Trade Shows

Association-sponsored trade shows enable marketers to display or demonstrate their goods and services to a targeted audience of prospective buyers. This type of informal education program may be held independently or in conjunction with an association meeting or convention. It may range from a half-day "table top" event, meant to educate more than sell, to a multi-day event that provides exhibitors with major marketing opportunities. It is often a good opportunity for organizations to provide educational programs to exhibitors; such programs generally focus on marketing and sales techniques for trade shows or trends specific to the industry or profession, which are provided to assist vendors in marketing their products.

Although many association education programs are subsidized as part of their overall mission, trade shows tend to be financially rewarding. In fact, excess revenues help to underwrite many other association programs and services. Trade shows offer many opportunities to conduct business and have become an important time for decision-making and purchasing. These activities supplement the educational aspects that trade shows have always provided, particularly by identifying new products, services, and technologies available to the trade or profession. (For more information on trade show planning and logistics, see chapter 32.)

The Use of Technology

New technologies can provide a multitude of advantages, including quickly disseminating urgent information, reducing participants' costs, and enlarging the reach of educational programs. But before making a commitment to using technology, consider members' receptivity; your association's ability to manage new technology; and the fact that not all topics, speakers, and information lend themselves to technological applications.

Options include the following:

- **Computer-based training.** The computer screen may display just text or the latest in high-resolution graphics, sound, and video. Usually the computer presents displays to the learner and then responds to his or her input in various ways.
- **CD-ROM.** This offers a means of storing vast quantities of computer data, particularly the large files needed for video and audio.

- **DVD.** This advanced version CD-ROM can include almost any form of electronic media. Plus, this alternative avoids the Internet's occasional problems with delivering large multimedia files.

- **Virtual reality.** Together, a computer and multi-media create the illusion of being inside a world that actually exists in the bits and bytes of computer software.

- **Video-based training.** Many instructors show videotapes in their classes to explain information, demonstrate skills and techniques, or establish a starting point for discussions.

- **Satellite communications.** This technology enables you to simultaneously send educational programs to groups of people all over the country. After the broadcast has concluded, an on-site facilitator or teacher engages each site in active learning activities. Or, computer networks or electronic bulletin board systems can be used to supplement the satellite teleconference; experts and teachers can be available online to answer questions or lead discussions.

- **Videoconferencing.** Using telephone lines, you send video pictures from point to point or even link several sites at once.

- **Digitization.** This process of converting program material—ranging from text, to images, to video and audio—into digital format, makes it easier to preserve, access, and share information.

- **Webinar.** This type of web conferencing—in contrast to a Webcast, which transmits information in one direction only—is interactive between the presenter and audience. It is 'live' in the sense that information is conveyed according to an agenda with a starting and ending time. In most cases, the presenter may speak over a standard telephone line, pointing out information being presented on screen, and the audience can respond over their own telephones, preferably a speakerphone.

In considering these technologies as possible delivery systems, the message, speaker capability, participant receptivity, facility arrangements, and costs are all important considerations. In fact, the message to be delivered—not the technology itself—is the primary reason driving the use of one of these technologies.

References

American Society of Association Executives, *Association Education Handbook,* Washington, D.C., 1984.

———, *The Association Educators Tool Kit,* Washington, D.C., 1995.

———, *Principles of Association Management,* 2nd ed., Washington, D.C., 1990.

Convention Liaison Council, *The Convention Liaison Council Manual,* 6th ed., Washington, D.C., 1994.

Cox, John B., and Andrew Cohn, "Continuing Education Goes On-Line," *Association Management,* June 1996, American Society of Association Executives, Washington, D.C.

Ingram, Albert L., "Teaching with Technology," *Association Management,* June 1996, American Society of Association Executives, Washington, D.C.

Text-to-Art, Inc., www.text-to-art.com.

Digitization., www.whatistargettech.com.

About the Authors

Ralph J. Nappi, CAE, president of NPES—The Association for Suppliers of Printing, Publishing and Converting Technologies (NPES) Reston, Virginia, entered the association field in 1981. He previously served at the American Machine Tool Distributors' Association (AMTDA), Rockville, Maryland, as president, vice president, and director of education and communication.

Deborah B. Vieder, director of communications for NPES—The Association for Suppliers of Printing, Publishing and Converting Technologies (NPES) in Reston, Virginia, entered the association field in 1979. She previously served as director of education and communication for the American Machine Tool Distributors' Association (AMTDA), Rockville, Maryland.

Review Questions

1. What methods can be used to collect data to assess the educational needs of members?

2. What key components of an educational program should be evaluated?

3. What factors should be considered when determining the delivery method of a program?

Publishing Professional Magazines, Books, and Other Media

Debra J. Stratton

A SSOCIATION PUBLICATIONS HAVE POWER—the power to create and maintain an association's image, enhance its credibility within the industry or profession, and establish it as a valuable source of information. Publications link an association with its members, providing member value and keeping the association viable and visible as competition for members' time and attention grows more intense. Finally, publications can provide added revenues from advertising, subscriptions, sponsorships, and more in both print and electronic form.

The most effective association communication programs include a variety of vehicles and formats that appeal to members' special interests and needs. Arriving at the right mix of publications means adapting to the ever-changing interests and concerns of association members, whether they require a comprehensive textbook on the profession, an in-depth magazine or scholarly journal, a brief and timely electronic newsletter, or a lively blog. Ensuring the right mix also requires a depth of understanding about members and their information needs, a clear vision of the association's goals and overall mission, well-defined objectives and business plans for operations, and a strategic communications marketing plan for achieving those objectives.

General Guidelines for a Publishing Operation

Most professional societies and trade organizations promote their publications as the major benefit of membership—with good reason. When asked to rank important association services, members typically place publications at or near the top of the list. The association's newsletter, magazine, or journal represents a tangible benefit to members and reminds them of what the association accomplishes on their behalf. Publications may, in fact, be the only link some members have with an association or society. Given their important role, publications need to be timely, authoritative, credible, well-designed, highly readable, and carefully focused on members' needs.

Understanding those specialized needs begins with an objective and fundamental understanding of your readers: Who are your members? What kind of information do they need and want from your association? Too many associations rely on anecdotal feedback or input from a few members or elected leaders in deciding these critical issues instead of regularly conducting basic research to objectively understand readers' needs.

A comprehensive membership or readership survey will provide basic information, including a profile of the average reader and his or her preference for various types of information as well as formats, such as late-breaking news in an e-newsletter, developing trends in a magazine, or in-depth issue analyses in an online journal. Focus groups, e-surveys, letters to the editor, conversations at meetings, and other less formal vehicles for getting feedback can further clarify information needs and help the editor shape a publication that fills a special niche, rather than duplicating what other publications already provide.

Publishing with a Purpose

Every publication—whether a magazine, an e-newsletter, or a monograph—needs a written statement of purpose: three or four sentences that describe the target audience, the types of information to be included, and the overall goals of the publication. The editorial mission statement for a technical magazine might seek to "explore the development, applications, and implications of new and emerging technologies. It anticipates trends; provides a forum for understanding, discussion, and leadership; and provides insight and analysis with a clarity that makes sense to anyone in any field of technology." Another magazine may focus on "delivering essential information, insights, and ideas that inspire and inform readers." A legislative newsletter may seek "to keep members up to date on legislative and regulatory developments."

The most effective publications are careful to define their purpose for both readers and advertisers and to communicate the purpose to top management, staff, and elected leaders. Many publications use a tagline just below the nameplate to communicate that editorial mission to readers as well—"*Practical strategies, applications, and trends for industry professionals.*"

A statement of purpose is the basis for determining what goes into a publication and evaluating how effective a publication is in meeting its objectives. A vague understanding of publishing goals leads to unfocused editorial content and confusion among readers, advertisers, and outside audiences. Worse yet, it can lead to battles between staff and volunteers over what is appropriate for the publication.

To avoid misunderstandings and unneeded conflicts, and to ensure staff know what is expected of them, develop a written statement of purpose for each periodical, review and update it regularly, and share it with readers, staff, and volunteers. Then use it to evaluate what editorial content is most appropriate in the publication.

It is not uncommon for association staff and leadership to disagree on a publication's purpose, especially if the publication is advertiser-supported. Some prefer a "house organ" that reports on association activities and services, while others believe strongly in the need for an independent trade or professional publication. Often a general membership newsletter serves as the house organ, reporting on association activities, advocating the association perspective, and promoting association services and programs, while the magazine or journal focuses exclusively on the trade or profession. Reports of association activities, if included at all in the magazine or journal, appear in an "Association News" column rather than in the feature well.

Clarifying the distinction between a house organ and an independent magazine is critical for publications that carry advertising and for those that serve a broader audience than just members. Is the publication primarily promotional, reporting on the association, or is it independent, reporting on the industry or profession? The more clarification that can be made initially, the more effective the publication ultimately will be.

Matching Needs and Formats

The type of information and the frequency of communication needed help determine a publication's format. If members are looking for the latest legislative news affecting their profession or their companies, a brief, weekly e-newsletter might be the perfect format. But if members want in-depth case studies on how to apply practices in their own settings, a bimonthly or monthly magazine may be more on target. Consider the function of the communication vehicle as well as members' preferences for print versus electronic communications as you review your current publication mix.

Newsletters are the most common format used by associations, and increasingly these are electronic newsletters. Many associations publish a dozen or more newsletters, each directed to a specialized segment of the membership or to nonmember subscribers. Newletters are fairly brief—usually ranging from two pages to 16 pages if print and even briefer if electronic—often simple in design and written to be scanned quickly. Generally, print newsletters do not include paid advertising, but paid sponsorships are becoming common in electronic newsletters.

Magazines and journals are a more formal means of communicating with members and may be published in print, online or in digital format, or a combination of both online and print. Nearly eight in 10 associations publish a magazine or scholarly journal as the official "flagship" publication of the organization, generally monthly (32%) or bimonthly (25%) (*Policies and Procedures in Association Management, Vol. 6, ASAE & The Center, 2006*). Although magazines and journals may contain news sections, their primary purpose is to provide in-depth coverage of selected topics. They vary in size, from as few as 24 pages to more than 200 pages, and often are supported by advertising (78% of flagship periodicals include advertising) and, at times, by subscription revenues as well (56% of flagship periodicals sell subscriptions to nonmember audiences).

Depending upon the publication's purpose and the changing needs of readers, an association may select a different format. **Tabloid newspapers,** for instance, are published by about 10 percent of associations. Sometimes referred to as "magapapers" or "newsazines," tabloids typically carry short news items up front and longer feature articles in the back. When publishing budgets tighten, this news/magazine format often proves appealing to smaller associations that cannot produce two separate publications. Medical societies also favor tabloids because the format offers a newsy complement to technical periodicals.

Electronic publications, especially newsletters, are becoming increasingly common with associations as a quick and relatively inexpensive way to deliver timely information that can be customized to meet specialized needs. According to the *Association Publishing Benchmarking Study* (Angerosa Research Foundation, 2005), 80 percent of associations publish at least one e-newsletter, generally in HTML format with graphics. The advantage of online publications is their timeliness and relatively low production cost; the disadvantage is that with the glut of electronic communications, they can easily be overlooked and considered one more marketing solicitation.

Other formats—especially electronic formats—are also gaining ground. Podcasting, blogs, Wikis, and RSS feeds provide easy access for communicating 24/7 with today's techno-savvy members. Format is largely dependent on members' needs, however. For instance, medical societies, whose members are interested in learning the latest techniques but are not always able to travel to meetings, may opt for a video version of their journal, or a **videojournal,** complete with advertising and printed supplements. More common, especially among technical and medical societies, are **CD-ROM versions** of the scholarly journal, which make searching and accessing research papers much more accessible.

Every organization has different communication needs at different times. The formats and frequencies selected must balance members' needs with the association's financial and staff resources. Furthermore, what's valuable to members must also be efficient for the association. A society of professional photographers, for example, may sacrifice other publications to produce a monthly, four-color magazine that showcases its members' work. An organization of scientists, on the other hand, might have staff produce a bimonthly newsletter, but rely on volunteers to prepare a book containing specialized research findings.

Is It Still Relevant?

A publication's format, and even its reason for being, may change over time and must regularly be assessed to ensure the publication remains on target. Publishing staff should periodically review each publication to determine relevance and effectiveness:

Is this publication still needed? Would another format better suit members' needs? Or has the publication outlived its purpose? Should it be published more often—or less frequently? Would the information presented in a newsletter be better suited for a magazine? How could the publication be repositioned to be more effective?

Regular, systematic review helps ensure that publications remain healthy. This may include using an outside specialist to conduct a readership study every two years or so, perform an audit of publications and publishing operations, or conduct an even broader review of all communication efforts in a communications audit. An objective outsider can provide insights into how to structure communications programs to be most effective.

Periodicals

Most associations publish a mix of periodicals, from journals and newsletters to magazines, directories, conference reports, and bulletins. Some associations publish twice as many newsletters as magazines, with many of those periodicals sent to fewer than 3,000 readers. No matter what the number produced, the staffs of all successful periodicals must first establish an editorial niche and develop appropriate editorial content to fill that niche.

There are several ways an association can identify industry trends and information of interest to readers. For example, staff can track the information requests the association receives to learn what members ask for. Readers can be interviewed in person by conducting focus groups or taking a "straw poll" at conventions or meetings. And by reading other trade publications, association publishers can stay one step ahead of the competition. This informal research, combined with editorial brainstorming sessions as well as more formal readership research, will help identify the topics and article formats that readers find most useful and appealing.

Other publications may opt to use an editorial board to keep it in touch with a technical field or to serve as a sounding board. Scholarly, scientific, or technical journals commonly use an editorial board, whose members function almost as editors to "peer review" articles before publication. Scholarly journals usually require at least three qualified reviewers to look at a manuscript before sending it to the editor—often a paid outside practitioner—for a final decision. This peer-review process helps protect a publication's credibility and integrity (See chapter 28).

Even some non-technical publications turn to an advisory board of volunteers for help in developing editorial content and locating expert authors and interviewees. A board, however, can't effectively manage a publication. Ultimately, the decision on what is published rests with a well-qualified, professional editor and staff—the people who know the readers and know the publication the best.

Building Editorial Content

Just as a publication's statement of purpose serves as its foundation, the articles filling its pages represent the bricks. Consistently well-written, high-quality editorial content builds reader interest and loyalty more than award-winning designs and colorful graphics. To generate the editorial content, an association may rely on a staff of editors and writers, freelance writers, members and suppliers, academicians, government leaders, and others. The content-development process should be continual, with the editor always on the lookout for new topics and different angles.

Editorial content should provide an appropriate mix of articles that appeal to readers with different interests and at different levels of experience. "How to" articles, for instance, may attract readers who are new to the industry or profession or who are investigating the uses of new technology, products, or systems. Case studies examine one person's or organization's problem and how it was solved. One association leader, author, or expert might be the focus of an in-depth interview, while several people might share their opinions in a roundtable discussion or open forum.

Although feature articles are the main attraction in a magazine or journal, departments devoted to ongoing issues are equally important. Departments, or standing columns, form the framework for a newsletter or magazine, giving the reader a familiarity and consistency that helps build reader loyalty. Readers know they can turn to a regular department each month for the latest on legal issues, book reviews, or a calendar of events.

Whether the association has a centralized approach to communications and marketing or operates under a more decentralized model, accuracy and consistency of style across all departments of an organization are critical for credibility. Establish content and design style guidelines for the entire association and adhere to them in all printed communications. Identify a dictionary and a style guide for grammar and usage that all staff members use as a reference source.

Some associations directly adhere to the standards of one source, such as *Chicago Manual of Style* or the *Associated Press Stylebook,* while others identify a basic source and then develop their own modifications or even write their own style guide. Consistency in application is more important than which dictionary or style guide is used. Also, if you frequently use outside contributors to your publications, develop author guidelines governing an article's length, format, tone, and audience.

Design for Readability

Packaging and presentation of publications—layout and design, paper stock, type face, use of photos and illustrations—are critical to readership. Good design and layout gets a publication noticed; solid editorial content keeps readers coming back. A good design—whether for print or electronic publications—not only provides the publication with an image that remains consistent from one issue to the next, but it helps encourage readability. Effective design employs easy-to-read type fonts, effective use of white space, and other design elements—such as color, headlines, art and photos, decks, callouts and sidebar boxes—to draw readers into the publication and keep them moving from one article to another.

Every publication needs a professional design as a starting point. When launching a new publication, for example, the initial design should include a logo/masthead, a front-page treatment, templates, and style sheets for feature articles and recurring departments and columns. And because design can easily become dated and ineffective, reexamine your publication's design every few years to ensure readers do not become complacent.

Larger associations may hire a full-time graphic designer or art director. Smaller associations that cannot afford this luxury can still produce attractive, readable publications by contracting with a design firm for each issue or by hiring an outside designer to develop a format and design look. The association may then choose to implement that design with in-house editorial/production assistants, according to the strict specifications established by the designer, or outsource the complete design and production operation.

With technology advances, in-house design capability is common in many associations; yet nearly half of associations (47%) report they outsource the ongoing design of their publications to design professionals (*Association Publishing Benchmarking Study*, Angerosa Research Foundation, 2005). The advantage of in-house design operations is increased control and the potential for reduced costs and quicker turnaround. The downside can be that to design in-house may put design in the hands of untrained editors and production personnel, resulting in reduced quality and delayed production.

And with printing technology's move to all-digital Computer to Plate (CTP) operations, many of the production-related steps that used to be done at the printer now move back to the designer. These include placement of ads and ensuring all materials in the publication are in appropriate press-optimized formats, all of which require more time and technical proficiency by design staffs. Be sure to provide appropriate training and support to ensure designers are skilled in technical requirements. Additionally, seek the advice and services of professional designers to create templates and overall formats that can then be used by in-house production staff to execute the layout.

Production

Decisions related to paper stock, scheduling, and distribution are the responsibility of the production manager. This area of publishing represents a key financial function and requires knowledgeable staff to identify and work with printers, mailing houses, and fulfillment companies. The production manager is responsible not only for selecting the most cost-effective ways to produce and distribute publications but also for ensuring consistent quality and timely distribution. To fulfill these needs, production managers need appropriate financial and publishing training to prepare and compare print specifications, determine press runs, and keep current with continually evolving digital print technology and postal and distribution issues.

To maintain credibility with their members and compete with commercial publications, associations must base their production decisions on financial data and strictly adhere to schedules. Making last-minute alterations at proof stage, for example, is costly and may delay distribution. A realistic production schedule accommodates many factors, allowing time for submissions from volunteers and outside writers, fact checking, proofreading, and alterations. Acquainting the entire editorial staff with the production process also helps; seeing firsthand how a magazine is printed should reinforce to staff writers the importance of meeting their deadlines.

Financial Management

Association publishing is a business. Like any business, it needs a financial plan to set goals and to help determine how well the publications department meets those goals. The financial well-being of the publishing operation must become the responsibility of all professional staff involved. Ultimately, however, it is the publisher—often called the editor or executive editor—who is responsible for ensuring the publishing operation meets its financial goals.

Financial management begins with preparing a budget that establishes financial goals for each publication. Although their parent organization may operate as a non-profit, most associations seek to generate a profit on their flagship magazine or journal. In fact, nearly half of magazines and journals generate a net profit after allocating direct expenses and staff salaries, according to the *Association Publishing Benchmarking Study* (2005), with a median profit of $420,000. And about one third (36%) generate net profit after overhead as well as direct expenses and staff salaries are allocated back to the publication, with a median profit of $360,000.

Even if the publication does not generate a profit, it provides an important service to the association and value to members. Clarify the financial goals of your publications to avoid misunderstandings:

- Is the association's intent to break even or to make money?
- How much revenue is expected?
- What level of investment in an existing publication or a start-up publication is the association willing to make over how many years to ensure a high-quality, valued publication?

Build a budget for each publication that takes a fresh look at the entire operation each year. Zero-based budgeting—as opposed to factoring in an across-the-board increase in income and expenses—makes staff reconsider each year how they are approaching the publishing process. To be effective, get as much input from staff and outside sources as possible, review the past performance of established publications, and keep well-informed on possible developments that could affect overall costs or income during the coming year.

For publications that include advertising income, track expenses that relate directly to editorial and expenses that relate to generating advertising income. On the advertising side, include all advertising income and all the costs associated with generating that income. On the editorial side, include income from nonmember subscriptions, royalties, reprints, licensing agreements, supplements, and other editorial sources as well as all the costs of producing the editorial portion of the publication. To reduce potential tax liabilities, ensure that appropriate expenses are charged against the advertising portion of the publication, including a percent of printing and distribution costs, salaries, overhead, and direct sales expenses.

Once the budget is established, use it as a management tool for controlling expenses and making key decisions. At any given time, the editor should know total production costs for each publication, the per-copy cost, and how each publication is financed (for example, fully subsidized by member dues or partially covered by advertising revenues). Hold key staff accountable for performance by comparing actual and budgeted figures each month, along with projections for year-end. Require staff to explain significant deviances from budget and what is being done to correct any shortfalls.

Some associations offer incentives to key staff for reaching or exceeding budgets. They may employ regular quarterly reviews of performance goals, financial income/expense reports, and significant variances along with revised year-end budget projections. Regardless of the system, the director of publications/communications (or publisher or editor) is responsible for all financial aspects of the publishing operation, including the development of realistic budgets and strategies for meeting those budgets. For instance, if advertising sales dip because of an overall slump in the economy, the director of publications must take steps to reduce the size of issues, to economize on paper stock, cut back on the use of color, and so forth.

Adhering to a predetermined advertising-to-editorial ratio in periodicals ensures advertising revenues will help offset production costs. Even if a magazine or journal does not rely solely on advertising to meet its income goals, having an established advertising-to-editorial ratio adds structure and balance to a publication. Publishers who seek to generate a net profit on their publications will generally adhere to a ratio of 45 to 50 percent advertising and 50 to 55 percent editorial in most issues. Others may opt for more editorial in each issue and less advertising, adhering to a ratio of 60 to 65 percent editorial to 35 to 40 advertising. Controlling the advertising-to-editorial ratio is an important factor in containing expense.

Advertising Sales

As pressure mounts to expand nondues sources of income, selling advertising becomes an increasingly popular way to partially or totally underwrite the costs of publishing. Nearly 80 percent of associations report selling advertising in their flagship periodical, which includes display advertising (95%) or classified advertising (47%) (*Policies and Procedures*, ASAE & The Center, 2006). For e-newsletters, about half of associations

(46%) sell advertising or sponsorships in the publication (*Association Publishing Benchmarking Study*, 2005). In addition to generating revenue for the association, advertising lends a look of professionalism to a publication and provides readers with information on the latest services and products available in their field.

The decision to sell advertising is a complex one, based on the market, the interest among prospects in reaching your market, competition for readers, perceived value of the editorial content, and demographics of readers. If you are considering selling advertising in a publication, conduct a feasibility study first to determine whether the potential revenue would sufficiently offset the investments of time and money involved in launching an advertising program.

With the pressures to sell advertising, conflict frequently develops between the editorial and the advertising portions of the publication. The greatest conflict is over issues of editorial integrity and whether to run editorial that is in some way supportive or promotional of advertisers. Credible association publications avoid any suggestion of advertising influence in editorial. However, general topic areas of interest to advertisers as well as readers are usually identified in an annual editorial calendar, which is provided to advertisers in a media kit. To avoid conflicts, clarify editorial and advertising policies in advance.

In addition, here are some other areas where conflicts may arise:

- **Ad placement.** Will all the ads be "stacked" in the back pages of the publication or integrated into the editorial pages? Will ads and editorial be clearly separated?

- **Positioning.** Covers and other premium positions are specially priced at rates substantially higher than the page rate. Some publishers also sell positions opposite well-read departments or columns for a premium of 10 percent or more over regular space costs. Determine if you will offer special positions and how to structure and promote these to advertisers.

- **Pricing.** Associations often undervalue their publications when setting advertising rates. Ensure you are selling a quality publication and then price advertising space for value and sell your "specialness"—your exclusive niche—to potential advertisers. Although association staffs and resources may be considerably smaller than a commercial counterpart, associations have a number of advantages over general trade publications. Price and position your publication to take advantage of the association's inherent strengths:

  - *Clout of organization:* As the official publication of the nonprofit organization, the periodical not only enjoys the recognition and visibility of the association but can also draw on its many resources. Promote this tie-in.

  - *Highly targeted readership:* Association members form a highly specialized group of potential buyers. Advertisers are willing to pay a premium to reach the top players in the industry or profession.

- *Quality of editorial and level of readership by members:* Traditionally, association publications are well-read. Conduct research to back up this claim and sell it to advertisers.

- *Paid circulation (by virtue of membership dues) as opposed to controlled circulation:* Association publications that are distributed as a part of membership dues are considered paid circulation and therefore represent a higher quality of distribution than controlled or free circulation trade and professional publications.

Audited circulation—a program whereby an outside firm regularly verifies the quality and accuracy of circulation figures—is even more desirable. As competition for ad dollars intensifies, more associations are moving to Audit Bureau of Circulations (ABC) or Business Publications Audit (BPA) auditing of circulation.

Marketing and Business Plans

To compete successfully, associations must do more than decide to "accept" whatever advertising comes in. Instead they must develop a strategy for aggressively soliciting advertising.

Incorporate a strategy for sales growth into a marketing plan that honestly assesses the strengths and weaknesses of your publication as well as the strengths and weaknesses of competitive publications. Based on this assessment, outline a strategy for long-term growth (during the next three to five years) that will maximize your publication's strengths and minimize its weaknesses to ensure growth in advertising, circulation, and editorial. The annual publication budget then becomes the short-term (one-year) plan for implementing the strategic plan and realizing long-term growth.

To implement the sales plan, hire experienced, well-trained salespeople or contract with an outside sales representative firm. Many associations begin by using a sales rep firm, paid on commission only of 20 to 25 percent of revenues, depending on the scope of work and revenue potential. Once a publication is established and billing substantial revenues, many associations choose to bring some or all of the ad sales force in house, often paying a base salary, plus a commission. According to *Association Publishing Benchmarking Study* (2005, Angerosa Research Foundation), 42 percent of advertising-supported association magazines and journals use outside sales reps, 38 percent use in-house sales staff, and 20 percent use some combination of in-house staff and sales reps. The median commission paid to reps is 20 percent; when both salary and commission are paid to a staff sales person, the median commission is 11 percent.

Both arrangements have advantages, depending upon the size of the publication, the geographic areas to be covered, and the revenue generated by the publication. Staffing considerations are critical to success so be sure to conduct a careful analysis of the costs and benefits of both options before you make the final decision.

In addition to selling display advertising, many publications sell print or electronic classified advertising, sponsorships in print publications or monographs, buyer's guide listings, electronic sponsorships, Web advertising, and convention-related advertisements. Increasingly associations are moving to integrated marketing plans where all marketing opportunities are integrated into a plan to encourage use of multimedia platforms and formats, both print and online.

Tax Considerations

Adding advertising to a publication introduces tax and legal issues. Advertising sold by tax-exempt organizations is considered unrelated business income, that is, unrelated to the purpose for which the organization was granted tax-exempt status. It is therefore subject to the Unrelated Business Income Tax (UBIT). Selling advertising does not jeopardize the tax-exempt status of an organization, but it may make the association liable for taxation.

According to regulations issued by the Internal Revenue Service in 1976, an association must allocate a portion of membership dues as subscription income. The allocation is not arbitrary but calculated according to a sequence of steps. In general, these regulations require taxation of net advertising revenues after expenses; editorial income is not subjected to taxation and therefore must be separated from advertising income.

Many nonprofit organizations, including the American Society of Association Executives and the U.S. Chamber of Commerce, have vigorously opposed the regulations, characterizing them as unfair; they can result in allocating so much of membership dues as subscription income that the publication shows a net profit when, in fact, it suffered a loss. Although the UBIT regulations continue to be tested in the courts, associations must still comply with them. Discuss the regulations with an accountant and legal counsel well-versed in association tax and legal matters. It is critical that an association's financial records clearly differentiate between advertising income and expenses and editorial income and expenses. The more that can be legitimately claimed as an advertising expense, the more net advertising revenue can be offset.

Circulation and Distribution

While most consumer publications rely on subscription income to help underwrite the costs of publishing, associations usually equate circulation with membership. Typically, a member's dues entitle him or her to receive a basic newsletter or magazine. However, in most cases, the publishing department does not receive part of those dues to apply toward publication expenses.

In recent years, however, more association publishers are looking to nonmember subscriptions as a means of not only expanding their reach but also generating additional revenue. More than half of associations report that they sell subscriptions to nonmembers (*Policies and Procedures*, ASAE & The Center, 2006). In addition, associations are beginning to sell access to publication content online, more commonly with scholarly and research journals. As of 2005, some 14 percent have pay-per-view options on their publication Web site whereby customers pay to access specific articles; this access model appears to be growing with an additional 16 percent planning to move to the pay-per-view approach (*Association Publishing Benchmarking Study*, 2005).

Several factors should be reviewed before embarking on a campaign to solicit nonmember subscribers, including:

- **Competition with the membership department.** The keenest competition for prospects usually arises between an association's publishing department and its membership department. The membership department may believe that selling an association benefit separately undermines membership recruitment. Often, however, when nonmember subscriptions are offered, subscribers convert to membership within the first year.

- **Not limiting promotions to potential members.** Suppliers to the industry or profession, government officials, the media, universities, libraries, and members of related organizations are all potential audiences. Purchasing commercial mailing lists will help define the universe of prospective subscribers.

- **Conducting a small sample mailing to test the potential for subscription sales.** Increasing nonmember circulation in increments, such as 10 percent per year, may be more realistic than a one-time effort to increase it 30 percent.

- **Evaluating additional expenses.** The cost of boosting circulation goes beyond a larger print run and increased mailing costs. Adjusting or expanding editorial content to attract nonmembers might require additional staff or outside writers, in addition to the costs of producing and sending direct-mail promotion pieces, purchasing mailing lists, entering subscriber data, and sending renewal notices.

- **Analyzing the long-term pay-offs.** Paid subscriptions translate into more revenue, and higher circulation figures attract more advertisers—but not immediately. Can the association wait several years before its investment in nonmember subscriptions pays off?

A program to attract nonmember subscribers is just one component of a publication's overall marketing plan. Although the plan will vary according to the type of publication and its audience, the plan should include an analysis of the market (including the competition), an analysis of the product (the publication), short- and long-term objectives, and strategies for accomplishing those goals.

Books

Unlike periodicals, which contain news that quickly becomes dated, books have a sense of permanence. An association that publishes books can influence a trade or profession for years to come by setting standards, preparing members for the future, and establishing itself as the main source for information. Books can also be an expensive undertaking, if they are not well-planned and marketed.

About half of associations sell books (55%), with about 75 percent of those sales being publications developed by the association itself and 25 percent resales of books published by another organization. The median number of titles offered is 20 (*Policies and Procedures*, ASAE & The Center, 2006).

Before accepting or rejecting any idea for a book, association staff members, in conjunction with a publications or special-projects committee, should follow several steps:

1. **Assess the need.** Many book publishing projects have their roots in other association activities, such as the results of a professional research survey, requests to the information department, or comments made during informal and formal discussions with members. What is the reason for publishing a book? What can a book do that an article in the association's magazine or journal cannot?

2. **Define the potential market.** Before any work begins, understand the proposed book's market. Is the book targeted exclusively to the association's members or other audiences as well? How large is the potential market? What is the book's shelf life—will the topic still appeal to buyers three or five years later?

3. **Examine the financial considerations.** As a business, a book publishing operation needs financial goals. Can the association afford to heavily subsidize or break even on the project? Some associations are willing to lose money on one book, calculating that sales of another book will more than offset the losses. In addition to financial resources, does the association have enough staff to devote to producing and marketing the final product?

The type of book published greatly affects production time and costs. **Collections** are the easiest to assemble and produce because they contain previously published articles or papers presented at a meeting or symposium. This "greatest hits" format is often popular among members but may have limited appeal outside the trade or profession.

Reference books, including manuals, handbooks, and glossaries, take longer to produce because they involve original submissions and a more rigorous approval process. Once published, however, such books often become the "bible" in the field and remain in print for several years.

Consumer-oriented books have the widest appeal and, consequently, the largest potential market. However, the costs of consumer marketing will be higher.

Among their members, associations have a natural resource for book authors. People who serve on the publications committee can identify experts in the field, or they may wish to write a chapter themselves. Members who are well-known in the field add to a book's credibility, even if they write only one section.

For long-term projects, associations often turn to outside contributors, such as consultants and freelance writers to draft original copy. To ensure consistency in copy, provide manuscript guidelines that discuss deadlines, style, length, tone, and the book's target audience. And require signed copyright release forms from all contributors and paid authors.

A staff member or an outside expert coordinates the book project. Typically, this editor ensures deadlines are met, keeps copy moving through the review process, and assembles all the book's pieces before production. If your association does not wish to maintain complete control of a book project, sign a publishing contract with a book manufacturer. The numerous companies that specialize in these book-publishing partnerships usually give the association editorial control but handle all the other production, distribution, and promotion details.

Whether working with a publishing company or venturing into book publishing on your own, address key issues in advance:

- **Timing.** Associations often schedule a book's release to coincide with a major convention or media event, allowing 12 to 18 months for development and production. If the book's topic is in the news, however, accelerate the production schedule.

- **Review and proofreading processes.** Determine who has the responsibility for approving final copy. Do all members of a publications committee need to review the book, or can that task be delegated to a subcommittee? Do authors have the opportunity to review or challenge changes to their work?

- **Copyright.** Clarify who holds the copyright for books, especially those that are a compilation of chapters written by volunteers. Generally, the association, as publisher, holds all copyright to the book once the authors sign the release form. This way, the association is free to reprint the materials, as needed, and use the information for other educational and information purposes.

- **Print run.** When considering how many copies to order, determine whether the topic or information will change or easily become dated. If that's the case, updates or revisions of the book may need to be scheduled and a smaller print run should be considered. Printing more than one year's supply can lead to storage problems and expenses. Determining factors may include the subject matter, marketing plans, members' purchasing habits, and response to pre-publication offers. Many associations use print-on-demand services where much smaller quantities can be printed quickly and relatively inexpensively.

- **Royalties and commissions.** Payment of contributors varies widely, depending upon factors such as the importance of the publication, the stature of the author(s)—consultants, well-known experts in the field, volunteers, and so forth—the size of the association, and the shelf life of the book, as well as the potential sales revenues anticipated from the publication. Overall, about a third of associations pay authors for their work. Payment is generally based on a flat fee (63%) or as a percent of gross book sales (30%) or net sales (29%) (*Policies and Procedures*, ASAE & The Center, 2006.) The majority—64 percent—do not pay authors because the work is considered a professional contribution to the field, but they may provide free or discounted copies for authors and/or contributors.

  When determining pay arrangements, clarify when contributors will be paid—upon acceptance of their work or upon printing of the book? Is compensation tied to the number of books sold? If the association has a co-publisher, what is the payment schedule?

- **Order fulfillment.** Does the association have the space, staff, and time to process book orders? How are orders shipped within the United States and abroad? If you anticipate high sales volume or offer numerous titles, consider contracting with a book distribution company. Agreements with co-publishers typically require customers to send their orders directly to the publishing company, bypassing the association completely.

Preparation and Printing

Options available for producing books vary widely, from a hard cover with acid-free paper and a sewn binding to a saddle-stitched soft cover. Consider the budget, the size of the manuscript, and the image to be presented with the book. Projects with quick turnaround times (less than six months), tight budgets, or short life spans might use spiral binding or offset stock with little or no color.

Technology has considerably changed the way books can be produced, speeding production time and reducing costs. Still, printers that specialize in books will provide the best value.

Setting the Price

Book pricing depends on demand for the material, the size of the market, production costs, and the association's goals. Most associations start with the book's direct costs—author's fees, illustration, design and layout, and printing—and calculate the per-copy cost. Next, they apply a multiplier that ranges from three to 10 times the per-copy cost. Because their smaller print runs represent higher per-copy costs, associations usually use smaller multipliers.

For example, 3,500 copies of a hardcover book may cost $45,000 to produce, or just under $13 per copy. Having researched what the market will bear, an association may price the book at $39 (a multiplier of 3) or at $65 (a multiplier of 5). Or it may use both prices: It's common to establish different prices for members and nonmembers, with the latter group paying no more than double the member price.

As with subscription and advertising rates, book prices should be competitive in the marketplace. Pricing a 150-page soft cover book at $3.50 to encourage sales could have the opposite effect. Would-be purchasers may not perceive value in a book that carries a low price tag.

Marketing a book begins long before it rolls off the presses. In fact, the level of response to a pre-publication sales offer can help determine the final print run or the book's price. A marketing plan should be in place while the book is still in outline form; the design of the cover, the popularity of contributors, and the title itself can all contribute to increased sales.

The marketing plan might also include these activities:

- Displaying the book at conferences.

- Cross-marketing or advertising the book in the association's publications and catalogs and on its Web site as well as in the publications of related organizations.

- Printing excerpts or news items in the association magazine and newsletter to pique readers' interest.

- Sending news releases to the press list and arranging interviews with authors.

- Sending review copies to specific people at key organizations, government offices, universities, and so forth.

- Organizing speaking tours for authors, members, or association staff to give presentations at regional conferences or chapter meetings. For consumer books, arrange interviews on local radio and television talk shows.

- Developing a direct-mail campaign to members and targeted outside audiences.

Considerations for the Future

Association publishers who enjoy long-range success—both financially and in terms of member satisfaction—are those who practice "smart publishing." That means they use the most innovative and cost-effective methods available to produce and distribute their publications. Some new technologies and management approaches to publishing are emerging as trends that warrant further investigation by association communicators:

- **Online publishing.** In this fast-paced world, members are increasingly asking for more specialized information delivered on demand. In response, many associations deliver information electronically on the Web. While some members may not have ready online access or may prefer print, online has opened extensive new areas for associations such as e-newsletters, RSS feeds, blogs, Pod casts, and more.

    Clearly, the advantages of electronic publishing are both speed and cost. Electronic bulletin boards, newsletters, or magazines allow association members to access news and information instantaneously, thus eliminating the cost of printing, mailing, and distribution. In addition, with online publishing, specialized newsletters to meet the targeted needs of a diverse membership group are less costly and less time-consuming to produce. Electronic communications may never replace traditional print formats, but they help supplement an association's offerings.

- **Outsourcing or contract publishing.** When a turbulent economy pressures association publishers to reduce costs and even eliminate staff, many consider alternative outside publishing arrangements, including contract publishing. This is an arrangement whereby an association agrees to turn all, or some, of its publication management over to an outside publisher in exchange for a fee or shared equity. While most associations create their own publishing staffs to manage responsibilities, 14 percent use some type of contract publisher (*Policies and Procedures*, ASAE & The Center, 2006). A contract publisher may, for example, manage all aspects of the publications—from editorial and design to printing, ad management, and circulation—or only parts of the operation. The association may continue to develop editorial content, for instance, while the outside firm handles production and advertising sales.

Usually outsourcing or contract publishing offers a major cost savings in salaries, benefits, equipment, and overhead and may reduce or eliminate the risk involved in launching a new publication. As the costs of staffing and equipment continue to escalate, more associations may consider the contract publishing alternative.

- **Web site as a communication tool.** While an association Web site is not a periodical, it is an integral part of an association's communication effort. Effective operations and management of the Web are central to communication success and member satisfaction. In more than half of associations, responsibility for managing the Web falls under the publications staff (54%). In other cases, management is placed in the IT, Web, or marketing and communications departments. (*Association Publishing Benchmarking Study*, 2005). Give careful consideration to how your Web site is managed and maintained. Ensure content is thoughtfully planned, placed, and updated since the Web will be a primary communication link to critical member and nonmember audiences.

A Strong Link

A well-planned and highly integrated publications program strengthens the link between an association and its members. To vie for members' attention in this world of increasingly sophisticated communications, associations must make professional communications a priority and regularly take a critical look at every area of operations, being willing to make changes to strengthen their communications program. A successful publishing program can ensure a healthy association.

About the Author

Debra Stratton is president of Stratton Publishing & Marketing, Inc./Stratton Research of Alexandria, Virginia. The firm is a leader in association publishing, marketing, and research. It specializes in providing strategic solutions to membership organizations. Stratton Publishing works with association publishers to strengthen their communications efforts, providing clients with reader, advertiser, and member research; communication and publication audits; consultation on publication repositionings and launches; and marketing support services. Stratton also serves as head of Angerosa Research Foundation, a 501(c)(3) foundation dedicated to conducting industry-wide research that advances the association publishing and communications fields. The foundation publishes the *Association Publishing Benchmarking Study* and *Electronic Publishing Trends & Practices.*

Review Questions

1. How often should associations conduct an assessment of member communications vehicles to assess whether publication content, format, delivery vehicle, and frequency are effectively addressing members' needs?

2. What areas should be addressed in the written editorial mission statement for each of an association's publications?

3. How can an organization position itself as the go-to source for information on a particular industry or profession?

Science, Technical, and Medical Publications

Don Hemenway

P UBLICATIONS PRODUCED FOR SCIENCE, technical, and medical readers—both members and nonmembers—are by their very nature different from the magazines, newsletters, and other types of publications an association may produce. While the material covered may be scientifically, technically, and/or medically oriented, for convenience sake, I'll simply refer to them here by their frequently seen combined form of STM. Both volunteers and staff have important roles to play in producing STM publications.

While there may be some subject expertise on staff, the content for these publications is mostly provided by specialists in the field, as also will the greater part of the overall tone and direction. They, the subject experts, whether members or not, will be involved in both creating and editing the materials. On the other hand, staff will be called upon for their business, managerial, and publishing expertise. Another factor that is typical of these kinds of publications is that their contents will be subject to peer-review. This chapter specifically does not address magazines and newsletters, as they typically contain non-peer-reviewed articles.

Topics covered herein:

- Types of STM publications and their life cycles
- Managing the STM publishing function
- The importance of peer review
- The production process
- Managing contractors
- Evaluating STM publishing programs
- Challenges and issues in STM publishing

Understanding the Basics

Types of STM Publications

While a journal may be frequently thought of as the most typical of STM publications, there are other types and hybrids among them as well.

Journals: The classic journal will provide peer-reviewed papers on a specific topic or theme. It will have an editor-in-chief who is an expert in the field, and may also have associate editors who are specialists within certain topical areas.

Some publishers find it beneficial and/or efficient to combine journals and magazines, though usually keeping the types of content very much separated, such that you may have a news section, a features section, and a peer-reviewed section. Examples of these sorts of publications include *Science*, *Nature*, and *Photogrammetric Engineering & Remote Sensing*. These publications are produced both in print and online, though the trend is in migrating toward online only.

Books: Sci/tech books may take many forms. One of the most popular among them is the collected work, where each chapter is written by a different expert or group of experts on a particular topic. Usually this sort of book will have an editor-in-chief who coordinates everything, outlining the scope, lining up and cajoling authors, and pulling all the pieces together. Each chapter is then like a separate paper from a journal, with its own author and reference list. These may be issued singly or as part of a thematic series.

Just as a single topic may be addressed by many authors over many chapters, so, too, may a single author or a few experts collaborating together address a topic. Such a book may be presented as a whole, with no single chapter identified with a particular author, and references may be gathered at the end of each chapter, or altogether at the end of the book.

Another type of STM book includes proceedings volumes, where papers from conferences are gathered together. Here the peer-review is often limited to a review of an abstract submitted prior to the meeting, and therefore these volumes are not considered to be as valuable or important. Simplest of all may be a conference volume that collects just the abstracts themselves.

Sci/tech books may also include such things as glossaries, guidebooks, field manuals, handbooks, and encyclopedias. Also, many of the types of books and journals already mentioned may be done in a hybrid fashion, combining their print contents with digital components, whether by inserting a CD or DVD with the printed volume, or publishing companion materials online.

Life cycle

A key area to consider is how often STM publications are produced and/or updated. Print journals vary from weekly to annual, while their online counterparts may be updated at any time, and the question of volumes and issues becomes an artificial constraint leftover from the days of print. For authors, this also means they need no longer wait until the next issue is ready to go to press, as once their papers are finished, they can be made immediately available.

With print publications tied to online versions, or with stand-alone online versions, the publications may become completely dynamic in terms of frequency. A manual or reference work that used to be updated every five or 10 years may now be updated on an as-needed basis. This is especially important in fields that are fast moving and/or affected by rapidly changing technology.

For this reason, STM publications exist in a variety of stages. Some may be one-time editions that are allowed to go out of print or are just allowed to remain online with no updating. Others go through the full cycle of startup, evolution, and eventually, if they lose their drive or readers/subscribers, may be allowed (or forced) to stop publication. Depending where a publication is in its lifecycle, you may be able to employ different strategies in managing it.

A big question related to the lifecycle that many publications now are facing in the early 21st century is how to respond to the digital publishing revolution. One offs, such as books, may readily exist in both print and digital (e-book) editions, but those that seek to remain current are more and more likely to move online.

However, online publishing can offer as many difficulties as it does opportunities. Maintaining subscriptions online and charging for them can be difficult. There is a strong Open Access movement afoot that is affecting many STM publishers, especially in the biological and medical fields, where the publishers are under pressure to make their contents freely available online.

Many associations are proceeding cautiously, continuing to issue publications in both print and online. If advertising has been a significant part of a print-based publication, it doesn't automatically transfer to the online edition. Also, publishers are experimenting with various models and types of open access. Nonetheless, many publishers are starting to forecast that most, if not all, of their print products will be online-only products within 10 years.

Rationale

So how do you decide what is the appropriate frequency or delivery method? Such decisions are informed by a good knowledge of your market—what do your potential readers, subscribers, and advertisers want? And, more importantly, what are they willing to support?

While some of this will be intuitive, market research can provide a good foundation for such decisions. Surveying the potential market, using focus groups, and analyzing the current and potential competition can all help you in figuring out what may be your possible and optimal strategies for managing your STM publishing efforts.

Service to the Members and Profession: The most basic reason for any publication to exist is information dissemination—your members have information they need to share with one another and others in their field. The STM publications are important to them for their careers, as publishing in books and journals, especially for academicians, is a major part of how they advance their careers.

Revenues: Another significant part of the publishing equation is the potential revenues they may generate, through sales of subscriptions, individual copies, reprints, author fees, possible associated advertising revenues, and perhaps sales of subscription lists. The publication may also help to attract members to the organization, resulting in ancillary monies from dues, conference attendance, and so forth.

Competition: A successful publications program can also help the association to compete in its marketplace. Competition comes from other associations, nonprofit organizations, government agencies, and commercial firms. Staying competitive means constantly evaluating your STM publishing program and its position in the market, keeping existing publications fresh, sunsetting those that have outlived their usefulness, and starting new ones as needed.

For an STM-oriented association, a successful publishing program is almost required. A small few may prove successful without a significant publications program, perhaps with seminars, tradeshows, and continuing education. But almost all such organizations will be significantly enhanced by a good program, which can pay dividends across all other aspects of the organization, enhancing its reputation, membership roster, and bottom line.

Managing the Sci/Tech Publishing Function

Management Structure: A typical management structure for association STM publications tends to be hierarchical and in many organizations provides for a publications committee that reports to the association's board of directors. This group of members will provide the guidance for how the association's publishing program is run. Depending on the size of the organization, there may be sub-committees or separate committees that differentiate between the STM publishing efforts and the more general publications, such as newsletters and magazines.

Each publication or series of publications within the STM publishing program may have its own editor-in-chief. That person may then have associate editors who help with the work. They all will then liaise with the appropriate staff and/or external contractors to manage the acquisition and production of the content.

It is important to be sure that each such group has a clear understanding of its responsibilities. Monitoring of schedules for workflows, delivery of content and its production, and all of the associated costs will help ensure a successful publishing program.

Finances: Each publishing project will need its own budget, which will also probably need approval as part of the association's standard budgeting process. Typically, a publications committee will work with the members to develop and approve new projects and work with staff to develop the budgets for those projects, including expense estimates and revenue projections. Expenses may include compensation for the editors, all production and delivery fees, along with the compensation for staff and consultants. Revenues then may consist of subscriptions, sales of reprints, author fees (page charges, color plate fees, and open access charges), advertising, and ancillary sales, such as charges for re-use of materials by other publishers.

All such budgets will have to be considered by the board of directors within the larger framework of the association's financial health, as it will do no good to plan and develop a project for which there is no funding or that will cause the organization financial hardship.

Peer Review: Key to an effective STM publishing program is to ensure that the best quality materials are published. The peer-review system requires that each item submitted is checked out by the researcher's colleagues for originality, completeness, logic, accuracy, and clarity.

A typical process works by having papers submitted to a central location. From there, they are sorted, such that appropriate reviewers may be identified for each. Often three reviewers are selected, such that a split decision may be decided by a majority of those who review the paper.

Although this process used to be conducted using hard copies, phone, and mail, it is now customary to have the entire review process managed electronically. Staff will typically serve as the hub and feed papers through the system in cooperation with the editorial staff and other subject-matter experts.

Once the reviewers are selected, and they agree to review a paper, copies are sent out to the reviewers, and deadlines are set for returning the papers. Once reviews are completed, there are several possible outcomes: The paper is accepted; the paper may be accepted if the author(s) agree to make required changes; or the paper may be rejected. Authors may appeal the recommendations or decisions made by the editors, and some papers may go back and forth several times.

When a paper is accepted and finalized in the review process, it then enters the production process, which is then usually staff managed, though much of the work may be contracted out. The text may be copyedited, references checked for accuracy, and graphics cleaned up and sometimes even redesigned. Animations and movies are checked for length and appropriate file type(s). When all is done, then the paper is ready for publication.

A peer-review system may be run with something as simple as a set of 3×5 cards or a spreadsheet. But nowadays, it's usually done using a Web-enabled database. Often a staff person will be designated to a position called something like "manuscript coordinator." That position then becomes the catalyst for the entire system. Papers come in and are logged into the system (probably using information entered by the author(s) online). From there, the paper must be classified for review, as to who will review it. This may be done by the editor-in-chief or perhaps by the associate editors. The suggested reviewers are then logged in the system, and when enough accept, the paper is sent out with a deadline for its return. Again, it may have to go through the loops of the process several times before reaching its final status of acceptance or rejection.

The speed of time-to-publication is of great interest to the authors, and the peer-review process, as you can see from its complexity, can be a cause of many headaches in that respect. While part of the difficulty may lie with slow reviewers, it is up to the staff to stay on top of the schedule at every stage, reminding and cajoling reviewers and editors at every stage to keep things on track. Regular monitoring of the flow of manuscripts through their various stages is critical to having a successful STM publishing program.

Publications Boards/Committees: Association members will assist in the STM publishing program by giving it direction and supporting it by acting as editors, reviewers, and contributors. Managing the editorial and reviewing functions will be a cooperative effort between staff and members, and soliciting contributions may well be too.

An STM publishing program may be directed by its own group of members or as part of a larger publishing program committee. Whether there are multiple groups most likely will depend on the size of the organization, as a larger one may be more likely to have separate groups. But whether they are separate or combined, it will be necessary for staff to work with the members on an ongoing basis.

Such a group of members will probably be made up of people from various backgrounds, but in all likelihood, if it's a volunteer group, obviously they'll all at least have a strong interest in the publishing program. In addition, it may be a good idea to include a nonmember or two on your publications committee who are consultants or representatives with professional publishing experience. These kinds of people can provide a certain amount of leavening to the group by offering insights that may help balance the less-informed opinions of the group.

In arranging for such a committee, it is important to ensure a variety of member participants to get a broad selection of opinions. Young, old, new, and long-time members all can bring something to the table. In addition, it will be good to have specific terms for each member, with a staggered set of terms, such that new members can rotate in while there are still old hands on board. Also, it would be helpful to have procedures in place such that someone can be replaced or removed, should they either not participate or cause problems.

Editors and Reviewers: Editors-in-chief for various projects will most likely need to be approved by one or more member administrative groups, whether the board of directors (or its equivalent) or the publications committee. The best candidates will be those people who have a high reputation within the field as well as some, if not extensive, knowledge of publishing processes. It will also be wise to ensure that they have a specific term of service, as well as specified procedures for their removal if needed.

Those editors-in-chief will probably then appoint or nominate associate editors to assist them in their labors. Such appointments may or may not need approval of the publications committee, depending on the needs of your organization and probably, in large part, how much the organization is willing to trust its editor-in-chief(s). The editor-in-chief, along with those designated as associate editors, will be called upon to find and convince other individuals to serve as peer reviewers and authors.

Generally, staff will provide the day-to-day coordination of the publishing process along with the business expertise and much, if not all, of the production management. All of the process may be contracted out, or it can nearly all be internally run. Most operations are a blend of such modes, depending on a variety of factors, including personal preferences, availability of qualified staff, expertise of existing staff, and predictability of work-flows. Copy editors, administrative assistants, graphic artists, and a program director may all be part of the typical staff.

Contractors and Contract Management: Key then is selecting appropriate contractors and managing them properly. Most often, work such as printing may be contracted out, but so, too, are copy editing and graphic arts, along with Web development and hosting.

Once you've decided what functions are to be outsourced, identifying potential providers is the next step. Certainly doing a Web search can yield some leads, but so too can industry directories and recommendations from colleagues.

Once you have a list of appropriate vendors, you'll then need to send them a request for proposal. A Request for Proposal (RFP) should provide all vendors with as much information as possible about your needs and processes, in order for them to provide you with an informed quotation. Depending on the scope of work, an RFP process may take a few short weeks or many months.

For large projects, it's not unusual to have a formal RFP process where a large group of possible providers are winnowed to a few for more detailed examination prior to making a final decision. Three primary factors will affect how each bidder is judged: time, quality, and cost. Some of them won't be able to do the type or quality of work you want, some may not be able to meet your schedules, and others may cost too much. Deciding on the correct balance is you and your staff's responsibility, and it will differ from project to project and organization to organization.

With a decision in hand, the next step is drawing up the agreement. Whether it is for a single project (such as a book) or an ongoing scope of work (such as a journal), it is important to get the contract right. While there's something to be said for simplicity, it is important to be sure that there is enough specificity to ensure both parties agree as to what is to be done, when, how often, to what accuracy and quality, and for what cost.

Trying to assess the intangibles in making a contracting decision—how well do they do what they say they'll do, what is their approach to customer service, how do they handle problem resolution, getting professional references and talking to other customers—can be one of the most useful things you can do. The final point is to be sure you have a dispute-resolution process agreeable to both parties. Typical may be a three stage process, beginning with mutual discussions, then mediation, and finally binding arbitration—with a goal of avoiding the costs of going to court.

Once awarded, then it's on to managing the contract and/or contractors. All those areas you outlined in your contract now are your guidelines for managing it. For the most part, if you've selected a good contractor, you shouldn't have to do more than monitor progress, tweaking the occasional situation or problem. If things do go south and pear-shaped, you've got your dispute-resolution process to fall back on. In a worst-case scenario, you may need to part ways and move on, perhaps to another contractor, or bring the work in-house.

It is even possible to license your publication(s) to another organization and let them run the operation from start to finish. Such arrangements are often made between a nonprofit organization and a commercial publisher. Such an arrangement may be successful for many years, but as with any other contract, it should be evaluated on a regular basis. You're typically giving up a good amount of control with such a contract, and as circumstances change, you may find that you wish to take that control back and/or look to reap more of the profits for yourselves, rather than ceding them to a commercial publisher. However, if you don't have the staff to produce the publication(s) yourselves, or the desire to, then this can prove an attractive option.

The contracting out option taken to its most extreme may include the ultimate sale of a publication. Such a divestiture shouldn't be taken lightly, as once a publication is sold, it will in all likelihood be nearly impossible to get back. But some organizations will divest themselves of a publication as a strategic move or in a time of financial crisis as a way to raise money to keep the organization alive.

Producing Sci/Tech Publications

Most STM publications are still produced in print, using a variety of presses, inks, papers, and bindings. Certainly any of the contents of books or journals may be delivered digitally, whether by CD/DVD or online, and perhaps even via audiotape. The advantages of these types of publications are many. The cost of color reproduction becomes negligible. So, too, do worries about excessive page counts.

Large datasets may be readily distributed digitally, as can multimedia files with sounds, animations, and movies. The added burden for digital production then is to be able to plan and prepare for the preparation, delivery, and production of these various types of content and their files. And, many authors may need help with them, as some will still be accustomed to just delivering word processor files, will have little or no concept of PDFs, GIFs, MPEGs, and WAVs (more to come on those later), and may not have considered publishing to involve spreadsheets and databases.

Selecting Formats: Given the various formats available—print, CD/DVD, and online (and all their variations), it is important to understand what options the various formats may provide your organization. As is happening more and more, a single product may exist in more than one format and may have different features in its different formats. Following are some of the elements to consider:

Format	Strengths	Weaknesses	Archiving	Appropriate Uses
Print	• Known production processes • Not as easy to duplicate as many digital files for the purposes of piracy	• Very difficult to update • Must be shipped to users • Requires physical storage space and inventory control • Color costs are expensive • Cannot handle sound or movies or animation without inserts of digital media	• With good quality paper, provides excellent archiving	• Still used on all types of publications • It is best used if your market is still uncomfortable with electronic delivery methods and if print advertising revenues are significant and difficult to move online
CD and DVD	• High amounts of data storage • Allows for easy distribution of sound, movies, and animations • Color reproduction costs are minimal	• Somewhat difficult to update • Must be shipped to users • May require physical storage space and inventory control (unless created in an on-demand mode)	• May prove fragile • It is not accurately known how long these will last • Playback issues may occur in the future as new media evolve and old players disappear	• Particularly good for distribution of sound and multimedia files • Good for products that may have anticipated life spans in terms of years rather than decades or centuries
Online	• Relatively easy to update • Doesn't require shipping and handling or inventory management • Color, sound and animation files are made readily available	• Vulnerable to hackers and pirates • Production methods and standards are still evolving • Because production methods are evolving, it can make changing vendors, providers, and software packages awkward	• Dealing with today's file formats in the future may be problematic • How reliable backups of digital files are is also an open question, partly affected by how often copies are made and also where they are stored	• Best for publications concerned with currency and frequency of updating, such as journals • Also good for distributing digital copies of other types of publications (sound files, e-books) so as to avoid costs related to shipping, handling, and inventory

Preparing Content for Publication: The type of publication and its planned medium(s) will drive the production processes involved. For print, the process is usually to receive a document in electronic form and then to have it copyedited in the same way. It may then be transmitted as individual documents for typesetting (for a journal) or in complete pages prepared with desktop publishing software (such as InDesign or QuarkXPress). Another popular way to deliver files is to send them to the printer as PDFs, which the printer then uses to make the plates for the presses.

If text is sent to the printer for typesetting and layout, then images may also be sent as originals, which the printer can then scan. If authors are submitting digital files for their figures, then typically accepted types are Adobe Illustrator, Freehand, Photoshop, TIFF, JPEG, Postscript, or Encapsulated Postscript (EPS).

Files may then be delivered via the Internet by sending them to a server at the printer's facility, usually using the Internet's File Transfer Protocol. Also, such files are sometimes delivered on CDs or DVDs.

Once the printer has prepared your material, then you're usually given a proof copy to review prior to the actual printing. It may be provided in a variety of formats, but the basic idea is to give you the chance to review a complete copy prior to printing in order to catch any last minute errors. If you have color pages, their proofs may come as separate materials because the printer is using a significantly different process than what is used to produce simple, black and white pages.

If you're rendering your publications online simultaneously with what's being done in print, then you can usually move fairly smoothly from one to the other. The same word processing and/or desktop publishing files may be used as the basis for what you put online. Depending on the sophistication and variety of things you may want to do online, there are many paths to move from one to the other.

Typical for many publications nowadays, especially journals, is to provide two versions of each article: one rendered in hypertext markup language (HTML) and the other as an Adobe Portable Document Format (PDF) file. The HTML is more flexible, allowing for a variety of links and easy updating. However, many readers prefer a PDF, especially when printed, as it looks more like the print edition of the publication.

The text of these publications may be coded in several ways in digital files. While it is beyond the scope of this chapter to address the various coding types in detail, you may hear from time to time of files or publications being prepared in HTML, which is a subset of SGML (standard generalized markup language) and SGML's more modern and Web friendly spin-off, XML (extensible markup language).

Today, more and more STM publications are moving to using XML. This is because XML allows you to separate the appearance of the information from its meaning, making it easy to exchange the information between applications and users. It can then be used just as easily in a database as in a Web site or printed in a book. There are also many tools available for adding XML coding to your documents. Also, within the realm of STM publishing, a standard is emerging for how such documents are formatted or defined, using a standard Document Type Definition (DTD).

This emerging standard, now adopted by the Library of Congress and the British Library, along with more and more nonprofit and commercial publishers, is the National Library of Medicine DTD. It exists in two flavors, one for serials and one for monographs. For more information about DTD, and to download a free copy, visit www.dtd.nlm.nih.gov.

Transitioning Between Print and Online: Of course one of the big questions many publishers face today is when or if they will stop publishing in hard copy and move to an online-only mode. This is proving to be a particularly enticing option for journals, and there is a growing number of journals that already exist only in the digital realm, with little or no printing happening, at least in terms of the publisher's own operations.

The reasons for such a transition are many. Researchers can access the material from wherever they may be and without having to go to a physical library. Hyperlinking between articles makes it much easier to research a topic. From the publisher's standpoint, there is no longer a need to be concerned with the cost of paper, ink, postage, and warehouse space.

However, there are difficulties or problems that still need to be overcome, which include a variety of areas:

- Many readers still prefer hard copy. Advertising may not readily transition from print to online.

- Subscriptions revenue may become harder to come by, in part because users may no longer purchase individual subscriptions as they gain access via their institutional libraries and are accustomed to getting nearly everything online for free.

- The open access movement may restrict the opportunities for revenue generation, especially as that model tends to drive publishers toward an author-supported (author fee paid) model, which can be difficult for some authors, and therefore some publishers, to support.

- Many libraries, too, are resistant to online-only editions, in part for fear that such publications may some day disappear, and they'll have nothing to show for their subscription monies; this makes for discussions about "perpetual access" to content and the need for reassurances of archiving and backup of material, even to the extent of contractually providing for offline copies of materials (perhaps provided on DVDs or CDs), should such a copy be required.

Nonetheless, it is apparent that the online publishing is becoming more and more the way to go in terms of STM publishing, and the pluses seem to far outweigh the minuses. Many publishers of journals foresee most, if not all, print editions disappearing within the next decade. Managing the negatives is therefore the important next phase in the transition process.

Fulfillment: Ensuring that those who've paid for your publications actually get them is referred to as the fulfillment process. At its most basic, it means maintaining an accurate list (database) of sales. For sending out print journals, it is used to create mailing labels that are used to send out the publications. Much the same is true of single copy sales, whether of a journal or book. The system is also then used to track expirations of subscriptions so that renewal notices may be sent out.

For online publications, the fulfillment process is then tied into what's often called "access control." That is, the system whereby your Web site or hosting service knows that such-and-such a user is entitled to view or download your content. For an ongoing publication such as a journal, the expiration date may often be hard coded into the Web site, such that if subscribers don't renew their subscriptions, their access expires on the designated day. And again, the same system should be used for sending out renewal notices.

Digital Rights Management: Not only is access-control managed online, but also the actual vending of the content using electronic-commerce systems. Such a system will allow a user to check off items they desire, place them into a virtual shopping cart, and when ready to complete the purchase, enter their credit card information via a secure Web page that will enable them to complete the transaction.

Another type of security is also becoming more prevalent in the online sales of content, and that is digital rights management (DRM). This is a type of software that will help publishers protect their content from being illegally copied and shared. It is currently used a lot with electronic books, but its application in areas such as online reprints of journal articles is increasing. If illegal file sharing is a concern for your organization, then DRM is something you should seriously consider, whether having someone else do it, or acquiring the ability to do it yourselves.

Managing Web Resources: One of the more awkward situations faced by many association publishing programs is managing the areas where publishing and technology overlap. For some larger organizations, the association Web site and the STM Web site may appear similar for the sake of branding, but will be run separately, as their needs can be quite different. If both are run in-house, then there can be a fair amount of friction between the STM staff, the association publication (magazine/newsletter) staff, and the IT department. Add to that the Web needs of the meetings, membership, marketing, and education departments, as well as other groups that may have a vested interest in your organization's Web presence, and you can have quite a hairball on your hands.

Ideally, each group should have an appreciation and understanding as to what the other is trying to accomplish and work together in an atmosphere of cooperation and collegiality. Unfortunately, that doesn't always happen. It's management's job to see that the various bits of the system work together as smoothly as possible. Sometimes the disputes between departments can become rather acrimonious, and difficult decisions will have to be made as to which direction the program will go. If management isn't knowledgeable enough about the issues involved (such as deciding on a DRM approach), then calling in independent consultants for advice may be useful. Certainly, at the end of the day, the most important question to ask is, what is the best (most efficient and cost effective) way to accomplish what the members want from the organization?

Evaluating Publications Products and Programs

Any association publications program will benefit from regular reviews if it is to remain vital. A variety of qualities may be assessed, including the quality, usage, frequency, features, usability, and relevancy, all of which can lead to an overall indication of viability, both of individual publications and a whole program. Another reason to examine these sorts of things is if you, or your members, believe the goals for publishing something have changed, as changes in goals may mean some changes in the way the business is run.

The first, and perhaps easiest, way to evaluate publications is by looking at data you already have in hand. Such statistics compiled and compared over time can provide snapshots of the health of your publications. Some of the questions to ask or statistics to track:

- How many copies and/or subscriptions are being sold?
- How much advertising is being sold?
- What is the expense/revenue ratio?
- For journals, what is the impact factor (a ranking of how much the articles in your journal are being cited by researchers; more citations are thought to mean more significant quality of research)?
- How much usage are your Web pages getting?
- How much press coverage are your publications getting?
- How many book proposals are being submitted; how many papers are being submitted to your journals?
- How is your site faring in the rankings of major search engines?

Checking such numbers on a regular basis may help you identify trends in how things are going. Statistics, however, have their limits, so more informative methods may be useful:

- **Expert Evaluations:** Many associations find it useful to call in independent experts to assess their publishing operations. They may have a more long-term, broader, or more in-depth range of experiences to bring to the process. If member buy-in is important, whether you or your staff likes it or not, the opinions of an external expert often carry far more weight than the same opinions if expressed by staff. There are many consultants out there, and some will fit some needs better than others. To start the process, it would be best to develop the most detailed and specific request for proposal you can come up with.
- **Surveys:** Even without an assessment by an independent expert, you may have a good idea as to what sorts of questions need asking. Surveys of members and users are a frequently used tool. They may be conducted by mail, telephone, face-to-face

(often at tradeshows and/or conferences), e-mail, and web-based form. These are particularly useful for obtaining simple, preferably non-free-form answers, such as multiple choice or yes/no, or ranking questions (for ease of quantification), which can be used to help develop ideas as to what to follow up on.

Ideally, you should use a random sample of members/users of large enough size to receive a statistically significant response. Consultants are available to help with constructing and analyzing such instruments if your staff lacks the capacity or expertise. Without those factors, you may still be able to get some useful information, but it will be less reliable. All too often, when incorrectly performed surveys are used, decisions are made based on poor or insufficient information.

- **Focus Groups:** If you need to get opinions or detailed answers rather than simple multiple choice or yes/no responses from members/users, then focus groups can be the way to go. These are often used as follow-ups to surveys to explore important issues in more detail. Gather together a group of people from your target audience, maybe offer them breakfast or lunch (or a cash payment, to encourage them to show up), a set of questions, and a facilitator to present the questions, keep things moving, and keep the group on track.

  Such conversations are then usually recorded and often videotaped as well for later viewing and transcription. These long-form, information gathering sessions will allow you to be able to hear in-depth the whats and whys of how your users/members are thinking. The interactions between the people in the room may bring out insights that otherwise you'd never have discovered. Running multiple focus groups over a few weeks may allow you to get input from various geographic regions, as well as to fine-tune the questioning based on earlier responses.

- **Usability Testing:** For digital products, especially Web sites, usability testing will enable you to get an understanding of how users really work with your products. These exercises can be useful in evaluating current products/sites as well as designs and pre-production versions for the purposes of fine-tuning. These tests may be conducted in person or remotely across the Internet.

  Such a test will be run with users working their way through a set of specified tasks:

  – Please find an article on topic X and print it out.
  – Who was the author of the paper in volume 32, no. 3, on page 235?
  – Find the online letters to the editor page, and write a brief response to the first item you see there.
  – Download four abstracts from the current issue.

Again, these tasks are then monitored and recorded. A facilitator is available to monitor and question them as the users work through the tasks. Upon completion, the results are then codified, and trends, problems, and suggestions may be found to act upon.

Acting on Reviews and Evaluations

After collecting your data, you need to decide what to do with it. If you don't like what it's telling you, it can always be put on a shelf and ignored. That may not be the most ethical thing, but it's happened more than once. "Bad data," "statistically unreliable," and "the consultants screwed up," have all been used as excuses.

Provided you really want to make something of what you've got, you'll now need to decide what actions to take based on the information you've gathered. The basic steps are to prioritize your possible projects, create plans for implementing your prioritized projects, followed by actual implementation, and then to evaluate how well you've met your goals.

You'll need to prioritize your possible actions based on various factors: which are the most important, which are the most affordable, which are the most achievable, which will take the longest and shortest amounts of time, and which will give you the most return on your investment(s).

Depending on the organization and its situation, each of those factors may have different weights. Some things you'd like to do, you'll find you can't, or shouldn't. Others that you might readily accomplish, you'll find aren't worth the time, effort, or money. So maximizing your choices is the critical point.

Once you've made your choices, then you need to work your way through the planning process. Typically this will involve staff, members, and perhaps consultants, based on the task(s) chosen and dollars available. Assuring buy-in with both members and staff will be critical in achieving success, so throughout the process, you'll need to keep communications in mind. Key points to consider will be staff availability and expertise, funding, and scheduling, all in conjunction with outlining the steps required to complete the project. As with any good plan, be sure to allow yourself some flexibility, especially in terms of dollars and time, to allow for unforeseen developments.

At the implementation stage, you follow your plan. Unfortunately, to paraphrase Field Marshal Helmuth von Moltke, "No plan survives the first contact with reality." A successful implementation will probably rely on your ability to handle the unexpected occurrences as much as it does on a good plan up front.

Finally, when your project is complete, it's time to start over—evaluate how you got there and where you're going.

About the Author

Don Hemenway has more than 20 years experience working for nonprofit organizations and associations, both on staff and as a consultant. He is currently executive director of GeoScienceWorld, a nonprofit organization offering an online portal of geoscience journals published by associations and university presses.

Review Questions

1. What are some of the strengths and weaknesses of the various formats of publications?

2. What factors should you consider when taking a publication online?

3. What are the typical member roles in the publishing function?

4. Why is peer review an important factor in scientific/technical publications?

29

Association Marketing

Alan R. Shark, D.P.A., CAE

Author's Note

Much time has passed since this chapter was first published, and it's good to see that for the most part it is as relevant today as it was when conceived. This chapter takes a classic approach in reviewing what marketing is and who should be responsible—and more importantly how and why. What has changed, however, are the many dramatic advances in technology affecting how members and nonmembers obtain information, achieve a sense of recognition and a sense of community, or feel that they have weighed in on issues without leaving their home or office.

One major advance is, of course, the Internet, which provides key information—mostly for free—that was once the domain of associations that could charge a modest price. Convergence has dramatically altered how we communicate with one another as voice, data, and video merge together in ever-changing creative devices. Broadband deployment provides the "pipes" necessary to move voice, data, and video across the planet in mere seconds—be it wired or wireless. While not a technological advance, mobility is another key factor that must be considered in marketing, as we find our members and customers moving about as never before.

The advent of technology and how we embrace it in association marketing management opens the door to vast opportunities as well as enormous challenges.

Opportunities include completely new and personalized service offerings that include video-on-demand as well as video conferencing and training. Internally, customer relationship management systems that track members' basic information, preferences, and purchasing habits are the new tool of choice in having an up-to-date integrated and comprehensive member/nonmember information system. From a marketing perspective, the more we know about our customers—be they members or nonmembers—and our competitors, the more effective we can be in delivering the right product or service, at the right time and right price, and in the best medium.

All of this requires an even greater degree of marketing management leadership than ever before.

While e-mail communications have become commonplace as the "address of choice," mostly due to the relatively low cost of delivery, they also have their drawbacks. Many well-intended e-mail communications never make it past a spam filter or go unread because many people are increasingly becoming overwhelmed with out-of-control inboxes. And in an ever-changing environment where people are moving around and changing e-mail addresses, there is no cost-savings approach for capturing such changes. Some marketing staff are returning to mailing as opposed to e-mailing while others are moving to a more balanced and coordinated approach using various mediums.

Leadership in marketing management requires that associations stay abreast of and be in compliance with state and federal laws aimed at protecting consumers receiving unwanted faxes and e-mail solicitations. The CAN-SPAM Act is designed to limit "spam," but it also limits an association's ability to send e-mails without first establishing a relationship. Even if that is done, the e-mails (and faxes too) must provide an opt-out option. Telemarketing involves similar compliance issues as well.

Member, consumer, and customer preference tracking is but another growing concern. Strategies must be carefully considered to achieve effective and meaningful results while at the same time staying ahead of the prevailing rules and regulations.

So while the principles remain mostly the same, the tools have changed. And while I've said you really can't delegate marketing, I need to add that you can never know too much about technology as both a means of delivering outstanding products and services and understanding the needs and wants of your targeted audience.

I N AN ASSOCIATION, MARKETING involves all the same principles used by modern profit-oriented corporations. There are differences, however, in the way nonprofit organizations carry out their missions. For-profit companies exist primarily to seek profits for their shareholders and, generally, have distinct products and services. Associations, by comparison, view their members as stakeholders. They exist to meet the needs of their members—whether by advancing a cause, promoting an industry, or serving as a collective force to fight for or against laws and regulations that affect the industry or profession. Their products and services are not always clear-cut.

Just because an association is deemed nonprofit does not mean it can survive without using the latest marketing concepts to realize revenue above and beyond expenses. In the past, dues income provided the main source of revenue for associations. But most associations have had to turn to other revenue streams to survive. For many organizations, conferences, expositions, publications, and research services account for at least a third or more of total association income.

As associations have grown in size and sophistication, so too have member needs and expectations. Furthermore, associations have discovered that they are also dependent on customers who, for many reasons, are not members. These customers actively purchase association products and services even though they are usually paying a higher nonmember price. Associations also have found themselves in competition with the ever-growing service sector in terms of providing publications, information services research, training, conferences, and consulting. Marketing is as critical a component for associations as for-profit corporations. No body of association management knowledge can be complete without a fundamental understanding of what marketing is, who is responsible for it, and why marketing planning is vital to an association's existence.

Understanding Marketing

Marketing is the discipline where ways are found—through the introduction of a product or service—to satisfy a need within a targeted group of customers, whether they are members or nonmembers. Satisfying needs is achieved through market research, distribution, product development, promotion, and pricing strategies.

The function of marketing examines the offering (*product* or service), determines the relative value that one may be willing to pay (*price*) and the method that should best reach customers (*place* or distribution), and plans the best way to make the product or service known and desired by the intended customers (*promotion*). These elements are referred to in marketing as the four Ps, and they are essential in determining which markets will drive an association's product and service offerings.

A market-driven association is directed by the needs of its members and other constituents or customers that members wish to serve. Depending on the particular association and its members' desires, it also may be directed by the broader needs of a profession, by philanthropy, or by society. A market-driven association actively scans the environment for changes that will affect its members and other constituencies. It makes decisions on strategy, products, services, and organizational processes based on constituents' perceptions of their own needs.

In addition, the market-driven association is proactive, not reactive. It aggressively engages in marketing research and strategic planning to define the present and future needs of its members and other constituents and offers a program of services tailored to those needs.

All associations can become "market-directed." The term "market-directed" emphasizes the proper role of marketing as one of the key instruments that supports the need of management, rather than being an end in itself.

The Management of Marketing

What does management have to do with marketing? Quite a bit. While most textbooks focus on the principles of marketing—what it is, what it involves, and its terminology— little has been written about who is responsible for marketing. Is it the chief executive officer (CEO), a deputy, a marketing professional, selected department heads, a committee, a board, or all—or a combination—of the above?

Association marketing is the responsibility of every association staff member and volunteer. But this statement, taken alone, leaves a vacuum of confusion, because staff and volunteers already play many roles in association management. If an organization wants to become market-driven, how would staff help achieve this transformation? What would be the role of volunteers?

Like any corporate structure, associations typically are divided by both function and department. Each function or department carries out some marketing on its own. In a typical association, the membership department seeks new members or looks for new services to satisfy existing members. The meetings and conferences department seeks better programs and promotions to increase attendance. The publications department attempts to find timely material that will attract loyal readers and thus advertisers. Public relations attempts to promote the association or a particular cause or position in a way that makes members want to continue their support. Even top management strives to make its administrative procedures and policies more appealing and user-friendly to members. But the effectiveness of each department's marketing efforts is multiplied if the departments are woven together in a strategically cooperative group.

Achieving association-wide marketing requires a high degree of orchestration throughout the organizational structure. Ideally, someone should have the responsibility of coordinating departmental efforts to ensure that members and customers feel they are dealing with one association and not a collection of uncoordinated groups. A strong commitment from the highest levels also is required for meaningful change.

The Role of the CEO

The chief executive officer must assume responsibility for association marketing. Realizing the magnitude of what is involved with becoming market-driven strengthens the argument for the CEO to be more fully aware and involved. Specifically, here are 10 ways association CEOs can help create or improve on a marketing environment:

1. **Serve as the central marketing staff person.** More and more CEOs now have marketing management experience, a skill that's especially needed in small and mid-sized associations. Because market-driven management differs from more traditional forms of association management, it stands to reason that such leadership must come directly from the top.

2. **Provide for appropriate staff and reporting relationships.** Many associations, especially large ones, require CEOs to have talents in areas other than marketing, such as government relations. In such cases, someone else should be assigned the marketing task and be given abundant support and commitment from the top.

3. **Provide the necessary staff support and budget.** It takes considerable staff resources, time, and financial resources to plan and conduct research and to develop, implement, and evaluate strategic plans.

4. **Create an environment in which marketing receives high priority in decision making.** Association-wide marketing should not be hidden in some obscure area of management. Everyone on the staff and the volunteers must understand what is required of them.

5. **Set realistic goals and objectives.** Market-driven management is not magic. Membership will not double overnight nor will income suddenly come pouring in.

6. **Ensure that market planning is synchronized with other planning.** For example, market planning should tie in with the association's strategic- and budget-planning cycles.

7. **Reward marketing achievement.** Market-directed management is everyone's business. One strategy is to link marketing accomplishments to a bonus incentive plan, which provides extra funds for staff when the association has met or exceeded certain financial goals.

8. **Insist on sound market research as the basis of strategic planning.** Associations that conduct market research, but then do not reflect what that research reveals about members' needs in all important decisions made by the board, staff, and volunteers, are not achieving their full potential as market-driven associations.

9. **Monitor and evaluate results of marketing plans and revisions.** Even the best of plans needs to be routinely evaluated against new information, so view a marketing plan as fluid. Adjustment is ongoing.

10. **Understand that the best of plans can fail when poorly executed.** Proper execution requires an emphasis on planning and evaluation. Staff need to understand that great ideas, new products, and services must have solid follow-through. Carefully consider distribution and administration: Can the new product or service be produced in a timely fashion? Can you deliver what you promised? More important, can you guarantee what you deliver? Many details need to be thought of in advance and all possible contingencies provided for.

Evaluating Marketing Structures

Each organization needs to assess what type of structure will best support a market-driven environment. Six basic models exist; all but one assumes that the CEO has delegated the primary, day-to-day responsibility for marketing management to someone else. Some of these models, whose pluses and minuses are spelled out below, can be intermixed to best meet an association's needs.

Model 1: Membership Orientation

Marketing frequently falls to the person who is primarily responsible for membership marketing.

Opportunities: Membership-oriented staff are usually closest and most familiar with overall membership needs. This knowledge, combined with marketing training, can be valuable in identifying new products and services or improving existing ones. This person also may be the most familiar with individual members and, therefore, able to personally recruit volunteers for the marketing project.

Limitations: The membership marketer usually has no authority over other departments' efforts and does not play a key role in the association's strategic planning. The position carries marginal responsibility for market research and assessment and has little direct involvement in product or service planning. Membership marketers usually view nonmembers as opportunities for membership, not as potential customers for other association offerings.

Model 2: In-house Consultant

This staff person provides consultation services to the various program departments throughout the association. For instance, he or she assists departments in writing or editing promotional copy, planning for new products and services, reviewing plans and concepts, and assisting with developing marketing strategies. This person may also take responsibility for conducting market research to support other departments.

Opportunities: An in-house consultant provides association staff with important professional resources. Friction is minimized because he or she is not threatening to the departments' status quo.

Limitations: This person is kept quite busy responding to staff needs; he or she more often reacts than coordinates and initiates. Sometimes, little use is made of this individual's sophisticated marketing skills.

Model 3: Separate Marketing Department

Staff have responsibility for developing, implementing, and coordinating all or most of the association's marketing activities. The department usually has considerable budget responsibility not only for promotion and distribution but also for revenue generation.

Opportunities: This department can be very effective when it has both the responsibility and authority to carry out a coordinated marketing program, including developing plans and making final determinations on budget projections on either side of the ledger.

Limitations: Usually this department is positioned at the same level as program departments. In effect, the director of marketing has little formal authority in relation to the responsibility given. Considered a peer by other department heads, the marketing department's director spends considerable time negotiating or bargaining with others to accomplish goals. Other departments tend to ignore marketing unless they see a direct benefit.

Model 4: Senior Marketing Staff Person

This person has the responsibility and authority to plan, coordinate, and execute an association-wide marketing plan and program. He or she works closely with all program departments, finance, administration, the CEO, and the board and usually belongs to the CEO's "cabinet."

Opportunities: This structure can be quite effective when the position enhances the effectiveness of various program departments and when department heads realize it is in their best interest to support and participate in the marketing program.

Limitations: Marketing professionals are considered relatively new players in association management. Their roles usually are misunderstood, and the expectations placed on them often are unrealistic. Also, there usually is insufficient staff to effectively carry out all necessary tasks and activities.

Rarely does an association hire a marketing professional when it perceives that all is well. More typically, it hires the marketer in an atmosphere of low-grade panic. If, in a very short time, sales or membership revenue goes down—despite many other contributions he or she makes—the marketing professional's position is in jeopardy. Instead of regarding the marketing professional as a luxury that can be justified only by immediate results, associations need to see it as a necessary position that requires a long-term investment in patience.

Model 5: Outside Consultant

This person is given the task of developing a marketing program within a specified time. The plan might be for a particular department, product line, or for the entire association. The consultant will make recommendations and may be asked to stay on to help implement the program.

Opportunities: Consultants can provide analysis, objectivity, and strong marketing skills. They also can reduce staffing requirements within the association and fulfill the need for high-level marketing expertise on an as-needed basis. Unencumbered with internal politics, they usually can move freely among departments.

Limitations: A consultant usually does not have sufficient time to really get to know staff, the specific project, or member needs. Even if the consultant's recommendations are well-received, execution remains a problem: Who will carry out the plans? What happens once the consultant has gone?

Model 6: The CEO as Marketing Director

A small association may have no choice but for the CEO to also wear the hat of marketing director.

Opportunities: Regardless of staff size, the CEO is viewed as an association's principal orchestrator, leader, innovator, and motivator. When the CEO is also the marketing director, there is no doubt about who is in charge. Acting as the head marketing person enables the CEO to quickly steer the association in new directions as opportunities arise. And, if true market research is indeed a cornerstone for any type of planning or action, the CEO will have valuable information to substantiate his or her policies or programs.

Limitations: The CEO may have been hired more for his or her skills in lobbying or knowledge of a profession. This person may feel uncomfortable—even resentful—about being burdened with the responsibility of strategic marketing, a skill in which he or she has no or limited training. Plus, given the nature of a CEO's responsibilities, he or she may simply not have enough time to perform the required duties.

The Planning Process

Good marketing stems from good planning. In turn, good planning begins with a strategic plan.

Strategic plans and strategic marketing plans often refer to the same document. In large organizations, the strategic plan gives a "big picture" view of the association and its future. In contrast, the strategic marketing plan may focus on specific association functions—usually products and services.

A strategic marketing plan is a program of action for reaching members, prospective members, and customers or nonmembers. It addresses all association operations—from membership and meetings to exhibits, education, and publications—whether they entail products or services or communicate a message.

Today's strategic marketing plan must also include a relatively new term to associations—branding. Branding is a term imported from the corporate side to denote the building of emotional ties between customers (members) and a product or service. Branding might be as simple as a new logo or name. When we think of a Volvo, we think of a safe car. When we think of Verizon Wireless, we are led to think of network reliability and a team to back it up. In both examples, a brand is only successful if it lives up to its promise in the minds of consumers. Associations too must look at branding as a way to reach members and prospects. Branding involves something far greater than a cosmetic makeover, and it should be very much an integral part of any strategic marketing plan.

Finally, the budget is the association's overall strategic plan represented in financial terms. Accounting for all sources of revenues and expenses, the budget is the clearest indication of how and where the association allocates its resources. If the budget is the most important plan an association has, then the marketing plan rates a close second. It prompts the association to rely on market research to develop a database for information, which provides tools for well-reasoned decision making.

Properly used, the marketing plan puts an end to old-fashioned, incremental decision making that frequently plagues an association budget process. Instead of arbitrary "cut the budget across the board" decisions, strategic plans provide for sound business decisions that focus on revenue with as much certainty as expense.

The marketing plan drives much of the budget process. With the plan, an association states operating assumptions, such as trends in membership and conference attendees, and ties them to the budget. The antithesis of a marketing plan is a system that merely counts up all the known expenses, adds a percentage factor to cover the unanticipated, and arrives at a revenue figure to cover the known expenses. In other words, budgets that take into account marketing plans focus on revenue and revenue potential. Budgets developed in a vacuum emphasize expenses; they focus on the past rather than on the future.

Key Components of a Marketing Plan

A strategic marketing plan can be as short as 10 pages or as long as 100, depending on the association's size and complexity and the amount of available data. Whatever the plan's length, it should include the following elements:

Introduction

This section states overall marketing goals and discusses how the plan ties into the association's mission statement or general strategic plan. Given the amount of information disclosed, it's wise to include a statement of confidentiality and nondisclosure.

Business summary

This section explains the marketing environment in which the association operates. It covers areas such as the overall business outlook as determined by inflation, interest rates, the association's competitors, its business partners, public confidence in the economy, and association-specific indicators.

The general business climate needs to take into account the nation or state, compared to that of the industry or profession the association represents. State any and all aspects of the association affected by the business climate: Is membership up or down?

What about publications sales? Did the organization lose an important staff person? If so, might it take time to complete a search and bring a new staff person up to speed?

Next, describe the members, nonmembers, or customers the association is trying to target and the rationale behind those decisions. The rationale generally takes the form of a judgment call by the CEO or marketing professional, in concert with board or committee input.

Each membership segment needs to have a unique strategy and message; you might, for instance, make some offerings available only to targeted members, such as chapter leaders or new members. One year, the plan may call for more resources devoted toward an emerging membership class, such as international members. Sending one message to all members is not effective. The more you can identify subgroups of members, the more effective the association will be in customizing its appeal to specific classes of members and customers, thus leading to more effective marketing of products and services.

The business summary should also describe the association's product mix. List the various membership categories, along with the product offerings and services for each. Mention new products and services that are in the works as well as those due to be discontinued. Describe the market position and sales revenue for each category. In some areas, the association may have no real competition and will be the primary source; in other areas, its market position may be secondary if competition is heavy.

Understanding market share or position helps the association focus on its strengths and weaknesses. If an association has a market penetration of only 20 percent of members in a given membership category, for example, it may want to develop strategies to increase that number through more aggressive recruitment programs and membership offerings.

Research

In this section, which constitutes one of the most critical aspects of a sound marketing plan, delineate characteristics of the overall markets or segments in which the association competes. What does the competition charge for its products and services? How many members belong to other organizations or purchase the services of others? What else is known about the association's members?

All too often associations spend an inordinate amount of time surveying members to determine how well they rate its products and services. It is even more important to ascertain membership's preferences and needs with respect to others' products and services. For example, what publications do they read? How often? What industry meetings do they attend? What other associations do they belong to? What do they want and need that is not being offered?

To be truly effective, marketing research must be ongoing and its results used to update the marketing plan regularly. The fluid nature of the plan, which stems from continual research, ensures its viability. The more that is known about members, nonmembers, and customers, the more effective decision-making tools will be available for developing strategies. Yet market research need not be expensive. You can use simple telephone surveys, focus groups, and fax-back surveys to obtain information about members and customers alike.

Marketing Strategies and Projections

This section of the plan lists the product and service line, including each offering's strengths and weaknesses. It outlines objectives and strategies for each component of the product mix (product, promotion, distribution, and price). The section also presents the marketing budget, noting how marketing dollars will be spent and what is expected in return.

Most associations find the promotion budget the most challenging. They wrestle with questions such as: How much should be allocated for membership recruitment? What are the anticipated results? How much will be spent on direct mail, advertising, public service announcements, telemarketing, and other related activities? Listing previous results for each product and service will help build more effective plans.

Strategic decisions that require additional resources for developing new or improved products and services must be linked to an association's mission statement and strategic plan. Although generally focusing on the bottom line, marketing plans must sometimes allow for some products and services to be offered at a loss. Some products and services that accomplish the goals of the association and fill an important need may never be able to "make a profit." Some intangible benefits may be necessary to recruit or retain members.

Of course, if it has too many intangible benefits that lose money, the association may need to develop strategies for turning losses into goals. For instance, one association offered a "free" six-month membership that entitled people to member discounts on an upcoming conference. On the surface, it would appear that this association would stand to lose six months' worth of membership plus the difference between member and nonmember conference fees. But the strategy was to provide trial memberships while at the same time increasing conference attendance (which would make exhibitors happy). The strategy worked in the long run. Half of those who took advantage of the trial membership renewed, and the conference gained about 50 new attendees.

As another example, consider two associations that created Web sites on the Internet. The first association did not see itself as making any money up front and viewed the Web site as a loss. On the other hand, the association successfully promoted the industry; made existing members feel good; and promoted membership, publications, and conferences. Later, the association learned that the Web site helped achieve its goal of recognition, with some evidence of increased interest in its activities.

The second association considered its Web site a failure: It had projected measurable results from increased online sales of memberships, publications, and conference registrations. Each association had a different strategy. While both endeavors appeared similar, one was considered a success and the other a failure.

The rationale for developing a strategy helps to determine whether it is considered a loss or a success. Each association must pursue its own rationale. Not every activity can be expected to bring in direct financial results—some strategies acknowledge that certain activities can lead to other goals.

Monitoring and Evaluation Techniques

General progress reports on the marketing plan should be issued monthly or quarterly. The frequency will depend on the size, complexity, and scope of the association. Remember, a marketing plan is not a static document, so it can be modified at any time.

If, for example, meeting attendance appears to be down compared to prior years, the association may want to try new marketing techniques (if time permits) or adjust its revenue projections and scale down costs. If the association envisions a long-term trend versus an isolated situation, it may want to adjust price. Some associations can raise their registration fees without too much political fallout, while others have actually increased attendance by lowering fees or by offering large discounts on multiple registrants from the same organization. Still others have found that offering low-cost alternative lodging helps boost attendance.

Marketing budgets usually require modification within the fiscal year: Numbers must be changed to reflect outcomes related to the success or failure of certain strategies. When this is accomplished, confusion can arise concerning the association's overall budget: Should it be changed, too? The answer is no. Just add notes to the budget to reflect important changes in the strategic marketing plan. Making notes to the budget may mean marking a budget line item and adding a corresponding note at the end of the budget document. This technique preserves historical data while alerting staff and board members to changes.

A good strategic marketing plan presents many opportunities to evaluate results. For example, expected revenues from specific programs and services should be broken out into fiscal quarters; any product or service that falls short of projections needs to be reevaluated. Were the strategies to blame? Did some unintended event cause a shortfall (for example, was a meeting canceled because of a blizzard)?

Although the strategic marketing plan can continue to change, at some point it should be presented as a new model. The best time to unveil such a plan is well before the budget process begins.

Marketing by Department

For larger associations, or those with separate subsidiaries, it makes sense to have each product- or service-driven department create its own marketing plan. For instance, an association might develop a separate marketing plan for large conventions or for its publications department.

Any plans that segment information need to be part of a larger marketing information system: Membership should be able to access information about meetings;

meetings should be able to coordinate with publications, and so forth. A centralized database with information about members and customers helps pinpoint purchasing trends and proves invaluable for planning.

Departmental marketing plans contain all the elements of the association-wide plan and are rooted in the overall strategic plan. The best method for generating departmental plans is to give each program and service department general guidelines for substance and format. Each departmental plan is incorporated into a master plan: Goals and objectives are coordinated among departments for the CEO's approval.

In today's fast-moving business world, the trial-and-error marketing methods of the past won't work. Without an ongoing marketing planning system, an association will base its decisions on past information, making assumptions that are groundless and highly subjective. With well-orchestrated plans, however, associations can count on noteworthy results.

Pitfalls to Avoid

Several pitfalls commonly plague a strategic marketing plan. Avoid a plan that:

- **Lists only goals, not strategies.** Such plans often fail to support assumptions with factual research.

- **Lacks support from the top.** Adequate resources have not been allocated to make the plan work. Perhaps the person in charge of the planning process has not been given sufficient authority to move ahead or lacks support staff.

- **Is out of sync with the budget cycle.** If the plan is completed after the budget has been approved, it will be of little use to association managers.

- **Disenfranchises staff.** Even if the marketing planning process is a centralized effort, staff from every department must provide input and support. A sound centralized function is open and embraces coordination and facilitation. Every staff member has some responsibility for marketing, regardless of the association size.

- **Is based on flawed assumptions.** A good marketing plan must be more than a wish list or goal statement. Successful plans contain information about how conclusions were derived. Financial data should not be accepted without supporting information as to how and on what basis assumptions were drawn.

- **Relies on poor quality market research.** Some staff leaders fall into the trap of believing that market research will be too costly or take up too much time. Associations must be willing to commit to ongoing, quality market research. Remember the old saying: No research is better than bad research.

- **Is not comprehensive.** If a plan is developed for a one-time event or opportunity, it may do more harm than good. The plan must be integrated with all activities of the association.

- **Gives no one the responsibility for marketing planning.** Another old saying to keep in mind: If everyone is in charge, no one is in charge.

References

Foundation of the Greater Washington Society of Association Executives, *Marketing the Nonprofit Association,* Washington, D.C., 1992.

Kotler, Philip, and Alan Andreasen, *Strategic Marketing for Nonprofit Associations,* 4th ed., Prentice-Hall, Inc., Englewood Cliffs, New Jersey, 1991.

Kotler, Philip. *Kotler on Marketing: How to Create, Win, and Dominate Markets* (1999, 272 pages).

Norris, Donald M., *Market Driven Management: Lessons Learned from 20 Successful Associations,* American Society of Association Executives Foundation, Washington, D.C., 1990.

About the Author

Dr. Alan R. Shark, D.P.A., CAE, is the executive director of the Public Technology Institute (PTI). Dr. Shark, whose career has spanned more than 28 years, is a highly recognized leader in both the nonprofit management and technology fields with an emphasis on technology applications and solutions for nonprofits and businesses as well as government agencies at all levels.

Review Questions

1. What are the four P's of marketing?

2. Is an association marketing plan a static document?

3. Does the CEO have an important role in association marketing? Why or why not?

CHAPTER

30

Membership Recruitment and Retention

Mark Levin, CAE, CSP

SINCE ASSOCIATIONS, SOCIETIES, CHAMBERS of commerce, and most nonprofit organizations are, by definition, *membership* organizations, the importance of establishing and maintaining effective membership recruitment and retention systems cannot be overstated. Organizations need a steady influx of members to help accomplish the organization's goals and to provide a voice for the industry, profession, community, or cause these organizations represent.

Your membership efforts also have a dramatic impact on the financial status of your organization. This is true even if the majority of your organization's income isn't coming from membership dues. Organizational leaders who believe that their organization "is not dependent on membership" might want to look a little more closely at their organization's financial reports. In most cases, the majority of the revenue generated by nondues income sources comes from members and the companies or institutions for which those members work. Insurance programs, meetings and conventions, educational programs, and so forth, all support the organization financially, but it's current members who make up the largest number of participants in these programs and events. What this means is that while your organization may not be dependent on membership *dues* to be financially viable, it *does* depend on membership.

While the actual number of members is certainly an important part of the membership function, you have to look way beyond the statistical aspects of membership to get a real appreciation for the impact that the membership function has on your organization. Membership growth is also about the momentum of an organization. When the membership function is working in your organization, there will be a growing number of new members and a steady or rising number of renewing members each year.

This membership growth increases the human resources of the organization, works as a tool to recruit other new members and influence the organization's various publics, and, as was stated earlier, has a dramatic effect on the organization's financial status. Since most associations, societies, chambers of commerce, and other nonprofit organizations have limited financial resources, they have to depend upon the volunteer work of their members to help achieve the organization's goals. Without a steady stream of new members, the group inevitably faces the problem of volunteer burnout. It is the new members joining this year who will become the leaders of the organization in the years to come.

Membership recruitment and retention needs to be systematic, well-planned, and efficiently managed if the organization is going to be successful. Membership must also be linked to all of the other activities of the organization. It is imperative for leaders to establish a *membership development culture* within the organization. This means that everyone in a leadership role in the organization—whether staff members or volunteer leaders—has to make membership growth an integral part of the organization's long- and short-term goals.

Once you have established that membership development culture in your organization, you need to develop an ongoing system to attract and keep members. Here are seven basic steps to follow in any effective membership recruitment and retention system.

Step 1 – Take an Assessment of Your Situation

Effective membership management requires a good understanding of the challenges the organization faces and identifying what opportunities it has to attract and keep members. Every organization should try to identify:

- The current status of membership, including the current number of members and prospective members, last year's retention rate, and the number of new members who joined last year
- A historical perspective of the organization's successes and failures in membership efforts in the past using data to track trends and changes
- An analysis of the organization's market penetration (i.e. the number of members versus the universe of potential members)
- The organization's level of effectiveness in attracting and keeping members from various membership categories, geographic areas, and length of time in the industry or profession
- A profile of which programs are most used by what membership groups
- The organization's norms for member participation and retention
- Who or what are the organization's major competitors

This membership assessment should be conducted by the staff and some level of volunteer leadership (either the board or a membership committee) at least every two years on a formal basis and annually on an informal basis. The formal assessment should come in the form of a report to the board. The informal assessment can be done as an annual exercise and discussion by the membership committee as it does its planning for the coming year.

It is essential to capture as much information as possible about your membership environment. Having this information allows you to accomplish two goals: 1) gain a better understanding of your membership challenges and 2) establish the baseline measurements for evaluating the effectiveness of your membership plan.

Step 2 – Develop a Plan

The next thing you need to do to assure success in membership development is to establish a plan of action. If there is no road map to guide staff and the membership committee, there can be a tendency to wander from one effort to another hoping that something will work. If there is no definition of what success is, how will you know when you have succeeded?

Having a membership plan is also important because it helps ensure some continuity in the membership function. If a two- or three-year membership plan can be established, then each year the people in charge of the membership function can be guided by the plan. Your organization's membership challenge then becomes determining which elements of the plan to implement each year in order to accomplish the established goals. This also assists your organization when there is a change in who is in charge of the membership function. Rather than having the new membership committee chair or staff person focus on some completely new aspect of membership, the plan allows these new people to take their creative energy and apply it to a specific part of your plan.

The overall goal of the membership function would seem to be pretty obvious—try to recruit and retain as many members as possible. This really should be the membership goal, but you need to determine what is meant by "as many as possible" and whether there are any limitations on how you get there. Membership goals and the strategies used to accomplish them are the basis of a structured plan of action.

Plan elements should include:

- An objective statement, defining your overall membership objective;
- Measurement criteria, which might include such measurements as net growth, retention rates, dues dollars generated, and membership by category;
- Identification of the current status of each measurement criteria;
- Setting goals for the next one to three years in each measurement category;
- An indication of who (staff, membership committee, etc.) is responsible for accomplishing the goals; and
- A detailed plan of action to achieve the goals.

Step 3 – Find and Target Good Prospects

It's important to personalize and customize your membership message as much as possible. Yes, you can go out and try to get every person, company, or institution that meets your membership requirements to join, but if that's your membership marketing strategy, you'd better have plenty of money and a lot of time. There is actually a name for that technique. It's called "buy or die marketing." You send all of your material to everyone who qualifies, and you keep sending them materials until they either join or die! (In some cases, even dying doesn't assure that they'll be dropped from your mailing list). Buy or die marketing is great if you have unlimited resources. Most organizations don't, so they have to work smarter.

You need to create a profile of your prospects—and not just a data profile (name, address, phone, e-mail, and so forth). Here are some of the characteristics you'd like to know about prospects (or groups of prospects) before you think about asking them to join your association:

- What type of business or practice setting are the prospects in?
- How long have they been in the business, profession, or community?
- What are the people's or company's areas of specialization?
- How large of a company or practice do they have?
- Are they self-employed or employees?

Obviously, this list will change from organization to organization. Your organization's bylaws spell out the various membership categories (i.e. regular, voting, active, associate, and so forth), and these categories provide a very basic way of segmenting and targeting prospective members.

Regardless of what your organization's purpose is, that message won't get through effectively if you try to have one value message for everyone who qualifies to join. (Note: Consult your organization's bylaws regarding who is eligible to join your organization. You should also know under what conditions an application for membership can be denied. Your organization's legal counsel can give you guidance on these matters.) You need to think about the person making the membership decision, and focus on getting through with a message that's meaningful to him/her.

Step 4 – Create an Effective Membership Message

The attention span of Americans is growing shorter and shorter. It's a long way from the time when prospective members would open their mail and carefully read everything before making any type of purchasing or joining decision to the scan-and-delete mentality of most of today's consumers. In some cases, according to direct marketing research, prospective members will spend as little as 2.5 seconds reading something before they decide if they even want to keep reading, much less join or buy. Add to that the explosion of information and the vast number of entities trying to get their attention, and it's no wonder that our membership message doesn't seem to be getting through.

Developing Meaningful Membership Messages

Here is a technique you can use to help you target your prospects and develop a meaningful membership message for each targeted member or group of members.

• Identify your prospective membership categories. This doesn't necessarily mean the membership categories as listed on your membership application (although it might). Instead, identify the most common business or professional groupings and use those as your targeted markets.

• For each prospective member category, try to list one or two things that you know about their everyday challenges, be they professional or personal.

• Now, match up (where you can) your organization's programs/products or services that can help these prospects meet these specific challenges.

Here is how a "targeting grid" might look.

Types of Prospect	Key Challenges	Ways to Help
New to profession	Getting first job No money Few contacts	Employment services Discounted first-year dues Networking opportunities
Mid-career professional	Lack of recognition Career path/future Keeping current	Leadership positions Publications Continuing education
Senior level professional	Recognition Generational differences	Leadership involvement Awards programs Mentoring programs

By creating a targeting grid like this one, you can focus your membership message on areas that are important to a specific prospect or group of prospects. If you can identify your best potential members and pinpoint some problems that your organization might be able to help them solve, then creating an effective membership message should follow fairly easily.

An even bigger challenge is getting the organization's message across in electronic formats. Those 2.5 seconds that you have to catch a reader's attention are shortened even more when trying to get prospects to open your e-mail or wade through your Web site. When trying to communicate membership value online, the key is to use graphics and links to keep the prospect engaged somehow in your Web site until the message has a chance to get through.

To really get the attention of prospective members—whatever format you're using—your message has to convey a real sense of *empathy*.

Empathy, according to the dictionary, means understanding another's feelings or motives. But membership empathy means that they *believe* you understand their feelings or motives. There is a major difference in those two definitions. Having empathy is a characteristic. Communicating empathy is a skill. Organizations that can master two primary techniques of communicating empathy will be the successful ones in today's membership marketplace.

- **Start with the prospect, not with the organization.** Before even trying to articulate all the programs and services your organization offers, you have to come to the realization that membership is not about the organization; it's about the member. Don't think like a membership marketer; think like a prospect. The prospect doesn't care what you do. The prospect only cares about what you can do for him or her. To be able to communicate this message, you have to know the prospect and what's important to him/her. One way to determine if your current membership messages are effective is to read through your organization's membership literature and see if the lists of benefits really tell your story. Are these lists merely a repackaging of the programs and services, or are they really creating empathy with the prospect(s)?

- **Get to the point.** Tell prospects the value of what you do, not what you do. To do that, you have to know what members value. In a professional society/organization, people value personal recognition, access to continuing education, career advancement, and a chance to support their profession. In trade associations and chambers of commerce, people/companies value increased sales, cost reduction or control, higher profits, and a chance to support their industry or community. In nonprofit organizations, people value personal recognition, a chance to make a difference, an opportunity to be part of an affinity group, and a chance to accomplish their own personal or organizational goals.

So that's what you should tell them. Tell them what your organization can do to help them, not simply what your organization does.

Step 5 – Develop Effective Membership Materials

While member-to-prospect recruiting is probably still the most effective recruitment method any organization can have, there is a limited amount of time volunteers will give to recruitment efforts, so organizations still need to develop effective membership recruitment materials. In addition to being supporting materials for your recruiters, your membership literature will most likely be the first impression most prospects will have of your organization. Most organizations introduce themselves to prospects through some type of mailing that contains a brochure and a cover letter. Here is a checklist of some elements to keep in mind when preparing a new or revised membership marketing brochure.

- **Make it memorable.** Have something that gets the reader's attention, whether it's a slogan, a logo, a photo, or a testimonial. In order to get prospects to look at your materials, you need to get their attention right away.

- **Be creative.** There is a huge amount of competition out there for your membership materials. Every day your prospects are bombarded with ads, solicitations, and e-mail requests. Try to be different from the other written materials and electronic images your prospect will see each day.

- **Make your materials "scannable."** This doesn't refer to scanning through an electronic scanner. This means that few prospects are going to take the time to read every word in your brochure. Break up the copy with photos, charts, and quotes. As the prospects glance through your brochures, they should see several key points highlighted that they will remember.

- **Get to the point.** Don't hide your message in a mass of copy or photos. Identify the key values of membership in a simple, direct way. That's the message you want to get across. Don't make the prospect have to search for it in all the clutter.

- **Be unique.** Use statements and images that show the prospect that your organization knows what is important to people in your industry, profession, or community. Highlight key buzzwords or statements that only an organization or person in your field could use.

- **Keep within your culture.** Every organization is somewhat unique, if not for who its members are then for the way it does things. As important as it is to make your membership materials readable and creative, be sure to keep within your organization's culture. Certain industries, professions, or organizations have a special way they communicate with members/prospects, a certain style that is appropriate within their industry, profession, or community. Don't lose that in your materials. Instead, build on it.

- **Be consistent.** One way to create an image or brand for your organization is through repetition. Use consistent colors and slogans in your various marketing pieces.

Step 6 – Deliver Your Message Effectively

There are a number of options available for delivering your organization's message:

- **Direct mail**—the most basic and widely used membership marketing technique. The key to having a good direct mail campaign is to do test marketing of various membership solicitation packets. Try various combinations of cover letters and enclosures with varying prospect lists, and identify the combinations that get the highest return. Then expand those successful elements to a broader campaign.

- **Telephone**—an overlooked opportunity in many organizations. In today's communications-overloaded environment, it is getting harder and harder to reach people via the telephone. This is due to several factors, including caller-identification systems, call waiting, voice messages, and the emergence of e-mail as the primary form of business communications. However, the telephone does have one advantage over direct mail: The telephone allows you to listen to the prospect, instead of just talking to the prospect.

- **Electronically**—almost a necessity in today's membership marketing environment. An online option for joining and renewing membership in your organization is needed because an entire generation of potential members has grown up with computers and the Internet, and this generation (and the ones that follow) represents the majority of your future members. Web sites need to be user friendly, engaging, and informative. These sites also need to be able to get the prospective member to want to join while on the site, so an effective membership marketing message is a must. You want to increase the Web site visitor/prospect's interest to the point where he or she wants to join, but you don't want them to have to leave your Web site to do that.

- **Member-to-prospect**—still the best (statistically) method of recruiting, but also the most difficult, in many cases. No membership message is more powerful than a current member telling his or her peer how much value there is in membership in your organization. Aside from the time factor, the single biggest reason members don't want to recruit is that they are afraid of being turned down, saying the wrong thing, or jeopardizing their relationships with others in their profession, trade, community, or social circle. In order to get members to help in the recruitment of other new members, you have to help them overcome these fears.

Materials for Member-to-Member Recruitment

Here are some suggestions on what you can provide to your members to give them some confidence in their ability to recruit their colleagues.

- Provide supporting written materials for recruiters, which might include a how to guide, job descriptions for membership committee members, specific tips on how to overcome the most common objections, various membership brochures, and sample membership ads that can be used in newspapers and so forth.
- Coordinate public relations efforts to create a positive environment for recruitment.
- Host a telephone seminar where recruiters can call in and talk about successful techniques, as well as discuss common objections.
- Develop a videotape or DVD for recruiters.
- Send weekly e-mails to recruiters with a "tip of the week" on how to overcome objections.
- Hold a membership institute to train all of your membership committee chairs and members.

Step 7 – Have a *System* for Retaining Your Members

Since the retention of members and supporters is one of the most important and ongoing challenges for any association, there should be no limit on the effort these organizations make to keep their membership base satisfied. Successful organizations of all types believe that good member service has to be part of that *membership development culture*, not just a slogan. These organizations understand that every employee plays a part in good member service, regardless of his or her position in the organization. There are some important techniques that organizations can use to establish and foster a culture of good member service.

Develop Some Member Service Policies and Standards

This can't be just a reminder to the staff to answer the phone quickly and be polite. Real commitment means identifying as many ways as possible to actually measure good member service and then setting standards of good performance. Try to identify what top-level performance means in areas like turnaround time on orders, how many times a phone rings before it's answered, how many times a caller gets transferred before speaking to the right person, and how accurate the member listings are in the organization's database and directory.

If the top leaders in the organization (board members, officers, and senior staff) aren't committed to better member service through a systematic approach, then the other staff and members are unlikely to be as concerned about it as they should be. The organization's board of directors and senior staff need to adopt a formal, specific, written set of customer service policies and guidelines. These need to be developed with input from various sources and then communicated to everyone in the organization's staff and volunteer leadership. These policies should be reviewed frequently and used as part of the evaluation of the organization's retention efforts.

Part of good member service is assuring that all of the organization's staff is empowered to help solve problems for members. This doesn't mean that the staffer who is the first contact with the member and his/her problem has to be the person with the answer to the problem. It's very possible that the member's problem is better handled by another staff person or volunteer leader. It does mean that the person who first interacted with the member is responsible not just for transferring the problem to someone else, but also for making sure that the problem is solved.

It also means that everyone on the membership organization's staff needs to buy into the concept of top-level member service. It means that the days of "It's not my job" are over. It means that staff can no longer consider themselves or their departments separate entities dedicated to only one area such as legislation or education. It means that all leaders, volunteers, and staff have to be willing to accept reminders and inquiries from others who have asked them to help solve a member problem. It means that the organization's leadership needs to establish a teambuilding system that will create a culture that focuses not on the organization, but on the members.

Get the Membership Off to a Good Start

Try to reduce that period from the time a member fills out an application and sends it to your organization until the time that the member is finally and officially welcomed in as a member (at all levels of the organization). This includes receiving welcoming correspondence, being up-to-date on all of the various organizational databases, and getting current publications and correspondence at the *correct address*. Here are some suggestions on ways to show new members how responsive and professional your organization can be.

- Acknowledge the application immediately (within one to two days if at all possible) via e-mail, fax, or phone.

- Have a current member who is geographically close to the new member, runs a similar-sized company, or is in the same specialty area as the new member write or call the new member and offer congratulations.
- Do a 30-day follow up contact to be sure that new members are getting all current correspondence.
- Make sure that each level of the organization (where applicable) notifies the other levels when welcoming contacts are made.

Find Ways to Get Members Involved

There is an old saying that "an involved member doesn't drop out." That saying might need to be modified slightly to "an involved member rarely drops out," but for the most part, it is still an accurate statement. Therefore, a big part of member retention is getting members involved.

In today's membership world, organizations have to be careful about equating the term involvement with leadership. In fact, it's getting harder and harder to get members to become active volunteer leaders. In that case, organizations need to change their focus from getting members involved to getting members engaged. Once a member becomes engaged, there is a better chance of getting them involved. Some ways to get members engaged include:

- Encouraging them to get active in state and local affiliates;
- Sending periodic short, online surveys to get members' opinions on important issues in the industry, profession, or community;
- Asking members to take on small tasks, such as handling registration at one event;
- E-mailing members a summary of an important issue and including in the e-mail a link to the organization's Web site where the member can get more information and details about the issue; and
- Identifying the least active members and doing some online or telephone focus groups to get their input on important industry/professional issues or organizational matters.

Don't forget to thank members who become engaged, as well as those who become involved. If they believe you appreciate their time, you might get more of it.

Have an Effective Dues Renewal Process

Collecting dues for the next year should be a smooth and painless part of the retention program of every organization. To ensure this, take these steps to establish standard, effective renewal communications:

- Be sure to send at least three renewal requests to members.
- Consider having an incentive for early renewals.

- Send a pre-renewal communication to members summarizing the organization's accomplishments during the past year and telling members that their renewal notice will be arriving soon.

- Personalize the renewal letter (versus "Dear Fellow Member").

- Ask current members to contact late paying members.

- Be sure that members can renew online.

- Allow members to use credit cards to renew.

- Be sure to acknowledge the renewal payment.

In addition to the steps outlined here, to be successful in membership, your organization needs to be in control of as much information as possible. It is critical to have a

The Globalization of the Association World

Membership marketing has become much more of a global challenge for virtually every membership organization. This doesn't mean that all membership organizations are becoming international. Many organizations don't have—and don't necessarily want to have—members outside of their home country. Yet today's Internet-connected world makes every organization global, if not officially international. There are no geographic boundaries on the Internet, no racial or ethnic minorities, no physically challenged, and no gender bias. There is just information, and people (as well as companies and institutions) don't care about the source of the information in a geographic sense. They just want quick access to useable information.

This isn't a brand new trend, but it is one that continues to have a huge impact on association marketing. The Internet has replaced other membership organizations as the biggest competitor for members' time and money. There is increasing pressure on organizations to keep up with technological changes because their members have to keep up. The ability to work 24 hours a day means that members want 24-hour access to information and resources.

In today's world, associations have to make a step up from being U.S.-based associations with members in other countries to becoming truly global organizations. Here is a short list of changes that organizations need to make to achieve that goal.

U.S. Organizations with Members Outside the U.S.	International Organizations
Variable dues	Equal dues
USD only payment	Accepts other currencies
English-only communications	Multi-language options
Periodic non-U.S. Conventions	Regular non-U.S. meetings
Non-U.S. designated seat(s) on board	Full access to all leadership positions
English-only speakers/presenters	Multi-language options
U.S. advocacy only	Works with other government entities
U.S. headquarters	Non-U.S. offices
Business as usual	Systematic, planned outreach to other cultures

good membership database management system, one that allows you to track member and prospect activity and to use that information to focus your membership resources. Quick retrieval of important demographic and participation information is a key to being responsive to opportunities to attract and keep members.

By being able to quickly access member and prospect information, your organization can target specific prospects with specific services and programs, identify non-participants and likely drops, track buying habits and create profiles of members' needs, cross-sell products and services, and create personalized communications for members and prospects.

In addition to the administrative aspects of membership, your organization's membership efforts should be under the direction of a trained professional staff member, someone who can coordinate your overall membership efforts. This person should have the skills, knowledge, and experience to use all of your resources efficiently and effectively. These resources include your other staff members, too. The membership director needs to be able to get the entire staff to understand the various roles they play in membership recruitment and retention. Membership growth is still the best path to organizational success. Using all of the resources available and having a planned, well-supported membership effort is the shortest road down that path.

About the Author

Mark Levin, CAE, CSP, has more than 30 years of experience in association and nonprofit organizational management. This includes service as a local chapter director, national membership and chapter relations director for a major construction trade association, membership and new unit development executive for the Boy Scouts of America, and chief executive officer for three organizations.

He is the author of four books: *Membership Development: 101 Ways to Get and Keep Your Members, The Gift of Leadership, Millennium Membership,* and *Retention Wars: The New Rules of Engagement.*

A graduate of the University of Maryland, he served on the faculty of the U.S. Chamber's Institute for Organization Management for 15 years and currently is executive vice president of the Chain Link Fence Manufacturers Institute, Columbia, Maryland.

Review Questions

1. How often should your organization conduct a membership assessment?

2. Why is a membership plan so important?

3. What are some key elements to consider when developing membership marketing materials?

CHAPTER
31

Going International

Carolyn A. Lugbill, CAE, MAM

T HE WORLD GROWS SMALLER by the day. And thanks to technology and the many ways available to communicate with members (electronic mail, Web sites, listservers, Web conferencing, Web casting, teleconferencing, chat rooms, fax, and so forth), associations have an unprecedented opportunity to capitalize on their international potential.

The various kinds of communication technology available have thrust associations into the global arena whether or not they want to be there. To capitalize on the opportunity, the association must be ready and know how to position itself in the global marketplace.

What It Means

What does the phrase "going international" really mean—conducting an off-shore meeting every two years? Creating specific products and services to serve international members? Changing the association's name to include the word *international*? Revising the association's governance structure to allow international representation on the board? Providing statistical data to help members penetrate new markets?

The term, "international," by itself usually means two or more countries. "International" often refers to an organization that is beginning to extend itself to other countries or that operates in a few countries but not necessarily worldwide. Although it conducts activities or has members in other countries, it retains a major focus on its home country. For example, an international association could be one that operates programs in one or more countries or regions where the association is headquartered.

Because of the tremendous diversity of focus, mission, and membership that associations have, not all organizations will have the same entry point for their international work. For one association, it may mean expanding its educational programs to reach groups of overseas members. Another association might go through a complete top-to-bottom restructuring, enabling it to engage in international activities in all areas.

Going international can encompass all these activities or focus on just a few of them. It is not an "all or nothing" proposition. Perhaps the key questions to ask are:

- What opportunities are there for our association to expand our membership, programs, or mission at the international level?
- What aspects of our association could benefit most from being 'internationalized'?
- What information do we need to better assess our potential in the international arena?

Defining "going international" will differ for a trade association, a professional society, and a philanthropic organization, as appropriate for their unique context and mission. For a professional society, translating the association's publication into several languages as a way to recruit and serve international members may be a priority. For a trade association, holding export seminars on specific target markets or organizing U.S. pavilions in other countries may be what members need to showcase their products and services. For a philanthropic organization, the goal might be building new types of partnerships overseas to better achieve their mission.

Going international affects every functional area of the association, from finance, communications, and marketing to publications, education, and chapter relations. For example, if your association holds a meeting outside domestic borders, the education and convention areas aren't the only departments involved. The finance department may have to assess exchange rates, make payments in a foreign currency, and possibly open up an overseas bank account. The marketing department must consider printing the meeting's promotional brochure in one or more languages and giving careful consideration to marketing techniques.

Going international is also a business strategy that needs to be reflected in an organization's strategic plan. Sample indicators of when an association has gone international are when:

- There is a compelling and clear mission that is international in scope;
- The board and committees have international representation and include a focus on international trends and activities;
- International activities are integrated strategically within the organization's priorities and throughout internal departments;
- Publications and communications are written for a culturally diverse audience; and an
- International mindset exists throughout the staff.

Thinking about International Expansion

Here are some critical issues that associations should keep in mind as they contemplate expanding internationally:

1. Associations that invest in international activities should pursue a strategy that reflects the interests of their overall membership. Not all members will have the same degree of interest in international opportunities.
2. As with any new expansion project, an international strategy will create new expenses. The cost of participating in international meetings, setting up operations overseas, and maintaining regular contact with staff and volunteer leadership may be far greater than doing so domestically.
3. Associations will encounter cultural differences as they expand into new regions or welcome new members from overseas. The values and expectations of international members will be different, and associations must be prepared to effectively service their needs.
4. Structure is a tool for strategy. Organizational models should be tools to accomplish goals and not an "end" in and of themselves. Also, just because one option may make the most sense now doesn't mean that it's definitive for the future. Each model should be evaluated and revisited on a regular basis as the association's membership grows and needs change.
5. Buy-in from the leadership, membership, and staff is essential regarding the pace, growth, and financial investment of the association's international activities.
6. Play to your association's strengths. If you have been successful in a particular country or with a specific activity such as a meeting or education program, analyze what has been working well and why, and see if that strength can translate to other countries.
7. Engaging more internationally is a calculated risk and involves changes. Have persistence and stay focused on your outcome.

Assessing Your International Potential

While it often goes without saying, there is no single "right way" for an association to go international. Strategies will vary with the unique opportunities and environment surrounding each individual association, including its mission, membership, needs, and many other factors.

- Associations that are already international in scope, such as with their membership and meetings, may find themselves entering a whole new phase in their international expansion, by taking their certification programs overseas or translating their online resources into additional languages, for example.

- Associations that are at the beginning stages of exploring their international opportunities will want to assess all their options very carefully and prioritize their best opportunities.

Successfully going international is part art, part science, and a lot of hard thinking, planning, and work. An association can assess its potential in the international arena by doing a basic strategic analysis of its membership, internal and external environment, and competition. By asking a series of key questions, association staff, in conjunction with their board and volunteer leadership, can assess issues such as:

- The extent to which the association represents an industry or profession that is international in scope—and where the opportunities lie;

- How active or interested the membership is in international activities in general or a particular type of international expansion;

- The opportunities that exist for the association and its members in the global economy; and

- The resources available to expand internationally to meet the demands of new issues, programs, and membership.

This type of assessment tool has many benefits. It helps evaluate your organization's strengths, weaknesses, opportunities, and threats. It asks questions to help you determine whether international activities fit into your association's current mission and strategic plan, whether new international activities will benefit the membership, and what market research may still need to be conducted before launching new international activities. It can also provide the supporting evidence to help a board make wise decisions about the organization's international potential and possible international activities to initiate.

Keep in mind that this strategic assessment tool will not give you final answers to all the complex questions and challenges inherent in international work. What it will do is provide you with a compass to help you evaluate the direction you need to go in as you work to fulfill your association's international potential.

Strategic Assessment Tool

Below is a list of questions that should be answered by the association staff in conjunction with its board and volunteer leadership to help determine an association's international potential.

Questions about the Profession or Industry

Geographic Considerations

- What percentage of your members by number comes from different geographic regions (countries)?
- What percentage of your revenue can be allocated to those same regions (countries)?
- What percentage of your organization's investment (expenditures) can be allocated to those same regions (countries)?
- If you could start from a fresh beginning, which regions would be your most promising potential markets for stakeholder / revenue development today?
- What percentage of your industry or profession is represented in association?
- What percentage of your profession or industry is international by nature?

The association may find that it should only target initially one country or a few countries before it decides to research a whole region or continent such as Europe, Asia, or Latin America. It's important to start small and then grow slow.

Differences in Practice of Profession or Industry Operations Geographically

- Are there significant differences in the sophistication and practice of the profession or industry operations by country, region, or continent?
- Are there geographic differences in how technology is applied or information is disseminated?
- For a professional society, is there a difference in the basic, graduate, and post-graduate education systems that impact your profession and how it is practiced?
- What are the reasons for these differences?

For example, in some parts of the world where you'd like to distribute your publications, some countries may have a very slow or unreliable postal system. The association may have to look at using an international mail distribution company or the Internet to ensure its publications get to members in a timely and accurate manner.

Partnership Potential

- Does the profession or industry have counterpart associations or related organizations in other countries?
- What is the environment or context in which the profession or industry is organized in these countries?
- How do members of the profession or industry communicate, share information, network with their peers, and lobby their government?
- Have you had the opportunity to evaluate first-hand the strengths and weaknesses of your potential partners (due diligence on their finances, programs, products, services, reputation, etc.)?
- Do you have strong relations with the current leaders of the organizations you are considering partnering with? How, when, and by whom are decisions made in those organizations?
- What cultural and regional differences exist among the profession or industry in various countries?
- What about the use of benchmarking with associations in other, although somewhat closely related, professions or industries?
- Is there an interest or need to develop international professional standards and credentials?
- Is this being driven by the needs of member companies, individuals, or both?
- Do you involve universities and other institutions of higher learning?

It is almost a given that a counterpart association in Europe or Latin America, for example, will have a different *modus operandi* or philosophy towards the profession or industry than in Asia, and the association will have to develop a different strategy for working with the various groups.

Benefits of Membership

- Is your country generally considered the world leader in this profession or industry?
- Will international members recognize what they have to gain by joining your organization?
- How will your members benefit from their counterparts (or firms abroad) in other countries? Sharing of expertise and information?

The next four sets of questions relate to trade associations.

Competition Issues

- Does the industry face significant competition from international competitors?
- Who is your members' competition?
- Will international liaison with those competitors strengthen the industry as a whole, or will your members be damaged?

Internal Barriers to International Membership

- Do your members oppose membership from international firms? Why?
- What percent of your members share this feeling?
- What will be the consequences of proceeding against this opposition?
- What will your members lose if the counterparts have equal access to the association's benefits?

Market Share

- What percent of worldwide market share do members of your industry in your country enjoy? Why?
- What is the potential worldwide market, and what factors influence it?
- To what extent is the world market saturated?

Raw Material/Resource Considerations

- Does the industry depend upon raw materials or other resources that are not readily available or competitively priced in your country?
- Are there sources outside your country that could be tapped to the advantage of members but are not because of shipping, customs, technological difficulties, or other problems?
- Can the association help to alleviate these problems?

Questions About the Association

Number and Monetary Value of International Members

- Does the association currently have members from other countries?
- What percent of the membership and of total dues do they represent?
- Do they pay equal, lesser, or greater dues?

International Membership Participation and Governance

- Are the international members active?
- How are they represented in the association?
- Can they (and do they) serve on committees and in other leadership positions?
- Are there any challenges or special restrictions associated with their involvement?

Membership Potential/Interest in Products/Services

- Are international nonmembers at your conventions, meetings, and educational seminars?
- Do they subscribe to your periodicals or buy your materials?
- Do they communicate with you electronically or access your Web site on a regular basis?

Assessing External Market

- Do your international members seek out the association's products and services?
- Do you actively market the association's products and services to international members and nonmembers?
- Is market data available that would shed light on differences in interest and need between members in and out of your country?
- Have you surveyed the market potential or conducted trend analyses?

External Competitive Environment

- Is any other organization, association, company, or government agency supplying goods and services to your international members?
- How do the quality, accuracy, price, and delivery system compare to what the association is able to offer?
- Is there an advantage in working cooperatively?
- To what extent have they penetrated the particular market they serve?
- Could members in your country benefit from their products and services?
- Is national pride or identity a significant factor that will influence your relative ability to compete?

Organization/Structure/Culture/Budget

- Can the organization's structure and culture accommodate international involvement?
- Can the association's budget handle the variances in currency value, international travel, mailing costs, overseas meetings, satellite offices, and the possibility of additional staff?
- Where is your membership on the question of international expansion?
- Can the organization's staff adjust (be more tolerant) to the language and cultural differences of international members?
- Should consultants be considered for helping the association rethink its governance structure and staff responsibilities?
- Does the mission and vision reflect an international perspective?
- Will the association's mission have to change?

Motivation for International Expansion

- What is driving the need to consider expanding internationally? The board? Other volunteer leaders? The chief staff executive?
- What "champions" are there within your organization for internationalization?
- What is the motivation? Additional revenue for the organization? Access to new markets? Exchange of information or expertise?
- Is there a consensus among your membership?

Thoughtful and thorough responses to the assessment questions will provide the blueprint for determining your organization's international objectives. However, your association may find that 'going international' is not consistent with the organization's current mission or long-range strategic plan. Or, that the timing is not right, that your association needs to strengthen certain areas, reach consensus among the membership, create a fundraising plan, or begin to identify overseas partners first. It is better to save the organization valuable time, energy, and money by focusing initially on areas where there is a strong business case.

50 Steps and More To Get You Started "Going International"

Once your association has conducted a strategic assessment and concluded it should become international in some form or at some level, here are some steps to consider pursuing:

Headquarters

- Make someone or some group accountable for international work within your organization. Put international goals in their performance evaluation. Also work at incorporating at least one international objective into each of the other staff functions, not just those with specific international responsibility.

- To get started, develop a simple international strategic plan as a complement to your organizational-wide strategic plan—and then work to integrate it back into the organizational-wide plan.
- Decide the five or ten time-specific, measurable goals you need to achieve this year to move your organization forward internationally.
- Discuss with senior management your organization's motivation for "going international." Make sure there is consensus and the reasons are communicated to the entire staff.
- Teach all staff how to complete and receive an overseas phone call and/or fax.
- On your internal phone list, identify staff who speak a second and third language for easy reference internally when that language skill is needed.
- Keep the board informed of progress in achieving international goals with periodic updates.
- Have the key international staff person serve on the organization's strategic planning committee to infuse the plan with an international perspective.
- Look at your international membership roster and identify candidates for inclusion in your succession planning model for board participation. Start the process to get them involved.
- Consider forming an international committee or advisory council within the association who can provide input on specific needs of international members. These members can also be good candidates for board positions.
- Provide international resources in your association's library.
- Make sure that your association's membership database allows for international addresses, phone, fax, postal, and country codes.
- Encourage interns from outside the U.S. to serve in the association from overseas counterparts or universities.
- Internationalize the "look" of your organization's reception area with world time clocks, flags of member countries, world maps, etc.

Communications and Printed Materials

- Include your country name in the return address on all printed matter going out from your organization.
- Expand the space available for mailing addresses on all reply vehicles.
- Don't include an 800 number without also including a direct dial number to facilitate incoming calls from international locations.
- Remember that slang is rarely universal.
- Beware of seasonal references in your communications—one reader's fall is another's spring. Use month names instead.
- Watch abbreviations (for example, program listings of "TBA" may confuse international attendees).
- If using a world-map graphic, don't show the U.S. or North America as the center around which all other countries revolve.

- Always spell out dates (10 August 2006)—the U.S. abbreviation of 8/10/06 is the opposite in many other countries (10/8/06).
- Write with a culturally diverse audience in mind.

Publications

- Consider starting an international column in your monthly publication.
- Suggest international "sidebars" to domestic stories.
- At least once a year, include at least one feature article or cover story dedicated to an international issue.
- Seek out international titles in your field to include in your publications catalog and bookstore at your meetings.
- Include international events in the calendar section of your association's publication.
- Appoint an international editorial advisory board to provide ongoing feedback and input into your publications.
- Include a listing of your overseas counterparts and other international organizations in your membership directory.
- Participate in international book fairs.

Meetings

- Whatever you do to internationalize your meetings is as important for your domestic members to see as your international members to experience.
- Provide international programming at your annual convention and other smaller meetings. Find speakers outside the U.S. who can present papers at your annual convention.
- Arrange greeters at the airport to welcome international attendees on arrival.
- Provide an international orientation and get-acquainted function at the opening of your annual meeting. Consider offering "buddies" on site to welcome international attendees.
- Consider having a special registration area for international attendees and staffing with individuals who speak other languages.
- Make your board aware of any special international guests and functions.
- Recognize international members at your meetings with a reception, flag ceremony, speaker, etc.
- Provide "international" ribbons, language buttons, or flag pins to designate international attendees.
- Establish an International Welcome Center or "lounge" at your annual convention for networking and meeting with internationally-minded attendees.
- Decorate "lounge" with clocks of different time zones, flags from various countries, or a world map.
- Ensure that your registration materials are internationally friendly (i.e., space for country name, and for country and city phone codes, etc.). Designate on your

registration form the official language of the meeting and advise whether there are any accommodations for other languages.

- Consider arranging post-meeting site visits for international attendees as this may help to justify the added expense of international travel.
- Invite international attendees to participate in an on-site focus group to help determine their continuing needs.
- Arrange for a group photo opportunity of all international attendees; publish it in your conference daily or monthly publication.
- Prepare an on-site guide to international events, attendees, and activities for international attendees.
- Translate promotional meeting materials and presentation papers into one or more languages as appropriate.
- Highlight international activities and seminars in a special section of your pre-conference publicity brochure.
- Provide a special welcome letter to international members in registration packets.
- Provide multilingual signage in key areas at your meetings.

International Visitors

- When possible, host international visitors at your headquarters and ensure that they are welcomed by senior level staff, including a greeting by the CEO.
- Always ask each staff person meeting with them to provide their business card to the visitor.
- When possible, brief those responsible for hosting the international visitor by providing general information on the country of the visitor.
- Provide information to staff on language capabilities of each visitor as well as professional background and interpretation needs.
- Post a sign at your reception desk that reads, "Welcome to Association ABC, Guest X, Country Y." You would be surprised at the significance of such a small gesture.
- Ask your publication staff to be available to take photos of the visit which can be used in your association publication. Use the photos with a brief explanation of their visit.
- Advise staff that you'll be hosting an international visitor or delegation from Country X and include how to phonetically pronounce their name and the most common greeting in the visitor's language.
- Have available a gift that is representative of the association that you will want to present to the international visitor or head of the delegation as a thank you for their visit.

Overseas Counterparts

- Use *Gale's Encyclopedia of Association: International Organizations* to research your overseas counterparts.
- Build a database of those counterparts and their leaders for easy access on your Web site.
- Provide forums for leaders of overseas chapters or counterpart associations to meet at least once a year. Offer training on the fundamentals of managing a voluntary membership association.
- Provide complimentary registration to leaders of overseas counterparts at your association's meetings.
- Start a publications exchange program with counterparts to facilitate the exchange of information and publicize your organization.
- Start an electronic newsletter for all the counterparts and solicit input from them.
- Allow your international counterparts to post their own schedules of events, directories of members, and other contact information on your website.
- Develop listservers for domestic and international members who want to exchange ideas and information.

Membership

Before instituting an international membership recruitment campaign, think through these questions:

- Why does your organization want to grow its international membership?
- What do you know about your current international members? Why have they joined?
- What programs and services do they use and/or find valuable?
- What obstacles, if any, stand in the way of potential members joining your organization or existing international members who want to access your association's current programs, products and services? Internet access? Affordability of dues? Meeting unique expectations based on differences in how profession is practiced?
- What similar organizations may exist in other countries, and how will your role be different from theirs?
- What costs is your organization willing to absorb to recruit and retain international members?

Beginning to answer some of these questions should provide the strategic direction for determining how best to achieve your international membership goal. For example, you may find that your organization should consider developing geographic criteria for targeting membership expansion. Targeting particular geographic locations at the beginning of an internationalization process can help to ensure that the chosen areas are the best potential matches for the organization's goals and strengths and to avoid politicizing your decisions.

Other Steps

- Establish an awards program that recognizes members' "best practices" of operating in the international arena.
- Consider starting an international scholarship program that promotes the career development of individuals in your profession.

Organizational Models for "Expanding Internationally"

Here are some different ways that associations organize themselves, in terms of who they serve and their level of activity for expanding internationally:

- U.S. association with U.S. members and programs and services only.
- U.S. association with members inside and outside the U.S., with services essentially designed for U.S. members but offered to all members.
- U.S. association with members outside the U.S. whose unique needs are served. The association may have started chapters or developed affiliate relationships with counterparts outside the U.S. to meet unique needs. International activities are a priority focus of the association.
- International association—significant portion of membership based outside one region or members headquartered in one region with significant interests in other regions. International activities are integrated strategically within the society's priorities and programs may be delivered locally within regions through an office or service center.
- Federation—several national or regional associations as members; also called an umbrella association. Usually, associations want to preserve their national identity and unite solely through a neutral entity such as a federation.
- Hybrid—combining different organizational structural options (i.e., chapters, affiliates, strategic alliances, overseas offices, etc.) to meet the unique needs of association members and relationships with counterparts worldwide.
- Global association—direct membership spread over two or more regions of the world, more or less equally, and not one country majority on the board. The association rotates its meetings to various regions and has a pre-eminent brand and role in education, quality, and advocacy around the world.

These organizational classifications or models show varying degrees of involvement that associations may encounter as they expand internationally. At the top of the chart are associations that are primarily U.S. based but which are beginning to attract international members and consider programs and services uniquely designed for those members. At the bottom of the chart are associations that have either adapted their organizational structure to meet the varying needs of their members worldwide or have become truly global with members, programs, or operations in many different regions around the world.

In her book *Going Global for the Greater Good,* Bonnie Koenig has likened these classifications to a spectrum of increasing involvement that many organizations travel along as they pursue their international engagement. While we often think that organizations are either local or global in nature, Koenig suggests that many associations lie at different stages within these organizational classifications or along the spectrum. It is important to realize that several options exist to help guide you in choosing the model that is best suited for your association.

Some associations, by virtue of their international goals, will pursue options that are further down this chart, while others will find compatibility with their missions and programs at the top of the chart. Associations may pursue various international activities without altering their core membership base or organizational structure. The further along an association travels down these models, however, the more important it will be to get buy-in from its members, staff, and other stakeholder groups.

Model Examples

For instance, as a trade association representing U.S. manufacturers, your association may want to remain U.S.-based and have U.S. members only. Still, members might benefit from an office in Brussels that would provide advice on regulations, standards, and distribution networks for members' products in Europe. Even a U.S.-based association, with only U.S. members, can have international aspects to its services.

Or perhaps your association is currently U.S.-based, has members inside and outside the U.S., and gears its services primarily to a U.S.-based audience—but wants to move toward providing unique services to international members. Steps to take may include conducting a strategic assessment, and then depending on the outcome, determining whether to modify certain U.S.-based services or develop new international ones. You'll also need to assess whether these new services could be cost-effective and bring in additional revenue. As another example, your association may wish to become more of a truly international organization that serves the unique needs of its non-U.S. members. That would require having significant international representation at the board and committee level, looking at your dues structure to see if it can accommodate international members, and evaluating your products and services for their relevance and applicability to international members, as well as a mission, goals, and financial resources that reflect the organization's commitment.

Conclusion

To summarize, as you consider expanding internationally, think about these questions:

- What are your organization's motivating factors for developing an international strategy?
- What questions does your organization still need to research and/or address in the assessment tool?

- Where is your association on the list of organizational models? Where does it want to be? Is there a consensus among your board and senior leadership about the organization's international direction?
- What are your association's strengths that you can capitalize on within the international arena?
- What is your organization's financial resource capacity and staff's cross-cultural awareness level for pursuing your international goals?

The more clearly your association can define its objectives, the stronger the possibility that the money and time invested in going international will build toward an inevitable payoff. If your association doesn't know how much it can realistically accomplish, go slow in outreach and investment. Try one international activity before launching several simultaneously. Continuously monitor the feedback and results so that you can review and revise the association's strategic plan annually.

Recommended Reading

ASAE & The Center for Association Leadership's Web site: www.asaecenter.org

Balestrero, Greg. "A Globalization Strategy of Engagement," *Association Management Magazine,* November, 2003.

Barkan, Terrance A. Strategic Review on Association Development: International Trends, Issues and Options. Association Global Services, 2006.

Barkan, Terrance A. What is a Successful International Strategy? *ASAE Global Link Newsletter,* March 2006.

Carter, Virgil. "Assessing Your Association's Global Potential—Six Key Questions, *ASAE Global Link Online Newsletter,* June 2001.

Glade, Brian. "Making the Case for Global Work," *ASAE Global Link Newsletter,* March 2002.

Koenig, Bonnie. *Going Global for the Greater Good: Succeeding as a Nonprofit in the International Community,* Jossey Bass, California, USA. 2004.

Koenig, Bonnie. "Global Exchange: Targeted Strategy for International Growth." *Association Management Magazine,* August, 2003.

Johnston, Lynn Ly. "International Expansion: Need not Greed," *Executive Update Magazine,* August, 2003.

Long, John. "Member Ambassadors Support Global Growth," *ASAE Global Link Online Newsletter,* July, 2005.

Lugbill, Carolyn, CAE. "Successful Strategies for Growing Your International Membership," ASAE Global Link Online Newsletter, January, 2007.

Lugbill, Carolyn, CAE, and Bonnie Koenig. "Strategic Assessment: The Key to Evaluating Your International Engagement. *ASAE Global Link Newsletter, ASAE Global Link,* May, 2006.

Lugbill, Carolyn, CAE. "Global Exchange: Make the Call on International Chapters," *ASAE Global Link Online Newsletter,* June, 2003.

Lugbill, Carolyn, CAE and Steve Glover. "Keeping your Board on Board for Global Growth," *Association Management Magazine,* June, 2004."

Lugbill, Carolyn, CAE. "Expanding Internationally: Which Model Best Suits your Association? Part II," *ASAE Global Link Online Newsletter,* March, *2005.*

Lugbill, Carolyn, CAE. "Expanding Internationally: Which Model Best Suits your Association? Part I," *ASAE Global Link Online Newsletter*, January, *2005.*

Lugbill, Carolyn, CAE and Bonnie Koenig. "The International Journey: Different Paths to Take," *ASAE Global Link Online Newsletter*, September 2001.

O'Donoghue, Michael. "International Strategic Alliances," *Association Management Magazine,* November, 2003.

Moore, Rebecca. "Developing a Business Model for Globalization." *ASAE Global Link Online Newsletter*, September 2004.

Ward, Paul. "Making a Strong Case for Going Global: A Framework for Analysis," *Journal of Association Leadership*, Winter, 2006.

Worth, Steven M. "Cross-Border Collaboration." *Association Management Magazine,* November, 2003.

Worth, Steven M. "Key Ingredients to Globalization Success," *Association Management Magazine,* May 2002.

About the Author

Carolyn A. Lugbill, CAE, MAM, is president of Going Global Matters, a consulting firm that helps associations "go international" with their organizational structure, programs, and services. Ms. Lugbill has more than 15 years experience helping organizations assess their strengths and weaknesses in the international arena to develop new opportunities for international growth. Before that, she was international activities director for the American Society of Association Executives (ASAE), Washington, D.C.

Review Questions

1. What does the term "international" mean as defined in the chapter?

2. What are some of the functional areas within an association that are affected by the association's international activities?

3. What role should the board play in an association's international activities?

4. Which areas need to be assessed when an association considers expanding internationally?

5. What are some of the different models that associations use to organize themselves, in terms of who they serve and their level of activity for expanding internationally?

32

Meeting Planning and Management

Dawn M. Mancuso, MAM, CAE

A meeting without community is just a bunch of people breathing the same air.
– Seth Kahn

OUR SOCIETY'S INCREASING USE of technology would make the casual observer conclude that the importance of face-to-face meetings for conducting business affairs was waning. Interestingly, experience proves otherwise. Conventions, expositions, and meetings constitute a significant industry; in fact, they contributed more than $122 billion to the gross domestic national product in 2004 alone. Association-sponsored meetings generated a large majority of this figure (approximately $82 billion), and the revenue expected by associations from conventions, exhibits, and meetings accounts for 32% of associations' overall income. Almost all (98%) associations conduct an annual meeting, and in 2004 association-sponsored meetings, conferences, trade shows, and conventions were attended by 21 million people.

Meetings play a key role in an association's ability to fulfill its mission because they deliver educational programs to members. For example, professional societies often hold educational conferences as part of their credentialing program. Meetings also bring together members to conduct personal, professional, and association business. They establish forums for the development of industry and association policies or for the airing of controversial issues and concerns. Recognizing volunteers, rewarding professional or industry excellence, enhancing member relations, educating members' customers, and providing a showcase for products and services are other functions. In terms of member recruitment, meetings create an opportunity for prospective members to "test drive" the association before making the decision to join.

Additionally, the bylaws of most associations call for at least one annual business meeting of members, usually to elect board members and vote on bylaws amendments. While alternative methods of balloting are frequently used—including casting votes by mail, e-mail, or Web-based service—none has, as yet, rendered the traditional annual meeting obsolete.

Meeting Planner Competencies

Perhaps more so than any other staff specialist, today's successful meeting planner has to be adept at a number of different skills. No longer is it enough for a meeting planner to be an organized and efficient manager of logistics. He or she must now be able to:

- Assess and integrate technology enhancements into meeting planner operations as well as the content of learning opportunities;
- Identify and track trends within the members' industry or profession to provide educational programming and events that are timely and worthwhile;
- Build and execute budgets, marketing plans, crisis management plans, and strategic plans (complete with mission, goals, objectives, and strategies) for conferences and events;
- Expand current and generate new revenue streams;
- Develop and utilize facility in analyzing and reporting financial data that will guide a continual improvement process and maximize Return on Investment (ROI);
- Cultivate both written and oral communications skills;
- Maintain knowledge of current legal and ethical issues surrounding supplier contracting and meeting/event planning to minimize risk;
- Develop negotiating skills to help with all aspects of the event planning process—from contract negotiations to personnel management.
- Design a planning process using project management concepts and tools in order to maximize productivity and available resources; and
- Nurture and manage teams made up of paid staff, volunteers, and third-party vendors so that all work together seamlessly and effectively.

Program Development

What makes a meeting or convention successful? One survey identified these factors for success: stimulating programs, a format well-suited to the target audience and the message(s) to be delivered, well-planned and executed logistics, knowledgeable moderators and chairpersons, a good physical environment, and the opportunity to meet one's colleagues and exchange ideas. On the flip side, meetings that lacked clear objectives, had poor presenters, or were in an inadequate facility were deemed unsuccessful.

The key to hosting a successful meeting lies in the advance work. Adequate planning will deliver higher quality programs, streamline costs, maximize revenues and participation, and simplify the on-site logistics.

The objectives of the meeting should be clearly delineated and in keeping with the association's mission. Around these objectives, the association should develop a program and format that will deliver an event (or series of events) that meets participants' needs. To elicit excitement and entice attendance, you will need a solid understanding of the needs and expectations of all groups within the intended audience. For instance, a trade association whose members are businesses is more likely than a charitable organization to emphasize an exposition. On the other hand, many professional societies emphasize comprehensive meetings featuring multiple, concurrent training sessions. Regional groups may find their members most value the networking and social parts of their programs, while international groups may find their participants more interested in working on joint business challenges or learning from top-flight management experts.

The most common method for deciding on a meeting's program and format is to use a volunteer committee or task force. This group, comprised of members from various membership or audience sectors, carries different titles, depending upon the governance structure of the association and the event being planned: convention planning committee, education committee, special events task force, expo committee, exhibits advisory council, and so forth. In some cases, numerous committees have responsibilities for different aspects of the meeting; other committees involved might include those related to awards, the host city, certification, marketing, and fundraising.

Program content should be based on information gathered through a number of research techniques. Valuable input may come from program or education committees, member (and nonmember) surveys, focus groups, sampling techniques, evaluations of previous events, and other association departments that have special insight into "hot" topics or new trends. Other sources of information include industry suppliers, the association's credentialing program, computer bulletin boards/community listservers, responses to a call for presentations, chapter meeting agendas and evaluations, and the programs of meetings held in complementary industries or professions.

Planners often find a common theme underlying many of the educational topics identified through the research process. A logo designed to incorporate this theme can become an important part of the marketing for the meeting.

Finding a Format

The next step in planning is to design a meeting format that will deliver the chosen content in the most interesting and effective way. Consider the learning objectives identified during the needs-determination process, how interactive the format should be to foster this learning, the demographics of the attendees, the meeting's overall objectives, the character of the destination (once chosen), budget, and available delivery systems. Typical format options for *in-person* meetings are:

- **General Sessions.** *Formal* lectures usually highlight one expert or a celebrity speaker, who addresses a topic of general interest to all segments of the audience.

Plenary session is another name for a general session, although some associations use the term *plenary* to describe an interactive session following a formal lecture.

An *audience reaction* team refers to a group of members (usually three to five) seated on stage; they query the speaker with typical audience questions. A *panel discussion* includes a small group of experts, who discuss an issue from a variety of perspectives, while a *colloquium* involves a panel of experts and a panel of members, all of whom discuss and debate various issues related to a topic.

An *interview* may involve a presenter being questioned by a moderator or a team of members; it is an especially effective presentation format if the presenter is a controversial or visionary figure. Finally, a *debate* often makes a thought-provoking general session because it positions two individuals or teams on opposite sides of an issue.

- **Expositions and Trade Shows.** Standardized 8 × 10' or 10 × 10' *display booths*—the basic exhibit spaces—face an aisle on one side, with an 8'-high drape as the back wall and two 3'-high drapes as side walls. Some exposition managers organize the exhibits by product or service category; others ensure competitive exhibitors are not close to one another on the exhibit floor.

  Other common configurations include *island booths* (bordered by aisles on all four sides) and *peninsula booths.* The latter normally consist of two or more standard booths and are bordered by aisles on three sides and neighboring booth(s) on the remaining (fourth) side. Peninsula booths usually require special height regulations to protect the visibility of neighboring booths.

  Product demonstration sessions provide company representatives the opportunity to show a crowd of attendees how a product or service works. Some trade shows set aside space on the exhibit floor for *model facilities,* such as a futuristic store, a model warehouse, and so forth. Many times these models incorporate and showcase the products or services of several exhibiting companies.

  Association information centers give many associations a way to use their trade show to promote their benefits and services to attendees. In these centers, associations display information and sample products (books, tapes, and so forth) in or near the regular exhibits.

- **Educational Sessions/Breakouts.** In addition to general sessions, many meeting planners appeal to certain segments of attendees by scheduling multiple, concurrent sessions that cover more customized topics. These breakout sessions may follow the traditional general session formats noted above (formal lectures, panel discussions, and interviews, for instance), as well as these alternatives:

  - Workshops or roundtables, where a moderator leads a small audience in discussing one or more topics.
  - Teams or buzz groups, where the audience is broken down into small units and given assignments.

- Hands-on demonstrations, during which participants actually learn to use equipment or practice a new technique.
- Simulations, in which a trained facilitator leads attendees through hypothetical exercises.
- Poster sessions, whereby presenters provide written materials that are affixed to large display boards and exhibited in an area where all attendees may review them. Sometimes, authors also give short presentations.
- Fishbowl, in which an inner circle of members debates an issue while an outer circle observes the interchange.
- Competitions or Competitive Games, where participants actively vie against one another, either individually or in teams.

- **Open Space Meetings.** Meetings using *Open Space Technology (OST)*, identified by Harrison Owens in his book *Open Space Technology: A User's Guide,* are typically organized in a way that participants create and manage their own agenda of parallel working sessions around a central theme of strategic importance.

- **Guest Programs.** Many associations schedule activities for spouses, companions, guests, children, and other family members who accompany meeting participants. Active guests are less likely to draw the regular attendees away from your core programming. Plus, encouraging their participation in your meeting could lead to higher ticket sales for evening and social functions and boost overall meeting attendance.

  To understand the interests of these guests, consider conducting a survey. Talk to the area's convention and visitors' bureau, a local destination management company, a tour operator, or search the Web to find out what attractions are available in the vicinity for group tours. In addition, educational programming on topics such as personal finance, self-improvement, physical fitness, relationships, and new technologies are often popular. Just be careful not to over-schedule guests; they also like to have some unstructured time for their own pursuits.

- **Tours and Other Social Events.** A meeting delegate typically wants some social time mixed in with the educational or business events. In fact, many planners find they must schedule some visits to local attractions or risk losing attendees' participation at other functions. Aside from the obvious mental break they provide, such events offer attendees a means to network with old and new friends and to learn something about the local area. Sometimes a professional educational component is added when *study tours* are conducted of business operations of local members, suppliers, etc.

  Receptions are the traditional way of helping members network in a social atmosphere. *Tours,* whether incorporated into the regular program or offered as options (with a separate fee), may include local area "hot spots" or stops at the business facilities of local members or suppliers.

Fundraisers and *sporting events* are two more options to consider. Golf or tennis tournaments are very popular ways of involving participants in social functions outside the meeting room. Many groups also hold fundraising auctions, black-tie dinners, or special lectures to benefit the organization's foundation, scholarship fund, or a designated charity. In fact, some associations regularly partner with local members in the host city to raise money or get participants to volunteer to assist a nearby charity during the dates of a conference/meeting, while others sponsor/host fundraisers or community service projects to benefit a single national/international social welfare organization all year round.

The rapid advancement of technology has added a selection of new format choices for the delivery of information and education. More and more, associations are using video conferencing, advanced software, and the Internet to host meetings and provide *home-based study* or *distance learning* opportunities to members via their computers and handheld wireless devices, including their Blackberry™, cell phones, and even portable MP3 players.

Early on, there was a lot of fear that these new delivery mechanisms would render the traditional in-person conference, expo, or educational session ineffective. Experience has shown us that when these technologies are used to enhance the participant's experience, attendance at the conference/event is viewed as all the more important.

Once you have decided on the right mix of events, you need to set a schedule or agenda that includes the number of days the meeting will be held, the start and end times for each event, and the program format for each event.

Budgeting

The basic components of a meeting budget are income (or revenue), expenses, and net return.

It is crucial to set reasonable expectations for each revenue source: delegate registration (number of participants, minus any complimentary registrations offered, multiplied by the registration fee), special event ticket sales (including tours and guest program), exhibit space rental, exhibitor registrations, sponsorships, and other miscellaneous income (such as sales of convention proceedings, often on CD-ROMs or tapes). Detailed historic information about past meeting results will provide a good basis for setting realistic goals.

Meeting expenses typically fall into one of two major groupings: direct or indirect. Direct expenses are those owed for goods or services provided by outside suppliers. These include food and beverage costs (paid to the hotel, convention center, or an outside caterer), audiovisual equipment and labor, staff travel and accommodations, speakers' fees, entertainment, photography, decorations and signage, exhibition decorating services, printing of convention programs, facility rental, security, and insurance.

Indirect expenses are incurred by allocating salaries, benefits, and office expenses against the event. Indirect expenses are as much a part of the cost of putting on any event as direct costs; they must be taken into account to get an accurate picture of an event's effect on the association's bottom line.

Net return is the difference between income and expenses. Most associations rely heavily on their conventions and meetings to bring in a surplus; in fact, conventions and meetings were the largest source of non-dues revenue for nearly one third (32 percent) of associations in 2003.

The budget, along with information gathered on expenses during the logistics planning stage, should be used to set participant prices for the meeting. Calculate full registration (which includes all events), individual event ticket prices, meal prices, optional tour prices, guest program prices, and exhibit booth rental. Many associations offer a discounted price for early reservations and charge a premium for registrations received on-site. Similarly, members of the association often receive a discount on the price of registration or exhibit space rental offered to nonmembers.

It is also important for meeting planners to understand the basic differences between fixed and variable costs of a meeting. Variable costs are those that change based on the number of participants. Some typical variable costs are food and beverage charges and the costs for registration materials. By contrast, fixed costs are those that do not change based on the number of participants attending the meeting. These costs are borne by the association whether 250 or 500 people attend, so it is important to watch these costs carefully and work to minimize them whenever feasible. One reason the financial return on your event (or *ROI, return on investment*) should be better with a larger turnout is because the fixed costs will be a smaller percentage of the overall costs per person.

Site Selection

Identifying the most appropriate facility type, location, and time of year to hold a meeting requires gathering some basic information on the potential meeting audience.

Does the group comprise corporate CEOs looking for opportunities to network or individuals very interested in sports? A resort facility would offer lots of informal activities to foster that networking or fulfill recreational needs. A trade association with members who conduct much of the buying for their businesses at its trade show should entertain using a first-rate convention center or hotel with substantial facilities to house exhibits. Airport hotels offer the convenience of location for smaller, shorter meetings, but they often do not have meeting facilities big enough for a large annual convention.

Members' pocketbooks will affect their preferences: a five-star hotel in a large city would probably not be the best choice for a budget-conscious group. Locale, too, plays a big part in site selection. Many national groups rotate their conventions around the country so that no one group of members is required to travel long distances every year. Some groups prefer large cities, while others feel more comfortable in suburban or rural settings. Furthermore, some regions of the country may hold special significance to the members of a group; for example, the members may wish to visit an area where business is growing rapidly or where they hope to vacation after the meeting has concluded.

Timing may come into play as well. Conventions for educators may need to be held during the summer months or school breaks, while most lifeguards probably prefer to wait until their off-season to attend a convention.

Once you have zeroed in on a location or two, the local convention and visitors bureaus (CVBs) can assist in your quest for an appropriate meeting facility. Compile all the information on the meetings schedule, format, history, and preferred locations and dates into a Request for Proposal (RFP) and distribute it to the CVBs. The bureaus will identify and contact the most appropriate facilities for your meeting. Bureaus sometimes collect the proposals and put together a city-wide bid to host an association meeting that is likely to require multiple facilities to hold all the events. Other sources of site information that can prove useful are recommendations from other meeting planners, meeting management consultants, and information shared through meeting planning Web sites, trade shows, and resource guides/directories.

Historical data will be crucial in determining whether a facility is right for a meeting. Collect information such as the number and type of sleeping rooms used per night, the number and types of food and beverage functions held, the number and size of meeting rooms used each day, the number of hospitality suites utilized, the amount of space required for registration/ticket sales/information desks, and the number of exhibit spaces rented. Given this data, the dollar value of a meeting to a host city can be calculated—an important bit of information to use when negotiating with the facility.

Conducting a Site Inspection

The next step is to personally visit the most promising facility. Once again, the local CVB can help arrange a site visit.

Most meeting planners conduct their own site inspections. Some, however, rely on site-inspection teams of volunteers. No one is as familiar with a meeting as the meeting planner, so delegate this function only to those who are qualified, dependable, and as impartial as possible. Explicit job descriptions for these volunteers should be written and adhered to, and final contract negotiations should remain a staff function.

When selecting a meeting site, consider rates (prices for sleeping rooms, meeting rooms, food and beverage costs, exhibit space, and ancillary charges), dates (exact days for which sleeping rooms and meeting space are available to the group), and space (amount and configuration of meeting space being offered and the flow of that space from one event to another). In concert with the visit, review the meeting specifications or request for proposal and the hotel or facility's proposal and floor plan.

Site Inspection Checklist

Consider these issues when conducting a site inspection:

Sleeping Rooms

- Will the hotel commit a sufficient number of sleeping rooms to your group for the meeting?

- Are you being offered a single (flat) rate, or does the rate vary based on the type of accommodations (single, double, triple occupancy)? Most hotels in the United States quote room rates on a European plan, which doesn't include meals. Outside the U.S. and at some resorts, rates are for a Full American plan (including three meals daily) or a Modified American plan (including breakfast and dinner).

- Can you fit your entire sleeping room block in one hotel, or must you use multiple properties? If you need to use multiple properties, how will transportation to/from the event site be handled?

- Are there sufficient hospitality suites for your industry suppliers?

- What is the condition of the sleeping rooms? Will they be a good value for your participants?

- What amenities are offered (hair dryer, makeup mirror, iron, in-room safe, snack bar, cable television, telephone, high speed internet access—wired vs. wireless—voice messaging service, video check-out, parking, exercise facilities, and so forth). What are the charges for these services?

- Will other groups be holding meetings at the same time? Will there be any conflicts over public space (lobbies, lounges, foyers)? Are the sleeping room rates for the other groups comparable to yours?

- Historically, what has been the hotel's occupancy rate over the dates being considered? Is this the high season, shoulder season, or off-season?

- Are security and safety high priorities with the hotel? Does it have working smoke detectors, fire alarms, sprinklers, and adequate lighting? Are there sufficient fire extinguishers, and does the hotel meet the Hotel-Motel Fire Safety Act, as well as local fire and safety codes? Does the hotel have an emergency plan, an on-site security force, and a chain of command for emergency situations?

Meeting Space/Exhibit Hall

- Does the hotel or convention center have sufficient space to hold your various events at the times you want? Compare an actual room with the figures given on the facility's diagram. Many times these figures originate from architectural drawings or projections and do not account for any alterations made to the floor plan or for set up of additional staging or audiovisual equipment. The most accurate figures are usually available from the manager of convention services or catering.

- Will the flow from one meeting room to another be comfortable for your attendees, or must they do lots of extra walking to get from place to place?

- Are the meeting facilities in good shape? Are the air walls clean and in good repair? Do they provide sufficient soundproofing for your meeting? Will any other functions be held next door to your meeting?

continued on next page

continued from previous page

- Is the lighting sufficient? Can the lighting system be controlled individually in each room?
- Is there a sound system in each room, and does it work well?
- Is the ceiling height in each room sufficient for your audiovisual needs? For example, will the chandeliers interfere with any audiovisual presentations being planned?
- Is the temperature in each meeting room individually set? How is the thermostat controlled?
- Are the public facilities, especially the restrooms and foyer areas, clean and neat?
- Is the freight door or elevator large enough to accommodate exhibits? What is the weight limit for the exhibit floor?

Complying with ADA

According to the Americans with Disabilities Act (ADA), your association becomes a "public accommodation" when it leases a hotel or other facility for a meeting. Thus, the association is responsible for leasing a site that is accessible to disabled individuals covered by ADA, including the visually impaired, deaf or hard of hearing, and those in a wheelchair or with some mobility impairment.

- Do the meeting and exhibit facilities meet ADA requirements? Check for ADA compliance in parking lots; walks, curbs, and ramps; entrances, corridors, and stairs; the front desk; public restrooms; accessible guest rooms and meeting rooms; restaurants and lounges; elevators; and public telephones and water fountains. Facilities should also have specialized emergency procedures for disabled guests.
- Will the facility agree to comply with the ADA in its contract? Will it agree to hold the association harmless against any claims made against the association for the facility's non-compliance?

Finally, it is always wise to talk with other meeting planners who have held events at the facility you're considering to hear first hand how the property performed and what challenges can be expected on-site. The hotel, convention center, or CVB can provide the names of planners who have held recent meetings at the properties in question.

Signing on the Dotted Line

With the site inspections completed, it is time to narrow the field to one or two top choices, place a tentative "hold" on the space, and start contract negotiations. While not all meetings require a formal contract, every meeting should involve at least a letter of agreement signed by representatives of both parties (the hotel or facility and the association). Putting the agreement in writing helps clarify the terms and makes the terms binding and enforceable.

A clear offer must be made and accepted by both parties involved in the agreement. In layman's terms, the contract must detail what the hotel or facility will provide and what the association or its members will pay. Both parties must agree in writing to this offer. As with all contracts, consult legal counsel before signing any agreement on behalf of your association.

Negotiate fairly with a hotel or other property so the finished product—the contract—provides a fair profit for the services and facilities provided. Some meeting planners have discovered that driving a property to agree to a one-sided contract results in poorer quality service during the convention or a lack of interest in hosting future meetings. Remember, everything is negotiable: Concentrating on additional services and amenities can be a good alternative to strictly focusing on price. (For tips on effective negotiating, see chapter 10.)

In addition to rates, dates, and space—the three main negotiating points of all meetings contracts—address these issues:

- Does the contract cover a single meeting, or does it cover multiple meetings during the course of a year or more?

- How will room reservations be handled—by rooming list, online reservation service, housing bureau, or phone-in reservations? What is the cut-off date for reservations, and what happens to rooms in your block after that date? How can reservations be made after that date and at what cost? Will the hotel assure the association that its meeting participants will receive the lowest room rates available to any guests at the time of the meeting? Are special rates available for a small number of staff rooms? Will the hotel agree to give the association the right to approve any requests for suites during the dates of its meeting?

- Will the association earn complimentary sleeping rooms for use by staff or VIPs, based on actual rooms used? The industry standard is one complimentary room for every 50 paid rooms. Find out if comp nights are calculated on the total number of room nights blocked or on a night-by-night basis.

- What rules will govern the establishment of a master account for the association? Are any deposits required, and are they put into escrow? What are the payment terms? How will billing be handled? Make sure the payment terms require the association to pay only for undisputed charges within the prescribed time (normally 30 days) and that payment is contingent upon the association's receipt of a full post-convention report from the property.

- Confirm the availability and cost of additional services, such as parking, airport transfers, in-room telephone and Internet service, package receiving, fax services, and concierge services.

- Name the exact meeting, exhibit, and public space being held for the association and the costs associated with the use of that space.

- Agree on specific food and beverage quotes, a percentage discount off the published catering menus, or a date by which food and beverage prices may be negotiated.

- Include a paragraph confirming the hotel's or facility's compliance with the terms of the Americans with Disabilities Act as well as any fire, safety, and building codes.

- List the responsibilities of the hotel should a meeting delegate with a confirmed reservation be turned away because the hotel is filled or oversold. Most times, the hotel will agree to find the guest alternate accommodations of equal or better quality, provide transportation to and from the association's meetings, and offer a room amenity until it can once again offer a sleeping room.

- Address what the property is required to do when and if any renovations are planned. Also note whether any concurrent meetings sponsored by other groups may be booked.

- Hotels may require performance or "attrition" clauses for sleeping room pickup or food and beverage revenues in their contracts. Associations need to be careful that the performance levels set by the hotel are reasonable, attainable, and clearly listed. Any payments from the association required by the hotel should be based on lost profits; for some meetings, specifying damages in actual dollars will help to avoid disputes over profits that may or may not have materialized.

- Watch the wording of any cancellation clause. Usually, cancellation is permitted if it results from an Act of God (such as a hurricane), strikes, epidemics, terrorism, or declarations of war. If penalties apply to the association for canceling a meeting of substantial size or economic value within a set period of time (usually one year) for other reasons, similar penalties should be applied to the property that cancels the group's contract. The contract should clearly stipulate when cancellation fees must be paid.

  Cancellation clauses should require the hotel to attempt to resell the rooms and state that revenue from resold rooms will be deducted from the amount owed by the canceling association. Again, any payment due for a canceled meeting should be set as a specific dollar amount based on lost profits, not gross revenues. Special cancellation policies may apply in cases where the hotel management changes, the meeting outgrows the meeting space, the meeting requires space or sleeping rooms at more than one property, the property is facing bankruptcy, or the property does not perform satisfactorily at an earlier meeting.

  The contract should address appropriate notification policies in each of these cases, clearly state the procedures to be followed when disagreements occur, and designate the state given jurisdiction in cases involving such disagreements. Many planners stipulate that contractual disagreements be referred to the American Arbitration Association or similar provider of alternative dispute resolution services.

- The indemnification clause should say that the hotel will pay the legal fees and any judgments against the association if someone names the association in a lawsuit for something within the hotel's scope of responsibility. Likewise, it should say that the association will hold the hotel harmless if the lawsuit concerns something under the association's control.

- Convention center contracts often have stipulations that apply to events other than typical association meetings, such as sporting events and concerts open to the general public. Be sure to eliminate the provisions that do not apply to your meeting.

- Insurance clauses can require the association, the hotel, or both to carry a minimum amount of liability insurance and to name the other group and its representatives as additional insureds on the policy.

- The contract should specify that the people signing have the authority to do so on behalf of their companies. It should also spell out that the contract and any signed addenda constitute the entire agreement between the parties.

Most associations set up a master account at the host hotel or meeting facility. Against this they charge meeting expenses such as food, meeting room rental, and labor. A master account is set up by filling out a credit application and getting approval from the property in advance of the meeting. Be explicit with the hotel about what will and will not be charged to the master account and who has authority to charge items. Once on site, review the charges made to the master account each day.

Specialized Services

Many planners contract with additional suppliers, such as airlines, car rental agencies, destination management companies, travel agents or tour companies, caterers, entertainers, audiovisual companies, and trade show decorators for specialized meeting services. For instance, an airline might offer attendees a discount on travel to and from a meeting when the association names it the "official airline" for the meeting and helps promote travel on that airline. The association usually receives a complimentary ticket for use by staff or VIPs every time the number of airline tickets sold to members reaches a certain threshold. The standard formula is one complimentary ticket earned for every 50 tickets sold.

Because most planners are not experts in audio-visual equipment, such as LCD projectors, they typically hire an audiovisual firm to provide, set up, and operate the equipment. When choosing a firm, ask about equipment inventories, the firm's location (an in-house firm is likely to have a larger supply of labor and equipment available on the spur of the moment), labor costs, overtime policies, and any additional charges incurred for use of the hotel sound system.

Working with entertainers requires special expertise as well. Be sure to give the performers guidelines for appropriate entertainment (acceptable language, for instance), background information on the audience, the event start time and length of performance, and any expenses covered by the association beyond the arranged performance fee. Booking agents can recommend appropriate acts and offer additional services such as on-site coordination; they can also be helpful in emergency situations when a last-minute replacement is needed. Whether using an agent or booking the entertainer directly, always preview the act before confirming the booking.

Remember that providing any entertainment that includes the use of copyrighted music will require the sponsoring association to secure the necessary performance licenses from organizations such as the American Society of Composers, Authors and Publishers (ASCAP) and Broadcast Music International (BMI).

Contracts with suppliers should be carefully reviewed to ensure the terms of the agreement are clear and equitable. Like contracts with facilities, they should include clauses on indemnification, performance, cancellation, assignability of the contract, and compliance with the ADA and other pertinent regulations.

Booking Speakers

One group of service providers—speakers—merits special attention. When choosing a speaker for a general session or educational workshop, consider whether the speaker's message will help the association satisfy the meeting's objectives, if the speaker's participation will stimulate attendance or press coverage, if the audience will recognize and respect the speaker's expertise, and whether the speaker's style of delivery will hold the audience's attention.

Many associations find talented speakers through local and national speakers' bureaus that represent both the famous and the not-so-famous. Other speaker sources include professional organizations (such as the National Speakers Association), convention and visitors bureaus, universities and colleges, destination management companies, other associations, and association members and suppliers. Whenever possible, preview the speaker by seeing him or her give a presentation or by sending a committee member to do the preview.

Speaker contracts should cover the usual items, such as day, time, location, program length, and presentation format (lecture, Q&A, and so forth), as well as the following: liability issues (copyright/slander), security requirements of high-profile speakers, substitute speakers provided by the speakers' bureau, expenses covered in addition to the arranged speaking fee (for example, coach versus first-class travel), whether the speaker may market any ancillary products (books or tapes), preferred attire, audio-visual equipment needed, approval to record the presentation, cancellation by either party, and the type of background information to be provided to the speaker.

For any speaker to be successful, he or she needs to be briefed on the audience—its demographic profile, perspective on the topic, the industry's or profession's general concerns and jargon, and topics to avoid. Additionally, educate the speaker about the meeting itself, such as its theme, format, and program.

Marketing Your Meeting

An association may host the best meeting in history, but it won't be a success if no one attends. The elements of a marketing plan will vary based on the type of meeting. Annual conventions with expositions, for instance, require at least two separate marketing campaigns: one to potential exhibitors and one to potential delegates. Other potential audiences are past attendees, government employees, university professors and other instructors, and representatives from allied industries. Some of the marketing budget and resources should also be set aside for publicizing the meeting to the trade and consumer media.

Once again, an association's market data will help determine how much promotion to do and how best to do it. Factors that will help in the decision-making process include the purpose of the meeting, the budgeted attendance goals, the attractiveness of the meeting program and location to target audiences, the accessibility of the meeting location, the appropriateness of the meeting dates, the cost for attendees, the amount of competition for the audience's training and travel dollars, and the meeting's marketing budget.

As a point for comparison, most associations spend 10 to 15 percent of their meeting's expense budget on marketing. The convention planning committee can be an excellent resource in identifying new target audiences and promotional vehicles, as well as boosting the meeting's profile through word-of-mouth advertising.

Technological advances offer new ways to deliver the marketing message to prospective audiences. Many associations promote their meetings to members via association Web sites, electronic newsletters, and e-mail marketing, in addition to direct mail, advertising, and press releases.

Regardless of how the message gets out, meeting promotions should include the benefits an attendee can reasonably expect to gain by attending; the schedule of events, including their exact time and location; registration instructions and fees; information on air travel, sleeping room accommodations, airport transfers, car rentals, and other travel arrangements; recommended attire; other local activities or attractions that may prompt a person to want to visit the meeting location; and where to find more information.

The best way to manage the marketing function is to establish measurable goals, develop a marketing plan to meet those goals, design a budget, and set a calendar of deadlines for each activity in the marketing plan. For example, many associations start a year in advance with a "hold the dates" promotion for an annual convention and space out the other mailings, e-mails, and promotions throughout the year.

Marketing the convention does not stop the day the meeting begins. In fact, many meeting planners set up a newsroom for media that cover the meeting, provide special information kits and story lists, plan media-only events such as press conferences, and offer interviews with well-prepared volunteers and staff who serve as spokespeople for the association.

Exposition Management

If an exposition or trade show accompanies the meeting, a basic tenet must be understood: A buyer-seller relationship exists between the companies exhibiting and the people attending (or the companies they represent). The stronger that relationship, the greater the odds that the exposition will be a valued part of a meeting.

Big or small, trade shows should not be treated as an afterthought in the meeting planning process. From the beginning, the exposition should be an integral part of the meeting's objectives. For instance, a meeting facility with sufficient space to hold the planned exhibits must be selected. Larger trade shows and those featuring large products—such as vehicles or heavy equipment—may not be able to find a hotel with adequate exhibit space. In these cases, the association may hold its trade show and some events in a convention center—a facility with meeting and exhibit space but no sleeping rooms that is usually operated by a public entity.

When picking a site for exhibits, consider these factors:

- Amount of space available
- Quality of the space (column-free, contiguous, well-lit?)
- Ceiling height
- Floor load capacities and any weight limitations
- Size of freight doors, elevators, ramps, and other entrances
- Union work rules and rates, and other facility regulations
- Availability of T-l and ISDN telephone lines, as well as wireless Internet access in both the public space and exhibit areas
- Any exclusive contracts for suppliers you are required to use (electricians, caterers, security, drayage, and so forth)

Keeping exhibitors happy requires delivering a good supply of buyers to them on the exhibit floor. That means designing the meeting agenda so delegates have time to visit the trade show without the interruption of other sessions or seminars. To ensure high buyer turnout, many associations conduct advance marketing promotions and offer incentives for delegates to walk the show floor and place orders (such as free meals, prize drawings, and giveaways in the exhibit hall). The catch-22 of putting on a successful trade show is that while exhibitors will evaluate the show on the basis of the buyer turn-out, delegates will evaluate the show on the basis of the quality and quantity of products and services on display. Thus, any exposition marketing must use a two-pronged approach.

The marketing materials sent to potential exhibitors should include details about the show (show hours, set-up and tear-down times, floor plan, booth assignment procedures, and booth personnel registration arrangements), a buyer profile, an exhibit space rental agreement, and show rules. The contract should cover space price and payment terms; cut-off dates for deposits, payments, and cancellation refunds; cancellation due to acts of God; booth restrictions (size, perimeters, sight lines, display materials, performance of copyrighted music, excessive noise or heat); labor union requirements; assignability of contract; exclusive suppliers; a hold-harmless liability clause; restrictions on certain sales activities; insurance requirements for exhibitors; and restrictions on sharing exhibit space. Once again, consult legal counsel when developing this contract.

It is important to note that nonmembers of the association do not have to be solicited for booth rental; it is also legal to charge nonmembers a premium price if supplier dues are regularly used to defer exhibit show costs. The courts, however, view exhibiting privileges as a competitive advantage, so restricting exhibit space rental to members may open the association to the risk of an antitrust suit.

Almost all meeting planners organizing a trade show hire a trade show decorator, or exhibition service contractor, to assist in the planning and on-site logistics management. These contractors, for a fee, provide and set up the pipe and drape that creates the individual booth spaces on the exhibit floor, aisle carpeting, signage, lounge and booth furniture, registration counters, and special decorations.

In addition, the decorator creates and distributes a manual for exhibitors, which highlights the rules associated with show move-in and tear down and markets a number of services, such as drayage, furniture and equipment rental, and labor. The decorator usually makes most of its money by providing these services directly to exhibitors; make sure that these services are fairly priced and that service is of a quality, so exhibitors find participation in your show to be a good value.

Housing

There are several ways to handle the sleeping-room reservation process:

A *rooming list* includes the name of meeting participants along with their arrival and departure dates and any special needs (roll-away bed, crib, accessible facilities, and so forth). The association—or a destination management company employed by it—typically compiles this information and sends it to the hotel. Reservations are usually confirmed by the hotel and guaranteed by the association.

Participants are sometimes instructed to *reserve rooms directly* with the hotel, either via the Internet, the phone, or by mail. Remember to collect information from the participant that the hotel needs to comply with the Americans with Disabilities Act.

A *housing bureau* is a centralized reservation service operated by the association or outsourced to the local convention bureau or a destination management company. This option is often used for meetings that require sleeping rooms at more than one hotel or for associations that want to control the assignment of sleeping rooms (for example, by giving reservations only to those delegates who have pre-registered for the meeting). Maintaining a housing bureau within the association requires a commitment of staff and other resources, often used to set up the appropriate Web pages and to handle phone requests. These costs can be offset by collecting advance deposits (usually one-night's room rate) on reservations. Whatever the housing process used, the meeting planner should assign any VIPs to special rooms (upgrades or suites) before the room block becomes available for general reservations and make sure that those who register receive confirmations. Additionally, the planner should consider reserving a few extra sleeping rooms before the cut-off date in case a speaker, staff person, board member, or other participant forgets to make a hotel reservation for the meeting.

Food and Beverage Functions

These events often prove the most visible and memorable of functions. They also require close scrutiny on the part of the planner in order to safeguard the meeting budget.

Rooms holding meal functions should be the appropriate size: not so small that participants are uncomfortable, but not so large that empty space in the room overshadows the event. Additional space should be allowed for food stations, bars, dance floors, staging, and walking room for participants and wait staff. Check that restrooms are nearby and, if the event is scheduled for outdoors, have an indoor location reserved in case of inclement weather.

Local attractions often provide unique and memorable backdrops for a meeting function; be sure to alert the host hotel not to include the off-premise function in the list of meals it will provide. Preferably, give this notice to the hotel before contract negotiations commence.

The most common types of meal functions are:

- **Coffee/Refreshment Breaks.** Either held right in the meeting room or in a separate but adjacent area, these allow people to socialize freely while taking a break from attending sessions. Pricing for these functions varies. Coffee prices may be based on per-person or per-gallon consumption, while soft drinks (in cans or bottles) may be charged on a per-item price based on actual consumption.

- **Breakfast/Brunch.** This meal can be economical to serve. Because of increasing diversity in menu preferences among attendees, many planners offer a buffet for this meal. Plated breakfasts, however, are still an option.

- **Lunch.** Priced either by the plate or per person, lunch can be a plated function or a buffet.

- **Receptions.** These can range from simple networking events including drinks and conversation to elaborate mini-meals featuring hors d'oeuvres, entertainment, and decorations. They are priced either by the person (per hour) or by ordering a set quantity of food and drink

  A hosted beverage service—where the association pays the cost of all refreshments—is usually priced either by the head (person per hour), by the bottle consumed (or opened), or by the drink. Cash bars, which require attendees to pay for their own drinks, operate on a per-drink basis; in addition, the association will sometimes incur a labor charge for bartenders and cashiers. It is also important to know if the hotel will serve house, call, or premium brands of liquor, or what types of beer, wine, and soft drinks will be served—particularly if the meeting attendees have strong preferences. If paying for beverage service by the bottle, remember to take an inventory of bottles before and after the event to make sure you're being charged appropriately.

  Associations concerned about the liability associated with serving alcoholic beverages should work with the catering director to limit consumption. Options include decreasing the size of glasses, giving participants a limited number of drink tickets, or limiting the time the bar remains open.

- **Banquets.** When making arrangements with the catering staff for a sit-down meal function, consider the type of service required. Typical events are *plated service* (each plate is prepared in the kitchen and presented to an attendee), but fancier events could use *French service* (the wait person serves each item separately to each person at the table) or *Russian service* (diners serve themselves each item from a platter held by the waiter). The room is either set up for open seating, where attendees choose seats upon entering the room, or for assigned seating, which is done before the meeting.

  Banquet meals are priced according to the actual number of people served (called a "per plate" charge); thus, they require the planner to "guarantee" the number of meals to be served. Because hotels usually require guarantees 48 to 72 hours in advance, the planner must be adept at forecasting actual attendance. The idea is to guarantee the exact number of people to be served so the association doesn't pay for meals that aren't consumed; if the planner underestimates attendance, however, the hotel may not have sufficient food or table space to serve everyone wishing to attend. Hotels usually prepare a small number of meals over the guaranteed figure (five percent of the total guarantee is standard), but ask about the exact percentage before deciding upon the guarantee.

Meal functions can be priced on a per-ticket basis. In this scenario, the meeting participant receives a ticket for a meal function upon registration. The server waiting on the table or working at one end of a buffet line collects this ticket, and the association pays for the number of meals based on tickets turned in. Usually the association must still give a guarantee to the hotel so the catering staff knows how much food to prepare. If tickets are required for a food function, be sure to have a staff person or volunteer on hand to assist delegates who have forgotten or lost their tickets.

Selecting appropriate menus requires a good understanding of the meeting delegates. Younger, adventurous delegates are likely to appreciate trendier, more exotic menu items, while older attendees may prefer traditional fare. Menus can be tailored to fit any type of cultural or religious profile and are often picked to match an event theme. Frequently, participants are looking for lighter, healthier food such as low-fat meats, fruits, and vegetables. It is important to note if members actively follow new dietary trends, such as high-protein, low-carbohydrate diets.

The catering staff can assist with menu design and planning, the most effective room layouts, and ways to get the most amount of food for the association's budget. Most hotels and facilities will negotiate food and beverage pricing three to six months before the meeting dates; if a budget amount is needed further in advance, you may be able to negotiate a set percentage off the menu prices or a cap on price increases for a set menu. Remember to include taxes and gratuities when calculating costs—and find out if gratuities are taxable.

Finally, it is the meeting planner's responsibility to make sure adequate dining facilities exist to serve delegates when meal functions are not planned. Find out, for instance, if the hotel has sufficient restaurant capacity for a mid-day luncheon or if your group of early-risers will put a heavy demand on the room service staff in the morning. This information should be communicated to the hotel so that it can prepare in advance to meet your members' needs.

Registration

The first experience participants have with a meeting is the registration desk. Long lines, misplaced registration packets, and missing tickets or materials will not give delegates a positive first impression. Be sure to staff your registration desk adequately, offer separate areas for pre-registrants and on-site registrants, provide training for the desk staff, streamline registration procedures as much as possible, and make sure all participants are treated courteously.

Security

Awareness of safety and security measures during a site inspection will help a planner choose a facility that will meet participants' expectations. Look to see whether the facility has smoke alarms, well-lit hallways, and marked exits.

To minimize the possibility of theft, use bonded personnel, put all receipts in a safe deposit box, and reconcile registration receipts and other sales every evening. By hiring a security company, you can provide a secure environment for exhibitors during move-in, exhibit days, and tear down. Remember to get competitive bids, check references, and ask about company policies on overtime, breaks, employee longevity, dress code, and whether the guards are armed.

As another security measure, associations often require meeting participants to wear a name badge at all events.

Insurance Considerations

Meetings expose their sponsoring associations to a higher level of liability and risk. Among the areas of risk generally accompanying meetings are general liability (bodily injury and property damage), fire, medical expenses and malpractice, product liability, burglary and robbery, workers' compensation, accidental death and disability, exhibitor property loss, show cancellation, and liquor liability.

Periodically review your association's insurance coverage to ensure it is adequate. Also, have the association named as an additional insured on policies maintained by third-party vendors, such as exposition decorators and bus charters, and collect proof of insurance from all exhibitors.

Printed Materials

A plethora of printed items are produced for most meetings, especially large conventions. They range from imprinted specialty items (registration portfolios, bags, and pens) to direct mail marketing materials, from exhibitor contracts and manuals to printed meeting programs, exposition directories, convention proceedings, and evaluation forms. You might also produce registration and hotel reservation forms, badges, tickets, daily convention newspapers, and speaker handouts.

Meeting planners have devised alternative methods of providing many of these printed materials. For instance, proceedings can be made available on CDs/DVDs or USB flash drive, or on the association's Web site; educational seminars can be distributed on audiotape, videotape, or DVD. Attendees and exhibitors alike might access promotional information as well as online registration systems using the association's Web page.

Team Management

Meeting planners require the assistance of many people—other association staff members, committee members and other volunteers, hired temporaries, hotel/facilities staff, and staff from other suppliers such as show decorators and tour companies. Orchestrating all these people so that no detail is overlooked and that events run smoothly requires a lot of time, attention to detail, and coordination of resources.

Common wisdom says that volunteers are the most productive when they serve in an advisory capacity. For instance, they might identify customer needs (educational programming and site preference) and unique resources (potential exhibitors, speakers, or entertainers). Some associations also find it helpful to involve volunteers in the on-site management of functions, especially staffing welcome desks, hosting new members, and operating on-site tours of member facilities.

Before the meeting begins, the planner should develop job descriptions for each of the roles assigned to volunteers. This means that the convention planning committee, volunteer speakers, and the evaluation team (and everyone in between) have a clearly stated mission and list of activities for which they are responsible. These job descriptions help volunteers understand and accomplish their goals in relation to the meeting and clarify the working relationships between staff and volunteers.

Both volunteers and staff should know exactly what to do should an emergency strike. The emergency plan should include the chain of command, actions to take for various situations, and important telephone numbers to use on site.

The staff of the hotel or meeting facility needs to be involved in developing the emergency plan—one of the many roles they fill during the course of planning a large convention or meeting. Typically, the meeting planner conducts contract negotiations with a sales representative; once the contract is signed, the planner usually begins working with a convention services manager to plan the logistics. While most convention services managers serve as the main point of contact for a planner, sometimes the planner works directly with various department heads, such as the front desk manager (for reservations and special check-in arrangements), the catering manager (food and beverage functions), the security director, room service director (for small functions in hospitality suites), and so forth. With so many people involved, a detailed contract and accurate record keeping are essential.

For smaller meetings, or in smaller properties, the sales representative may assist with all arrangements for the meeting.

Convention Planning Tools

The meetings industry has developed a number of standard tools to assist with the management of planning and to simplify communications between the members of the meeting planning team.

The *meeting profile and specifications report* delineates the meeting's arrival/departure pattern, meeting room and sleeping room requirements, food and beverage functions, and exhibit space needed. It also includes historical data on past meeting locations and dates. The profile and specifications are the heart of a Request for Proposal when searching for a meeting site.

Standard Set-Ups

When specifying room set-ups, using common industry jargon will ensure clear communications with the hotel's set-up crew. Such terms include:

- *Theater style*—chairs are set in a succession of rows. These rows can be placed straight across, in a semicircle, or in a chevron (V-shape), with or without a center or side aisles.
- *Schoolroom or classroom style*—narrow tables are set in front of the chairs so participants have a place to put books, writing tablets, and so forth. Again, this set-up can be in rows straight across or in a V-shape.
- *U-Shaped*—regular-width tables are set out with chairs in a U-shaped configuration.
- *Hollow square or rectangle*—a U-shaped configuration where the open end has been closed off with tables. Chairs are placed all around the outside edge of the square, looking in toward the center.
- *Conference style*—a large table, or series of tables pushed together to create one large table, is set in a rectangular shape with chairs around the perimeter. Unlike the hollow-square set-up, there is no space in the center of the configuration.
- *Banquet style*—5' or 6' round tables that each seat 8 or 10 people around the circumference. As the name indicates, this set-up is typically used with food and beverage functions.
- *Crescent rounds*—Banquet rounds set with 4-5 seats around half the circumference of the table, facing the stage or podium.
- *Cocktail rounds*—small round tables and few chairs, used mostly for receptions and other social functions.

If you're using an unusual layout for a function, a floor diagram becomes imperative. Meeting planner templates and specialized computer software programs are available to help you design your own diagrams.

The *meeting timetable* or *activity calendar* is a schedule of beginning dates, deadlines, and names of the people responsible for each task related to planning the meeting. Project management techniques and tools, especially software programs, can streamline the creation of this calendar.

The *convention resume* is what planners use to communicate the specific work plan for each event during the convention. It includes a narrative overview of the meeting (with background on the meeting participants), contact information, VIP arrangements, master-account billing instructions, expected shipments or deliveries, special security requirements, anticipated outlet usage (restaurants, room service, lounges), lobby services requirements (bellmen and concierge), front desk instructions, planned use of the facility's public space, day and time of on-site pre-convention meeting between hotel staff and planner, and the function sheets for each event planned.

Function Sheets compile the myriad details surrounding each event at the meeting. Each sheet should carry the name of the association, the event name, the day and

International Destinations

Meetings held outside the United States pose special challenges. First and foremost, the association should determine whether the tax-deductibility of the meeting is an important consideration for participants. If so, the planner should choose a site in a country that meets IRS regulations. In general, the IRS denies tax deductions for travel expenses to meetings outside the North America area unless attendance relates directly to the conduct of business by the participant or unless it is as reasonable for the meeting to be held outside the North American area as within.

This "as reasonable" test incorporates several issues usually applied by the IRS in reviewing deducibility questions: the purpose of the meeting, the activities taking place during the meeting, the mission and activities of the sponsoring association, and the home country of the association's members and meeting participants. In other words, the meeting program should incorporate an international focus—through special study tours, involvement of professional colleagues from the host country, and other educational offerings that could not be easily duplicated in the United States.

The IRS has, however, expanded its definition of "North American area" to include any U.S. possessions, Canada, Mexico, and a number of Caribbean countries (Bermuda and the Bahamas, for instance). Any meeting held in these areas does not have to meet the "as reasonable" test in order for travel expenses to be deductible. Still, check with a tax attorney before planning an international meeting to verify the tax-deductibility status of the host country being considered.

IRS regulations are not the only challenge to planning a successful meeting abroad. You will also encounter language and cultural differences, substantial mailing and shipping costs and delays, customs and immigration regulations, duties and taxes, currency exchange rates, special insurance requirements, electricity and other utility systems disparities, and labor union regulations. Because of these added concerns, planners usually lengthen their planning timetable considerably and seek outside help from U.S. consulates, customs brokers, freight forwarders, professional conference organizers, and travel agencies. Members residing in the host city and local convention bureaus are generally good sources of additional assistance.

date, beginning and ending times, meeting room and floor number, desired set-up, a diagram of floor layout (if necessary), expected attendance, the person in charge of the event, audiovisual equipment needed, food and beverage needs, and any special requirements.

Other items to communicate to the convention services manager about room set-ups include: staging; head tables; lecterns or podiums (tabletop or freestanding); audiovisual equipment such as screens, projectors, and stands; special lighting requirements (darkened house lights, spotlights); entertainment scheduled in the room; centerpieces desired; smoking/non-smoking sections; and room and food station decorations.

The proliferation of affordable computer software has simplified coordination of meetings. Software programs can record and track registrations and ticket sales, print badges, diagram a meeting room set-up or exhibit show floor, maintain mailing lists, record pertinent sales information, create transcripts of continuing education credits, and schedule and organize the planning, marketing, and management functions (project management).

On-Site Management

Despite the long hours associated with planning, work days during the meeting itself can become grueling for the meeting planner, association staff, volunteers, and hired suppliers. Meetings place association staff in a highly visible position, where members and nonmembers alike watch and evaluate how the staff interacts with volunteers, customers, and each other. Staff's behavior becomes a reflection of the association itself. Proper rest, a positive attitude, and healthful meals go a long way toward making the on-site experience rewarding for everyone involved.

An organized on-site operation is crucial for the meeting to appear well-planned. The planner should arrive at the site one to three days in advance to set up the association's office, verify that all materials shipped to the hotel have arrived, meet with the hotel staff at a pre-convention meeting (commonly called the *pre-con*) to review all plans and provide updated counts and guarantees, arrange for a safe-deposit box or local bank account for daily receipts, conduct an orientation with staff and volunteers, and monitor exhibit hall set-up and move-in.

During the meeting, the planner needs to oversee all events and support services, such as registration and information desks; check that the hotel's information systems (such as the reader board and in-room video services) correctly list the daily events; check each meeting room's set-up at least 1 hour before the event start time; check all food and beverage set-ups 45 to 60 minutes before the function begins; set up cash boxes for each registration worker; make sure the cash boxes are balanced every day; have signs posted in appropriate places; make sure handouts, awards, and other items are in the right place; review the hotel's daily report on sleeping rooms; monitor on-site registration numbers and adjust guarantees; verify that speakers, entertainers, and VIPs arrive on time; and count attendance at each event for a historical record.

Just before returning home, the planner needs to spend time with the convention services manager and the accounting department to review the master account bill; prepare thank you notes and gratuities to hotel staff and other suppliers; make arrangements to return rented equipment such as computers, copy machines, and portable radios; conduct a post-convention meeting with volunteers and suppliers; pack up the remaining registration, office, and other materials for return shipping; and make arrangements to handle the cash receipts via wire transfer, cashier's check, or a credit on the master account. Planners often find it necessary to stay a day or two beyond the meeting dates to finalize all these arrangements.

Clearly, it would be impossible for one person to personally handle all the details of a large meeting. Planners regularly rely on other staff members, assistants hired from the local convention and visitors bureau or destination management company, and association volunteers. Because the planner cannot be everywhere at once, associations typically rent cellular phones, pagers, and portable radios to keep staff in touch during the meeting, especially when concurrent events are taking place.

A detailed plan of action that assigns specific duties to individuals helps ensure that all meeting events go smoothly. To implement this plan of action, the association chief executive officer must give the planner the authority to direct the on-site operations.

Evaluating the Meeting

No planning process is complete without a thorough evaluation of what transpired. This evaluation should tell the planner not only what happened, but *why* it happened. Include each audience segment—delegates, exhibitors, speakers, and members of the press—in the evaluation process.

Methods of evaluating a meeting range from small, single-event surveys distributed and collected on site to comprehensive, post-convention surveys e-mailed to meeting participants. Others include special focus groups, an evaluation team or committee, and personal interviews conducted on site or afterward by telephone or e-mail.

Consider all aspects of the meeting when designing the evaluation tool: the meeting site/city, facility, events, speakers, registration desk procedures, entertainment, exhibits, schedule of events, convention timing/dates, pricing, use of audiovisual aids, optional tours, official suppliers (travel agent, airlines, car rental agency), pre-convention promotions, and the printed program booklet.

The data collected in the evaluation process, along with the financial results and statistical data provided by the association, the hotel, and the CVB, should be compiled into a meeting history report. Those data will prove useful when planning future meetings.

Emerging Trends

Societal trends related to the quality of the environment and the importance of communities have prompted planners to make meetings more environmentally friendly and socially conscious. For instance, many meeting planners use recycled paper products in their convention materials, have recycling bins available for discarded handouts, collect badge holders at the end of a meeting to reuse or recycle, conduct fundraising and community service projects in the host locale, and distribute remaining meeting items left over from event functions to area charities. Likewise, some hotels and other members of the hospitality industry sponsor outreach programs in their local communities. Planners are finding it increasingly important to make their meetings as family-friendly as possible. This trend has spurred on an increase in spouse programs, on-site child care, social events including families, and individual event ticket pricing options.

Ethics has also become a watchword. Because of the industry's focus on hospitality and the competitive relationship among suppliers, meeting planners and their professional organizations have established guidelines related to accepting familiarization trips, free site inspections, gifts, and rebates.

On the legislative and regulatory front, the challenges include local governments' increasing taxation of tourists to offset general budgetary deficits, the deducibility of spouse travel to meetings, the deducibility of meeting and travel expenses for meetings held abroad or on cruise ships, and the increasing difficulty for participants from countries outside North America to acquire visas to come to meetings held in the U.S. Some of these threats have spurred planners and their professional societies to become proactive about educating legislators and the public about the role associations play in American society.

The future undoubtedly holds many changes for the meetings industry. Already, the Internet has changed how associations market their meetings, obtain site information, and communicate with hotels and vendors.

The methods of delivering educational programming to members are changing as well. Meetings proceedings are frequently offered via the Web and on CDs, in addition to the more traditional audio and video tapes. Associations are merging technologies such as Web casting, online learning systems, teleconferencing, and testing software to conduct and certify training for all different kinds of skills and knowledge. The future is bound to present newer and more efficient technological advancements to send the meeting to the member instead of having the member come to the meeting.

It has been said that the digital economy is all about creating new patterns of personal activity. No one really knows what technological advances will mean for meetings and conventions in the future. Associations and their meeting planners must keep abreast of the changes or risk getting left behind.

References

Key Findings from the 2005 Associations Advance America Survey. Available at http://www.asaecenter.org/AdvocacyOutreach/contentASAEOnly.cfm?ItemNumber=17481. Accessed April 2007.

Policies and Procedures in Association Management: Conventions and Meetings, Education and Professional Development, Certification, Accreditation, and Licensing, Vol. 6, American Society of Association Executives, Washington, DC, 2006.

ASAE, *Association Meeting Trends,* American Society of Association Executives, Washington, DC, 1999.

Finkel, Coleman L., *New Conference Models for the Information Age,* American Society of Association Executives, Washington, DC, 1998.

Foster, John S., III, *Law of Meetings, Conventions and Trade Shows: Meetings and Liability,* The Law Offices of John S. Foster, Atlanta, Georgia, 1995.

Owen, Harrison, *Open Space Technology: A User's Guide,* Berrett-Koehler Publishers Inc., San Francisco, California, 1997.

Power, Mary, "2006 Economic Forecast: A Strong and Growing Marketplace," *PCMA Convene,* November 2005.

Russell, Michelle, "Convene's 15th Annual Meetings Market Survey: Consistent Upward Trend," *PCMA Convene,* March 2006.

Scott, Bill, *Planning Accessible Meetings: A Guide to ADA Compliance,* American Society of Association Executives, Washington, DC, 1998.

Turner, Peter, "Meetings Professionals Examine Core Competencies," *Meetings & Expositions Newsletter,* American Society of Association Executives, August 1998.

About the Author

Dawn M. Mancuso, MAM, CAE is the executive director/CEO of the Association of Air Medical Services in Alexandria, Virginia.

Review Questions

The role of the association meeting planner has changed quickly in the last decade. Here are a few questions about this expanding role when looking at the meetings department:

1. What role should a meeting planner play in adding to the value proposition offered to members by his/her association?

2. How do meetings play a role in raising the visibility of the sponsoring organization? How can the meeting planner maximize the positive aspects of this enhanced visibility while mitigating the risks associated with the negative aspects of a higher profile?

3. What changes are taking place in the hospitality marketplace that are changing how meeting planners are doing their jobs? What tools are available to assist planners in coping with these external changes?

4. How would you define the core competencies of the meeting planner today? What would you project to be the core competencies needed in the decade ahead? What are some creative ways of building these core competencies?

33

Legal Issues in Association Standard Setting, Certification and Accreditation Programs, and Codes of Ethics

Jeffrey S. Tenenbaum & Beth A. Caseman

A SSOCIATION STANDARD-SETTING PROGRAMS, CERTIFICATION and accreditation activities, and member codes of ethics provide valuable benefits, not only to associations and their members, but also to industry, government, and the general public. However, to successfully establish, operate, and enforce such programs, association executives must have a basic understanding of, and take measures to protect the association from, the potentially significant legal risks.

Although clearly in the public interest and of benefit to members and others, standard setting by associations raises risks of legal liability under antitrust law, copyright and patent law, and under common law theories of due process, negligence, and warranty, among others. An association's certification and accreditation programs and code of ethics also may incur risk of legal liability under antitrust law and under theories of due process, negligence and warranty, and defamation. Courts generally are extremely reluctant to second-guess the reasonableness of an association's standard-setting and certification programs and member codes of ethics. Yet the costs, burdens, and distractions of mounting a defense to a lawsuit can be overwhelming. Fortunately, there are steps associations can take in structuring and administering such programs to minimize the risk of being sued in the first instance, and, if a lawsuit does materialize, to ensure that the association will prevail. In addition, appropriate errors and omissions insurance can help protect the association against the financial burdens of such litigation.

Outlined below are the principal areas of legal risk that associations encounter in connection with the operation of standard-setting programs, certification and accreditation programs, and member codes of ethics: antitrust, copyright and patent law, due process, negligence (liability to third parties), defamation, compliance with the

Americans with Disabilities Act, and tax. Other theories of liability exist as well—such as theories of warranty and enterprise liability—but the areas of legal risk outlined here make up the majority of claims filed against associations in connection with standard setting, certification and accreditation programs, and codes of ethics. Note that not all of these forms of liability apply to all three types of programs; for instance, the Americans with Disabilities Act applies to certification programs (i.e., testing), but not to standard setting or codes of ethics. The forms of liability as they apply to specific programs are made clear in each section below.

Antitrust

Antitrust laws generally prohibit anticompetitive acts in restraint of trade. The primary federal antitrust laws that affect associations are Section 1 of the Sherman Act and Section 5 of the Federal Trade Commission Act. Section 1 of the Sherman Act states, in part: "Every contract, combination in the form of trust or otherwise, or conspiracy, in restraint of trade or commerce among the several States, or with foreign nations, is hereby declared to be illegal." Associations are, by definition, combinations of competitors and thus particularly susceptible to allegations of antitrust abuse.

The key factor in an antitrust challenge to an association's standard setting, certification activities, or code of ethics is whether the association's actions in establishing or enforcing standards or rules of conduct are *unreasonably* anticompetitive within the meaning of the antitrust laws. Any standard or rule adopted by a group of competitors (e.g., a trade or professional association) that discriminates against, excludes, or damages other competitors may potentially violate the antitrust laws. Under the rule of reason, courts will look at all of the facts and circumstances to determine whether the association's program, on balance, restrains competition in the relevant market more than it promotes it.

For example, unsuccessful applicants for certification, or those whose certification is revoked, may seek to use the antitrust laws to obtain certification or to obtain damages for the failure to certify. An association may be held liable under the antitrust laws if the challenger can demonstrate that (i) certification is essential in order to effectively compete in the market, *and* (ii) the program's exclusion was the result of unreasonable or invalid standards or criteria or of unfair or inappropriate procedures.

Certifying bodies generally have broad discretion in setting and implementing certification requirements. Courts are reluctant to second-guess technical standards— such as those used as the basis for certification decisions—as long as the standards are objectively established and substantively justifiable. A certification program that is designed to, and does in fact, protect and promote the economic health of a particular industry or profession or the welfare of the industry's or profession's customers or clients generally will be deemed to be more pro-competitive than anticompetitive—even though those who fail to achieve certification may find it more difficult to compete in the market.

In contrast, certification programs that are anticompetitive, discriminatory, unrelated to objective standards, or implemented without fair procedures are likely to attract antitrust challenges. In addition, certification programs that charge an unreasonably high price to apply for or receive certification or recertification or that require membership in the sponsoring association as a prerequisite to obtaining certification ("tying arrangements") are subject to antitrust challenge.

Similarly, standards for conduct contained in an association's code of ethics, which seek to guard against immoral or unethical behavior, must be reasonably tied to a pro-competitive purpose, such as discouraging fraud or deception in the profession, and also must provide procedural fairness to affected members or applicants. An association's membership restriction may have strong pro-competitive justifications, but if the restriction is applied arbitrarily or subjectively, the association still may be at antitrust risk. The association's code of ethics and the process for enforcing the code should be stated plainly and objectively in publicly-available association documents. A well-drafted code of ethics will put members and applicants on notice not only of rules of ethical conduct all members must follow, but also the procedural steps the association will follow in resolving alleged violations of those rules.

In the standard-setting context, antitrust laws and enforcers acknowledge that standard-setting is generally pro-competitive. However, standard-setting bodies may provide a forum for collusion among competitors. For example, courts have found violation of the antitrust laws where members of an association conspired to release an interpretation of a standard that was unfavorable to a competitor and where an association recruited new members to vote for a standard that excluded certain competitors in the industry.

Standard Setting, Intellectual Property, and Antitrust. It is often necessary to incorporate intellectual property into standards. Standard-setting bodies are thus challenged with balancing (i) the individual ownership rights recognized by patent and copyright laws; (ii) the competition values protected by the antitrust laws; and (iii) the need for compatibility of competitors' products.

The law of patents requires an inventor seeking a patent to prove that the inventor has developed a novel, useful, and non-obvious process or product. The grant of a patent gives one the right to exclude others from making, using, or selling the claimed technology for 20 years from the date of application filing. Patent applications are secret during the period of review, which can take years. Typical types of patents include utility patents, design patents, plant patents, and the business methods patent, which has taken on tremendous importance in the digital economy.

Copyright law provides narrower protection than patent law—it merely protects "expression," defined as the original arrangement of symbols of communication based on the creative choice of the author. It does not protect ideas, processes, methods of operation, or facts.

There is a fundamental conflict between the exclusive rights granted to an inventor by patent and/or copyright law and the necessity of interoperability in the digital economy. Patent issues are implicated in standard setting where patented material is "essential" to a standard (i.e., those adopting the standard would not be able to implement it without infringing on the patent). The "essential facilities" doctrine says that denial of access to a resource essential to competition in a downstream market may violate the antitrust laws.

For example, an industry member's failure to disclose ownership of a patent design incorporated into a standard, when participating in the standard-setting process and promoting a standard that incorporates that design, may be seen as an anticompetitive act in direct violation of antitrust laws, particularly when the patent holder then seeks to enforce the patent against infringers adopting the standard.

This conflict can be reconciled at the outset of any standard-setting process by making sure that the process is fair, access to proprietary information is not unduly limited, and the standards adopted have good technical support. Standard-setting bodies should require members (and any other participants in the standard-setting process) to disclose any patents or pending patent applications involving a contemplated standard, and require either free licensing of intellectual property incorporated into a standard, or at minimum, licensing on "reasonable" and "nondiscriminatory" terms.

Due Process

As noted above, in addition to antitrust issues, associations also may incur legal risk for failing to afford members and others "due process" based on a lack of either substantive or procedural fairness. Substantive fairness requires the use of objective standards reasonably related to a legitimate organizational purpose, while procedural fairness requires the uniform application of such standards.

To minimize the risk of liability, it is critical for associations to carefully establish and strictly, consistently, and objectively follow their own written rules and procedures for the administration of any standard-setting or certification program or code of ethics. Associations are legally bound to follow their own rules and regulations in setting professional and product standards.

Courts usually will defer to substantive standards established by an association. However, standards set and decisions made by an association in applying those standards may be overturned if the standards, or the association's decisions in applying them, are arbitrary, capricious, or discriminatory, where they are influenced by bias or prejudice, or where they lack good faith. Courts are likely to scrutinize the fairness of the procedures (as opposed to the standards themselves) more closely because these are matters with which they are more familiar.

At minimum, procedural due process requires associations to provide notice of a potential adverse decision to a member, prospective member, or applicant for certification, to provide an opportunity for the affected individual to respond, and to provide the individual with an opportunity to appeal any adverse decision. Of course, it is incumbent on an association to both have the relevant procedures in place and actually follow all due process obligations it places on itself through such procedures. In addition, fundamental fairness requires that similarly-situated persons and entities be treated the same.

Negligence

Reliance on the fact of membership, certification, or accreditation of a professional, entity, product, or service can, in some cases, cause the association that granted the membership, certification, or accreditation to be held liable when a patient, client, or customer suffers harm (physical, financial, or otherwise) at the hands of the member or certified individual, entity, or product. The most common claim is that the association was negligent in granting membership, certification, or accreditation and should therefore be liable for resulting injuries.

This liability risk to third parties generally means negligence liability (a form of tort liability), but it is sometimes couched in claims such as misrepresentation, failure to warn, warranty, strict liability, and enterprise liability. For instance, the injured party may allege that the association *warranted* or *guaranteed* the individuals, entities, products, or services certified or granted membership by the association and therefore should be responsible (under a breach of warranty theory) for resulting injuries to those who purchase, utilize, or participate in them.

Court decisions holding associations and certifying bodies liable for negligence in the context of self-regulatory programs and certification programs are relatively rare. This type of liability is subject to a number of conditions and remains infrequent, although there have been several high-profile cases in recent years holding associations liable for negligence arising from their self-regulatory programs. In short, an association generally will be found liable under the tort of negligence only if the injured party can prove all of the elements of negligence liability:

1. **Duty.** The first question courts ask is whether the association owed a duty of care to the third party (the injured plaintiff who utilized the services of a certified vendor, for instance). While there is generally no duty of care owed to third parties, some courts have held that once an organization undertakes to set standards or inspect, test, or otherwise certify individuals, entities, products, or services, it should reasonably know that third parties might rely on those standards or certifications, and therefore must exercise reasonable care in doing so.

2. **Breach of duty (negligence).** The court will next determine whether the certifying body failed to act with reasonable care (i.e., acted negligently) in granting the certification or in setting a particular standard. In other words, the association is obligated to use due diligence and reasonable care in promulgating the certification standards and in applying them to applicants for certification. For instance, a mail-order certification program that establishes no meaningful standards or that exercises no real scrutiny in evaluating applicants could be at risk for breach of its duty of care.

3. **Reliance.** It must be proven that the plaintiff relied upon the association's certification in utilizing the certified individual, entity, product, or service. It generally is not sufficient for a plaintiff merely to show that the association certified a vendor, for instance, and later an injury occurred; the plaintiff must establish that it was because of the association's certification that the vendor's products or services were utilized. If the association can establish that the plaintiff did not know of the association's certification or that the certification was not a material factor in the decision to utilize the vendor's product or service, then it may be able to avoid liability.

4. **Causation.** The negligence of the certifying association must be considered to be a "proximate cause" of the injury to the ultimate user (the plaintiff). While the most direct cause of the plaintiff's injury generally is the negligence of the certified party or product—not the certifying association—where the certifying body expects the public to rely upon the certification, and the injured party does just that in selecting the certified party or product, the causation and reliance criteria both may be met. In other words, if reliance is established, causation likely will be as well.

If any one of these four elements cannot be established, then liability generally will not result. Finally, there must be measurable injury (physical, financial, or psychological) to the plaintiff for any damages to exist.

Defamation

Defamation is the oral utterance (slander) or written publication (libel) of false or misleading facts or false or misleading implied facts that are derogatory or damaging to an individual's, entity's, or product's reputation. Accusing someone of dishonesty or other moral deficiency or of professional or business deficiency raises significant risk of defamation liability.

The risk of defamation is likely to arise in the context of certification activities and codes of ethics (i) when an individual, entity, or product is denied certification or when an individual or entity is denied or expelled from membership, and then damaging statements are made (to one or more third parties) by a representative of the certifying body or association about the individual, entity, or product; or (ii) when sensitive, potentially damaging information about a member or an applicant for membership or certification becomes known to the certifying body or association during the certification or ethics enforcement process, and that information is subsequently disclosed to one or more third parties (intentionally or unintentionally).

Even those who believe they are communicating the truth may commit defamation. For a statement to be defamatory, it must be *actually* communicated to someone other than the speaker or author. The defamed individual or entity may sue anyone who publishes, prints, or repeats the defamation, and, depending on the circumstances, may recover from the speaker(s) or author(s) money damages to compensate for the harm to reputation and to punish the speaker(s) or author(s) as well. Truth is an absolute defense to any defamation claim.

In some circumstances, legal "privileges" apply that may protect the speaker or author from liability even where a statement might otherwise be defamatory. The three principal privileges in the association context are (i) where the speaker takes reasonable precautions to ensure the statement's accuracy, including making reasonable inquiry; (ii) where the statement concerns a public official or figure, the speaker will not be liable unless the speaker *actually knew* the accusations were false and made the statement in reckless disregard of its truth or falsity; and (iii) publication or communication of a derogatory statement within an association's governing body—for the purpose of promoting a common interest—may be protected by a "qualified privilege." For example, deliberations among a certification board concerning certification-related proceedings are likely protected by this qualified privilege. Where this privilege applies, statements may give rise to defamation liability only if motivated by spite or ill-will or if communicated to persons outside of the management or governing group.

Americans with Disabilities Act Compliance

Associations sponsoring and administering certification and accreditation programs are subject to the requirements of the federal Americans with Disabilities Act (ADA). The requirements of the ADA of most relevance to certifying bodies are the specific and extensive standards contained in the law for private entities that conduct examinations and courses relating to applications, licensing and certification, or credentialing for educational, professional, or trade purposes. The U.S. Department of Justice's regulations require that certifying bodies "offer such examinations or courses in a place and manner accessible to persons with disabilities or offer alternative accessible arrangements for such individuals."

Note that the ADA does not apply if an individual seeking certification does not have a covered disability. For instance, U.S. Supreme Court decisions have clarified that available corrective and mitigating measures, such as medication or medical aids, must be considered in determining whether or not an individual has a disability under the ADA. Thus, for example, the Court held that correctable myopia is not a disability, nor is high blood pressure controlled with medication.

A certifying body is responsible for selecting and administering the certification examination in a place and manner which ensures that the examination tests what the examination purports to measure, rather than testing the individual's disability, such as impaired sensory, manual, or speaking skills (unless those skills are what the examination is designed to test). This means ensuring that (i) testing places are accessible to individuals with disabilities and (ii) auxiliary aids and services are made available to enable individuals with disabilities to take the examination, in accordance with the ADA's requirements.

For example, for individuals with hearing impairments, oral instructions or other orally-delivered materials could be provided through an interpreter, assistive listening device, or other applicable means. For individuals with visual impairments, the examination and answer sheets could utilize large print or Braille, could be provided via audiotape, or could be provided through the use of qualified readers and transcribers to read questions and record answers.

A certifying body does not have to provide auxiliary aids and services in all cases. If providing a particular auxiliary aid or service would fundamentally change the examination or result in an undue burden on the certifying body, it does not need to be provided. This determination is case-specific.

Regarding who decides what type of auxiliary aid or service should be provided, when possible, the individual with the disability should be consulted to determine the type of aid or service that may be needed. When more than one type of auxiliary aid or service will enable a person with a disability to participate effectively, a certifying body may choose what aid or service to make available.

Aside from auxiliary aids or services, other types of modifications may be required. For instance, it may be necessary to modify the manner in which the test is administered. For example, if an individual has an impairment that makes writing difficult, it may be necessary to give that individual more time to complete the exam or to permit the typing of answers.

The individual with a disability may *not* be required to bear the cost of the aid or modification. The certifying body must bear the cost of the aid or modification. However, a certifying body is only required to provide auxiliary aids or modifications that do not pose an *undue burden* on a certifying body and do not *fundamentally change* the examination.

Examinations must be administered in facilities that are accessible to disabled individuals, or alternative accessible arrangements must be made. If the facility in which the examination is offered is not accessible, the exam may be administered to an individual with a disability in a different room or another location. The alternative location should provide comparable conditions to the conditions in which the test is administered to others.

All testing locations need not be accessible and offer specially designed exams; however, if an examination for individuals with disabilities is administered in an alternative accessible location or manner, it must be offered as often and in as timely a manner as other examinations. Examinations must be offered to individuals with disabilities at locations that are as convenient as the location(s) of other examinations.

Individuals with disabilities cannot be required to file their applications to take the examination earlier than the deadline for other applicants in order to enable accommodations to be made. However, a certifying body may require individuals with disabilities to provide advance notice to the certifying body of their disability and of any aids and/or modifications that might be required, so long as the deadline for doing so is not earlier than the deadline for others applying to take the examination.

A certifying body may require applicants to provide documentation of the existence and nature of the disability as evidence that they are entitled to an aid or modification, so long as the request is reasonable and limited to the need for the modification or aid requested. Appropriate documentation might include a letter from a doctor or other health care professional or evidence of a prior diagnosis or accommodation (such as eligibility for a special education program). The applicant can be required to bear the cost of providing such documentation, but he or she cannot be charged for the cost of any modifications or auxiliary aids provided for the examination.

Finally, the rules for courses (such as educational seminars of any type offered by associations) are similar to those for examinations. They generally require that modifications be made in courses offered by private entities to ensure that the place and manner in which the course is given are accessible to individuals with disabilities. The most significant difference is that the general rule for courses applies to *all* individuals with disabilities, not just those with "impaired sensory, manual, or speaking skills." Modifications in courses may include changes in the length of time allowed for completing the course, substitution of course requirements, or adapting the manner in which the course is conducted or materials are distributed. Advance notice of the opportunity to obtain materials in alternative formats must be provided to disabled individuals. Appropriate auxiliary aids also must be provided, unless to do so would fundamentally alter the course or create an undue burden. If courses cannot be administered in a facility accessible to individuals with disabilities, comparable alternative arrangements must be made. Such arrangements may include offering the course through the Internet, DVD, videotape, CD-ROM, or prepared notes. The selection or choice of courses available to individuals with disabilities may not be restricted.

Tax

It is conceivable, although very unlikely, that an association that is exempt from federal income tax under Internal Revenue Code ("Code") Section 501(c)(6) could run afoul of the Code restrictions that prohibit such organizations from providing substantial "particular services" to members. Such a restriction might apply in the event that the Internal Revenue Service (IRS) reviewed an association's code of ethics enforcement program and determined that in fact, the program's primary purpose is the mediation of intra-membership business disputes, as opposed to the promotion or furtherance of the industry or profession as a whole. Even if that were the case, an association would only be in danger of losing its tax-exempt status if the IRS were to determine that the activity constituted greater than 50 percent of the association's total activities. However, if the questioned activity accounted for less than 50 percent of the association's total activities, the IRS still might seek to tax fees received by the association in exchange for the provision of such services as (taxable) unrelated business income.

Steps to Minimizing Risk

Court decisions involving association standard setting, certification and accreditation programs, and codes of ethics suggest that taking the following steps in connection with such activities will significantly limit the association's liability risks and protect its interests:

1. **Ensure that valid, objective bases support each standard, certification requirement, and code of ethics provision, to the extent possible.** Standards, certification and accreditation requirements, and codes of ethics should be clear and unambiguous, reasonable, fair, and objectively grounded. If used in connection with a certification program, standards should be based on supporting data or on a respected body of industry or governmental opinion linking each particular standard to the qualities that the certification purports to measure. Where possible, standards should be directed at, and focus on, the *ends*, not the *means*. Where the means are specified, they must be legitimately, demonstrably, and directly related to the objectives. Equivalent standards or alternative paths to certification should be established wherever possible. As with the standards themselves, the determination as to whether requirements for certification have been satisfied should focus on the ends, not the means. There must be valid, demonstrable, and reasonable bases upon which to determine that applicants for certification have met the requirements. Standards, requirements for certification, and code of ethics provisions should never be arbitrary or capricious, or vague or ambiguous. Procedures should be developed that document the reasonableness of, and the objective basis for, the proposed standards, certification requirements, or code of ethics provisions.

2. **Make sure that standards, certification requirements, and code of ethics provisions are no more stringent or rigid than necessary** to ensure that the specified competency or quality levels have been attained or to ensure that minimum acceptable levels of conduct are met.

3. **Specific commercial or economic considerations should play no role in the setting of standards or certification requirements or in the setting or application of code of ethics provisions.** In addition, standards, certification programs, and codes of ethics should never be created or used for the purpose of raising, lowering, or stabilizing prices or fees, excluding competitors from the market, or limiting the supply of products or services.

4. **Prior to finalizing standards, certification requirements, and code of ethics provisions, provide interested parties with notice of the proposed standards or provisions and an opportunity to comment on them.** Fairly and objectively consider such comments in finalizing the standards, certification requirements, or code of ethics.

5. **Periodically review and update all standards to ensure that they are current and reflect new legal, technological, and other developments.** The association's code of ethics also should be reviewed and updated periodically to ensure that it is current. Provide appropriate opportunities for public notice and comment whenever standards or code of ethics provisions are modified, and carefully consider such comments in the revision process. In addition, document any and all complaints or concerns about the standards or code of ethics, and revise the standards or ethics provisions accordingly if appropriate.

6. **Administer each process objectively and uniformly without subjectivity, favoritism, or discrimination.** There must be no bias, partiality, or inconsistency in establishing or operating the association's standard setting, certification, or code of ethics program. Those administering the program must scrupulously, consistently, and objectively follow the rules governing the process.

7. **Require full disclosure by those involved in the standard setting, ethics enforcement, or certification process of any factor that might be considered bias or a conflict of interest.** Require recusal or removal if a bias or conflict is particularly severe or pervasive. Full disclosure and appropriate checks and balances generally are effective mechanisms for safely managing most potential conflicts of interest. In addition, reduced volunteer involvement and increased association staff involvement may assist in objectivity and the absence of bias in the ethics enforcement and certification process.

8. **Require participants in the standard-setting process to disclose any patents or pending patent applications involving a contemplated standard.** Require either free licensing of intellectual property incorporated into a standard or, at minimum, licensing on "reasonable" and "nondiscriminatory" terms.

9. **Before discipline is enforced or certification is denied or revoked, individuals who would receive such discipline or who seek certification should be provided due process.** This includes providing these individuals with (i) notice of an adverse decision and a meaningful opportunity to respond to the notice, (ii) a hearing before a panel of peers, none of whom has a direct economic or personal interest in the outcome of the proceeding, (iii) the right to be represented by another person, including an attorney, and to submit evidence and arguments in defense, (iv) the right to examine the evidence and to cross-examine witnesses (if applicable), (v) the right to a written decision explaining the reasons underlying it, and (vi) the right to appeal an adverse decision to a higher-level decision-making body within the association.

10. **Base decisions with regard to certification and ethics enforcement completely and exclusively on the record of review and not on extraneous, anecdotal, subjective, or other outside sources of information.** The proceedings and all adverse allegations, complaints, and actions that arise in connection with the process should remain strictly confidential. While nothing prevents a certification program

from publicizing the names of, and information about, those who are certified, care should be taken to avoid any explicit or implicit disparagement of those who are not certified. While it is acceptable for a certifying association to verify that an entity is not currently certified, no further details should be provided.

11. **Use a copyright notice on all standards and related materials (that are subject to copyright protection) and register such standards and materials with the U.S. Copyright Office.** With regard to standard setting and certification programs, this will minimize the risk of copyright infringement, maximize copyright rights, and facilitate enforcement of such rights. Be sure that the association owns or has the right to use the entire contents of such materials (*e.g.*, obtaining written copyright assignments from all non-association employees that participate in the standard-setting process). In addition, as listings of certified entities generally are not protectable under U.S. copyright laws, use a shrink-wrap license or other form of contractual commitment to place explicit, binding limits and conditions on the use of the list. The shrink-wrap license also can be a useful vehicle to disclaim any endorsement or guarantee of the certified entities by the association.

12. **Widely publicize the availability of the association's certification program and permit application to all who choose to apply.** Do not limit participation in the certification program to only members of the sponsoring association. Certification programs should be open both to association members and nonmembers on the same terms and conditions. Moreover, nothing in excess of a reasonable price should be charged to apply for or receive certification or recertification. However, fees charged to nonmembers for certification may be higher than those charged to association members to reflect any membership dues or assessments that contribute to funding the program.

13. **Avoid "grandfathering" of those who do not meet all current certification standards.** Require regular recertification as appropriate to ensure that those who are certified continue to meet the program's standards. In addition, review the certification process itself on a periodic basis to ensure it is being properly administered.

14. **Comply with the Americans with Disabilities Act.** Ensure that all certification examinations—as well as all courses that prepare applicants for certification exams—are administered in strict compliance with the specific requirements imposed by the federal Americans with Disabilities Act and implementing regulations.

15. **Maintain strict security regarding all aspects of the association's certification process.** Any missing, stolen, or copied examination booklets, for instance, can have a severe impact on the integrity of the certification process.

16. **Use a trademark notice in connection with any certification logo or seal, and register the mark with the U.S. Patent & Trademark Office (either as a certification mark or as a service mark).** Registering will minimize the risk of trademark

infringement, maximize trademark rights, and facilitate enforcement of such rights. Be sure the association's use of the mark does not infringe on anyone else's trademark rights. In addition, codify the terms and conditions of, and limitations on, use of the mark by certified entities in a written agreement, possibly as part of the certification application form or in connection with distribution of the mark. Be sure to include provisions, among others, designed to prevent false or misleading use of the mark and to prohibit any further use upon decertification. Note that the federal *Lanham Act,* and similar state laws, prohibit the use of any false or misleading terms, names or symbols, or any other false or misleading descriptions or representations, that are likely to deceive the public with respect to the affiliation of the user with a particular organization.

17. **Include binding limitation of liability and indemnification provisions in the certification application form (or other document)** to absolve the association from liability to those who are certified and to hold the association harmless from lawsuits by those injured by the acts or omissions of certified entities.

18. **Make it clear that it is voluntary.** Ensure that participation in and use of standards or a certification program are completely voluntary.

19. **Do not limit participation in the standard-setting process to members only.** Invite nonmembers of the sponsoring association to participate in the process.

20. **Use written disclaimers.** Where appropriate, use written disclaimers to clarify the association's limited role with respect to the use of, and responsibility for, the standards and to clarify the association's limited role with respect to lack of responsibility for, and absence of, guarantees or warranties of certified products, services, or entities. If and where appropriate, require use of similar disclaimers by those that receive certification.

21. **Where appropriate and feasible, consider utilizing and participating in the standard-setting procedures of the American National Standards Institute (ANSI).** Where a certification program is involved, consider obtaining accreditation of the certification program by ANSI.

22. **Maintain sufficient insurance to cover the liability risks of the standard-setting and/or certification program.** Some association professional liability insurance (APLI) policies provide coverage for certain (but not all) claims arising from standard-setting and certification programs as part of the basic policy, although some with coverage sub-limits. Other APLI policies will not cover such activities without an endorsement to the policy. Be sure to fully disclose the association's standard-setting and certification activities in the insurance application. Importantly, APLI policies do not cover bodily injury or property damage claims arising from these programs. Stand-alone standard-setting and certification insurance policies are available and may be necessary to insure against these particular risks. Adequate insurance should be a prerequisite to the operation of any association standard-setting or certification program.

23. **Avoid any implicit or explicit guarantee or warranty of certified products, services, entities, or individuals, including members.** To this end, avoid "puffery." Do not overstate how a product, service, professional, or company performs, and do not use superlatives such as "never fails" or "safest" in describing those that are members or certified. Do not allow members to express or imply that they are endorsed by the association by virtue of being accepted as a member.

About the Authors

Jeffrey S. Tenenbaum, Esq. is a partner, and **Beth A. Caseman, Esq.** is an associate, in the association practice group of Venable LLP. Both are resident in the firm's Washington, DC office.

This publication is not intended to provide legal advice or opinion. Such advice can only be provided in response to specific factual situations.

Review Questions

A disgruntled applicant for certification has taken the professional certification exam offered by your association on seven separate occasions and has failed each time, despite the fact that she's been a successful member of the profession for 15 years. She writes to the association demanding an accommodation. She's never been good at standardized multiple choice tests, she says, and she believes the association should allow her to take the test in a different format. In addition, she maintains the questions on the exam are subject to multiple interpretations. She also maintains that the test questions are designed to exclude certain members of the profession from becoming certified.

1. Is your association required to grant her an accommodation under the Americans with Disabilities Act? What if she sends a doctor's note along with the letter, indicating that she has attention deficit disorder or dyslexia? What if her doctor's note simply states that she has high blood pressure and does not handle stress well?

2. If she is able to show that the association's exam questions were written to exclude certain members of the profession (a tough burden), how might your association successfully defend an antitrust lawsuit? Does it matter that she's already a highly successful member of the profession?

3. In the course of the certification board's discussions of the applicant's request, one of the board members says, "Oh, I knew her in college. She's a complete loon." Is the statement defamatory? Is it protected by a qualified privilege? What if the comment is incorporated into the minutes, which are circulated to the association's senior staff members? What if the minutes are posted on a publicly accessible section of the association's Web site?

4. Is the association's certification board required to respond to the letter? May the applicant sue solely on the basis of the association's failure to respond? On what grounds?

34

Certification and Accreditation Programs

Michael S. Hamm, CMC

S THE WORLD GROWS in complexity, more people seem to be searching for reliable ways to measure the performance of individuals and institutions. The association world strives to meet this demand—and exhibit leadership in their respective fields at the same time—through the development of certification and accreditation programs.

Some confusion surrounds the meaning of these terms. *Certification* usually implies the measurement of competency for individuals; *accreditation* usually refers to a process of standards setting and compliance measurement for systems, organizations, or institutions. According to *Policies and Procedures in Association Management 2006,* a survey conducted by the American Society of Association Executives, the two top reasons that associations develop certification programs are to ensure professional competence/establish standards and to enhance the prestige of the profession. While typically developed for the same reasons, accreditation programs have traditionally been viewed as a regulatory and quality-enhancing mechanism for the educational world, although a variety of businesses and trades have implemented the concept as well.

Certification and accreditation programs are also referred to as *credentialing* activities, a broader term that encompasses the various licensure programs administered by government agencies. Education and training organizations also grant credentials, but these forms of recognition are not traditionally viewed as certification programs. Certificate programs offered by associations and academia can create confusion as well.

The *NOCA Guide to Understanding Credentialing Concepts* defines a certificate program as a training program on a topic for which participants receive a certificate after attendance and/or completion of the coursework. Some programs also require successful demonstration of attainment of the course objectives. One who completes a professional certificate program is known as a certificate holder. A credential is usually not granted at the completion of a certificate program. There are three types of certificate programs: knowledge-based, curriculum-based, and attendance- or participation-based.

Some organizations refer to completion of one of these programs as demonstrating certification in a particular field or discipline. In general, however, satisfactory completion of acceptable educational programs is only one component of a valid and reliable national certification program.

Questioning the Need

Certification and accreditation programs tend to be long-term commitments that an association should enter into only after careful evaluation and thought and with demonstrated evidence of membership support. Any organization considering the development of such a program should first conduct a thorough strategic analysis. During this analysis, raise the following questions:

- Does the proposed credentialing process fit into the current or new mission and objectives of the association?

- Do the volunteer leaders understand all of the ramifications of initiating a credentialing program?

- Is your association the best organization to meet this need? Should you seek partners or pursue this project as a joint venture with other national organizations respected in your field or discipline?

- Could your field or discipline accomplish the goals of a credentialing program with an alternative system?

- Will volunteer leaders commit the appropriate level of resources to develop a credible and defensible program? "Half-baked" credentialing efforts frequently create more problems than benefits for all of the parties concerned.

  A credentialing program developed without adequate planning and design can backfire when stakeholders and applicants question its basic validity and reliability. These issues may not be apparent in the beginning, but they certainly will arise if the credentialing process assumes a high stakes role in the field or discipline. It is always easier to develop a program based on this assumption, rather than assume that the process can be redesigned in the future if challenges develop.

- How will your association address the needs of all of the stakeholders who will interact with the credentialing system? Examples of stakeholder groups that frequently need to be considered include:
  - Association members
  - Members of similar and even competing organizations

- The public and consumers of the goods or services provided by your members
- Employers and businesses involved with your field or discipline
- Government agencies (local, state, and national)
- The media
- Educational organizations
- International interests (in some fields)
- Entities and organizations unique to your field or discipline

- What methods or means will you use to assess the competence of individuals or the performance of organizations in an accreditation program?
- How will a proposed private-sector credentialing effort supplement or work with existing or potential future licensure programs in the field of interest?

Credentialing systems can lead associations to a new and broader role in their respective fields. One of the most challenging aspects of developing a new credentialing system is adjusting to the fact that active standards-setting organizations will interact with a variety of stakeholders in the development of these programs; to be effective a credentialing system must address the varied needs of these groups in some fashion. In this sense, credentialing initiatives can quickly move beyond the traditional membership service focus of many associations. There is no legal requirement that a certification or accreditation program serve the particular needs of a broad community of stakeholders, but volunteer leaders will quickly understand that the program's credibility will suffer if its focus is limited to association members.

Benefits to Associations

Well-developed certification and accreditation programs can become the premier vehicles for defining excellence, quality, and acceptable performance in a field. In this sense, these programs have the potential to become one of the most important initiatives undertaken or supported by a national association. Credentialing programs can enhance the reputation of the association, provide a valuable public service and, in some cases, minimize or prevent government regulation of a field or discipline. The major stakeholder groups frequently rely upon and use strong credentialing programs.

Certification programs often increase the demand for new and targeted education/training programs to help candidates prepare for initial certification, and most certificants are interested in participating in advanced training to maintain their credentials. While independent certification bodies are not usually involved in encouraging association memberships, it is appropriate for certification bodies to identify approved organizations, including membership associations, which provide appropriate and timely education/training services. In this sense, certification bodies actually benefit from the existence of strong membership associations with comprehensive training resources. Associations also help support certification by citing the benefits of certification in their publications and including links to certification programs on their Web sites.

The relationship between associations and their credentialing programs can be mutually supportive, but all parties must be careful to avoid even the appearance of self-promotional activities that may not be in the best interests of the discipline and its other key stakeholders.

In the final analysis, a strong credentialing program has the potential to become a highly valued service for members. In some fields, the credential has become so important that members would give up their association membership before they would consider losing their certification or accreditation status. Keep this potential in mind during all aspects of the planning and evaluation of these programs.

Unfortunately, the potential power of these programs can lead to some abuses. Some stakeholders may place more importance on credentials than is warranted based upon an objective analysis of the outcomes achieved or the exaggerated claims made in promotional literature. For example, some people assume a certification guarantees that the individual who earned it is competent or believe an accreditation guarantees an organization will provide high-quality service. Credentialing bodies usually clarify the limitations of their recognition, but this "fine print" sometimes gets lost in promotional literature extolling the virtues of the credential.

Common Misconceptions

These seven misconceptions often arise in the course of program development:

1. **Credentialing programs are large sources of revenue for associations.** While certification programs can grow into strong revenue streams, there are no guarantees. Sound certification programs are expensive to develop, market, and operate, and the ultimate financial performance often depends upon a variety of factors related to the credential's importance within the workforce or job market. Generally, certification programs developed for larger target audiences have the best chance of generating profits.

   Accreditation programs sometimes take more time to develop, and the review process is usually more expensive and time consuming than that of a typical certification program. These factors tend to increase the costs of accreditation efforts and may create financial barriers for potential applicants. Larger programs can generate considerable amounts of revenue but, again, profitability depends upon a variety of factors related to the economics of the discipline or the field. Sometimes an association will develop an accreditation program for a small universe of applicants with the understanding that the effort may need to be permanently subsidized.

2. **"If we build it, they will come."** Associations often assume that a certification or accreditation program will thrive and grow based upon the group's sterling reputation rather than the real value conferred by the credential. This dangerous perception

is increased when the "blue ribbon" leadership of an organization is involved in creating and implementing the program.

While a strong organizational reputation and a well-respected standards-setting body can enhance interest in a credential, even the best programs need to invest in marketing and publicity efforts. No national association can assume that its strength and reputation are enough to persuade the market to accept a new credentialing effort.

3. **Our credentialing program can easily be managed by a staff member responsible for education or training.** Associations frequently underestimate the amount of time, money, and staff resources required to develop a sound certification or accreditation program. These false assumptions often lead an association to assign development and implementation responsibilities to a manager who already has a full plate of other duties, such as the director of education or membership. This person may quickly become overwhelmed upon realizing the magnitude of the challenge and the importance of the credentialing program to the sponsoring association. Association leaders need to allocate sufficient resources (both staff and dollars) if they expect to develop a credible and respectable credentialing initiative.

4. **If it doesn't work, we can end the experiment and move on to other projects.** Certainly, any service can be discontinued if it does not fulfill basic performance objectives. Credentialing programs, however, present some unique challenges in terms of their life cycles. Once your association has made a commitment to accredit organizations or to certify individuals, a growing population of stakeholders will come to rely on this service. Discontinuing this recognition raises a host of legal, financial, and public relations issues.

To an association, launching a new credentialing program is akin to a couple having a baby: The fundamental structure of the family changes forever, and the parents must assume the responsibilities and risks inherent in raising a child.

5. **The association will always control all aspects of the program.** The majority of credentialing efforts begin with the assistance of a parent association. Many programs evolve to the point where stakeholders' needs prompt the credentialing body to seek a separate and independent status. This issue is of particular importance when the credentialing body serves a significant population outside of the association membership.

Credentialing bodies also find it helpful to dissociate themselves from some of the lobbying and political concerns of the parent organization. While some association leaders would argue that management and control of standards-setting bodies is one of the highest priorities of a national membership organization, the public and other key stakeholders tend to be more comfortable with credentialing programs that are separate from the economic and political agendas of their respective associations. In many cases, it is best to plan for an independent status from the onset, to avoid the later complications of organizational change.

6. **The credential should be limited to members only.** While most credentialing efforts are developed to meet a need of the members, the most effective ones are not tied to any membership criteria for participation. The credibility of the credentialing effort is enhanced if it is viewed as a service to the public rather than a self-serving membership service.

Of course, members should be encouraged to participate in their association's credentialing program, and it is appropriate to offer discounted fees to members when an association is the primary sponsor of the effort—but no national certification program should limit participation to its members exclusively. Competency, quality, and acceptable performance have nothing to do with the payment of dues to an association or professional society.

7. **Credentialing will increase demand for other association services.** Certification and accreditation programs have the potential to boost interest in other services such as education and training, but they should not be developed for that purpose. A credible national credential should accommodate multiple concepts of quality, competency, and performance. This usually means that the parent association's educational resources are only one of many avenues available for achieving and maintaining competency or a level of performance in a particular field or discipline.

Associations cannot assume that competence can only be demonstrated by satisfactory completion of their particular course or educational program. You can build a certification or accreditation program around one association's or educational organization's model, but the reputation of the credential will never transcend this limited foundation.

Developing a Program

Here are the basic steps to follow:

- **Collect background information.** While the concept of credentialing is being considered, gather written materials and information from other association executives whose organizations sponsor similar programs. Staff as well as volunteer leaders can attend continuing education programs related to credentialing, and consultants can also assist in the information-gathering process.

- **Conduct market research.** After the governing body has made a commitment to pursuing a credentialing program, quantify the potential demand for the service and identify specific issues and concerns that need to be addressed during the development and implementation phases. Market research can include focus groups; individual conversations with members and representatives of the various stakeholder groups; and a formal feasibility study conducted by mail, fax, or computer. The feasibility study is, in essence, an insurance policy—it protects against "finger pointing" should a credentialing effort fail because of insufficient demand for the service.

- **Develop a business plan.** This document includes the relevant assumptions about the projected market for the credentialing activity, its place within the existing organizational structure, and assumptions about the expenses and revenues related to launching and sustaining the effort. Board approval of the business plan is usually secured prior to implementation of the program.

  The business plan should include strategies for marketing the credential—not only with the intention of telling the target audience and key stakeholder groups about it but also to create positive perceptions about the credential. Even a well-developed and credible certification or accreditation program can fail if it is not perceived properly by the target audience. Because the meaning of certification and accreditation often creates confusion, information regarding these concepts should be included in speeches, newsletters, journals, and annual meeting programs to help pave the way for this new service.

  Given the wide range of efforts required to reach the desired audiences, adequate funding is necessary in this area. Associations may use their existing marketing staffer or bring in specialized consultants with expertise in certification or accreditation marketing.

Additional actions to take during the planning phase include the following:

- Analyze the legal implications of launching a credentialing program, including the tax status of the new credentialing organization or its potential effect on the parent association's tax status. Consider consulting a specialist if your legal counsel does not have experience in credentialing issues.

- Review your directors' and officers' liability insurance to make sure that the policy covers this new service and the increased liability exposure it brings.

- Develop an appeals process and a supporting set of policies and procedures for its use. Legal counsel should, at a minimum, review all the appeals policies and procedures.

- Have legal counsel review promotional literature to make certain it does not misrepresent the true meaning of the new program. An example of misrepresentation would be a statement within the promotional literature claiming that certified individuals are more competent than practitioners who do not possess the credential. While this statement may be true in some cases, a certification organization could get into trouble if it became involved in a legal challenge and had no evidence to back up the claim.

- Decide what type of examination, assessment instrument, or format for the review process will be used.

- If applicable, incorporate the standards of government agencies or private recognition bodies into the credentialing initiative.

- Develop a policy for dealing with requests for "grandfathering"—waiving requirements for a selected group based on the assumption that the group's members have demonstrated some level of competence that merits special treatment.

  Obviously, grandfathering can potentially pose trouble for any new credentialing effort. Before waiving requirements for a large number of applicants in an attempt to build "buy-in" for a new credentialing effort, consider the likely reactions of the various stakeholder groups. The practice could influence the credential's credibility and acceptance by other recognition bodies.

- Establish policies for continuing competence. Most reputable certification and accreditation programs require holders of the credential to demonstrate ongoing compliance with certain criteria and standards.

- Develop a method for dealing with individuals or organizations that fail to demonstrate the qualities that permit continued maintenance of the credential. This discipline concept adds credibility to a credential, yet the legal aspects of removing a credential are significant. Give this matter careful attention and study.

One of the key issues to consider in planning a new certification or accreditation program is the use of technology to improve efficiency and reduce costs. Computer-based testing is quite common in the certification world. Examination development, as well as item-writing work, is increasingly being accomplished on the Internet. Also, online applications for certification candidates have contributed to an easier application process and reduced reliance on paper records. Accreditation applications are also available online, and accreditation Web sites are often used to provide updated training for site visitors. Use of this software does add additional cost to the development of a new program, but the benefits of using the most efficient technology will usually pay off over time.

Structure and Governance Issues

Some associations handle accreditation and certification services internally through a committee or special office. While this option may seem most desirable from a management and control perspective, the credibility of the credential will be limited if it is viewed as just another membership service.

Independent credentialing boards or commissions can be more credible in the world beyond the membership arena. Sometimes an association will develop an external board or commission but stay involved in the program by providing financial and staff support.

Management staff support for credentialing efforts can be provided by hiring a new CEO with credentialing experience or assigning this responsibility to a senior manager within the parent association. Another alternative is to contract with an association management company or a consultant to provide this service; this sidesteps political problems that might arise when the interests of the credentialing body and the parent association differ.

Governance is another critical area to address as part of a credentialing effort. The governing body of a credentialing program has a powerful role in the field. The success or failure of the effort depends, to a certain extent, upon the reputation this group has among the target audience and other key stakeholders.

Members of the governing body should be selected for their ability to ensure that the credentialing effort maintains the highest standards of performance and accountability to the stakeholder groups, not for political reasons. Their role is challenging at best, but even more so when the credentialing effort is primarily aimed at protecting the public. Including public members on the governing body is important to any credentialing effort; ideally, those members should not have any political or economic ties to the profession or field of interest.

Evaluating Program Performance

Any new association program or service should be developed with some form of evaluation in mind. Certification or accreditation programs should be given a reasonable amount of time to achieve the goals set forth in the original mission statement, with periodic reports on progress provided to senior management and the governing body of the association. Appropriate follow-up should take place depending upon the unique circumstances of each program.

Collecting feedback from the stakeholder groups is the most important aspect of performance evaluation. This can be done through surveys or focus groups conducted either by an association staffer or an external evaluator who has no direct stake in the results reported.

Developing successful credentialing programs is complex and time-consuming. The amount of time will depend upon the unique circumstances of each discipline or field, but most new programs require at least one to two years to achieve a break-even status.

In some fields, this time frame may be much longer if a lot of promotional work is required to build widespread acceptance of the credentialing effort's value.

Although the benefits of a strong and credible credentialing program are many, the original cast of staff and volunteer leaders may not see the fruits of their labors because of the lengthy life cycles these programs tend to have. That's why all individuals involved in the planning of these programs should adopt a philosophy of "taking the high road"—their efforts will have a long-lasting influence on key stakeholder groups and perhaps even the public.

Resources

Organizations

American National Standards Institute
1819 L Street, N.W., 6th Floor
Washington, D.C. 20036
(202) 293-8020

ASAE & The Center for Association Leadership
1575 I Street, N.W.
Washington, DC 20005
Phone: (202) 626-2723

Clearinghouse on Licensure, Enforcement and Regulation (CLEAR)
403 Marquis Avenue, Suite 100
Lexington, KY 40502
Phone: (859) 269-1289

Council for Higher Education Accreditation (CHEA)
One Dupont Circle, Suite 510
Washington, DC 20036-1193
Phone: (202) 955-6126

National Organization for Competency Assurance (NOCA)
2025 M. Street, N.W., Suite 800
Washington, DC 20036
Phone: (202) 367-1165

Publications

Council on Licensure, Enforcement and Regulation, and National Organization for Competency Assurance, *Principles of Fairness: An Examining Guide for Credentialing Boards,* Lexington, Kentucky, 1994.

Hamm, Michael S., *Fundamentals of Accreditation,* American Society of Association Executives, Washington, D.C., 1997.

Hamm, Michael S., and Larry A. Early, "Certification: Yes or No?," *Association Management,* December 1994, American Society of Association Executives, Washington, D.C.

Jacobs, Jerald A, *Certification and Accreditation Law Handbook,* American Society of Association Executives, Washington, D.C, 1992.

National Commission for Certifying Agencies, *NCCA Guidelines for Certification Approval,* Washington, D.C, 1991.

Pare, Michael A, ed. *Certification and Accreditation Programs Directory,* Gale Research, Inc., Detroit, Michigan, 1995.

Professional Examination Service, *Guidelines for the Development, Use and Evaluation of Licensure and Certification Programs,* New York, 1996.

About the Author

Michael S. Hamm, CMC is the principal of Michael Hamm & Associates, a Rockville, Maryland-based consulting organization specializing in meeting the unique planning and operational needs of certification and accreditation organizations. Hamm has more than 20 years of experience in association management.

Review Questions

1. How would an association determine whether to launch a certification or accreditation program?

2. Is it advisable to limit participation in a certification program to members only?

3. What are the primary steps to take in developing a certification or accreditation program?

CHAPTER

35

Affinity Programs

Matthew J. Rowan

The Dilemma

Association members are expecting an ever-increasing level of benefits and service, but without increases in dues. With limited options to support new member benefits, more and more associations have turned to nondues revenue from affinity programs as part of the solution. Through sponsorship of affinity programs, associations can generate nondues revenue, decrease the pressure to raise dues, and provide valuable benefits to members.

What Are Affinity Programs?

Affinity programs generally involve the association's sponsorship of a commercial company's product or service being marketed to members through the use of the association's name, logo, or mailing lists. The essence of a properly structured affinity program is the association licensing its intangible property (i.e., name, logo, and mailing lists) to the vendor company and receiving a royalty in return.

History and Trends

Pioneered in the United States by the insurance, car rental, and credit card industries, affinity marketing activity has exploded in recent years. Affinity programs have grown in popularity and acceptance to the point that it's rare to find an association without some type of sponsored program. Fueled by the demand from the large number of associations that have experienced the benefits of affinity programs, an increasingly diverse list of benefit programs are now being offered to associations. Joining the trend toward mass-marketed, consumer-oriented products and services, companies specializing in a particular industry are also expanding into affinity marketing. Publishers, education providers, and other industry-specific vendors have discovered the target marketing opportunities and the value in the marketplace of an association sponsorship. They benefit from the access, credibility, sales, and reduced costs that come with an affinity marketing program. The programs available to associations have grown to include an array of business services, financial services, and other industry-specific products and services.

Royalties and other licensing fees are paid to associations by companies willing to provide services to members. The nature and characteristics of the compensation are somewhat complex and are influenced by consideration of rules applicable to unrelated business income tax (UBIT), as described further below. Other associations couple sponsorship programs with in-kind services; one professional group had their Web site developed and maintained by a publisher that is active in the same industry. This saved the association the time and expense of establishing its Web site, enhanced member service, and generated more Internet traffic for the publisher.

Creating the Win-Win-Win Situation

The appeal of affinity marketing is that it represents a "win" situation for the association, the company offering the affinity program, and the association members.

How Associations "Win"

For associations, affinity programs enable associations to offer new services for members that generate nondues revenue with little investment of money or staff resources. By licensing the association's name, logo, and mailing list to an affinity program provider, associations benefit from the specialized expertise, financing, and delivery systems of the company administering the affinity program. The affinity program company also takes full responsibility for marketing and customer service. By sponsoring existing products and services, the association can focus its resources on satisfying member needs.

Affinity programs also help reinforce the bond between the association and the member. When members use an association's sponsored credit card, for example, it is a tangible reminder of their commitment and loyalty to their association. It also builds awareness by reminding members that the association is providing a good value and a useful benefit.

By generating nondues revenue, affinity programs can reduce pressure on associations to increase membership dues. Avoiding or minimizing dues increases has a direct impact on increasing membership retention and recruitment. It can also help avoid the organizational turmoil that can accompany dues increases.

How Affinity Marketers "Win"

For companies offering affinity programs, the primary benefit of an association's sponsorship is greater sales efficiency: generating more sales per promotional dollar.

The association's sponsorship gives a company enhanced credibility and recognition in the marketplace. Companies realize additional sales by tapping into the members' loyalty to the association and the association's credibility with its membership through the licensing of the association's logo, name, and mailing lists.

A direct mail promotion mailed using the association's logo is much more likely to be noticed and read by the members. Resistance to sales and consumer skepticism can be greatly reduced by the stamp of approval the association sponsorship represents. This results in higher response rates to all promotions, especially direct mail and telemarketing.

Association memberships are a ready-made target marketing opportunity for companies. Associations tend to be formed around homogenous groups with common characteristics such as level of education, profession, income, age, or interests. These demographics can be used to estimate potential member acceptance of an affinity program. Using these targeting techniques, the affinity marketer can generate profitable sales with reduced promotional costs. Since promotions include the association logo familiar to members, affinity marketers avoid the difficult and expensive process of establishing themselves in a new market.

Receiving the sponsorship of an association also serves to differentiate a company's product or service from its competition. Many affinity programs are offered on an exclusive basis which can pre-empt the affinity marketer's competition.

Affinity program agreements give the company a license to use the association's name and logo on all marketing material directed at the association's membership, which can greatly improve the effectiveness of sales and marketing activity. A concrete reflection of the association's sponsorship, the association logo is a powerful tool that gives the product or service being sponsored a "foot in the door" with members. Envelopes, brochures, and other promotions with the association logo are more likely to be read, members may be more open to the affinity program's product offering, and the likelihood of a purchase is increased.

Affinity marketers find association members tend to spend more money, create fewer bad debts, and turn into longer term customers than non-affinity customers. Member loyalty is demonstrated by the fact that many associations experience membership renewal rates in excess of 85 percent. This established link between members and their associations spills over into the relationship between the member and the affinity program. The potential for long-term profits from loyal customers increases the attractiveness of affinity marketing for the company offering the affinity program.

How Association Members "Win"

Association members benefit by the opportunity to receive a "better deal" on a product or service that is available to them only as a member of the association. This preferred service represents a better value either through a price discount, a special value-added package of products or services, or both. The member receives the benefit of the group purchasing power represented by the entire membership to which he or she belongs.

Being part of a larger block of business can result in better customer service for the member. Members can also rely on the leverage of the association sponsorship to be an advantage in settling any disagreements or customer service problems with the company providing the affinity program.

Non-dues revenue from affinity programs can help minimize the pressure to raise membership dues. When membership dues increases can be postponed, reduced, or eliminated altogether, it provides a direct benefit to the individual member.

Affinity programs also represent a convenience for members who often trust their association to compare the affinity program to similar products or services in the market, negotiate on behalf of the association's membership using their group purchasing power as leverage, and select the best value for its members.

Affinity Programs and UBIT

Unrelated Business Income Tax (UBIT) applies to income generated through activity typically outside the association's tax-exempt purpose. Activities that constitute a "trade or business" unrelated to the exempt purpose and that are "regularly carried out" are subject to UBIT. UBIT has special implications with regards to revenue from affinity programs.

The Internal Revenue Service (IRS) considers a broad range of activities to be unrelated marketing and promotion services subject to UBIT, such as advertising and promotions. However, "royalties" from the use of intangible property are provided a special exemption from UBIT, along with other passive income such as dividends and interest. The exemption has implications for how an affinity agreement is properly constructed and implemented, so it is advisable that associations consult with their financial and legal advisors to calculate a program's potential UBIT implications before the affinity program contract is signed.

Passive Income Is Tax Exempt

In general, the key distinction for characterization of revenue from affinity programs for tax purposes is whether the conduct of the association is "active" or "passive" in the affinity program. If the association is an active marketer of the affinity program, some or all of the income likely would be viewed by the IRS as a trade or business unrelated to the association's tax exempt purpose and, therefore, subject to UBIT. If, on the other hand, the association is merely licensing its name, logo, and mailing lists (i.e., intangible property) to the company running the affinity program, and not an active promoter of the program, the income would not be subject to UBIT.

For income to be considered passive, the association must not participate in the program's marketing activity. "Active" conduct such as free advertising, promotional letters from the association's officers, and insertion of marketing materials in mailings to members can cause the IRS to consider the association's income derived from that affinity program subject to UBIT.

If the association does become actively involved in promoting the affinity program, the association's expenses related to advertising, marketing, or promotion may be used to offset UBIT income, so the tax is paid only on the "net revenues." However, an excessive amount of UBIT could jeopardize an association's tax-exempt status, so it is advisable for the association to closely monitor its UBIT obligations and seek professional advice from financial, tax, and legal experts.

UBIT Considerations When Establishing Affinity Programs

Some helpful tips to apply in constructing a tax-free revenue stream from affinity programs include:

1. The agreement for an affinity program should be called a "Royalty Agreement" or "License Agreement," and the fees clearly referred to in the agreement as "royalties."
2. To maintain "passive" involvement in the affinity program, the contract should not require the association to assist the affinity program company in marketing its products or services.
3. The association should include provisions that permit prior review and approval of all marketing materials or documents that include the association's name or logo to protect the association's goodwill.
4. It is preferable to base royalties on gross proceeds and more risky to contract for a percentage of net profits from the activity.
5. The association should not share expenses with the affinity program provider, and the provider should pay fair market value for advertisements in newsletters or magazines and exhibit space.
6. Avoid use of the term "agent" in the agreement. Neither party should be referred to as the agent of the other.
7. The agreement should affirmatively state that it is not intended to create a joint venture or partnership between the parties.
8. The program should always be referred to as the outside service provider's program, and should not be referred to as the association's program.

Roles And Responsibilities: Who Does What?

The Association

In sponsoring an affinity program, the association agrees to sponsor a product or service to be marketed to its membership by licensing the use of the association's intangible property such as its name, logo, and trademarks. The association agrees to allow its logo to be used on all promotional material, including brochures, envelopes, letterhead, flyers, and advertisements. Announcements may be run in association magazines and periodicals.

For administrative purposes, often associations are also asked to identify a staff person to serve as primary point of contact. Usually a responsibility of the membership services, marketing, or membership development departments of the association, this staff function may serve as liaison, reviewing and approving use of the association's name and logo, and seeking member or committee approval as appropriate for new affinity marketing plans. Once programs are launched, their responsibilities include monitoring performance, executing the marketing plan, coordinating with the affinity marketer, and evaluating member satisfaction. Of course, any active marketing assistance provided by the association staff member—beyond permissible advance reviewing of the use of the association's intangible property—could jeopardize the tax-free status of revenues received. To avoid this, the association may want to consider having the affinity marketing conducted through the association's for-profit subsidiary, or to construct the marketing contract with the affinity program such that it is split into two agreements, a royalty agreement and a marketing agreement.

Companies Offering Affinity Programs

Affinity marketing companies are responsible for developing a high quality product or service. The affinity marketer usually pays the costs and handles the logistics of administering, operating, and promoting the program. This includes development of marketing materials, executing the marketing plan, providing customer service, general account servicing, sales tracking and reporting, and payment of royalties due the association.

Promoting Affinity Programs

The majority of the costs of promoting affinity programs are generally borne by the company offering the affinity program. This includes printing of materials, graphic arts, copy writing, postage, mailing services, and telemarketing. All promotions bearing the association's name or logo should be approved by the designated association contact before they are printed or mailed; the legal reason for this is to protect the "style and quality" of the association's trademarks.

The marketing plan and schedule the affinity program company plans to implement should be clearly spelled out in the contract between the company and the association. The affinity program company should have experience marketing its program to other groups and that experience should be reflected in the marketing plan. Samples of mailings, advertisements, and other marketing materials should also be provided to the association to illustrate the quality of promotional materials and exact display of the association logo. Web sites branded to the association program and e-mail marketing that adheres to the association's e-mail policies should also be discussed in advance.

Direct Mail

Associations rely heavily on direct mail to promote their educational programs for the same reasons affinity marketers do: It is pro-active, cost effective, and can be closely targeted.

For most affinity programs, direct mailings to the association's membership are the primary means of promotion. Catalogs, brochures, letters, and other materials may be mailed to the membership by the affinity program company using the association's logo. Marketers prefer direct mail because it allows for market segmentation and target marketing. Age, education level, income, job title, and past purchases are among the demographics most often targeted by affinity marketers. Targeting allows promotions to be tailored to the market segment most likely to purchase the product or service. The affinity marketer can avoid the expense of mailing to other market segments that are less likely to have purchasing responsibility or an interest in the product or service. Direct mail also has the advantage of being very cost effective. Sales can be accurately tracked to evaluate and monitor the promotion's effectiveness.

The downside of direct mail is member complaints about receiving too much "junk mail." This can be minimized by closely monitoring the number of direct mail promotions members receive. Mailings can also be spaced out so the membership receives these promotions at regular intervals. In some cases, several different affinity program companies may bundle their promotions in a single mailing to reduce the number of individual mailings.

Telemarketing

Calling an association's members to promote an affinity program can create extreme results, both positive and negative. For this reason, it's understandable that many associations are often reluctant to provide affinity marketers with member lists that include phone numbers.

Experienced affinity marketers, however, have trained their telemarketers in a softer, less aggressive approach that has made telemarketing a more viable promotional vehicle for association affinity programs, and associations should review and approve any telemarketing scripts that use the association's name.

Telemarketing has some built-in advantages over other promotional vehicles. The first advantage is speed. A telemarketing program can launch a program promotion in a matter of weeks as opposed to the months it takes for mailings and advertisements to reach members. Should telemarketing generate complaints, it can be halted at a moment's notice. The second advantage is that a telemarketing campaign can be monitored "live" as it happens (of course, in accordance with applicable telemarketing and "privacy" laws). The association's affinity program liaison can monitor the telemarketing calls to ensure that members are not being harassed or receiving a "hard sell." They can also participate in telemarketer training sessions to further sensitize them to the unique needs of the membership.

Advertising

Advertising in the association's publications is another popular promotional vehicle because of its low cost and high visibility. Advertisements of various sizes are developed and prepared by the affinity marketing company and approved by the association representative. Affinity program ads in the association's official publications further communicate to the membership the association's endorsement and commitment to the affinity program.

"Take One" Brochures

"Take ones" are small brochures or flyers produced by the affinity marketer to communicate discount offers and other special values. Take ones are very cost effective because the cost of printing is low, and they can be used in a variety of settings.

Choosing Affinity Programs

Selection Process

The process of selecting, evaluating, and launching affinity programs varies with the association. For more staff-driven associations, the decision-making process requires the staff to do much of the research and report its recommendations to a committee. In more member-driven associations, a committee of members becomes intimately involved in the evaluation and selection. It is important to recognize that the failure to exercise "due diligence" in selection of the vendor could give rise to tort or other liability (such as "negligent selection") if loss or damage is experienced by the members as a result of negligence by the vendor. In addition, if the association becomes too actively involved in the vendor's activities, it can be liable for "negligent supervision" or other negligence if the members suffer loss.

Member Demand

Anticipated member demand for an affinity program should be the primary driving factor in the association's decision to endorse an affinity product or service. If the program offers a valuable, tangible product or service that is in strong demand from the membership, revenue generation and membership retention will be enhanced. Should the member demand for the affinity program's offering be low, the benefits of affinity marketing will not accrue to the association.

Affinity Marketer Commitment

The affinity marketer's commitment to the association's sponsorship is also key. Does the company have many association clients or just a few? How long have they been involved in affinity marketing? The answers to these kinds of questions can help the association determine if the company has made the long-term commitment to provide top-notch service to the association's members. If the affinity marketing company appears to be looking for quick, short-term profits, securing association sponsorship may not be productive for either party. A visit to the affinity marketer's facilities may be one way to ascertain the company's commitment to the association market.

Reference Checks

An affinity marketing agreement is a long-term arrangement, and the association should have in-depth discussions with other association clients of the company offering the affinity program. The company should have a proven track record in product delivery, marketing, and customer service, and a reputation as a reliable provider and administrator of affinity programs for associations. If an affinity marketing company has a track record of paying royalties on time and has numerous satisfied association clients, it is probably a good indicator of future performance as an affinity marketing partner.

Legal Protection

Basics of Affinity Marketing Contracts

All association affinity marketing contracts should be reviewed by legal counsel to be sure the association has adequate protection. The contract should specify the exact responsibilities of the affinity marketer including marketing plans and schedule, discounts to be offered to members, performance standards, member pricing, royalty calculation, and payment schedule. Limits on the association's legal obligations and liability should be clearly detailed in the agreement, particularly through a comprehensive indemnification clause. Any and all ambiguities should be questioned and resolved, and appropriate changes should be made to the contract to accurately reflect the responsibilities of each organization in the affinity program.

Contract language regarding royalties should be clearly spelled out as payment for use of the association's logo, name, and mailing list, and not as compensation or fees for services rendered. As indicated, one strategy for protecting the tax-free nature of royalty income is to run marketing through a for-profit subsidiary; splitting the agreement into two, a royalty agreement and a marketing agreement, may also be a useful approach for this purpose.

Termination

A termination clause is particularly important for affinity marketing contracts. In the event that either party elects to end the affinity marketing relationship, the association's members would be accepting service from a company who has lost the sponsorship of the association. For this reason, the termination clause should specify the disposition of the members' accounts, make arrangements for continued servicing of members, and provide for any ongoing royalties to the association.

Particularly with insurance and other long-term financial products, the contract should specify whether the association's block of business stays with the affinity marketer or can move with the association to a new provider. It's best to investigate the association's options prior to signing a contract.

Conclusion

Affinity programs bring the product and marketing expertise and experience of corporations together with the market power of the association's sponsorship. By reinforcing the loyalty and bond between the member and the association, affinity programs have become a substantial source of revenue and goodwill for associations and corporate America. As association members continue to demand higher levels of service at a constant dues rate, affinity programs will play an ever-increasing role in the future success of associations.

References

Classic, Jefferson C., "Summary of Legal Aspects of Association Corporate Relations," Jenner and Block, Washington, DC, 1997.

Goedert, Paula Cozzi, "Update on Association Tax Issues," Jenner and Block, Chicago, IL, 1997.

McBride, J. Scott, "GWSAE Marketing Survey: Evaluating Your Association's Marketing Success," Greater Washington Society of Association Executives, Washington, DC, 1996.

Slaughter, Jodie Hirsch, "Managing Affinity Marketing Within the Association," McKinley Marketing, Chevy Chase, MD, 1996.

Slaughter, Jodie Hirsch, "Success in Association Affinity Marketing," McKinley Marketing, Chevy Chase, MD, 1996.

Slaughter, Jodie Hirsch, Paula Beste Cleave, and Henry Chamberlain, "Creating Profitable Affinity Relationships with Associations," presented at the School of Association Management: Understanding and Selling to the Association Market, American Society of Association Executives, Washington, DC, 1996.

Teagno, Gary C., *Profiting Through Association Marketing*, Irwin Professional Publishing, Illinois, 1994.

About the Author

Matthew J. Rowan is president and CEO of the Health Industry Distributors Association (HIDA). His 20-year association career includes experience in managing of association publishing, communication, advocacy, membership development, and marketing efforts.

Review Questions

1. What steps can an association take to limit its exposure to UBIT?

2. How should associations determine which affinity programs to offer?

3. Which specific areas should be addressed in an affinity marketing agreement?

CAE Content Outline

T HE COMPOSITION OF THE CAE exam is guided by extensive research on the job tasks performed and knowledge needed by association executives. This research, and the exam content outline, is updated approximately every five years. During 2003-2004, the CAE Commission oversaw a methodical and comprehensive investigation into the skills required for successful association management. This research included a literature review, interviews with key thought leaders, surveys of over 1,500 association professionals, extensive statistical analysis, and a thorough peer review. The research resulted in the identification of 185 essential association management tasks organized into ten knowledge domains. This outline presents the content covered on the CAE exam with the amount of the test devoted to each domain indicated in parentheses.

DOMAIN 1
Strategic Management (13–15%)

A. General Management
1. Identify and define the association's core competencies and ensure that association operations and activities support and capitalize on these competencies.
2. Identify and implement, when appropriate, other corporate entities to further the association's mission (e.g., foundations, service corporations).
3. Develop and analyze internal (operational) and external (leadership and membership) performance metrics for association operations and activities.
4. Work with board to develop a staff leadership succession plan.
5. Apply management theories for effective management of the association.

6. Develop and implement strategies to encourage best practices and introduce and manage change and innovation.
7. Utilize quantitative and qualitative tools and project management skills to achieve management goals.
8. Apply logical steps in the project management process, including needs analysis, planning, prioritizing, program development, implementation, management, and evaluation.
9. Plan and ensure that quality control procedures are implemented.
10. Establish and utilize a strong peer network to maintain knowledge of current association management practices.

B. Marketing/Branding
1. Define the scope of the market and identify target segments and key stakeholder groups in building membership and customers.
2. Identify the association's unique value proposition, preferred positioning, and distinctive brand.
3. Conduct environmental scans.
4. Research and identify strategies and tactics for increasing member return on investment (ROI).
5. Develop and implement a marketing plan to support the association's positioning and branding, enhance membership recruitment and retention efforts, and promote programs, products, and services.

C. Financial Management
1. Identify, retain, and/or manage accounting services.
2. Develop, recommend, implement, review, and manage budgets.
3. Develop systems, metrics, and tools (e.g., allocation of all-cost programs, budgeting by program) for monitoring and managing financial performance.
4. Determine oversight responsibilities related to subsidiary corporations (e.g., financial operations, business operations, consistency with mission).
5. Establish a financial reporting system that provides clear, accurate, and complete reports for the board, staff, and members.
6. Ensure that finances are independently reviewed and audited on a periodic basis.
7. Recommend, implement, and manage investment policies and activities and identify and retain investment management services.
8. Recommend, implement, and manage reserve policy.
9. Evaluate the impact of economic and budget factors on financial planning, investment policies, and financial performance.
10. Develop and establish policies and procedures to ensure strong internal financial controls.
11. Monitor and maintain adequate cash flow to meet the organization's disbursement needs.
12. Implement an antifraud policy.

DOMAIN 2
Planning and Research (7–9%)

A. Strategic Planning/Strategic Thinking

1. Establish and implement a strategic planning process that advances the association's mission and vision and is based on sound methodological principles.
2. Ensure that the association has a focused and well-articulated mission and vision that is communicated to members, staff, and the public.
3. Assist the board in setting and implementing short- and long-term association priorities based on a strategic planning process.
4. Align the association's annual business plan with the strategic plan to focus resource allocation.
5. Ensure that association activities, operations, and business plans support the strategic goals of the organization.
6. Evaluate the effectiveness of the strategic plan on an ongoing basis and revise as necessary.
7. Evaluate the need for, and feasibility of, working with other organizations through mergers, partnerships, acquisitions, and consolidations.

B. Business Planning

1. Identify business goals and objectives and strategies and tactics for achieving these goals.
2. Evaluate data from a variety of sources (e.g., needs assessment, trend monitoring, benchmarking, evaluations) and utilize these data to develop business plans.
3. Prepare business plans (including financial projections, breakeven points, and total costs) for new and existing programs, products, and services.
4. Develop long-range funding and needs plans.
5. Develop strategies to incorporate fund-raising vehicles into revenue planning, as appropriate.
6. Develop a business continuity plan.

C. Research, Evaluation, and Statistics

1. Develop a research agenda that benefits the internal operations of the association, advances the profession or industry, and provides needed information for members and other stakeholders (e.g., needs assessment surveys, market analyses, benchmarking studies, best practices studies, compensation surveys).
2. Identify and utilize appropriate research methodologies (e.g., interview, focus group, survey) and data collection methods (fax, e-mail, Internet based).
3. Implement statistical and quality control procedures to ensure accuracy of research results and manage research conducted by contracted research consultants.
4. Prepare and deliver customized research reports tailored to the needs and interests of stakeholders (e.g., members, government agencies, partners).
5. Design and implement a data reporting system that is flexible and customizable.

DOMAIN 3
Leadership (11–13%)

A. General Leadership
1. Utilize qualitative and quantitative data in decision-making.
2. Take actions based on decisions made in the best interests of the association and, when appropriate, take risks.
3. Practice and demonstrate collaborative leadership.
4. Promote an organizational culture that is sensitive and responsive to the needs, interests, and values of the entire membership.
5. Integrate the interests and goals of stakeholders to achieve success for the association.
6. Support and reinforce the board's stewardship responsibilities.

B. Ethics
1. Lead by example through maintaining the highest degree of personal integrity and professional ethics and identify/resolve ethical dilemmas.
2. Adhere to the American Society of Association Executive's Standards of Conduct.
3. Establish and implement conflict of interest policies.

C. Diversity
1. Ensure that association communications, programs, products, and services reflect sensitivity to diversity (e.g., race, ethnicity, gender, religion, age, sexual orientation, nationality, disability, appearance, geographic location, professional level).
2. Create a climate of inclusiveness that promotes understanding and respect for diversity.

D. Interpersonal Relationships and Dynamics and Group Facilitation
1. Support individuals' professional and personal development (e.g., mentoring, career counseling and advancement, leadership development).
2. Coach and mentor staff, board, and members and model appropriate skills in interactions with these groups.
3. Provide opportunities to develop interpersonal skills and cross-cultural competence.
4. Promote and facilitate individual participation, contributions, and ownership toward group efforts and decisions.
5. Provide informed consultation to the board to facilitate board activities, process, and objectives.

E. Negotiating
1. Practice and ensure the use of effective and ethical negotiation skills for self and others (e.g., to resolve conflict, to achieve consensus).

2. Coach and model the use of negotiation skills in contract negotiations and other interactions.
3. Utilize mediation to resolve conflicts, where appropriate.

DOMAIN 4
Administration (12–14%)

A. Human Resources
1. Maintain a work environment that fosters staff teamwork, communications, efficiency, and effectiveness.
2. Ensure clear delineation of accountability and organizational responsibilities within the office.
3. Promote work/life balance for staff.
4. Develop, implement, and evaluate personnel policies and procedures.
5. Recruit, hire, and train association staff.
6. Supervise and coach staff and provide job descriptions based on essential competencies needed to perform effectively.
7. Provide formal performance review process.
8. Discipline and/or terminate association staff.
9. Develop, implement, and manage compensation administration program.
10. Comply with municipal, state, and federal laws related to employment (e.g., ADA, Family Medical Leave Act).
11. Evaluate association work procedures and systems and implement improvements, as necessary.

B. Technology
1. Identify and contract for technology consultation and technical support services.
2. Determine the appropriate information technology system (i.e., information systems, databases, communication technologies, Web technologies) needed to support association goals and activities.
3. Oversee the selection, purchase, installation, maintenance, and upgrading of information technology.
4. Conduct ongoing analysis to confirm that information technology system is performing in line with staff and member needs and expectations.
5. Develop and implement policies and procedures to maintain system security and integrity.
6. Identify areas in which new technology tools can improve design, development, and delivery of products and services.

C. Legal
1. Identify, retain, and effectively manage legal counsel.
2. Review and ensure proper use and execution of contracts, including employment contracts.

3. Develop policies and procedures to ensure compliance with local, state, and federal laws.
4. Monitor association actions and activities to protect not-for-profit status and compliance with antitrust laws.
5. Maintain required documents (e.g., articles of incorporation, bylaws, minutes, and contracts).
6. Maintain appropriate insurance coverage to protect the fiduciary interests of the association, members, and staff.
7. Ensure that the association's intellectual property is protected.

D. Facilities Management
1. Develop and implement an organization-wide continuity plan to protect human and physical assets of the organization in case of a disaster.
2. Maintain proper security for the workplace and develop and implement crisis prevention and safety programs.
3. Evaluate the benefits of owning and leasing options for association facilities and equipment.
4. Ensure an accessible work environment that is compliant with ergonomic and ADA guidelines.

E. Vendor/Supplier Management
1. Determine the benefits, implications, feasibility, and advisability of outsourcing association functions.
2. Establish procedures for the appropriate utilization and evaluation of requests for proposals (RFPs).
3. Establish procedures and criteria for reviewing the performance of vendors, suppliers, and consultants.

DOMAIN 5
Knowledge Management (5-7%)

A. Knowledge Management System
1. Identify the diverse information needs and preferences of the association's membership and other stakeholders.
2. Develop, implement, and manage a knowledge management (KM) program to advance association goals and objectives and serve stakeholder information needs through the dissemination of intellectual and knowledge-based assets.
3. Utilize the knowledge management system to share leading edge profession or industry learning, insight, and best practices and deliver high-quality products and services with speed, efficiency, and effective customer service.
4. Assemble, review, and repackage information in a timely fashion for customized responses to requests for information.

5. Conduct ongoing evaluation of KM services based on quantitative and qualitative data to assess and manage knowledge assets and support continuous improvement.

B. Professional Development Programs and Delivery Systems

1. Evaluate and plan the use of multiple methods and delivery systems (e.g., face-to-face seminars, distance learning, selfdirected learning, Web-based courses).
2. Develop and enhance the content of professional development products and integrate various delivery systems.
3. Incorporate an understanding of the conditions necessary for successful adult learning into the planning and development of professional development offerings.
4. Plan and implement procedures and preventive education to help members maintain compliance with laws and regulations (e.g., in-service training for members).

DOMAIN 6
Governance and Structure (10–12%)

A. Volunteer Structure

1. Establish, integrate, and maintain an effective and representative governance system (e.g., officers, board of directors, executive committee, nominating committee, house of delegates) to guide the mission of the association.
2. Establish and maintain an effective system of organizational units (e.g., committees, task forces, sections, special interest groups) to develop and/or implement the mission of the association.
3. Work with board to develop a volunteer leadership succession plan.
4. Serve as liaison with the board and executive committee to achieve the association's goals.
5. Conduct on-going review of governance documents (e.g., association constitution, bylaws) to ensure that they reflect current practice in association management.
6. Identify and propose effective and flexible ways for communicating and conducting meetings (using technology, where appropriate) to facilitate the activities of the association's board of directors, committees, task forces, and special interest groups.
7. Establish and maintain an appropriate volunteer recruitment, training, recognition, and accountability system.
8. Educate and orient board members, volunteers, and staff regarding their respective roles and responsibilities.

B. Chapters, Divisions, Interest Groups, and Communities of Practice

1. Determine policies and criteria regarding the formation of association chapters, divisions, interest groups, and communities of practice.

2. Develop and implement effective relationships, delineating, where appropriate, lines of authority and responsibility vis a vis association chapters, divisions, interest groups, and communities of practice.
3. Identify and determine the best methods for responding to the needs and interests of association chapters, divisions, interest groups, and communities of practice.
4. Identify strategies for tailoring products and services to the unique needs of association chapters, divisions, interest groups, and communities of practice.
5. Provide relevant and timely research to support the success and activities of association chapters, divisions, interest groups, and communities of practice.
6. Utilize a variety of communication channels to facilitate regular and accurate exchange of information between the association and its chapters, divisions, interest groups, and communities of practice.

DOMAIN 7
Public Policy and Government and External Relations
(7–9%)

A. Public Policy
1. Identify and analyze the need for public policy development activities.
2. Identify and foster advocacy sources that support the profession or industry and implement association-sponsored advocacy programs.
3. Recommend and implement public policy programs.
4. Plan, implement, and evaluate government relations programs consistent with board-approved policies.
5. Monitor city, state, and national legislation and regulations.
6. Report to membership and other interested parties on the current political environment, the actions of relevant regulatory bodies, and the impact of proposed and enacted legislation to their bottom line and operations.
7. Manage association lobbying activities, including the identification and retention of registered lobbyists.
8. Determine the advisability of, establish, and manage political action committees (PACs).
9. Determine the need for, and feasibility of, grass roots activities and implement and evaluate such activities.

B. Coalition Building
1. Identify and bring together groups with a common interest to develop a plan to reach mutual goals.
2. Communicate mutually advantageous goals and objectives to appeal to new allies.
3. Form short- and long-term coalitions to address single, time-limited, or long-term issues of common interest.

4. Develop a coalition-building model that is responsive and flexible and which may include partnerships, alliances, and/or informal and formal relationships.

DOMAIN 8
Membership (10–12%)

A. Member Relations
1. Strategically position members in relation to the media, government, and public affairs.
2. Integrate the context and cultural norms of potential members, partners, and other stakeholders into outreach efforts.
3. Create a variety of opportunities for member contribution to association activities and advancement (e.g., focused, short-term volunteer opportunities; committee participation, leadership roles).
4. Develop communication strategies to keep members engaged and informed.
5. Ensure compliance with the association's privacy policy.

B. Membership Recruitment and Retention
1. Conduct needs analysis to determine current members' needs in the context of the association's mission and objectives.
2. Plan and implement membership recruitment and retention program (e.g., resources, logistics, audiences, design and content, pilot testing, integration with other programs and services, legality) based on the strategic plan and results of the needs analysis.
3. Utilize market segmentation and targeting to develop appropriate strategies, messages, and delivery vehicles for current and potential members.
4. Communicate the value and relevance of the association to diverse populations of members and potential members.
5. Evaluate member recruitment and retention utilizing a variety of measures, including customer satisfaction and new member and renewal volume and revenue.

C. Globalization
1. Analyze the impact of global, social, cultural, and economic trends on the association.
2. Investigate applicable laws, regulations, ethical standards, and cultural and language differences in countries in which the association is planning to, or currently conducting, business.
3. Consider the implications and feasibility of expanding association membership beyond current national borders, including the development of international partnerships, alliances, and relationships.

DOMAIN 9

Programs, Products, and Services (12–13%)

A. Development of Programs/Products/Services

1. Identify and prioritize the need for programs/products/services based on the association's goals and the needs and interests of members and stakeholders.
2. Conduct needs assessment/market research to evaluate the feasibility of introducing, modifying, or discontinuing programs/products/services.
3. Create a program/product/service development and implementation plan (e.g., resources, logistics, audiences, design and content, pilot testing, integration with other programs and services, legality).
4. Develop marketing plans for programs/products/services.
5. Conduct periodic review and evaluation of programs/products/services and make recommendations regarding maintenance, improvement, or discontinuation.
6. Identify, develop, and monitor revenue sources (e.g., membership dues, sales, programs, grants).

B. Fundraising/Development Programs

1. Identify qualitative and quantitative data and motivating factors associated with giving, and incorporate these factors into development strategies, including determination of appropriate fundraising vehicles.
2. Develop a management plan specific to fundraising (e.g., target groups, fundraising vehicles, volunteers needed, impact, costs, risks, recognition, legal aspects).
3. Develop criteria for establishing foundations and endowments within the not-for-profit legal structure and the philosophy and strategies of the association and ensure that funds are spent in accordance with the donors' intent.

C. Meeting and Event Planning

1. Determine meeting/event program, format, and speakers based on meeting/event purpose, content, and audience; develop contracts; and use standard planning tools (e.g., meeting/event profile and specifications report, meeting timetable, convention resume, sleeping room pick-up report, function sheets).
2. Evaluate options for site selection, taking into consideration food and beverage, hotel accommodations, security, insurance, etc. and contract with facility for rates, date, space, and services.
3. Employ strategies to enhance revenue generated by the meeting/event and minimize attrition.
4. Develop Internet-based tools and resources to provide the association with data for decision-making and assist attendees in accessing information about the meeting/event.
5. Provide on-site management for meeting/event operations (e.g., registration, information desk, food and beverage setups, scheduled speakers, events).

6. Conduct post-meeting/event evaluation, including a survey of attendees, vendors, and exhibitors and a review of the financial results.

D. Technical Journals and Publications

1. Identify the need for technical journals and publications in specific areas of association interests.
2. Develop a publication management system with appropriate editorial and peer review structure.
3. Determine the most effective and feasible publication format (e.g., print, electronic) based on the type of information, the time sensitivity, and intended audience.
4. Periodically review and assess publication quality, usefulness, and relevance, and implement changes as appropriate to meet revised publication goals and objectives.

E. Ethics/Self Regulation Programs

1. Implement and manage an association ethics and discipline program.
2. Foster an environment in which members are encouraged to identify and adhere to high standards of ethical behavior.
3. Plan and implement procedures and preventive education to help members maintain compliance with the association's ethical standards.
4. Monitor and evaluate the impact of professional and industry practices on the public good.

F. Standard-Setting Programs

1. Investigate the legal implications and liabilities associated with standard-setting activities.
2. Develop, implement, and manage voluntary standards program.
3. Maintain currency of the standards program by periodic review and monitoring.

G. Industry Awards and Member Recognition Programs

1. Identify and analyze need for industry awards and member recognition programs.
2. Develop, implement, manage, and evaluate industry awards and member recognition programs.

H. Credentialing (Certification, Accreditation, and Licensure)

1. Investigate and evaluate the legal implications and liabilities associated with credentialing programs.
2. Develop, implement, and manage credentialing programs, including credential renewal and revocation procedures, and maintenance of records of credential status.
3. Ensure that credentialing programs meet technical standards (e.g., tests are psychometrically sound).

I. Affinity Programs (e.g., Endorsements, Joint Ventures, Sponsorship)

1. Determine policies and criteria for selecting, sponsoring, and continuing affinity programs.
2. Develop, implement, manage, and evaluate affinity programs.

DOMAIN 10
Public Relations and External Communications (6–7%)

A. Public Relations Programs

1. Identify the target groups and individuals that must be positively influenced to achieve the goals of the association.
2. Plan, implement, and evaluate a credible public relations education and information program to positively influence groups and individuals and enhance public trust.
3. Develop a crisis communications and management plan.
4. Manage and execute appropriate responses to media inquiries.

B. Non-Technical Publications and Other Media

1. Evaluate consumer and trade media outlets (e.g., television, radio, print, Web-based) and develop and implement media approaches to advance the association's goals.
2. Integrate the publications program to achieve the editorial mission and develop a variety of publications, media programs, and delivery systems to meet the diverse needs and interests of members and stakeholders.
3. Manage or outsource publications and other media and determine the most effective and feasible publication format (e.g., print, electronic) based on the type of information, time sensitivity, and intended audience.
4. Plan, implement, and monitor the strategy and applications associated with association Web site development and maintenance.

Index

A

Accidents, preventing, 245
Accounting, information management, 230
Accreditation, defined, 433
Action plan, 52–53
Activity ratios, 135
Ad hoc groups, 5
Adobe Portable Document File (PDF), 342
Adult learning, 303–305
    child learning compared to, 303–304
    industry trends, 304
    motivation for, 304
    needs assessment, 304–305
    readiness to learn, 304
    role of experience in, 304
Adverse selection bias, 42, 43
Advertising
    affinity programs, 452
    in association publications, 315, 321–323
    defined, 264
Advocacy roles, 41
Affiliates, and subsidiaries compared, 73
Affiliation agreement, 68
Affinity programs, 445–454
    advertising, 452
    association responsibilities in, 449–450
    benefits to associations, 446
    benefits to marketers, 446–447
    benefits to members, 447–448
    CAE exam, content outline, 466
    choosing a program, criteria for, 452–453

    contracts, 453
    defined, 445
    direct mail promotion, 451
    history and trends, 445–446
    marketer commitment, 452
    marketer responsibilities in, 450
    member demand for, 452
    process for selecting, 452
    promoting, 450–452
    "Take One" brochures, 452
    telemarketing, 451
    termination of, 453–454
    and unrelated business income tax
        (UBIT), 446, 448–449
Affirmative action, defined, 283
Age Discrimination in Employment Act, 175
American Association of Pharmaceutical
    Scientists, 239
American Competitiveness and Corporate
    Accountability Act of 2002. *See*
    Sarbanes-Oxley Act
American Dental Association, 298
American National Standards Institute
    (ANSI), 431
American Society for Interior Design (ASID),
    43
American Society of Association Executives,
    Standards of Conduct, 86
American Society of Civil Engineers, 54
Americans with Disabilities Act (ADA), 147,
    169–170

compliance, 246–247, 419–420, 425–427, 430
defined, 283
education programs and, 307
meetings and conventions, 401
reasonable accommodation, defined, 170, 307
Analysis paralysis, 82
Andragogy, 303
Annual business meeting, 391
Antink, Adrienne, 71
Antitrust, 42, 63–64, 222–223, 419, 420–422
Antitrust compliance policy, 57, 64
Articles of incorporation, 6, 58
Assembly of delegates, 4
Associate members, role of, 14
Association information centers, trade shows, 394
Association professional liability insurance (APLI), 61, 431
Attitudinal archetypes, 84
Audit(s)
codes of ethics, 112
committee, 8, 16
financial, 137
legal, 57–58
social responsibility program, 113
Audit Bureau of Circulations (ABC), 323
Authenticity, 279

B

Background checks, 150
Backup systems, 232
Balakgie, Carla, 93
Balance sheet, 134
Banquet style room set-up, 412
Barry Posner, 80–81
Benchmark positions, 155
Benjamin, Maynard H., 234
Berry, Kathie, 140
Blogs, 125, 254, 316
Blue sky thinking, 118
Board of directors, 3
chief executive officer and, 3
code of conduct, 84
ex-officio board members, 3
government relations and, 252
leadership in, 88–90
members as chairs of standing committees, 4
orientation, 77
professional liability insurance, 61
selection of, 3
and subsidiary corporations, 75
written job descriptions, 84

Bonus(es)
cash system, 157, 160
employee, 153
reasons for awarding, 158
Boy Scouts of America, 298–299
Branding, 356
Breach of duty, 423. *See also* Negligence
Bridgespan, 43
Bridging, 268
Brooks, Beth, 11
Budget and finance, 131–141
accounting practices, 16, 137, 230
affiliated and subsidiary organizations, 140
annual budgets, preparing, 131–132
audit, 137
billing and accounts receivable information management, 230
budgeting, 59, 131–133
CAE exam, content outline, 456
capital budget, 132, 133
cash budget, 132, 133
in coalition building, 293
compilation, 137
controls, oversight, and independent evaluation, 136–137
direct expenses, 396
education programs, 305–306
financial reporting, 134–136
financial transactions, segments of, 136
fixed costs, 305, 397
formulating a budget, 132
governance policies, 15
implementing and monitoring the budget, 133
incremental budgeting, 132
independent evaluation of financial information, 137
indirect expenses, 396–397
internal financial controls, 136
investments, 139
for marketing, 357, 360
for meetings and conventions, 396–397
nondues income, sources of, 363
operating budget, 49, 132–133
publishing operations, 320–321
reserves, 138
review, 137
risks, protection from, 74
salary planning, 156–157
technical publications, 336–337
strategic budgets, 49
and tactical planning, 126–127
unrelated business income tax, 60, 132, 446, 448–449

variable costs, 305–306, 397
zero-based budgeting, 132, 320
Business planning, CAE exam, content
  outline, 457
Business Publication Audit (BPA), 323
Butterfield, Bruce, 30
"Buy or die" marketing, 366
Bylaws, 6, 84
  annual business meeting, 391
  annual review of, 16
  changes to, 1
  chapters in, 58
  common elements of, 1–2
  legality of, 58
  purpose of, 1
  standing committees, 4
  state mandates for, 2
  tax-exempt purpose, specifying, 2

C

CAE exam, content outline, 455–466
  administration, 459–460
  governance and structure, 461–462
  knowledge management, 460–461
  leadership, 458–459
  membership, 463
  planning and research, 457
  programs, products, and services,
    464–466
  public policy and government/external
    relations, 462–463
  public relations and external
    communications, 466
  strategic management, 455–456
Campaign-finance reform, 250
Cancellation clauses, contracts, 62
CAN-SPAM Act, 350
Capital budget, 132, 133
Capturing positive externalities, 32
Careers, and jobs compared, 35
Case management, 162
Cash budget, 132, 133
Cash flow statement, 135–136
CD-ROMs, 309, 316
Center for Research on Education, Diversity,
  and Excellence (CREDE), 279
Certification and accreditation programs,
  433–443
  accreditation, defined, 433
  ANSI accreditation, 431
  antitrust concerns, 419, 420–422
  application form, 431
  benefits to associations, 435–436
  business plan for, 439
  CAE exam, content outline, 455–466

certification, defined, 433–434
  collecting feedback, 441
  common misconceptions about, 436–438
  computer-based testing, 440
  continued maintenance of credential, 440
  continuing competence, policies for, 440
  credentialing bodies, 437–438
  and demand for other association
    services, 438
  denial or revocation of certification,
    422–423, 429
  developing a program, steps in, 438–440
  grandfathering, 430, 440
  incorporating government standards into,
    440
  information management, 229
  legal issues, 64, 439–440
  liability surrounding, 431, 439
  lifecyles of, 437
  long-lasting influence of, 442
  membership criteria for, 438
  need for, determining, 434–435
  program performance, evaluating,
    441–442
  as a reflection of association's reputation,
    436–437
  resource organizations, 442
  as a revenue source, 436
  risk, steps to minimizing, 428–432
  security and, 430
  staff involvement in, 437, 441
  structure and governance issues, 441
  type of examination, 440
  voluntary participation, notice of, 431
Champoux, Tom, 85, 86
Change drivers
  demand-networks and, 32–38
  identification of, 23
Change, types of, 24
Channels of distribution, selection of, 39–40
Chapters
  bylaws and, 58
  CAE exam, content outline, 461–462
  information management, 228–229
Charter, 68
Chemers, Martin, 79
Chief executive officer (CEO)
  accountability of, 15
  appropriate protection against liability, 65
  board of directors and, 3
  compensation issues, 160–161
  as designated spokesperson, 18
  employment contract, 15, 160
  as liaison between board and members,
    10

role of in marketing, 352–353, 357
as social entrepreneur, 32
and subsidiary corporations, 74
succession planning, 15, 383
Chief Knowledge Officer (CKO), 238
Child labor, 174
Civil Air Patrol, 298
Civil disorder, 247
Civil Rights Act of 1964, Title VII, 177–178
Climate, of inclusiveness, 87
Clipping services, 265
Coalition building, 287–295
   bottom up, 291–292
   CAE exam, content outline, 462–463
   central coordination, need for, 292–293
   core issues, redefining, 289
   financing, 293
   flexibility, need for, 293
   focus, need to create and maintain,
     290–291, 294
   goals of, 287–288, 290–291
   moving beyond, 294–295
   National Coalition of Music Education
     (NCME), 288–289
   self-definitions, 288–289
   strategy for, 287
   unique contributions of disparate
     organizations, 289
   visibility, importance of, 292
Cocktail rounds, room set-up, 412
Codes of ethics, 6
   adoption of, 84
   auditing, 112
   committee responsibilities, 110
   enforcement of, 110–111, 429–430
   ingredients of, 109
   integration of with association's mission
     and objectives, 106, 108
   management and ownership of, 108
   risk, steps to minimizing, 428–432
   scope of, 106
Codes of Professional Responsibility, 105
Co-evolutionary shared networks, 33
Collaborative economy, 34
Collins, Jim, 81, 83, 88
Commercial general liability (CGL)
   insurance, 61
Commitment form, 9
Committees
   audit, 8, 16
   CEO search, 15
   code of conduct, 84
   code of ethics, 110
   commitment form, 9
   conflict of interest statement, 9

government relations, 253
information management, 228–229
meetings and conventions, 393
nominating, 3
publications, 338
standing, 4
written job descriptions for, 84
Communication(s). *See also* Public relations
   with components, 70–71
   and computing, interrelation of, 231–232
   in a crisis, 269–271
   diversity in, 282
   e-mail, 350
   with employees, 165–166
   employee training in, 165
   government relations, 255, 257–258
   international expansion and, 383–384
   and knowledge management, 237
   labeling, use of in negotiations, 98
   with members, 17, 258
   membership message, empathy in, 367
   during negotiation, 103
   with outside suppliers, 205–207
   via satellite, 310
   between staff and volunteers, 9, 10
   targeted, 255
   Web sites as tool for, 330
Community relations, defined, 264
Community service, 297–301
   benefits of, 297, 301
   community groups needing help, list of,
     299
   financial support as, 298
   getting involved in, steps to, 299–301
   in-kind services, 298
   Internet, use of, 301
   long-term relationships with nonprofit
     organizations, examples of, 298–299
   mission statements and, 299
Compensation
   benchmark positions, 155
   bonus payments to employees, 153
   cash bonus system, 157, 160
   employee incentive programs, 153
   Equal Pay Act, 174
   equity increase, 156
   executive issues, 160–161
   formal salary administration plan,
     154–155
   incentives, 157–160
   market rate, 155
   merit type, 157
   pay practice, 156
   policy, determination of, 154–156
   salary planning, 156–157

stock options, 157
targeted income replacement ratio, 160
Competitive competencies, 34
Compilation, financial, 137
Component relations, 67–71
  affiliation agreement, 68
  communication, 70–71
  duplication, elimination of, 68
  effective, steps to, 68–69
  importance of, 67–68
  leader orientation, 69
  performance expectations, 68, 69
  recognizing/dissolving components,
    68–69
  reporting requirements, specifying, 68
  services, 69
  staff responsibilities, 69
  volunteer recognition, 69
Computer-based training, 309
Conference style room set-up, 412
Conflict, 97
Conflict of interest statement, 9
Conflict resolution, 84
Conflicts of interest, 9, 43–44, 59, 84, 111,
  259, 429
Consolidated Omnibus Budget Reconciliation
  Act of 1985 (COBRA), 174
Consultants
  for information management, 231
  knowledge management, 236–237
  lobbyists, 259
  marketing, 354, 355–356
Consumer-oriented books, publishing, 326
Consumer Protection Act, 169
Continuous improvement, 49
Contract manufacturing, 33
Contracts, 61–62
  affinity programs, 453
  cancellation clauses, 62
  employment, CEO, 15, 160
  information management technology, 233
  limited liability provisions, 62
  publishing, 329–330
  for space, meetings and conventions,
    400–403
  with suppliers/vendors, 207–208
Convenience sample, 218
Convention and visitor bureaus (CVBs), 398
Convention resume, 413
Convergence, 349
Copyrights, 62, 327, 419, 421–422, 430
Corporate culture
  attracting staff and volunteers to support,
    84, 90

creating a climate for diversity in,
  279–281
  of customer service, 91
  government relations and, 252
  management, components of, 85
  success, determinants of, 87
  successful vs. traditional, 86
Corporate Culture and Performance, 86
Cox, John B., 130
Credentialing, 16–17. *See also* Certification
  and accreditation programs
Crescent rounds room set-up, 412
Crisis communication(s), 269–271, 272
  accountability and responsibility in, 270
  examples of good and bad, 271
  no comment responses, 270
Crisis management, 20, 128–129
  crisis communications, 269–271, 272
  crisis phase, 128–129
  objectives, 271
  post crisis phase, 129
  pre-crisis phase, 128
Cross-firm decision-making, 33
Cross-sectoral coalition networks, 34
Culture. *See* Corporate culture
Customer-centric demand networks, 38
Customers' Customers Analysis, 32, 38
  advantages/disadvantages of, 32
  and demand network building, 38–41
  need for, 22
  risks of, 41–43
Customer satisfaction surveys, 22
Customer service, 165
Customer service culture, 91
Cycles, 24

D

Dalton, James G., 56
Data collection methods
  e-mail (Internet) polling, 215
  fax surveys, 215
  instant-response units, 216
  interactive, 215
  mail surveys, 215
  mixed mode, 216
  Web-based, 215
Data-driven decision making, 82
Data security, 232
Daybook, 267
Deception, media, 421
Decision making, 81–83
  data-driven, 82
  effective, checklist for, 82
  risk analysis in, 82
Defamation, 419, 424–425

Defined benefit plans, 162
Defined contribution plans, 162
Demand-driven network, 38
Demand networks, 31, 32–38
    Customers' Customers and, 38–41
Demographic shifts, 26
Determination letter, tax-exempt status, 60
Digital rights movement (DRM), 344
Digitization, 310
Direct expenses, 396
Direct mail, 369, 451
Directors and officers (D&O) insurance.
    See Association professional liability
    insurance (APLI)
Direct supply chain providers, 34
Discrimination
    age, 175
    allegations of, 62
    Civil Rights Act of 1964, 177–178
    intentional, 146
    unintended but actual, 146
Disparate impact, 146
Disparate treatment, 146
Display booths, trade shows, 394
Distance learning, 37, 232, 396
Distributive negotiation, 102
Diversity, 275–285
    accountability for, 280
    business case for, 278–279
    CAE exam, content outline, 458
    in communications, 282
    creating a climate for, 87, 279–281
    defining, 276–278, 283
    employee training in, 166, 280
    Four Layers of, 276–277
    in hiring, 146
    implementing initiatives for, 281
    importance of, 278–279
    in information gathering activities, 280
    leadership buy-in, 280
    measuring success, 282–283
    in mission and vision statements, 280
    motivation and, 278
    print materials and, 280
    risks associated with, 283–284
    transparency and, 280
    visual images and, 280
    weaving the message throughout the
        organization, 281–282
Document Management Industries
    Association (DMIA), 35
Document Type Definition (DTD), 342
Double bottom line, 32, 41–42
Downsizing, 34
Drucker, Peter, 21, 27, 49, 194

Due process, 64, 419, 422–423, 429
Dues, 17, 41
Duty, 423
DVDs, 310

E

Eadie, Doug, 88
E-commerce, information management, 229
Education, defined, 304
Education association, 288
Education programs, 303–311
    ADA requirements, 307
    adult learning, 303–305
    budgeting, 305–306
    evaluation and review, 308–309
    implementation and management, 307
    marketing and promotion, 306–307
    program design and development, 305
    speakers, assisting, 306
    technology, use of, 309–310
    at trade shows, 309
Efficiency, 44, 202, 244
Electronic Data Interchange (EDI) data
        sharing practices, 33
    standards, 42
    value-added networks (VANs), 35
Electronic publications, 316
E-mail communications, 167, 350
Embezzlement, 59
Emergency lighting, 246
Emergency plan, 246, 247, 411
Emergency preparedness, 246
Employee manual, 62
Employee record requirements, Fair Labor
        Standards Act, 173–174
Employee Retirement Income Security Act of
        1974, 175
Employees. *See also* Personnel
    in annual review of policies and
        procedures, 16
    attitude survey, 165
    benefits, 161–163
    child labor, 174
    communications with, 165–166
    compensation policy, 76, 154–156
    competency, cultivation of, 90
    components, relationship with, 69
    corrective discipline, 163–164
    dissatisfaction, 153, 154
    eligibility to work, proof of, 176
    e-mail, privacy and, 167
    employee manual, 62
    feedback, 165–166
    flextime, 91, 166
    as important resource, 143

incentive compensation programs, 91, 153, 321
in international programs, 383
involvement of in certification programs, 437, 441
leadership, 90–91
minimum wage, 172
morale problems, 77
orientation, 152
overtime, 62, 172–173
performance, 152–153
performance appraisals, 153–154
privacy, 167
professional advancement opportunities, 90
professional development activities, 90, 164–165
recognition of, 90
record requirements, Fair Labor Standards Act, 173–174
sanctions against, 163
satisfaction, markers for, 165
in subsidiary corporations, 76–77
telecommuting, 91, 166–167
termination of, 62, 163–164
training, 90, 91, 164–165, 166, 280
vacation policies, 62
volunteer relationship, 9, 10
worker's compensation, 166
work/life balance, 91
Employment applications, 145
Employment at will policy, 151, 164
Employment contract, CEO, 15, 160
Endorsements. See Affinity programs
Entrepreneurial management style, 32
Environment, 90, 91
Environmental health and safety, 245–246
Environmental Protection Agency (EPA), 245
Environmental scanning, 23, 24–26
Equal Employment Opportunity Commission (EEOC), 147
Equal Pay Act, 174
Equity increase, 156
Ergonomics, 245–246
Essential facilities doctrine, 422
Ethics, 105–115. See also Codes of ethics
appearance of unethical behavior, 111
barriers and drivers in, 112
CAE exam, content outline, 458, 465
conflicts of interest, 9, 43–44, 59, 84, 111, 259, 429
defined, 106
government relations, 260
international considerations, 114
lapses in, 105

laws, regulations, and executive orders impacting, 113–114
meetings and conventions, 416
research, role of, 111–112
social responsibility, 107
social responsibility program audits, and, 113
Evaluation
of certification and accreditation programs, 441–442
of education programs, 308–309
formative, 308
four levels of 308
independent, of financial information, 137
of marketing structures, 353–356
of meetings and conventions, 415
in public relations, 265, 272
summative, 308
for tactical planning, 127–128
of technical publications, 345–347
Event planning. See Meetings and conventions
Event sequence, 52–53, 55
Exclusivity, 41
Executive committee, 4
Executive compensation, 160–161
Executive leadership, 81
Exhibit space, trade shows, 394, 401
Ex-officio board members, 3
External problems, 120
External research, 210

F

Facilities management, 243–248
ADA compliance, 246–247
aesthetics, 245
building security, 246
CAE exam, content outline, 460
custodial service, 245
emergency preparedness, 246
environmental health and safety, 245–246
ergonomics, 245–246
facilities resources, 248
facilities services, 245
fire protection, 246
HVAC systems, 244
leasing, 243
lighting, 244
occupancy satisfaction, 244–245
owning, 243
parking, 245
productivity, checklist for, 244
recycling, 245
renting, 243

visitor access, 246
Fair Credit Reporting Act, 151, 169
Fair Labor Standards Act, 171–174
  minimum wage, 171
  overtime, 172–173
Family and Medical Leave Act, 175–176
Federal Election Campaign Act, 64
Federal Election Commission, 249, 260
Federal Insurance Contributions Act of 1935
  (FICA), 170–171
Federal labor laws
  Age Discrimination in Employment Act,
    175
  Americans with Disabilities Act (ADA),
    169–170
  compliance calendar, 181
  Consolidated Omnibus Budget
    Reconciliation Act of 1985 (COBRA),
    174
  Consumer Protection Act, 169
  Employee Retirement Income Security
    Act of 1974, 175
  Equal Pay Act, 174
  Fair Labor Standards Act, 171–174
  Family and Medical Leave Act, 175–176
  Federal Insurance Contributions Act of
    1935 (FICA), 170–171
  Immigration Reform and Control Act,
    176–177
  list of, by number of employees, 168
  National Labor Relations Act, 177
  Occupational Safety and Health Act, 177
  Pregnancy Discrimination Act of 1978,
    178
  reporting requirements, 180
  sexual harassment, 178
  summaries of, 169–179
  Title VII, Civil Rights Act of 1964,
    177–178
  Uniformed Service Employment and
    Reemployment Rights Act, 179
  Uniform Guidelines on Employee
    Selection Procedures, 179
Federal Trade Commission, 420
Fee-for-service income, 40, 41
Fee-for-service products, 42
Fiduciary responsibility policy, 84
Fiedler, Fred, 79
File Transfer Protocol, 342
Finance. See Budget and finance
Financial reporting, 134–136
  accrual vs. cash basis of accounting, 134
  balance sheet, 134
  cash flow statement, 135–136
  ratios for analysis, 135

statement of activities (income
  statement), 134, 135
Fire alarms, 246
Fire protection, 246
Fixed costs, 305, 397
Flagging, 268
Flexible spending accounts (FSAs), 162
Flextime, 91, 166
Focus groups, 214, 266, 346
Follow-up, 70
Formative evaluation, 308
For-profit subsidiary, 14, 15, 60
401(k) plans, 162–163
Fraud, 59, 421
Freedom of Information Act, 249
French service, banquets, 409
Function sheets, 413–414
Fundraising, 191–200
  CAE exam, content outline, 464
  challenges to, 199
  creating an entity for within the
    association, 199
  donor information management, 228
  donor types, 195
  establishing an affiliate nonprofit
    organization for, 198
  events at meetings and conventions, 396
  integration of into overall strategic plan,
    193
  marketing principles and, 194
  methods, pros and cons of, 197
  motivation and, 195
  reasons for, 191
  sources of funds, 191
  strategic marketing plan for, 196
  tactical planning for, example of, 123
Future
  defining, 21–30
  preparing for, 21–23
Futures analysis, 21, 22
  change drivers, identification of, 23,
    26–27
  components of, 23–24
  cycle, 23
  environmental scanning, 23, 24–26
  objectives, 23
  scenario planning, 23, 27–30
  strategic planning, 23

G

Garnishments, of wages, 169
Gelatt, James P., 199
General membership survey, 210
Glassie, Jefferson C., 65–66

Globalization, 21, 32, 36–38, 373. *See also*
    International expansion
    CAE exam, content outline, 463
    "Viagra Lesson," 37
Going Global for the Greater Good, 388
Governance and structure, 1–11
    ad hoc groups/task forces, 5
    articles of incorporation, 6, 58
    association management, 15
    board of directors, 3, 4, 61, 75, 77, 84,
        88–90, 252
    bylaws, 1–2, 6
    CAE exam, content outline, 461–462
    CEO search committee, 15
    codes of ethics, 6, 84, 106, 108, 109,
        110–111, 428–432
    executive committee, 4
    for-profit subsidiaries, 14, 15
    house (assembly) of delegates, 4
    incorporation, advantages and
        disadvantages of, 2, 14
    management fees, 15
    membership categories, 14
    membership sections, 5
    nonprofit foundations, 14
    officers, 3–4
    organizational units, 3–5, 14
    policies and procedures, developing, 6,
        13–20
    recordkeeping, 14–15
    special interest groups, 5
    staff-volunteer relationship, 9, 10
    standing committees, 4
    subsidiary corporations, 74–76
    succession planning, 15, 383
    trends affecting, 8
    volunteer relations, 1, 5–9, 14
Government affairs, 16
Government relations, 249–261
    associations' role in, 250
    briefings, 258
    CAE exam, content outline, 462–463
    candidate events, 258
    coalitions, 257
    committee, 253
    conflicts of interest, 259
    defined, 264
    government interaction, 255–256
    grassroots networks, 257, 260
    increased activity, 249–250
    informational activity, 253
    informing members, 258
    issues identification and analysis, 254
    legal issues, 251
    lobbying, 250, 251, 260

    management and administration, 259
    member involvement, 257
    members and staff, roles of, 253, 259
    need for, 249
    plans and procedures, 251–253
    political action committees (PACs), 249,
        259, 260
    position statements, 252, 254–255
    proactive approach to, 253
    program components, 254–259
    public relations activities surrounding,
        255, 257–258
    purpose of, 254
    reactive efforts, 253
    regulatory, 256
    showing value of to the board, 252
    site visits by government officials, 257
    speakers, 258
    spokesperson, designating, 253
    tax status and, 251, 258, 260
    testimony, 256
    trainings, 258
    trends in, 260–261
    types of programs, 253–254
Government services
    contractual relationships with, 41
    privatization of, 40–41
Graham, John H., 275
Greenspan, Alan, 33

H
Hamm, Michael S., 443
Hart, Velma R., 284
Hazards, 245
Health care reimbursement arrangements
    (HRAs), 162
Health insurance, employee, 161–162
    Consolidated Omnibus Budget
        Reconciliation Act of 1985 (COBRA),
        174
Health savings accounts (HSAs), 162
Hemenway, Don, 347
Heskitt, 86
High Impact Governing in a Nutshell—
    17 Questions that Board Members and
    CEOs Frequently Ask, 88
Hiring
    acceptable and unacceptable interview
        questions, 149–150
    background checks, 150
    credit reports, 151
    disparate impact, 146
    disparate treatment, 146
    diversity in, 146
    employee recruitment, 144–146

interviewing, 146–150
job bidding/posting, 145
making the offer, 151
from outside the association, 146
persons with disabilities, 150
pre-employment physical examination, 147
promoting from within, 145
references, checking, 147, 150–151
telephone screening, 146
Holding company, creation of, 75
Hollow square room set-up, 412
Holtz, Shel, 271
Home-based study, 396
House of delegates, 4
Housing bureau, 407
Human resource management, 143–190. *See also* Employees; Personnel
  CAE exam, content outline, 459
  compensation policy, determining, 76, 154–156
  corrective discipline, 163–164
  diversity, 166
  emerging trends in, 166–167, 169
  employee benefits, 161–163
  employee development, 90, 164–165
  employee privacy, 167
  employment orientation, 152
  employment performance, evaluating, 152–153
  executive compensation, 160–161
  federal labor laws, 168–179, 181
  federal reporting requirements, 180
  feedback mechanisms, 165–166
  flextime, 91, 167
  formal employment applications, 145
  HR policy, 163
  incentive compensation, 91, 157–160
  independent contractors, 167, 169
  interviewing, 146–150
  job bidding/posting, 145
  job descriptions, 154
  making the offer, 151
  outsourcing of, 144
  performance appraisals, 153–154
  professionals in, 143
  promotion from within, 145
  recruitment, 144–146
  references, checking, 147, 150–151
  risks and consequences associated with, 144
  salary planning, 156–157
  sample forms for, 184–190
  telecommuting, 166–167
  vacation replacements, 145

Hyde, Barbara, 273

I

Illegal drugs, use of, 170
Immersion education, 90
Immigration Reform and Control Act, 176–177
Incentive compensation, 157–160
Incentive target, 158
Inclusiveness, 87
Incorporation, advantages and disadvantages of, 2
Incremental budgeting, 132
Indemnification, 62
Independent contractors, 167, 169
Indirect expenses, 396–397
Indirect suppliers, 34
Individual behavior, paradigm for explaining, 26
Individual interviews, 213–214
Industry association, 288
Information, and technology compared, 37
Information management, 225–234
  accessing, upgrading, or acquiring systems for, 230–233
  accounting, 230
  backup systems, 226
  billing and accounts receivable, 230
  committee and chapter management, 228–229
  donor management, 228
  education and certification management, 229
  employees responsible for, 233
  marketing, 229
  meetings and events, 229
  membership management and activity tracking, 227
  online searches, 233
  order and inventory management, 229–230
  overview of, 223–227
  privacy, 226
  reporting, 230
  security, 226, 232
  technology, understanding, 232
  time sensitivity, 226
  value, 226
  Web content and e-commerce activities, 229
Information reporting, 222
Insurance
  association professional liability policies, 61, 431
  legal issues, 60–61

liability, need for, 8
meetings and conventions, 410
for standard setting and certification
programs, 431
Intangible property, 63
licenses for use of, 62
Integrated marketing communications,
263–264
Intellectual property. *See also* Copyrights;
Patents
antitrust concerns, 421–422
development, 36
legal issues, 63
Internal financial controls, 136
Internal problems, 120
Internal research, 210–211
Internal Revenue Code (U.S. Tax Code)
independent contractors vs. employees,
distinction between, 167, 169
international meeting destinations, 413
Section 501(c)(3), 2, 60, 427
Section 501(c)(6), 2, 60
unrelated business income tax (UBIT),
60, 132, 446, 448–449
Internal Revenue Service (IRS), 14, 59, 73,
427, 448
International expansion, 375–390
accountability for, 382
association concerns, 381–382
communications and printed materials,
383–384
competition issues, 380, 381
cultural differences, 377
geographic considerations, 378–379
goals for, 383
"going international," defined, 375–376
international membership, 380, 381, 383,
386
international potential, assessing, 377–378
international visitors, 385
key questions to ask, 376, 378–382
leadership buy-in, 377
market share, 380, 381
meetings, 384–385
membership and, 377, 380, 383
motivation for, 382, 383
organizational models for, 387–388
organization structure and culture, 382
overseas counterparts, 386
partnership potential and, 379–380
publications, 384
raw material/resource considerations, 380
risks of, 377
staff, role of, 383
strategic assessment tool for, 378–382

strategic plan and, 376, 383
in succession planning, 383
Internet, 125, 225, 254, 301, 349
Interviewer bias, 213
Interviewing
prospective employees, 146–150
for surveys, 213–214
Inventory, information management,
229–230
Investments, 139
Island booths, trade shows, 394

J
Job bidding, 145
Job candidate evaluation form, sample, 184
Job descriptions, 152
committees, 84
components of, 154
in defining compensation policy, 155
for volunteers at meetings and
conventions, 411
worksheet for creating, sample, 189
Job opportunities, 240
Job posting, 145
Joint ventures. *See* Affinity programs
Journals, 315–316, 334. *See also* Technical
publications
Just-in-Time (JIT) relationships, 31, 32–35

K
Kaine, Jack W., 104
Knowledge management, 235–241
AAPS Career Network case study,
240–241
AAPS MemberNet case study, 239–240
CAE exam, content outline, 460–461
consultant, hiring, 236–237
cultural hurdles to, 237
defined, 235
electronic-based sources, 237
enablers, 238
existing knowledge repositories, analysis
of, 236
financial resources and human assets
necessary for, 238–239
job opportunities, 240
knowledge transfer, 235, 237
meeting topic database, 236
membership directory, 239
mission critical knowledge, 236
motivations for, 236
outcome of, 235
paper-based sources, 237
relevancy of, 238
search capabilities, 238

taxonomy and, 237
Knowledge Management Officer (KMO), 238
Knowledge transfer, 235, 237
Knowles, Malcolm, 303
Koenig, Bonnie, 388
"Koffee klatch" meetings, 166
Kouzes, James, 80–81, 86, 88

L
Langlois, Richard, 34
Lanham Act, 431
Lawson, Richard V., 241
Leadership, 79–93
    attributes of, 79–81
    board of directors, 88–90
    building relationships among leaders,
       87–91
    CAE exam, content outline, 458–459
    code of conduct, 84
    as a community effort, 83–84
    conferences, 70
    decision making, 81–83
    diversity, 87
    executive style, 81
    hierarchy, 81
    inherent vs. learned, 92
    key to effective, 34
    leader orientation, 69
    leaders as go-betweens, 83
    legislative style, 81
    and management compared, 53
    modeling, 85–87
    ongoing development, 88–89
    personal competencies needed for, 80–81
    quality of and organizational success, 79
    staff, 90–91
    strategic planning and, 84
    structural requirements, 80
    success in, determinants of, 88
The Leadership Challenge, 80–81, 86
Legal audits, 57–58
Legal issues, 57–66
    ADA compliance, 419–420, 425–427, 430
    affinity programs, 453–454
    alcoholic beverages, serving at receptions,
       408–409
    antitrust, 42, 63–64, 222–223, 419,
       420–422
    appropriate protection against liability, 65
    association programs, 63–65
    CAE exam, content outline, 459–460
    contracts, 61–62
    copyrights and patents, 419,421–422, 429,
       430
    corporate status, 58–59

    defamation, 419, 424–425
    due process, 64, 419, 422–423, 429
    essential facilities doctrine, 422
    finances, 59
    in government relations, 251
    insurance, 60–61
    intellectual property, 63
    legal audits, 57–58
    liability risks, 57
    litigation, 61
    lobbying, 64
    membership, 64
    negligence, 419, 423–424
    personnel, 62
    political activities, 64–65
    in research and statistics, 222–223
    risk, principal areas of, 419
    risk, steps to minimizing, 428–432
    in standard setting, certification and
       accreditation programs, and codes of
       ethics, 419–432
    supplier relations, 207–208
    taxes, 59–60, 427
    trademarks, 62, 430–431, 450
    warranty, 62, 419, 432
Legal privilege, 425
Legislative leadership, 81
LEGO-relationships, 31
Leroy, Wayne E., 11, 248
Levin, Mark, 374
Liability
    appropriate protection against, 65
    risks of, 57
Libel, 151, 424
Licenses, for use of intangible property, 62
Lifecycle, component, 68–69
Limited liability contract provisions, 62
Limited liability protection, 58
Linear supply-chain relationships, 31
Link-relative method, 220
Liquidity and current ratios, 135
Litigation, 61
Load factoring, 220
Lobbying, 250, 251, 260, 437
    defined, 264
    goals of, 287
    by Section 501(c)(6) organizations, 64
Lobbying Disclosure Act, 64
Logical incrementalism, 48
Long-term projections, 28
Losey, Michael R., 182
Lugbill, Carolyn A., 390

M
Magazines, 315–316

Mahlmann, John J., 295
Mancuso, Dawn M., 417
Market-directed association, defined, 351
Market-driven association, defined, 351
Marketing, 349–362
  affinity programs, promotion of, 450–452
  association vs. for-profit, 350–351
  association-wide, 352
  branding, 356
  budgeting for, 357, 360
  business summary, components of,
    357–358
  "buy or die," 366
  CAE exam, content outline, 456
  chief executive officer, role of, 352–353,
    357
  defined, 264
  by department, 360–361
  of education programs, 306–307
  function of, 351
  information management, 229
  in-house consultant, 354
  management of, 351–352
  with membership orientation, 354
  meetings and conventions, 404–405
  monitoring and evaluation techniques,
    360
  outside consultant, 355–356
  overview, 351
  pitfalls in planning for, 361
  plan, key components of, 357–360
  planning process, 356–357
  of publications, 323–324, 328–329
  research and, 358–359, 361
  by a senior marketing staff person, 355
  by a separate marketing department,
    354–355
  staff, role of, 361
  strategic plan for, 356, 361
  strategies and projections, 359–360
  structures, evaluations of, 353–356
  to trade show exhibitors, 406
  trends affecting, 349–350
  trial memberships, 359
  volunteers, role of, 355
  Web sites as, 359
Market rate, 155
Matrix of Opportunities, 122, 124, 126
Maynard, Dr. Bill, 85, 86
Media relations, 18, 20, 266–268
  deadlines, 267
  defined, 264
  media advisory, 267
  media directories, 267

media interviews, ten commandments of,
  268
  at meetings and conventions, 405
  press conferences, 267
  press releases, 266–267
  spokesperson, designation of, 18, 20, 253,
    267
  spokesperson, training, 267–268
Meeting profile and specifications report, 412
Meetings and conventions, 16–17, 391–418
  ADA compliance, 401
  advance work, importance of, 392
  alternatives to in-person, 416
  annual business meeting, 391
  attendance, declines, 360
  attendance, tactical plan to boost, 124
  audio-visual equipment, 403
  banquets, type of service, 409
  budgeting, 396–397
  buzz groups, 394
  CAE exam, content outline, 464–465
  cancellation, 402
  colloquium, 394
  committee, 393
  contract negotiations, 400–403
  convention center contracts, 403
  convention resume, 413
  diversity in planning, 87
  educational sessions, breakouts, 394–395
  emergency plan, 411
  emerging trends in, 416
  entertainers, booking, 403–404
  environmentally friendly, 416
  ethics in, 416
  evaluating, 415
  exhibit space, 401
  exposition management, 405–407
  food and beverage functions, 401,
    408–410
  formal lectures, 393
  format, 392, 393–396
  function sheets, 413–414
  fundraisers and sporting events, 396
  general sessions, 393–394
  guest programs, 395
  host organization, 17
  housing bureau, 407
  information management, 229
  insurance considerations, 410
  internationalization of, 384–385
  international meetings, 16–17, 413–414
  marketing the meeting, 404–405
  master accounts, 401, 403
  media relations, 405
  meeting objectives, 393

meeting planner competencies, 392
meeting profile and specifications report, 412
meeting room set-ups, 412, 414
meeting timetable/activity calendar, 413
menu design and planning, 409
name badges, 410
"official" airline, 403
on-site management, 414–415
open space meetings, 395
performance licenses, 404
planning tools, 412–414
plenary session, 394
pre-convention meeting, 414
printed materials, 411
program development, 392–393
receptions, 395, 408–409
registration, 410
role of in association mission, 391
rooming list, 407
room reservations, 401, 407
security, 410
site inspection, conducting, 398–400
site selection, 397–398
speakers, booking, 404
specialized services, 403–404
tax deductibility issues, 416
team management, 411–412
tours and social events, 395–396
trade shows and expositions, 394
volunteers, role of, 393, 411
workshops, 394
Meeting timetable/activity calendar, 413
Member recognition, 387
    CAE exam, content outline, 465
Member relations
    affinity programs, benefits of, 447–448
    associate members, 14
    CAE exam, content outline, 463
    chapters, 17
    code of ethics, 84
    communication with members, 17, 258
    disciplinary actions, 64
    information management and activity tracking, 227
    international expansion and, 377
    international members, 380, 381, 383
    legal issues, 64
    member satisfaction, research to determine, 210, 211
    members' customers, 31
    needs assessment, 22, 210
    new customers, 43
    noncompliant members, adversarial relationships with, 41

publications, role of, 330
    sections, 5
Member recruitment and retention, 227, 363–374
    application process, streamlining, 371–372
    CAE exam, content outline, 463
    coordinating efforts, 374
    creating an effective message, 366–368
    database management system, importance of, 373–373
    delivering the message effectively, 369–370
    direct mail solicitation, 369
    dues renewal process, 372–373
    electronic messages, 369–370
    eligibility decisions, 64
    finding and targeting prospects, 366, 367
    globalization and, 373
    goals, setting, 365
    identifying opportunities, 364–365
    international campaign, 386
    member involvement as a retention mechanism, 372
    member service policies and standards, 371
    membership materials, developing effective, 368–369
    membership growth, 363–364
    member-to-member recruiting, 370
    member-to-prospect recruiting, 368, 370
    plan, developing, 365
    plan, example of, 122
    retention system, developing, 370–374
    telephone solicitation, 369
    trial memberships, 359
Membership development culture, 364, 370
Mentoring, 6, 87, 90
Message boards, 125
Milestones, timeline of, 30
Millennial generation, 21, 27, 29
Minimum wage, 171
Model facilities, trade shows, 394
Monthly Absenteeism Tracking Form, sample, 190
Multiplier effect, 124, 128
Music Educators National Conference (MENC), 288

N

Nappi, Ralph J., 311
National Academy of Recording Arts & Sciences, Inc. (NARAS), 288
National Association of Music Merchants (NAMM), 288

National Business Forms Association (NBFA), 34
National Coalition of Music Education (NCME), 288–289
National Council for Interior Design Quality (NCIDQ), 44
National Education Association, 299
National Labor Relations Act, 177
National Library of Medicine DTD, 343
National Restaurant Association, 298
Natural element emergencies, 247
Needs assessment, 210
    adult learning, 304–305
    member, 22, 210
Negligence, 419, 423–424
Negotiation, 95–104
    agenda, need for, 102
    assumptions, 103
    CAE exam, content outline, 458–459
    climate, 101–102
    common mistakes in, 102–103
    communication in, 103
    concession making, 103
    conflict escalation, 97
    cooling-off period, need for, 97
    counterproposals, 99–100
    deadlines, 101
    defined, 95
    dissecting information, 102
    distributive, 102
    dress, 101
    effective negotiators, traits of, 96
    ego and, 102
    gains from, 95
    golden rules of, 96–102
    handling disagreements, 99
    inflexibility, 102
    labeling communications, 98
    negative approach to, 102
    overconfidence, 103
    persistence in, 96
    point of view, 97, 103
    power position, 100–101
    practice, importance of, 103–104
    pre-negotiating solutions, 100
    preparation, 96
    principles of, 97
    questioning in, 99, 103
    redefining the issue, 104
    saving face, 98
    scarce resource in, 95
    space contract for meetings and conventions, 400–403
    strongest positions, 100
    successful, requirements of, 95
    summarizing, 103
    thinking ahead, 104
    trust and, 96–97, 100
    varied terms, 95
    walk-away position, 98
    win-win vs. equal win, 96
    workable agreements, 100
    with yourself, 103
Net return, 397
Newsletters, 315
NOCA Guide to Understanding Credentialing Concepts, 433
Nominating committee, 3
Nominating procedures, 84
Non-duplication of benefits, employee health insurance, 161
Non-probability sample, 218
Non-tariff barriers (NTBs), 36–37
Nth name sample, 217

O

Occupational Safety and Health Act of 1970, 177, 245
Occupational Safety and Health Administration (OSHA), 245
Offer letter, sample, 186
Office administration, 18
Officers, 3–4
    first vice president/vice chair(man)-elect, 3
    president/chair(man) of the board, 3
    secretary/treasurer, 3
    vice presidents/directors, 4
    written job descriptions, 84
Online learning systems, 416
Online publishing, 329
Online voting, 8
Open access movement, 343
Open Space Technology (OST), 395
Operating budget, 49, 132–133
Organizational behavior, paradigm for explaining, 26
Orientation
    diversity training, 87
    employee, 152
    new board members, 77
    new component leaders, 69
Orientation checklist–human resources, sample, 187
Orientation checklist–supervisors, sample, 188
O'Sullivan, Richard, 45
Out clause, 62
Outcome statements, 54
Outsourcing, 33, 34

benefits of, 201–202
developing win-win relationships in, 206
of human resource management, 144
managing the relationship, 205–207
of the publishing function, 329–330
of the public relations function, 271–272
requests for proposals, soliciting, 203–205
research function, 221
Overtime, 171–173
exemptions to, 172–173

P

Partner relationships, 34
Passive income, 448–449
Passive revenues, 60
Passwords, 232
Patents, 419, 421–422, 429
Payment terms, 62
Pay practice, 156
Pedagogy, 303
Peer relationships, 34
Peer review, technical publications, 333, 337–338
Peninsula booths, trade shows, 394
Pensions, 162
Performance appraisals, employee, 153–154
Performance expectations, employee, 152
Personal integrity, 85
Personal liability, risk of, 8
Personnel. *See also* Employees
legal issues, 62
policies and procedures, 18
records, privacy and, 167
Plated service, banquets, 409
Podcasting, 125, 316
Policies and procedures, 6, 13–20, 84
annual review of, 16
business and finance operations, 140
crisis management, 20
development and review process, 14
governance, 14–15
guidelines for developing, 19
importance of, 13
media relations, 18, 20
office administration, 18
operations and management, 14, 15–18
personnel, 18
policies, defined, 13
procedures, defined, 13
public image and public policy, 14, 18, 20
purpose of, 13
role of volunteers and staff in developing, 13
services, 18
Policy, defined, 13

Political action committees (PACs), 16, 64, 249, 259, 260
Political activities
legal issues, 64–65
lobbying, 64
Portable skills, 35
Portfolio analysis, 43–44
Portfolio planning, 41
Position statements, 252, 254–255
Posner, Barry, 86, 88
Pregnancy Discrimination Act of 1978, 178
Press conferences, 267
Press releases, 266–267
Price fixing, 63, 222
Primary research, 211
Probability sample, 217
Procedure, defined, 13
Product demonstration sessions, trade shows, 394
Professional development programs
CAE exam, content outline, 461
employee, 90, 164–165
Professional ethics, 85
Professional societies, growth of, 36
Profitability ratios, 135
Promotion, defined, 264. *See also* Marketing
Proprietary information, 37
Proxy tax, 64
Public affairs, defined, 264
Public image, 14, 18, 20
Public policy, 14, 18, 20
Public relations, 263–273
CAE exam, content outline, 466
clipping services, 265
crisis communications, 269–271, 272
defined, 263
evaluation, 265, 272
focus group research, 266
goal of, 264–265
in government relations, 257–258
integrated marketing communications, 263–264
as a management function, 263
mark-up for services, 272
media relations, 18, 20, 266–268
outsourcing, 271–272
plans, 265–266
press releases, 266–267
retainer fees, 272
specific campaign plans, 265, 266
strategic communications plan, 265–266
terminology, 264
as a two-way process, 263
Web sites as, 268–269, 272
Publications. *See* Publishing

Publicity, defined, 264
Publishing, 313–331
    advertising rates, setting, 322–323
    advertising sales, 315, 321–323
    advertising-to-editorial ratio, 321
    audited circulation, 323
    books, 325–329, 334
    CAE exam, content outline, 466
    circulation and distribution, 324–325
    contracts, 329–330
    copyrights, 62, 327, 419, 421–422, 430
    design for readability, 318–319
    editorial content, 318
    electronic publications, 316
    financial management, 320–321
    flagship publications, 315
    general guidelines for, 313–314
    in-house design capability, 319
    international expansion and, 384
    magazines and journals, 315–316, 334
    marketing and business plans, 323–324,
        328–329
    matching needs and formats, 315–316
    and member relations, 330
    newsletters, 315
    nonmember subscribers, 325
    online, 329
    order fulfillment, 328
    outsourcing, 329–330
    pay-per-view Web publications, 324
    periodicals, 317
    policies and procedures, 18
    preparation and printing, 329
    prices, setting, 328–329
    printing technology, 319
    production, 319–320, 321
    reader loyalty, building, 318
    readers, importance of, 314
    relevance of publications, 316–317
    royalties and commissions, 327–328
    sales growth strategy, 323
    staff incentives, 321
    statement of purpose, 314–315
    style guides, 318
    tax considerations, 324
    technical publications, 333–347
    Web sites as, 330

Q

Quantitative surveys, 213
Quick Response (QR) relationships, 31, 32
Quinn, James Brian, 48
Quota sample, 218

R

Rational-analytical system, 48
Reasonable accommodation, Americans with
    Disabilities Act (ADA), 170, 307
Recognition
    employee, 90
    member, 387, 465
    volunteers, 8, 69
Recruitment. *See also* Member recruitment
    and retention
    of employees, 144–146
    volunteers, 6
Reference books, publishing, 326
Reference checking form, sample, 185
Reference checks
    affinity marketers, 453
    pre-employment, 147, 150–151
Reporting, information management, 230
Requests for proposal (RFPs)
    site selection for meetings and
        conventions, 398
    vendors/suppliers, 203–205
Research and statistics, 209–224
    accuracy and precision of results, 218–220
    archives, 211
    CAE exam, content outline, 457
    on certification and accreditation
        programs, 438–440
    contracted research, 221
    data collection techniques, 215–216
    external research, 210
    focus groups, 214, 266, 346
    information reporting, 222
    internal research, 210–211
    for issues management, 210
    legal issues, 222–223
    link-relative method, 220
    load factoring, 220
    for marketing purposes, 358–359, 361
    for meetings and trade shows, 211
    on member satisfaction, 211
    planning, 212
    primary research, 211
    sampling methodology, 212
    sampling terminology, 217–218
    secondary research, 211
    setting objectives, 212
    special considerations, 220
    for strategic planning, 211
    survey logistics, 221
    survey methods, 213–214
    survey sampling, 216–217
    surveys, types of, 209
    survey subjects, 209–210
    trade publications and, 211

Reserves, 138
Restraint of trade, 63, 420. *See also* Antitrust
Retirement plans, 162–163
Return on investment, 397
Review, financial, 137
Risk analysis, 82
Riska, Stacey, 208
Robinson, William T., 78
Role clarification, 9
Rowan, Matthew J., 454
Royalties and commissions, 60, 327–328, 446
RSS feeds, 316
Rudolph, Deborah, 261
Russian service, banquets, 409

S

Salaries. *See* Compensation
Sampling, 216–217
    accuracy and precision of results, 218–220
    confidence error, 218, 219
    convenience sample, 218
    error, 218
    frame, 217
    margin of error, 218, 219
    non-probability sample, 218
    nth name sample, 217
    population, 217
    probability sample, 217
    quota sample, 218
    sample size, 218, 219
    simple random sample, 217
    stratified, 218
    systematic sample, 217
    terminology, 217–218
Sarbanes-Oxley Act, 8, 13, 57, 59, 137
Satellite communications, 310
Savings Incentive Match Plans for Employees
    (SIMPLE plans), 163
Scanning dashboard, 25, 26
Scanning gauge, 25
Scenario planning, 23, 27–30
    association matrix, 28–29
    benefits, 27–28
    creating scenarios, 28–29
    defined, 27
    principles required for, 28
    value of scenarios, 27–28
    working with scenarios, 29–30
Scholarship program, international, 387
Schoolroom room set-up, 412
Schools, Randolph R., 301
Science, technical, and medical (STM)
    publications. *See* Technical publications
Secondary research, 211
Security

building, 246
certification program, 430
data, 232
information management, 226, 232
meetings and conventions, 410
Self-concept, 303
Self-regulation programs, legal issues, 64
*7 Measures of Success—What Remarkable
    Associations Do that Others Don't*, 83
Sexual harassment, 178, 283
Shared network environments, 34, 37
Shark, Alan R., 362
Sherman Antitrust Act, 420
Sherman, Michael, 223
Sienkiewicz, Jone R., 20
Simple random sample, 217
Single-point forecasts, 27
Site inspection
    checklist for, 399–400
    meetings and conventions, 398–400
Site selection, meetings and conventions,
    397–398
Site visits, by government officials, 257
Skip level interviews, 166
Slander, 151, 424
Smoke detectors, 246
Social entrepreneurs, 32
Social networking, 125, 239
Social responsibility, 107
Social responsibility program audits, 113
Social Security, 170
Society for Interventional Radiology (SIR), 36
Solution in search of a problem approach, 38
Spam filters, 350
Speakers
    booking, for meetings and conventions,
    404
    education programs, 306
    fees, 306
    government relations program, 258
Special interest groups, 5
Specific campaign public relations plans, 265,
    266
Spokesperson(s), 18, 20, 253, 267
Sponsorships, 60. *See also* Affinity programs
Sprinkler systems, 246
Standard-setting programs
    antitrust concerns, 421
    CAE exam, content outline, 465
    legal issues, 64
    liability insurance for, 431
    nonmember participation in, 431
    risk, steps to minimizing, 428–432
    written disclaimers regarding, 431
Standards of conduct

antitrust concerns, 421
ASAE, 86
Standing committees, 4
Statement of activities (income statement), 134, 135
State of the society (association) meetings, 165
STEEP (sociodemographics, technology, economics, environment, and politics) categories, 25
Stock options, 157
Strategic budget, 49
Strategic communications plan, 265–266
Strategic issues, 50–51
    classification of, 51
    defined, 50
    monitor, 51, 55
    priority, 51, 55
    research, 51, 55
Strategic management, CAE exam, content outline, 455–456
Strategic marketing plan, 356
Strategic planning, 23, 47–56
    action plan, 52–53
    CAE exam, content outline, 457
    event sequence, 52–53, 55
    evolution of, 47–48
    failures of, 38
    four elements of, 51–56
    fundraising program, integration of, 193
    international expansion, 376, 383
    issues on the radar screen, 54
    ongoing programs in, 48–49
    outcome, 52
    outcome statements, 54
    principles, 52
    research and statistics for, 211
    strategic issues, 50–51, 52
    and tactical planning, need for, 117
Strategy, defined, 51
Stratified sampling, 218
Stratton, Debra, 331
Structural emergencies, 247
Structure and governance, for certification and accreditation programs, 441
Structure → Conduct → Performance model, 26, 39
Sturgeon, Timothy, 33, 34
Sturzi, Scott R., 115
Subsidiary corporations, 73–78
    and affiliates compared, 73
    budget and finance, 140
    chief executive officer and, 74
    governance and structure, 74–76
    holding company, creation of, 75

    management and staffing, 76–77
    outside experts in, 77
    potential perils of, 77
    reasons for forming, 73–74
    "second guessers," 77
    start-up capital, 77
Succession planning, 15, 383
Summative evaluation, 308
Supplier management, CAE exam, content outline, 460
Supplier relations, 201–208
    communication in, 205–207
    contracts, 207–208
    deciding on a supplier, 204–205
    legal issues, 207–208
    managing the outsourcing relationship, 205–207
    minimum standards, 207
    outsourcing, benefits of, 201–202
    requests for proposals (RFPs), soliciting, 203–205
    supplier assessment form, 204–205
    target goals, 207
    unacceptable standards, 207
Surveys
    by fax, 215
    focus groups, 214
    individual interviews, 213–214
    interactive, 215
    by mail, 215
    popular techniques compared, 214
    quantitative, 213
    sampling, 216–217
    technical publications and, 345–346
    telephone interviews, 213
    Web-based, 215
Sustainability, 31–45
    customers' customers and demand network building, 38–41
    customers' customers strategy, risks of, 41–43
    demand-networks, necessity of, 32–38
    portfolio analysis, 43–44
Systematic sample, 217

T
Tabloid newspapers, 316
Tabor, Janis L., 261
Tactical planning, 117–129
    accountability, 128
    attendance at annual convention, example of, 124
    blue sky thinking, 118
    budgeting to, 126–127

commitment and continuity, need for, 118

competition, identifying and measuring, 120

creating, 122–125

crisis management, 128–129

different approaches to, 118

economic impact, 126

evaluation, 127–128

flexibility, need for, 126

fundraising/endowment building campaign, example of, 123

internal vs. external problems, 120

key audiences, identification of, 120–121

length of, 125

membership recruitment/retention plan, example of, 122

NASA approach to calendaring, 125

scheduling, 125–126

setting goals and objectives, 119

shortcuts to, 125–126

situation analysis/problem definition, 119–120

and strategic plans, relationship to, 127–128

technological tactics, 125

vehicles and tactics, identification and development of, 121–122

"Take One" brochures, 452

Targeted income replacement ratio, 160

Task forces, 5

Taxable wage base, 171

Tax-deductible contributions, 501(c)3 status and, 198

Taxes, 59–60, 427. *See also* Internal Revenue Code (U.S. Tax Code)

deductibility issues, meetings and conventions, 416

lobbying dues nondeductibility laws, 64

proxy, on lobbying expenditures, 64

publications, 324

unrelated business income tax (UBIT), 60, 132, 446, 448–449

Tax-exempt status, 2, 59–60

determination letter, 60

501(c)(3), 2, 60, 73, 198, 241, 258, 259

501(c)(4), 251

501(c)(6), 2, 60, 73, 251, 427

Form 990, 59

and government relations, 251, 258, 260

nonexempt activities, 60

passive income, 448–449

purpose, specifying, 2

Taxonomy, 237

Team building, 90

Teamwork, 10, 165, 166

Technical publications, 333–347

access control, 344

books, 334

CAE exam, content outline, 465

collected works, 334

contractors and contract management, 339–340

digital (e-book) editions, 335

digital files, using, 342

digital rights management, 344

editors and reviewers, 338–339

evaluating publication products and programs, 345–346

expert evaluations, 345

finances, 336–337

focus groups, 346

formal RFP process for, 339–340

format, selecting, 340

frequency and delivery method, 335

fulfillment, 343–344

hyper-text markup language (HTML), 342

journals, 315–316, 334

in libraries, 343

lifecycle of, 334–335

management structure, 336

managing web resources, 344

as member service, 335–336

online versions, 335

open access movement and, 343

peer review, 333, 337–338

preparing content for publication, 342–343

proceedings, 334

production, 340–344

publications board/committee, 338

rationale for, 335–336

revenues from, 336

reviews and evaluations, acting on, 347

staff expertise, 333

subscription revenue, 343

surveys, 345–346

transitioning between print and online, 343

types of, 334

usability testing, 346

as a way to stay competitive, 336

Technology, 21, 26, 349

CAE exam, content outline, 459

in education programs, 309–310

Telecommuting, 91, 166–167

Teleconferencing, 416

Telemarketing, 451

Telephone interviews, 213

Telephone systems, 232
Tenenbaum, Jeffrey S., 432
Termination
    affinity programs, 453–454
    contract clauses, 62
    employees, 62, 163–164
Testing software, 416
Theater style room set-up, 412
Title VII, Civil Rights Act of 1964, 177–178
Trade association, 288
Trademarks, 62, 430–431, 450
Trade secrets, 63
Trade shows, 394. *See also* Meetings and
    conventions
    booths and exhibit space, 394
    decorators, 407
    education programs at, 309
    management of, 405–407
Training. *See also* Education programs
    computer-based, 309
    employee, 90, 91, 164–165, 166, 280
    in government relations, 258
    media (spokesperson), 267–268
    outside consultants, use of, 6
    video-based, 310, 349
    volunteer orientation, 6
Transparency, 85
Trust, 70, 96–97, 100

U

Uniformed Service Employment and
    Reemployment Rights Act, 179
Uniform Guidelines on Employee Selection
    Procedures, 179
Unreasonably anticompetitive, defined, 420
Unrelated business income tax (UBIT), 60,
    132, 446, 448–449
Usability testing, 346
U-shape room set-up, 412
U. S. Tax Code. *See* Internal Revenue Code
    (U.S. Tax Code)
Utility emergencies, 247

V

Value chain, 31
Values, 86
Variable costs, 305–306, 397
Vendors. *See* Supplier relations
Vertical disintegration, 33, 34
Veterans' Reemployment Rights Act, 179
"Viagra Lesson," 37
Video-based training, 310
Videoconferencing, 37, 310, 349, 396
Videojournals, 316
Video-on-demand, 349

Vieder, Deborah B., 312
Viral marketing, 125
Virtual reality, 310
Vision statements, 30
Volunteers. *See also* Member relations;
    Member recruitment and retention
    CAE exam, content outline, 461
    communication with, 9, 10
    importance of, 1
    information management, 228–229
    at meetings and conventions, role of, 393,
    411
    orientation, 6
    recognition of, 8, 69
    recruitment of, 6, 84
    role of in marketing, 355
    selecting effective, 7
    strengthening the relationship with, 5–9
    support, 8–9
    training of, 84

W

Warranty, 62, 419, 432
Web casting, 416
Web content, information management, 229
Webinars, 233, 310
Web masters, 229, 233
Web page, 225
Web sites, 229, 254, 268–269, 272, 330, 359
Welch, Jack, 90
Wheatly, Margaret, 87
Whistleblower policies, 8, 59
Wikis, 316
Wildcards, 24, 28
Workers' compensation, 166
Workforce, professionalization of, 32, 35–36
Workshops, 394. *See also* Meetings and
    conventions
World Wide Web, 254

X

XML (extensible markup language), 342

Z

Zero-based budgeting, 132, 320

For Additional Reading

ASAE & The Center for Association Leadership offers these and numerous other publications for additional reading at **www.asaecenter.org**:

7 Measures of Success: What Remarkable Associations Do That Others Don't
ASAE & The Center for Association Leadership

Association Law Handbook, 4th edition
Jerald A. Jacobs

Association Tax Compliance Guide
Jeffrey Tenenbaum

The Business of Certification: A Comprehensive Guide to Developing a Successful Program
Lenora G. Knapp and Joan E. Knapp

The Component Relations Toolkit: Tools and Tips for the Component Relations Professional
ASAE & The Center for Association Leadership

Core Competencies in Association Professional Development
Edited by Terri Tracey, CAE and Kathleen M. Edwards, CAE

Financial Management Handbook for Associations and Nonprofits
Craig Stevens, Kate Petrillo, and Dawn Brown

From Scan to Plan: Integrating Trends into the Strategy-Making Process
James G. Dalton, Jennifer Jarratt, and John B. Mahaffie

From Scan to Plan: Managing Change in Associations
James G. Dalton

The Fundamentals of Accreditation
Michael S. Hamm

A Guide to Periodicals Publishing for Associations, 2nd edition
Edited by Frances Shuping, CAE

High-Impact Governing in a Nutshell: 17 Questions That Board Members and CEOs Frequently Ask
Doug Eadie

International Legal Issues for Nonprofit Organizations
Jefferson C. Glassie

Millennium Membership: How to Attract and Keep Members in the New Marketplace
Mark Levin, CAE

Outsourcing: Using Outside Resources to Get More Done
Stacey Riska

Operating Ratio Report
ASAE & The Center for Association Leadership

Policies and Procedures in Association Management: A Benchmarking Guide
ASAE & The Center for Association Leadership

Principles of Association Management, 4th edition
Henry Ernstthal

Strategic Planning for Association Executives
Gerald L. Gordon

The Will to Govern Well: Knowledge, Trust, and Nimbleness
Glenn H. Tecker, Jean S. Frankel, and Paul D. Meyer, CAE